Functional Programming in Java

HOW TO IMPROVE YOUR JAVA PROGRAMS USING FUNCTIONAL TECHNIQUES

PIERRE-YVES SAUMONT

MANNING
SHELTER ISLAND

For online information and ordering of this and other Manning books, please visit
www.manning.com. The publisher offers discounts on this book when ordered in quantity.
For more information, please contact

> Special Sales Department
> Manning Publications Co.
> 20 Baldwin Road
> PO Box 761
> Shelter Island, NY 11964
> Email: orders@manning.com

Manning Publications Co.
20 Baldwin Road
PO Box 761
Shelter Island, NY 11964

Development editor:	Marina Michaels
Technical development editor:	Mark Elston
Project editor:	Janet Vail
Copyeditor:	Andy Carroll
Proofreaders:	Katie Tennant and Melody Dolab
Technical proofreader:	Alessandro Campeis
Typesetter:	Dottie Marsico
Cover designer:	Leslie Haimes

ISBN 9781617292736
Printed in the United States of America
1 2 3 4 5 6 7 8 9 10 – EBM – 22 21 20 19 18 17

brief contents

contents

v

preface

Writing programs is fun and rewarding. Programming is an activity that many people would do for fun, and yet are paid for. In this sense, a programmer is a bit like an actor, a musician, or a professional football player. It seems like a dream until you, as a programmer, begin to have real responsibilities. Writing games or office applications isn't really a big deal from this point of view. If your application has a bug, you simply fix it and release a new version. But if you write applications that people depend on, and if you can't simply release a new version and have your users install it themselves, it's another story. Of course, Java isn't meant for writing applications for monitoring nuclear plants or flying airplanes, or any system in which a simple bug could put human life at risk. But if your application is used to manage internet backbones, you wouldn't like a nasty bug to be discovered one day before the Olympic Games open, causing a TV transmission failure for a whole country. For such applications, you want to be sure that your program can be proven correct.

Most imperative programs can't be proven correct. Tests only allow us to prove programs incorrect when they fail. Successful tests don't prove much. What you release are programs that you weren't able to prove incorrect. With single-threaded programs, extensive tests may let you show that your code is mostly correct. But with multithreaded applications, the number of possible condition combinations makes that impossible. Clearly, we need a different way to write programs. Ideally, it would be a way that allows us to prove that a program is correct. Because this is generally not fully possible, a good compromise is a clear separation between parts of the program that can be proven correct and parts that can't. This is what functional programming techniques offer.

Functional programming has about as many definitions as there are functional programmers. Some say that functional programming is programming with functions. This is true, but it doesn't help you understand the benefits of this programming paradigm. More important is the idea that functional programming involves pushing abstraction to the limit. This allows a clear separation between the parts of a program that can be proven correct and the other parts whose output depends on external conditions. This way, functional programs are programs that are less prone to bugs, and in which bugs can only reside in specific, restricted areas.

Many techniques can be employed to reach this goal. The use of immutable data, although not specific to functional programming, is such a technique. If data can't change, you won't have any (bad) surprises, no stale or corrupted data, no race conditions, no need for locking on concurrent accesses, and no risk of deadlocks. Immutable data can be shared without risk. You don't need to make defensive copies, and you don't risk forgetting to do so. Another technique is abstracting control structures so that you don't have to write the same structures again and again, multiplying the risk of messing with loop indexes and exit conditions. Completely removing the use of null references (whether implicit or explicit) will free you from the infamous NPE (NullPointerException). With all these techniques (and more), you can be confident that if your program compiles, it's correct (meaning that it has no implementation bugs). This doesn't remove all possibility of bugs, but it makes things much safer.

 Computers have used the imperative paradigm from the beginning, based on mutating values in registers. Java, like many other programming languages known as "imperative languages," seems to rely heavily on this paradigm, but this isn't essential. If you're an experienced Java programmer, you might be surprised to hear that you can write useful programs without ever changing the value of a variable. This isn't a mandatory condition for functional programming, but it's so comfortable that functional programmers nearly always use immutable data. You might also have difficulty believing that you can write applications without ever using an if ... else structure or a while or for loop. Again, avoiding such structures isn't a condition for using the functional paradigm, but you can avoid them if you want, and this leads to much safer programs. So even if Java is generally seen as an "imperative language," it's not. No language is imperative, and no language is functional. Believing that they are is like thinking that English is better for business texts while Italian would be better for singing opera, French for love poetry, and German for philosophy (or whatever combinations you can imagine). Differences may exist, but they're mostly cultural, and the same is true for programming languages. Java is an imperative language because most Java programmers are imperative programmers, and the Java culture is mostly imperative. In contrast, Haskell programs are generally written in a functional style because programmers choose this language with functional programming in mind. But it's possible to write imperative programs in Haskell, and it's possible to write functional programs in Java. The difference is that Haskell is more "functional-friendly" than Java.

So the question is, "Should you use Java for functional programming"? Surprisingly (given the subject of this book) the answer is no. With the freedom to choose any language, I'll say that you shouldn't chose Java for this purpose. But you generally won't have this freedom. Most of the negative comments I received when writing articles about using Java for functional programming were along the lines of "You should not use Java for this. This is not the way Java was intended to be used," or "Why are you using Java for this? Better to use Haskell, or Scala, or whatever."

In reality, you generally don't have a choice of language. If you work in a company, you probably have to use the corporate language, or at least the one chosen by your team for the project you're working on. Haskell is never an option from this point of view. Often, you'll have no choice but to use Java. And if you're in a position to choose the language, you likely won't have any choice besides using a language you know, or using a language that allows the reuse of some legacy code, or a language that suits the environment, or some other condition. This book is aimed at you, the Java programmer who has no real choice other than using Java, although you want to benefit from the safety of functional programming.

Using functional programming techniques in Java will often cause you to go against so-called "best practices." Many of these practices are, in fact, useless, and some are very bad practices indeed. Never catching errors is one of them. As a Java programmer, you probably learned that you shouldn't be catching OOME (Out Of Memory Error) or other kinds of errors you can't deal with. Maybe you even learned that you shouldn't catch NPEs (NullPointerExceptions) because they indicate bugs, and you should let the application crash and fix it. Unfortunately, neither OOME nor NPE will crash the application. They'll only crash the thread in which they occur, leaving the application in some indeterminate state. Even if they occur in the main thread, they'll possibly fail to crash the application if some non-daemon threads are running. This "best practice" was true when all applications were single-threaded. It's now a very bad practice. You should catch all exceptions, although possibly not in a `try ... catch` block. In functional programming, the mantra is, "Always catch, never throw."

There are many other best practices that will be challenged during our functional programming journey. One of them, although not directly related to Java or imperative programming, is, "Don't reinvent the wheel." Think about it. Once, someone invented the wheel. At that time, it was probably something roughly circular made of some rigid material and turning on an axle. The wheel has been reinvented many times since then. If it hadn't, you'd have no cars, no trains, and nearly nothing using wheels. So you should continue trying to reinvent the wheel again and again. Not only will this give us better wheels in the future, but it's challenging, rewarding, and fun. (And if you believe that modern cars have circular wheels, you'd better think again. No car could ever run on circular wheels!)

acknowledgments

I would like to thank the many people who participated in making this book possible.

First, a big thank you to my developmental editor, Marina Michaels. Besides your wonderful work on the manuscript, it's been a real pleasure to work with you.

A big thank you, too, to Mark Elston, my technical editor, and to Alessandro Campeis, my technical proofreader, both of whom helped me make this book much better than I could have done alone.

To all the reviewers, MEAP readers, and everyone else who provided feedback and comments, thank you! This book would not be what it is today without your help. Specifically, I'd like to thank the following people who all took the time to review and comment on the book: Aditya Kumar, Al Krinker, Andy Kirsch, Andy Knight, Anthony Moralez, Arun Allamsetty, Barry Kern, Boris Vasile, Bruce Hernandez, Charles Feduke, Chris Kirk, David Drummond, Davide Fiorentino lo Regio, Erwin van Eijk, Gualtiero Testa, Ivan Milosavljević, Jan Vorwerk, Jérôme Baton, Joshua McAdams, Julian Templeman, Maria Gemini, Norbert Kuchenmeister, Philippe Charrière, Piotr Bzdyl, Rambabu Posa, Sebastian Hähnel, Sebastian Metzger, Simeon Leyzerzon, Tarin Gamberini, Ursin Stauss, William Wheeler, Zach Schwartz and Zorodzayi Mukuya.

about this book

This isn't a book about Java. This book is about functional programming, which is a different way to write software programs. "Different" means different from the "traditional" way of writing software, which is called the imperative paradigm. This book is about applying the functional paradigm to Java programming.

There's no such thing as a "functional language." There are only languages that are more-or-less functional-friendly. Although I use Java in this book, you can apply all the principles I teach to any other language. Only the way in which you implement these principles would be different. You can write functional programs in any language, even those said not to be functional at all; you can similarly write imperative programs with the most functional-friendly languages.

With the release of Java 8, some functional features have been added to the Java language. But just as this book isn't about Java, it's also not about these specific Java 8 features. In this book, I make heavy use of some of these features, and I mostly ignore others. If your goal is to learn how to use the functional features of Java 8, this is not the right book. Urma, Fusco, and Mycroft's *Java 8 in Action* (Manning, 2014) would be a much better choice.

On the other hand, if you want to learn what functional programming is, how to build functional data structures, and how the functional programming paradigm will help you write better programs (sometimes using the Java 8 features and sometimes avoiding them), this is the book for you.

Audience

This book is intended for readers with some programming experience in Java. A good understanding of Java generics is necessary. If you find yourself not understanding a

Java construction (such as generic constants implemented as methods, or parameterized method calls), don't be afraid: I'll explain what they mean and why they're needed.

You don't need to have prior experience in functional programming, or to be aware of the mathematical theory that underlies it. Chapter 2 will act as a reminder of what a function is, and that's it. No other math will be used.

I present all functional techniques in relation to their imperative counterparts, so I expect you to have experience with imperative programming in Java.

How to use this book

This book is intended to be read sequentially, because each chapter builds upon the concepts learned in the previous ones. The only exceptions are chapters 14 and 15, in which what you'll learn in chapters 12 and 13 isn't used. This means you can skip chapters 12 and 13 if you want; they present more-advanced techniques that are useful to know but that you might prefer not to use in your own programs.

I've used the word "read," but this book isn't intended to just be read. Very few sections are theory only. To get the most out of this book, read it at your computer keyboard, solving the exercises as you go. Each chapter includes a number of exercises with the necessary instructions and hints to help you arrive at the solution. All the code is available as a separate free download from GitHub (http://github.com/fpinjava/fpinjava) and from the publisher's website at https://www.manning.com/books/functional-programming-in-java. Each exercise comes with a proposed solution and JUnit tests that you can use to verify that your solution is correct.

The code comes with all the necessary elements for the project to be imported into IntelliJ (recommended), NetBeans, or Eclipse, although at the time of this writing, Eclipse (Mars 4.5.1) is not yet fully compatible with Java 8. Projects may be imported "from source" or using Gradle. Any version of Gradle may be used, because Gradle is able to download the correct version automatically.

Please note that you're not expected to understand most of the concepts presented in this book by just reading the text. Doing the exercises is probably the most important part of the learning process, so I encourage you not to skip any exercises. Some might seem quite difficult, and you might be tempted to look at the proposed solutions. It's perfectly OK to do so, but you should then come back to the exercise and do it without looking at the solution. If you only read the solution, you'll probably have problems later trying to solve more-advanced exercises.

This approach doesn't require much tedious typing, because you have nearly nothing to copy. Most exercises consist of writing implementations for methods, for which you are given the environment and the method signature. No exercise is longer than a dozen lines of code; the majority are around four or five lines long.

Once you finish an exercise (which means when your implementation compiles), just run the corresponding test to verify that it's correct.

One important thing to note is that each exercise is self-contained with regard to the rest of the chapter, so code created inside a chapter is duplicated from one exercise to the next. This is necessary because each exercise is often built upon the preceding one, so although the same class might be used, implementations differ. As a consequence, you shouldn't look at an exercise before you complete the previous ones, because you'll see the solutions to yet-unsolved exercises.

You can download the code as an archive, or you can clone it using Git. I highly recommend cloning, since the code is subject to change, and it's much more efficient to update your code with a simple pull command than to re-download the complete archive.

The code for exercises is organized in modules with names that more or less reflect the chapter titles, rather than the chapter numbers. As a result, IDEs will sort them alphabetically, rather than in the order in which they appear in the book. To help you figure out which module corresponds to each chapter, I've provided a list of the chapters with the corresponding module names in the README file accompanying the code (http://github.com/fpinjava/fpinjava).

Setting expectations

Functional programming is no more difficult than imperative programming. It's just different. You can solve the same problems with both paradigms, but translating from one to the other can sometimes be inefficient. Learning functional programming is like learning a foreign language. Just as you can't efficiently think in one language and translate to another, you can't think imperatively and translate your code to the functional approach. And just as you have to learn to think in a new language, you have to learn to think functionally. Learning to think functionally doesn't come with reading alone; it comes with writing code. So you have to practice.

This is why I don't expect you to understand what's in this book just by reading it, and why I provide so many exercises; you must do the exercises to fully grasp the concepts of functional programming. This isn't because the topic is so complex that it isn't possible to understand it through reading alone, but because if you could understand it just by reading (without doing the exercises), you probably wouldn't need this book.

For all these reasons, the exercises are key to getting the most out of this book. I encourage you to try solving each exercise before you continue reading. If you don't find a solution, try again rather than going directly to the solution I provide. If you have a hard time understanding something, ask questions on the forum (see the next section). Asking questions and getting answers on the forum will not only help you, it will also help the person answering the question (along with others who have the same question). We all learn by answering questions (mostly our own questions, by the way) much more than by asking them.

Author Online

Purchase of *Functional Programming in Java* includes free access to a private web forum run by Manning Publications, where you can make comments about the book, ask technical questions, and receive help from the author and other users, or even provide help to other users. To access the forum and subscribe to it, point your web browser to https://forums.manning.com/forums/functional-programming-in-java. This Author Online page provides information on how to get on the forum once you're registered, what kind of help is available, and the rules of conduct on the forum.

Manning's commitment to our readers is to provide a venue where a meaningful dialog among individual readers and between readers and the authors can take place. It's not a commitment to any specific amount of participation on the part of the authors, whose contribution to the forum remains voluntary. I, as the author of this book, will be monitoring this forum and will answer questions as promptly as possible.

The Author Online forum and the archives of previous discussions will be accessible from the publisher's website as long as the book is in print.

What is functional programming?

Not everybody agrees on a definition for functional programming (FP). In general terms, functional programming is a programming paradigm, and it's about programming with functions. But this doesn't explain the most important aspect: how FP is different from other paradigms, and what makes it a (potentially) better way to write programs. In his article "Why Functional Programming Matters," published in 1990, John Hughes writes the following:

Functional programs contain no assignment statements, so variables, once given a value, never change. More generally, functional programs contain no side effects at all. A function call can have no effect other than to compute its result. This eliminates a major source of bugs, and also makes the order of execution irrelevant—since no side effect can change an expression's value, it can be evaluated at any time. This relieves the programmer of the burden of prescribing the flow of control. Since expressions can be evaluated at any time, one can freely replace variables by their values and vice versa—that is, programs are "referentially transparent." This freedom helps make functional programs more tractable mathematically than their conventional counterparts.[1]

In the rest of this chapter, I'll briefly present concepts such as referential transparency and the substitution model, as well as other concepts that together are the essence of functional programming. You'll apply these concepts over and over in the coming chapters.

1.1   *What is functional programming?*

It's often as important to understand what something is not, as to agree about what it is. If functional programming is a programming paradigm, there clearly must be other programming paradigms that FP differs from. Contrary to what some might think, functional programming isn't the opposite of object-oriented programming (OOP). Some functional programming languages are object-oriented; some are not.

Functional programming is sometimes considered to be a set of techniques that supplement or replace techniques found in other programming paradigms, such as

- First-class functions
- Anonymous functions
- Closures
- Currying
- Lazy evaluation
- Parametric polymorphism
- Algebraic data types

Although it is true that most functional languages do use a number of these techniques, you may find, for each of them, examples of functional programming languages that don't, as well as non-functional languages that do. As you'll see when studying each of these techniques in this book, it's not the language that makes programming functional. It's the way you write the code. But some languages are more *functional-friendly* than others.

What functional programming may be opposed to is the imperative programming paradigm. In imperative programming style, programs are composed from elements that "do" something. "Doing" something generally implies an initial state, a transition,

---

[1] John Hughes, "Why Functional Programming Matters," from D. Turner, ed., *Research Topics in Functional Programming* (Addison-Wesley, 1990), 17–42, www.cs.kent.ac.uk/people/staff/dat/miranda/whyfp90.pdf.

and an end state. This is sometimes called *state mutation*. Traditional imperative-style programs are often described as a series of mutations, separated with condition testing. For example, an addition program for adding two positive values a and b might be represented by the following pseudo code:

- `if b == 0, return a`
- `else increment a and decrement b`
- `start again with the new a and b`

In this pseudo code, you can recognize the traditional instructions of most imperative languages: testing conditions, mutating variables, branching, and returning a value. This code may be represented graphically by a flow chart, such as figure 1.1.

On the other hand, functional programs are composed of elements that "are" something—they don't "do" something. The addition of a and b doesn't "make" a result. The addition of 2 and 3, for example, doesn't *make* 5. It *is* 5.

The difference might not seem important, but it is. The main consequence is that each time you encounter 2 + 3, you can replace it with 5. Can you do the same thing in an imperative program? Well, sometimes you can. But sometimes you can't without changing the program's outcome. If the expression you want to replace has no other effect than returning the result, you can safely replace it with its result. But how can you be sure that it has no other effect? In the addition example, you clearly see that the two variables a and b have been destroyed by the program. This is an effect of the program, besides returning the result, so it's called a *side effect*. (This would be different if the computation were occurring inside a Java method, because the variables a and b would be passed by value, and the change would then be local and not visible from outside the method.)

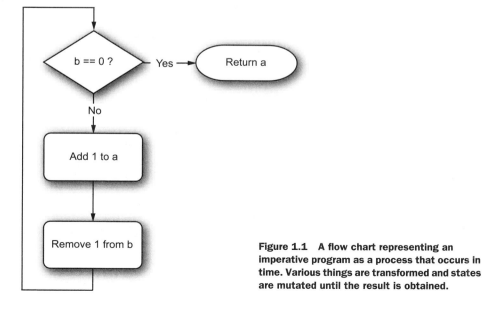

Figure 1.1   A flow chart representing an imperative program as a process that occurs in time. Various things are transformed and states are mutated until the result is obtained.

One major difference between imperative programming and FP is that in FP there are no side effects. This means, among other things,

- No mutation of variables
- No printing to the console or to any device
- No writing to files, databases, networks, or whatever
- No exception throwing

When I say "no side effects," I mean no observable side effects. Functional programs are built by composing *functions* that take an argument and return a value, and that's it. You don't care about what's happening *inside* the functions, because, in theory, nothing is happening ever. But in practice, programs are written for computers that aren't functional at all. All computers are based on the same imperative paradigm; so functions are black boxes that

- Take an argument (a *single* one, as you'll see later)
- Do mysterious things inside, such as mutating variables and a lot of imperative-style stuff, but with no effect observable from outside
- Return a (single) value

This is theory. In practice, it's impossible for a function to have no side effects at all. A function will return a value at some time, and this time may vary. This is a side effect. It might create an out-of-memory error, or a stack-overflow error, and crash the application, which is a somewhat observable side effect. And it will cause writing to memory, registering mutations, thread launching, context switching, and other sorts of things that are indeed effects observable from outside.

So functional programming is writing programs with no *intentional side effects*, by which I mean side effects that are part of the expected outcome of the program. There should also be as few non-intentional side effects as possible.

1.2   *Writing useful programs with no side effects*

You may wonder how you can possibly write useful programs if they have no side effects. Obviously, you can't. Functional programming is not about writing programs that have no observable results. It's about writing programs that have no observable results other than returning a value. But if this is all the program does, it won't be very useful. In the end, functional programs have to have an observable effect, such as displaying the result on a screen, writing it to a file or database, or sending it over a network. This interaction with the outside world won't occur in the middle of a computation, but only when you finish the computation. In other words, side effects will be delayed and applied separately.

Take the example of the addition in figure 1.1. Although it's described in imperative style, it might yet be functional, depending on how it's implemented. Imagine this program is implemented in Java as follows:

```
public static int add(int a, int b) {
  while (b > 0) {
    a++;
    b--;
  }
  return a;
}
```

This program is fully functional. It takes an argument, which is the pair of integers a and b, it returns a value, and it has absolutely no other observable effect. That it mutates variables doesn't contradict the requirements, because arguments in Java are passed by value, so the mutations of the arguments aren't visible from outside. You can then choose to apply an effect, such as displaying the result or using the result for another computation.

Note that although the result might not be correct (in case of an arithmetic overflow), that's not in contradiction with having no side effects. If values a and b are too big, the program will silently overflow and return an erroneous result, but this is still functional. On the other hand, the following program is not functional:

```
public static int div(int a, int b) {
  return a / b;
}
```

Although this program doesn't mutate any variables, it throws an exception if b is equal to 0. Throwing an exception is a side effect. In contrast, the following implementation, although a bit stupid, is functional:

```
public static int div(int a, int b) {
  return (int) (a / (float) b);
}
```

This implementation won't throw an exception if b is equal to 0, but it will return a special result. It's up to you to decide whether it's OK or not for your function to return this specific result to mean that the divisor was 0. (It's probably not!)

Throwing an exception might be an intentional or unintentional side effect, but it's always a side effect. Often, though, in imperative programming, side effects are wanted. The simplest form might look like this:

```
public static void add(int a, int b) {
  while (b > 0) {
    a++;
    b--;
  }
  System.out.println(a);
}
```

This program doesn't return a value, but it prints the result to the console. This is a desired side effect.

Note that the program could alternatively both return a value and have some intentional side effects, as in the following example:

```
public static int add(int a, int b) {
  log(String.format("Adding %s and %s", a, b));
  while (b > 0) {
    a++;
    b--;
  }
  log(String.format("Returning %s", a));
  return a;
}
```

This program isn't functional because it uses side effects for logging.

1.3   *How referential transparency makes programs safer*

Having no side effects (and thus not mutating anything in the external world) isn't enough for a program to be functional. Functional programs must also not be affected by the external world. In other words, the output of a functional program must depend only on its argument. This means functional code may not read data from the console, a file, a remote URL, a database, or even from the system. Code that doesn't mutate or depend on the external world is said to be referentially transparent.

Referentially transparent code has several properties that might be of some interest to programmers:

- It's self-contained. It doesn't depend on any external device to work. You can use it in any context—all you have to do is provide a valid argument.
- It's deterministic, which means it will always return the same value for the same argument. With referentially transparent code, you won't be surprised. It might return a wrong result, but at least, for the same argument, this result will never change.
- It will never throw any kind of Exception. It might throw errors, such as OOME (out-of-memory error) or SOE (stack-overflow error), but these errors mean that the code has a bug, which is not a situation you, as a programmer, or the users of your API, are supposed to handle (besides crashing the application and eventually fixing the bug).
- It won't create conditions causing other code to unexpectedly fail. For example, it won't mutate arguments or some other external data, causing the caller to find itself with stale data or concurrent access exceptions.
- It won't hang because some external device (whether database, file system, or network) is unavailable, too slow, or simply broken.

Figure 1.2 illustrates the difference between a referentially transparent program and one that's not referentially transparent.

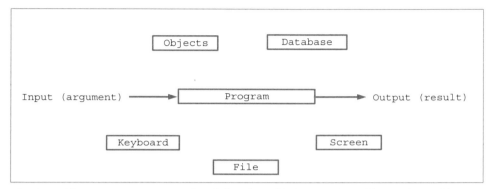

A referentially transparent program doesn't interfere with the outside world apart from taking an argument as input and outputting a result. Its result only depends on its argument.

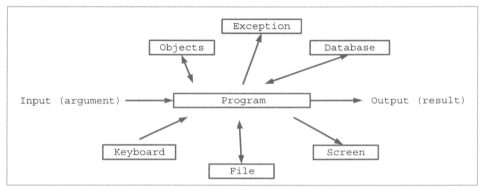

A program that isn't referentially transparent may read data from or write it to elements in the outside world, log to file, mutate external objects, read from keyboard, print to screen, and so on. Its result is unpredictable.

Figure 1.2   Comparing a program that's referentially transparent to one that's not

1.4   The benefits of functional programming

From what I've just said, you can likely guess the many benefits of functional programming:

- Functional programs are easier to reason about because they're deterministic. One specific input will always give the same output. In many cases, you might be able to prove your program correct rather than extensively testing it and still being uncertain whether it will break under unexpected conditions.
- Functional programs are easier to test. Because there are no side effects, you don't need mocks, which are generally required to isolate the programs under test from the outside.

- Functional programs are more modular because they're built from functions that have only input and output; there are no side effects to handle, no exceptions to catch, no context mutation to deal with, no shared mutable state, and no concurrent modifications.
- Functional programming makes composition and recombination much easier. To write a functional program, you have to start by writing the various base functions you need and then combine these base functions into higher-level ones, repeating the process until you have a single function corresponding to the program you want to build. As all these functions are referentially transparent, they can then be reused to build other programs without any modifications.

Functional programs are inherently thread-safe because they avoid mutation of shared state. Once again, this doesn't mean that all data has to be immutable. Only shared data must be. But functional programmers will soon realize that immutable data is always safer, even if the mutation is not visible externally.

1.5   *Using the substitution model to reason about programs*

Remember that a function doesn't *do* anything. It only has a value, which is only dependent on its argument. As a consequence, it's always possible to replace a function call, or any referentially transparent expression, with its value, as shown in figure 1.3.

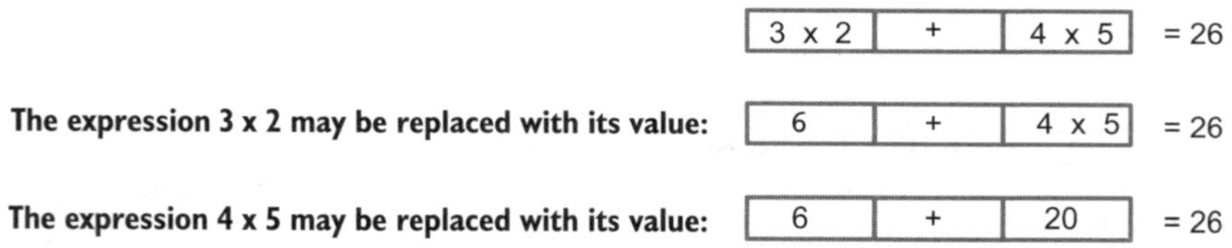

	3 x 2	+	4 x 5	= 26
The expression 3 x 2 may be replaced with its value:	6	+	4 x 5	= 26
The expression 4 x 5 may be replaced with its value:	6	+	20	= 26

Figure 1.3   Replacing referentially transparent expressions with their values doesn't change the overall meaning.

When applied to functions, the substitution model allows you to replace any function call with its return value. Consider the following code:

```
public static void main(String[] args) {
  int x = add(mult(2, 3), mult(4, 5));
}
public static int add(int a, int b) {
  log(String.format("Returning %s as the result of %s + %s", a + b, a, b));
  return a + b;
}
public static int mult(int a, int b) {
  return a * b;
}
```

```
public static void log(String m) {
  System.out.println(m);
}
```

Replacing `mult(2, 3)` and `mult(4, 5)` with their respective return values doesn't change the signification of the program:

```
int x = add(6, 20);
```

In contrast, replacing the call to the `add` function with its return value changes the signification of the program, because the `log` method will no longer be called, and no logging will happen. This might be important or not; in any case, it changes the result of the program.

1.6 *Applying functional principles to a simple example*

As an example of converting an imperative program into a functional one, we'll consider a very simple program representing the purchase of a donut with a credit card.

Listing 1.1   A Java program with side effects

```
public class DonutShop {

  public static Donut buyDonut(CreditCard creditCard) {
    Donut donut = new Donut();
    creditCard.charge(Donut.price);        ← ❶ Charges the credit card as a side effect
    return donut;                          ← ❷ Returns the donut
  }
}
```

In this code, the charging of the credit card is a side effect ❶. Charging a credit card probably consists of calling the bank, verifying that the credit card is valid and authorized, and registering the transaction. The function returns the donut ❷.

The problem with this kind of code is that it's difficult to test. Running the program for testing would involve contacting the bank and registering the transaction using some sort of mock account. Or you'd need to create a mock credit card to register the effect of calling the `charge` method and to verify the state of the mock after the test.

If you want to be able to test your program without contacting the bank or using a mock, you should remove the side effect. Because you still want to charge the credit card, the only solution is to add a representation of this operation to the return value. Your `buyDonut` method will have to return both the donut and this representation of the payment.

To represent the payment, you can use a `Payment` class.

Listing 1.2   The `Payment` class

```
public class Payment {

  public final CreditCard creditCard;
  public final int amount;
```

```
  public Payment(CreditCard creditCard, int amount) {
    this.creditCard = creditCard;
    this.amount = amount;
  }
}
```

This class contains the necessary data to represent the payment, which consists of a credit card and the amount to charge. Because the buyDonut method must return both a Donut and a Payment, you could create a specific class for this, such as Purchase:

```
public class Purchase {

  public Donut donut;
  public Payment payment;

  public Purchase(Donut donut, Payment payment) {
    this.donut = donut;
    this.payment = payment;
  }
}
```

You'll often need such a class to hold two (or more) values, because functional programming replaces side effects with returning a representation of these effects.

Rather than creating a specific Purchase class, you'll use a generic one that you'll call Tuple. This class will be parameterized by the two types it will contain (Donut and Payment). The following listing shows its implementation, as well as the way it's used in the DonutShop class.

Listing 1.3 The Tuple class

```
public class Tuple<T, U> {

  public final T _1;
  public final U _2;

  public Tuple(T t, U u) {
    this._1 = t;
    this._2 = u;
  }
}
public class DonutShop {

  public static Tuple<Donut, Payment> buyDonut(CreditCard creditCard) {
    Donut donut = new Donut();
    Payment payment = new Payment(creditCard, Donut.price);
    return new Tuple<>(donut, payment);
  }
}
```

Note that you're no longer concerned (at this stage) with how the credit card will actually be charged. This adds some freedom to the way you build your application. You could still process the payment immediately, or you could store it for later processing. You could even combine stored payments for the same card and process them in a single operation. This would allow you to save money by minimizing the bank fees for the credit card service.

The combine method in the following listing allows you to combine payments. Note that if the credit cards don't match, an exception is thrown. This doesn't contradict what I said about functional programs not throwing exceptions. Here, trying to combine two payments with two different credit cards is considered a bug, so it should crash the application. (This isn't very realistic. You'll have to wait until chapter 7 to learn how to deal with such situations without throwing exceptions.)

Listing 1.4   Composing multiple payments into a single one

```
package com.fpinjava.introduction.listing01_04;

public class Payment {

  public final CreditCard creditCard;
  public final int amount;

  public Payment(CreditCard creditCard, int amount) {
    this.creditCard = creditCard;
    this.amount = amount;
  }

  public Payment combine(Payment payment) {
    if (creditCard.equals(payment.creditCard)) {
      return new Payment(creditCard, amount + payment.amount);
    } else {
      throw new IllegalStateException("Cards don't match.");
    }
  }
}
```

Of course, the combine method wouldn't be very efficient for buying several donuts at once. For this use case, you could simply replace the buyDonut method with buyDonuts(int n, CreditCard creditCard), as shown in the following listing. This method returns a Tuple<List<Donut>, Payment>.

Listing 1.5   Buying multiple donuts at once

```
package com.fpinjava.introduction.listing01_05;

import static com.fpinjava.common.List.fill;
import com.fpinjava.common.List;
import com.fpinjava.common.Tuple;

public class DonutShop {

  public static Tuple<Donut, Payment> buyDonut(final CreditCard cCard) {
    return new Tuple<>(new Donut(), new Payment(cCard, Donut.price));
  }

  public static Tuple<List<Donut>, Payment> buyDonuts(final int quantity,
                                     final CreditCard cCard) {
    return new Tuple<>(fill(quantity, () -> new Donut()),
                                new Payment(cCard, Donut.price * quantity));
```

```
        }
}
```

Note that this method doesn't use the standard java.util.List class because that class doesn't offer some of the functional methods you'll need. In chapter 3, you'll see how to use the java.util.List class in a functional way by writing a small functional library. Then, in chapter 5, you'll develop a completely new functional List. It's this list that's used here. This combine method is somewhat equivalent to the following, which uses the standard Java list:

```
public static Tuple<List<Donut>, Payment> buyDonuts(final int quantity,
                                             final CreditCard cCard) {
    return new Tuple<>(Collections.nCopies(quantity, new Donut()),
                    new Payment(cCard, Donut.price * quantity));
}
```

As you'll soon need additional functional methods, you won't be using the Java list. For the time being, you just need to know that the static List<A> fill(int n, Supplier<A> s) method creates a list of n instances of A by using a special object, Supplier<A>. As its name indicates, a Supplier<A> is an object that supplies an A when its get() method is called. Using a Supplier<A> instead of an A allows for *lazy evaluation*, which you'll learn about in the next chapters. For now, you may think of it as a way to manipulate an A without effectively creating it until it's needed.

Now, your program can be tested without using a mock. For example, here's a test for the method buyDonuts:

```
@Test
public void testBuyDonuts() {
  CreditCard creditCard = new CreditCard();
  Tuple<List<Donut>, Payment> purchase = DonutShop.buyDonuts(5, creditCard);
  assertEquals(Donut.price * 5, purchase._2.amount);
  assertEquals(creditCard, purchase._2.creditCard);
}
```

Another benefit of making your program functional is that it's more easily composable. If the same person made several purchases with your initial program, you'd have to contact the bank (and pay the corresponding fee) each time. With the new functional version, you can choose to charge the card immediately for each purchase or to group all payments made with the same card and charge it only once for the total.

To group payments, you'll need to use additional methods from your functional List class (you don't need to understand how these methods work for now; you'll study them in detail in chapters 5 and 8):

```
public <B> Map<B, List<A>> groupBy(Function<A, B> f)
```

This instance method of the List class takes a function from A to B and returns a map of key and value pairs, with keys being of type B and values of type List<A>. In other words, it groups payments by credit cards:

```
List<A> values()
```

This is an instance method of Map that returns a list of all the values in the map:

```
<B> List<B> map(Function<A, B> f)
```

This is an instance method of List that takes a function from A to B and applies it to all elements of a list of A, giving a list of B:

```
Tuple<List<A1>, List<A2>> unzip(Function<A, Tuple<A1, A2>> f)
```

This is a method of the List class that takes as its argument a function from A to a tuple of values. For example, it might be a function that takes an email address and returns the name and the domain as a tuple. The unzip method, in that case, would return a tuple of a list of names and a list of domains.

```
A reduce(Function<A, Function<A, A>> f)
```

This method of List uses an operation to reduce the list to a single value. This operation is represented by Function<A, Function<A, A>> f. This notation may look a bit weird, but you'll learn what it means in chapter 2. It could be, for example, an addition. In such a case, it would simply mean a function such as f(a, b) = a + b.

Using these methods, you can now create a new method that groups payments by credit card.

Listing 1.6   Grouping payments by credit card

```
package com.fpinjava.introduction.listing01_06;

import com.fpinjava.common.List;

public class Payment {

  public final CreditCard creditCard;
  public final int amount;

  public Payment(CreditCard creditCard, int amount) {
    this.creditCard = creditCard;
    this.amount = amount;
  }

  public Payment combine(Payment payment) {
    if (creditCard.equals(payment.creditCard)) {
      return new Payment(creditCard, amount + payment.amount);
    } else {
      throw new IllegalStateException("Cards don't match.");
    }
  }
}
```

```
public static List<Payment> groupByCard(List<Payment> payments) {
    return payments
        .groupBy(x -> x.creditCard)
        .values()
        .map(x -> x.reduce(c1 -> c2 -> c1.combine(c2)));
}
}
```

Changes a List<Payment> into a
Map<CreditCard, List<Payment>>
where each list contains all payments
for a particular credit card

Reduces each List<Payment> into a
single Payment, leading to the overall
result of a List<Payment>

Changes the Map<CreditCard,
List<Payment>> into a
List<List<Payment>>

Note that you could use a method reference in the last line of the groupByCard method, but I chose the lambda notation because it's probably (much) easier to read. If you prefer method references, you can replace this line with the following one:

```
.map(x -> x.reduce(c1 -> c1::combine));
```

In listing 1.6, the portion after c1 -> is a function taking a single parameter and passing that parameter to c1.combine(). And that's exactly what c1::combine is—it's a function taking a single parameter. Method references are often easier to read than lambdas, but not always!

1.7   *Pushing abstraction to the limit*

As you've seen, functional programming consists in writing programs by composing pure functions, which means functions without side effects. These functions may be represented by methods, or they may be *first-class functions*, such as the arguments of methods groupBy, map, or reduce, in the previous example. First-class functions are simply functions represented in such a way that, unlike methods, they can be manipulated by the program. In most cases, they're used as arguments to other functions, or to methods. You'll learn in chapter 2 how this is done.

But the most important notion here is abstraction. Look at the reduce method. It takes as its argument an operation, and uses it to reduce a list to a single value. Here, the operation has two operands of the same type. Except for this, it could be any operation. Consider a list of integers. You could write a sum method to compute the sum of the elements; you could write a product method to compute the product of the elements; or you could write a min or a max method to compute the minimum or the maximum of the list. But you could also use the reduce method for all these computations. This is abstraction. You abstract the part that is common to all operations in the reduce method, and you pass the variable part (the operation) as an argument.

But you could go further. The reduce method is a particular case of a more general method that might produce a result of a different type than the elements of the list. For example, it could be applied to a list of characters to produce a String. You'd need to start from a given value (probably an empty string). In chapters 3 and 5, you'll learn how to develop this method (called fold). Also note that the reduce method won't work on an empty list. Think of a list of integers—if you want to compute the sum, you need to have an element to start with. If the list is empty, what should you return? Of course, you know that the result should be 0, but this only works for a sum. It doesn't work for a product.

Also consider the `groupByCard` method. It looks like a business method that can only be used to group payments by credit cards. But it's not! You could use this method to group the elements of any list by any of their properties, so this method should be abstracted and put inside the `List` class in such a way that it could be reused easily.

A very important part of functional programming consists in pushing abstraction to the limit. In the rest of this book, you'll learn how to abstract many things so you never have to define them again. You will, for example, learn how to abstract loops so you won't have to write loops ever again. And you'll learn how to abstract parallelization in a way that will allow you to switch from serial to parallel processing just by selecting a method in the `List` class.

1.8 Summary

- Functional programming is programming with functions, returning values, and having no side effects.
- Functional programs are easy to reason about and easy to test.
- Functional programming offers a high level of abstraction and reusability.
- Functional programs are more robust than their imperative counterparts.
- Functional programs are safer in multithreading environments because they avoid shared mutable state.

Using functions in Java

This chapter covers

- Understanding functions in the real world
- Representing functions in Java
- Using lambdas
- Working with higher-order functions
- Using curried functions
- Programming with functional interfaces

To understand how functional programming works, we could use functional components provided by some functional library, or even the few that have been made available in the Java 8 library. But instead, we'll look at how you can construct things rather than how to use these provided components. Once you've mastered the concepts, it will be up to you to choose between your own functions and the standard Java 8 ones, or to rely on one of the existing external libraries. In this chapter you'll create a Function very similar to the Java 8 Function. It will be a bit simplified in how it handles type parameters (avoiding wildcards) in order to make the code easier to read, but it will have some powerful capacities that are absent from the Java 8 version. Apart from those differences, they'll be interchangeable.

You might have trouble understanding some parts of the code presented in this chapter. That's to be expected, because it's very difficult to introduce functions without using other functional constructs such as `List`, `Option`, and others. Be patient. All the unexplained components will be discussed in the following chapters.

I'll now explain in greater detail what a function is, both in the real world and in a programming language. Functions aren't only a mathematical or programming entity. Functions are part of everyday life. We're constantly modeling the world in which we live, and this is true not only for programming. We construct representations of the world around us, and these representations are often based on objects that mutate their state as time changes. Seeing things this way is human nature. Going from state A to state B takes time, and it has a cost in terms of time, effort, or money.

Consider addition as an example. Most of us see it as a computation that takes time (and sometimes intellectual effort!). It has a starting state, a transition (the computation), and a resulting state (the result of the addition).

To add 345, 765, and 34,524, we certainly need to perform a computation. Some of us can do it in little time, and others will take longer. Some might never succeed, or will get an erroneous result. Some will make the computation in their head; others will need to write it down on paper. All will probably mutate some state to achieve this, whether it's a sheet of paper or some part of their brain. But to add 2 and 3, we don't need all this. Most of us have memorized the answer and can give the result immediately, without doing any computation.

This example shows that computation isn't the essential element here. It's just a means to calculate the result of a function. But this result existed before we made the computation. We just generally don't know what this result is beforehand.

Functional programming is just programming using functions. To be able to do this, we first need to know what a function is, both in the real world and in our programming language of choice.

2.1 What is a function?

A *function* is generally known as a mathematical object, although the concept is also ubiquitous in everyday life. Unfortunately, in everyday life, we often confuse functions and effects. And what is even more unfortunate is that we also make this mistake when working with many programming languages.

2.1.1 Functions in the real world

In the real world, a function is primarily a mathematic concept. It's a relation between a source set, called the function *domain*, to a target set, called the function *codomain*. The domain and the codomain need not be distinct. A function can have the same set of integer numbers for its domain and its codomain, for example.

WHAT MAKES A RELATION BETWEEN TWO SETS A FUNCTION

To be a function, a relation must fulfill one condition: all elements of the domain must have one and only one corresponding element in the codomain, as shown in figure 2.1.

This has some interesting implications:

- There cannot exist elements in the domain with no corresponding value in the codomain.
- There cannot exist two elements in the codomain corresponding to the same element of the domain.
- There may be elements in the codomain with no corresponding element in the source set.
- There may be elements in the codomain with more than one corresponding element in the source set.
- The set of elements of the codomain that have a corresponding element in the domain is called the *image* of the function.

Figure 2.1 illustrates a function.

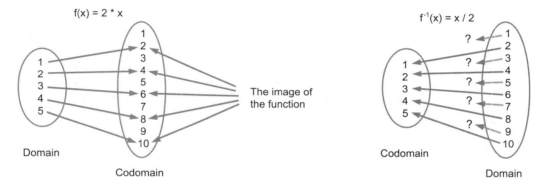

f(x) is a function from N to N.

f⁻¹(x) isn't a function considering **N** as the domain. It is, however, a function considering the set of even numbers (the image of f) as the domain.

Figure 2.1   All elements of a function's domain must have one and only one corresponding element in the codomain.

You can, for example, define the function

```
f(x) = x + 1
```

where x is a positive integer. This function represents the relationship between each positive integer and its successor. You can give any name to this function. In particular, you can give it a name that will help you remember what it is, such as

```
successor(x) = x + 1
```

This may seem like a good idea, but you shouldn't blindly trust a function name. You could alternatively have defined the function as follows:

```
predecessor(x) = x + 1
```

No error occurs here, because no mandatory relationship exists between a function name and the definition of the function. But, obviously, it would be a bad idea to use such a name.

Note that we're talking about what a function is (its definition) and not what it does. A function does nothing. The `successor` function doesn't add 1 to its argument. *You* can add 1 to an integer to calculate its successor, but *you* aren't a function. The function

```
successor(x)
```

doesn't add 1 to x. It is only equivalent to x + 1, which simply means that each time you encounter the expression `successor(x)`, you can replace it with `(x + 1)`.

Note the parentheses that are used to isolate the expression. They aren't needed when the expression is used alone, but they might be necessary on some occasions.

INVERSE FUNCTIONS

A function may or may not have an inverse function. If `f(x)` is a function from A to B (A being the domain and B the codomain), the inverse function is noted as $f^{-1}(x)$ and has B as its domain and A as its codomain. If you represent the type of the function as A -> B, the inverse function (if it exists) has the type B -> A.

The inverse of a function is a function if it fulfills the same requirement as any function: having one and only one target value for each source value. As a result, the inverse of `successor(x)`, a relation that you'll call `predecessor(x)` (although you could just as well call it xyz), isn't a function in N (the set of positive integers including 0) because 0 has no predecessor in N. Conversely, if `successor(x)` is considered with the set of signed integers (positive and negative, noted as Z), the inverse of `successor` is a function.

Some other simple functions have no inverse. For example, the function

```
f(x) = (2 * x)
```

has no inverse if defined from N to N. It has an inverse if you define it as a function from N to the set of even integers.

PARTIAL FUNCTIONS

A relation that isn't defined for all elements of the domain but that fulfills the rest of the requirement (no element of the domain can have a relationship with more than one element of the codomain) is often called a *partial function*. The relation `predecessor(x)` is a partial function on N (the set of positive integers plus 0), but it's a total function on N*, which is the set of positive integers without 0, and its codomain is N.

Partial functions are important in programming because many bugs are the result of using a partial function as if it were a total one. For example, the relation `f(x) =` `1/x` is a partial function from N to Q (the rational numbers) because it isn't defined for 0. It's a total function from N* to Q, but it's also a total function from N to (Q plus error). By adding an element to the codomain (the error condition), you can transform the partial function into a total one. But to do this, the function needs a way to return an error. Can you see an analogy with computer programs? You'll see that turning partial functions into total ones is an important part of functional programming.

FUNCTION COMPOSITION

Functions are building blocks that can be composed to build other functions. The composition of functions f and g is noted as f ∘ g, which reads as f *round* g. If f(x) = x + 2 and g(x) = x * 2, then

```
f ∘ g (x) = f(g(x)) = f(x * 2) = (x * 2) + 2
```

Note that the two notations f ∘ g (x) and f(g(x)) are equivalent. But writing a composition as f(g(x)) implies using x as a placeholder for the argument. Using the f ∘ g notation, you can express a function composition without using this placeholder.

If you apply this function to 5, you'll get the following:

```
f ∘ g (5) = f(g(5)) = f(5 * 2) = 10 + 2 = 12
```

It's interesting to note that f ∘ g is generally different from g ∘ f, although they may sometimes be equivalent. For example:

```
g ∘ f (5) = g(f(5)) = g(5 + 2) = 7 * 2 = 14
```

Note that the functions are applied in the inverse of the writing order. If you write f ∘ g, you first apply g, and then f. Standard Java 8 functions define the compose() method and the andThen() method to represent both cases (which, by the way, isn't necessary because f.andThen(g) is the same as g.compose(f), or g ∘ f).

FUNCTIONS OF SEVERAL ARGUMENTS

So far, we've talked only about functions of one argument. What about functions of several arguments? Simply said, there's no such thing as a function of several arguments. Remember the definition? A function is a relation between a source set and a target set. It isn't a relation between two or more source sets and a target set. A function can't have several arguments.

But the product of two sets is itself a set, so a function from such a product of sets into a set may appear to be a function of several arguments. Let's consider the following function:

```
f(x, y) = x + y
```

This may be a relation between N x N and N, in which case, it's a function. But it has only one argument, which is an element of N x N.

N x N is the set of all possible pairs of integers. An element of this set is a pair of integers, and a pair is a special case of the more general *tuple* concept used to represent combinations of several elements. A pair is a tuple of two elements.

Tuples are noted between parentheses, so (3, 5) is a tuple and an element of N x N. The function f can be applied to this tuple:

```
f((3, 5)) = 3 + 5 = 8
```

In such a case, you may, by convention, simplify writing by removing one set of parentheses:

```
f(3, 5) = 3 + 5 = 8
```

Nevertheless, it's still a function of one tuple, and not a function of two arguments.

FUNCTION CURRYING

Functions of tuples can be thought of differently. The function $f(3, 5)$ might be considered as a function from N to a set of functions of N. So the previous example could be rewritten as

```
f(x)(y) = g(y)
```

where

```
g(y) = x + y
```

In such a case, you can write

```
f(x) = g
```

which means that the result of applying the function f to the argument x is a new function g. Applying this g function to y gives the following:

```
g(y) = x + y
```

When applying g, x is no longer a variable. It doesn't depend on the argument or on anything else. It's a constant. If you apply this to $(3, 5)$, you get the following:

```
f(3)(5) = g(5) = 3 + 5 = 8
```

The only new thing here is that the codomain of f is a set of functions instead of a set of numbers. The *result* of applying f to an integer is a function. The *result* of applying this function to an integer is an integer.

   $f(x)(y)$ is the *curried* form of the function $f(x, y)$. Applying this transformation to a function of a tuple (which you can call a function of several arguments if you prefer) is called *currying*, after the mathematician Haskell Curry (although he wasn't the inventor of this transformation).

PARTIALLY APPLIED FUNCTIONS

The curried form of the addition function may not seem natural, and you might wonder if it corresponds to something in the real world. After all, with the curried version, you're considering both arguments separately. One of the arguments is considered first, and applying the function to it gives you a new function. Is this new function useful by itself, or is it simply a step in the global calculation?

   In the case of an addition, it doesn't seem useful. And by the way, you could start with either of the two arguments and it would make no difference. The intermediate function would be different, but not the end result.

Now consider a new function of a pair of values:

```
f(rate, price) = price / 100 * (100 + rate)
```

That function seems to be equivalent to this:

```
g(price, rate) = price / 100 * (100 + rate)
```

Let's now consider the curried versions of these two functions:

```
f(rate)(price)
g(price)(rate)
```

You know that `f` and `g` are functions. But what are `f(rate)` and `g(price)`? Yes, for sure, they're the results of applying `f` to `rate` and `g` to `price`. But what are the types of these results?

`f(rate)` is a function of a price to a price. If `rate = 9`, this function applies a tax of 9% to a price, giving a new price. You could call the resulting function `apply9-percentTax(price)`, and it would probably be a useful tool because the tax rate doesn't change often.

On the other hand, `g(price)` is a function of a rate to a price. If the price is $100, it gives a new function applying a price of $100 to a variable tax. What could you call this function? If you can't think of a meaningful name, that usually means that it's useless, though this depends on the problem you have to solve.

Functions like `f(rate)` and `g(price)` are sometimes called *partially applied functions*, in reference to the forms `f(rate, price)` and `g(price, rate)`. Partially applying functions can have huge consequences regarding argument evaluation. We'll come back to this subject in a later section.

If you have trouble understanding the concept of currying, imagine you're traveling in a foreign country, using a handheld calculator (or your smartphone) to convert from one currency to another. Would you prefer having to type the conversion rate each time you want to compute a price, or would you rather put the conversion rate in memory? Which solution would be less error prone?

FUNCTIONS HAVE NO EFFECTS

Remember that pure functions only return a value and do nothing else. They don't mutate any element of the outside world (with *outside* being relative to the function itself), they don't mutate their arguments, and they don't explode (or throw an exception, or anything else) if an error occurs. They can return an exception or anything else, such as an error message. But they must return it, not throw it, nor log it, nor print it.

2.2   *Functions in Java*

In chapter 1, you used what I called *functions* but were in fact methods. Methods are a way to represent (to a certain extent) functions in traditional Java.

2.2.1   Functional methods

A method can be functional if it respects the requirements of a pure function:

- It must not mutate anything outside the function. No internal mutation may be visible from the outside.
- It must not mutate its argument.
- It must not throw errors or exceptions.
- It must always return a value.
- When called with the same argument, it must always return the same result.

Let's look at an example.

Listing 2.1   Functional methods

```java
public class FunctionalMethods {

  public int percent1 = 5;
  private int percent2 = 9;
  public final int percent3 = 13;

  public int add(int a, int b) {
    return a + b;
  }
public setPercent2(int value) {
  percent2 = value;
}
  public int mult(int a, Integer b) {
    a = 5;
    b = 2;
    return a * b;
  }

  public int div(int a, int b) {
    return a / b;
  }

  public int applyTax1(int a) {
    return a / 100 * (100 + percent1);
  }

  public int applyTax2(int a) {
    return a / 100 * (100 + percent2);
  }

  public int applyTax3(int a) {
    return a / 100 * (100 + percent3);
  }

  public List<Integer> append(int i, List<Integer> list) {
    list.add(i);
    return list;
  }
}
```

Can you say which of these methods represent pure functions? Think for a few minutes before reading the answer that follows. Think about all the conditions and all the processing done inside the methods. Remember that what counts is what's visible from the outside. Don't forget to consider exceptional conditions.

Consider the first method:

```java
public int add(int a, int b) {
  return a + b;
}
```

add is a function because it always returns a value that depends only on its arguments. It doesn't mutate its arguments and doesn't interact in any way with the outside world. This method may cause an error if the sum a + b overflows the maximum int value. But this won't throw an exception. The result will be erroneous (a negative value), but this is another problem. The result must be the same each time the function is called with the same arguments. This doesn't mean that the result must be exact!

EXACTNESS The term *exact* doesn't mean anything by itself. It generally means that it fits what is expected, so to say whether the result of a function implementation is exact, you must know the intention of the implementer. Usually you'll have nothing but the function name to determine the intention, which can be a source of misunderstanding.

Consider the second method:

```java
public int mult(int a, Integer b) {
  a = 5;
  b = 2;
  return a * b;
}
```

The mult method is a pure function for the same reason as add. This may surprise you, because it seems to be mutating its arguments. But arguments in Java methods are passed by value, which means that values reassigned to them aren't visible from outside the method. This method will always return 10, which isn't useful because it doesn't depend on the arguments, but this doesn't break the requirements. When the method is called several times with the same arguments, it will return the same value.

By the way, this method is equivalent to a method with no argument. This is a special case of function: f(x) = 10. It's a constant.

Now consider the div:

```java
public int div(int a, int b) {
  return a / b;
}
```

The div method isn't a pure function because it will throw an exception if the divisor is 0. To make it a function, you could test the second parameter and return a value if it's null. It would have to be an int, so it would be difficult to find a meaningful value, but that's another problem.

Consider the fourth method:

```
public int percent1 = 5;

public int applyTax1(int a) {
  return a / 100 * (100 + percent1);
}
```

The `applyTax1` method seems not to be a pure function because its result depends on the value of `percent1`, which is public and can be modified between two function calls. As a consequence, two function calls with the same argument could return different values. `percent1` may be considered an implicit parameter, but this parameter isn't evaluated at the same time as the method argument. This isn't a problem if you use the `percent1` value only once inside the method, but if you read it twice, it could change between the two read operations. If you need to use the value twice, you must read it once and keep it in a local variable. This means the method `applyTax1` is a pure function of the tuple `(a, percent1)`, but it's not a pure function of a.

Compare that with the `applyTax2` method:

```
private int percent2 = 9;

public int applyTax2(int a) {
  return a / 100 * (100 + percent2);
}
```

The `applyTax2` method is no different. You might see it as a function, because the `percent2` property is private. But it's mutable, and it's mutated by the `setPercent2` method. Because `percent2` is accessed only once, `applyTax2` can be considered a pure function of the tuple `(a, percent2)`. But if considered as a function of a, it's not a pure function.

Now consider the sixth method:

```
public final int percent3 = 13;

public int applyTax3(int a) {
  return a / 100 * (100 + percent3);
}
```

The method `applyTax3` is somewhat special. Given the same argument, the method will always return the same value, because it depends only on its arguments and on the `percent3` final property, which can't be mutated. You might think that `applyTax3` isn't a pure function because the result doesn't depend only on the method's arguments (the result of a pure function must depend only on its arguments). But no contradiction exists here if you consider `percent3` as a supplemental argument. In fact, the class itself may be considered a supplemental implicit argument, because all its properties are accessible from inside the method.

This is an important notion. All instance methods can be replaced with static methods by adding an argument of the type of the enclosing class. So the `applyTax3` method may be rewritten as

```
public static int applyTax3(FunctionalMethods x, int a) {
  return a / 100 * 100 + x.percent3;
}
```

This method may be called from inside the class, passing a reference to `this` for the arguments, such as `applyTax3(this, a)`. It can also be called from outside, because it's public, provided a reference to a `FunctionalMethods` instance is available. Here, `applyTax3` is a pure function of the tuple `(this, a)`.

And finally, our last method:

```
public List<Integer> append(int i, List<Integer> list) {
 list.add(i);
 return list;
}
```

The `append` method mutates its argument before returning it, and this mutation is visible from outside the method, so it isn't a pure function.

OBJECT NOTATION VS. FUNCTIONAL NOTATION

You've seen that instance methods accessing class properties may be considered as having the enclosing class instance as an implicit parameter. Methods that don't access the enclosing class instance may be safely made static. Methods accessing the enclosing instance may also be made static if their implicit parameter (the enclosing instance) is made explicit.

Consider the `Payment` class from chapter 1:

```
public class Payment {

  public final CreditCard cc;
  public final int amount;

  public Payment(CreditCard cc, int amount) {
    this.cc = cc;
    this.amount = amount;
  }

  public Payment combine(Payment other) {
    if (cc.equals(other.cc)) {
      return new Payment(cc, amount + other.amount);
    } else {
      throw new IllegalStateException(
                      "Can't combine payments to different cards");
    }
  }
}
```

The `combine` method accesses the enclosing class's `cc` and `amount` fields. As a result, it can't be made static. This method has the enclosing class as an implicit parameter.

You could make this parameter explicit, which would allow you to make the method static:

```java
public class Payment {

  public final CreditCard cc;
  public final int amount;

  public Payment(CreditCard cc, int amount) {
    this.cc = cc;
    this.amount = amount;
  }

  public static Payment combine(Payment payment1, Payment payment2) {
    if (payment1.cc.equals(payment2.cc)) {
      return new Payment(payment1.cc, payment1.amount + payment2.amount);
    } else {
      throw new IllegalStateException(
                          "Can't combine payments to different cards");
    }
  }
}
```

A static method enables you to make sure no unwanted access exists to the enclosing scope. But it changes the way the method can be used.

If used from inside the class, the static method can be called, passing it the `this` reference:

```java
Payment newPayment = combine(this, otherPayment);
```

If the method is called from outside the class, you must use the class name:

```java
Payment newPayment = Payment.combine(payment1, payment2);
```

This makes little difference, but it all changes when you need to compose method calls. If you need to combine several payments, an instance method written as follows

```java
public Payment combine(Payment payment) {
    if (this.cc.equals(payment.cc)) {
      return new Payment(this.cc, this.amount + payment.amount);
    } else {
      throw new IllegalStateException(
                          "Can't combine payments to different cards");
    }
  }
```

may be used with object notation:

```java
Payment newPayment = p0.combine(p1).combine(p2).combine(p3);
```

That's much easier to read than this:

```java
Payment newPayment = combine(combine(combine(p0, p1), p2), p3);
```

Combining one more charge in the first case is also simpler.

2.2.2   *Java functional interfaces and anonymous classes*

Methods can be made functional, but they're missing something that keeps them from being able to represent functions in functional programming: they can't be manipulated besides being applied to arguments. You can't pass a method as an argument to another method. The consequence is that you can't compose methods without applying them. You can compose method applications, but not the methods themselves. A Java method belongs to the class where it's defined, and it stays there.

You can compose methods by calling them from other methods, but this must be done while writing the program. If you want different compositions depending on particular conditions, you have to lay out these compositions at writing time. You can't write a program in such a way that the program itself will change during execution. Or can you?

Yes, you can! Sometimes you register handlers at runtime to handle specific cases. You can add handlers to handler collections, or remove them, or change the order in which they'll be used. How can you do this? By using classes containing the methods you want to manipulate.

In a GUI, you often use listeners to handle specific events such as moving the mouse, resizing a window, or typing text. These listeners are generally created as anonymous classes implementing a specific interface. You can use the same principle to create functions.

Let's say you want to create a method to triple an integer value. First, you have to define an interface with a single method:

```
public interface Function {
  int apply(int arg);
}
```

You then implement this method to create your function:

```
Function triple = new Function() {

    @Override
    public int apply(int arg) {
        return arg * 3;
    }
};
```

This function can then be applied to an argument:

```
System.out.println(triple.apply(2));

6
```

I must admit that this isn't spectacular. A good old method would have been easier to use. If you want to create another function, you can process it exactly the same way:

```
Function square = new Function() {

    @Override
```

```
    public int apply(int arg) {
        return arg * arg;
    }
};
```

So far, so good, but what's the benefit of this?

2.2.3 Composing functions

If you think about functions as methods, composing them seems simple:

```
System.out.println(square.apply(triple.apply(2)));
```

```
36
```

But this isn't function composition. In this example, you're composing function applications. Function composition is a binary operation on functions, just as addition is a binary operation on numbers. So you can compose functions programmatically, using a method:

```
Function compose(final Function f1, final Function f2) {
    return new Function() {
        @Override
        public int apply(int arg) {
            return f1.apply(f2.apply(arg));
        }
    };
}

System.out.println(compose(triple, square).apply(3));
```

```
27
```

Now you can start seeing how powerful this concept is! But two big problems remain. The first is that our functions can only take integer (int) arguments and return integers. Let's deal with this first.

2.2.4 Polymorphic functions

To make our function more reusable, you can change it into a polymorphic function by using parameterized types, which are implemented in Java using generics:

```
public interface Function<T, U> {
    U apply(T arg);
}
```

Given this new interface, you can rewrite our functions as follows:

```
Function<Integer, Integer> triple = new Function<Integer, Integer>() {
    @Override
    public Integer apply(Integer arg) {
        return arg * 3;
    }
};
```

```
Function<Integer, Integer> square = new Function<Integer, Integer>() {
  @Override
  public Integer apply(Integer arg) {
    return arg * arg;
  }
};
```

As you see, we switched from `int` to `Integer` because `int` can't be used as a type parameter in Java. Hopefully, auto-boxing and auto-unboxing will make the conversion transparent.

EXERCISE 2.1
Write the `compose` method by using these two new functions.

> **NOTE** Solutions follow each exercise, but you should first try to solve the exercise by yourself without looking at the solution. The solution code also appears on the book's website. This exercise is simple, but some will be quite hard, so it might be difficult to refrain from cheating. Remember that the harder you search, the more you learn.

SOLUTION 2.1

```
static Function<Integer, Integer> compose(Function<Integer, Integer> f1,
                                          Function<Integer, Integer> f2) {
  return new Function<Integer, Integer>() {

    @Override
    public Integer apply(Integer arg) {
      return f1.apply(f2.apply(arg));
    }
  };
}
```

Problem with function compositions

Function composition is a powerful concept, but when implemented in Java, it presents a big danger. Composing a couple of functions is harmless. But think about building a list of 10,000 functions and composing them into a single one. (This could be done through a fold, an operation you'll learn about in chapter 3.)

In imperative programming, each function is evaluated before the result is passed as the input of the next function. But in functional programming, composing functions means building the resulting function without evaluating anything. Composing functions is powerful because functions can be composed without being evaluated. But as a consequence, applying the composed function results in numerous embedded method calls that will eventually overflow the stack. This can be demonstrated with a simple example (using lambdas, which will be introduced in the next section):

```
int fnum = 10_000; Function<Integer, Integer> g = x -> x;
Function<Integer, Integer> f = x -> x + 1;
for (int i = 0; i < fnum; i++) {
```

```
  g = Function.compose(f, g);
};

System.out.println(g.apply(0));
```

This program will overflow the stack when `fnum` is around 7,500. Hopefully you won't usually compose several thousand functions, but you should be aware of this.

2.2.5 *Simplifying the code by using lambdas*

The second problem you have is that functions defined using anonymous classes are cumbersome to use in coding. If you're using Java 5 to 7, you're out of luck, because there's no other way to go. Fortunately, Java 8 introduced lambdas.

Lambdas don't change the way the `Function` interface is defined, but they make implementing it much simpler:

```
Function<Integer, Integer> triple = x -> x * 3;
Function<Integer, Integer> square = x -> x * x;
```

Lambdas aren't just a syntax simplification. Lambdas have some consequences in terms of code compilation. One of the main differences between lambdas and the traditional way of writing anonymous classes is that the types on the right side of the equals sign can be omitted. This is possible because Java 8 comes with new capabilities regarding type inference.

Prior to Java 7, type inference was possible only when chaining identifier dereferencing, such as this:

```
System.out.println();
```

Here, you don't need to specify the type of `out`, and Java is able to find it. If you were to write this without chaining, you'd have to specify the type:

```
PrintStream out = System.out;
out.println();
```

Java 7 added a bit of type inference with the *diamond syntax*:

```
List<String> list = new ArrayList<>();
```

Here, you don't need to repeat the type parameter `String` for the `ArrayList` because Java is able to infer it by looking at the declaration. The same thing is possible with lambdas:

```
Function<Integer, Integer> triple = x -> x * 3;
```

In this example, the type of `x` is inferred by Java. But this isn't always possible. When Java complains that it isn't able to infer the type, you have to write it explicitly. Then you must use parentheses:

```
Function<Integer, Integer> triple = (Integer x) -> x * 3;
```

SPECIFYING FUNCTION TYPES

Although Java 8 introduced lambdas to ease function implementation, it's missing the same kind of tool to simplify writing function types. The type of a function from an `Integer` to an `Integer` is

```
Function<Integer, Integer>
```

and the function implementation is written like this:

```
x -> expression
```

It would be nice to be able to apply the same simplification to the type, which would allow you to write the whole thing as follows:

```
Integer -> Integer square = x -> x * x;
```

Unfortunately, this isn't possible in Java 8, and it's something you can't add yourself.

EXERCISE 2.2

Write a new version of the `compose` method by using lambdas.

SOLUTION 2.2

Replacing anonymous classes with lambdas is straightforward. Here's the code of the first version of the `compose` method:

```
static Function<Integer, Integer> compose(Function<Integer, Integer> f1,
                                          Function<Integer, Integer> f2) {
  return new Function<Integer, Integer>() {
    @Override
    public Integer apply(Integer arg) {
      return f1.apply(f2.apply(arg));
    }
  };
}
```

All you have to do is replace the return value of the `compose` method with the argument of the anonymous class's `apply` method, followed by an arrow (`->`) and the return value of the `apply` method:

```
static Function<Integer, Integer> compose(Function<Integer, Integer> f1,
                                          Function<Integer, Integer> f2) {
  return arg -> f1.apply(f2.apply(arg));
}
```

You can use any name for the argument. Figure 2.2 shows this process.

```
public static final Function<Integer, Integer> compose(final Function<Integer, Integer> f1,
                                                       final Function<Integer, Integer> f2) {

  return new Function<Integer, Integer>() {

    @Override
    public Integer apply(Integer arg) {
      return f1.apply(f2.apply(arg)) ;
    }
  };
}



public static final Function<Integer, Integer> compose(final Function<Integer, Integer> f1,
                                                       final Function<Integer, Integer> f2) {

  return arg -> f1.apply(f2.apply(arg));
}
```

Figure 2.2 Replacing anonymous classes with lambdas

2.3 *Advanced function features*

You've seen how to create apply and compose functions. You've also learned that functions can be represented by methods or by objects. But you haven't answered a fundamental question: why do you need function objects? Couldn't you simply use methods? Before answering this question, you have to consider the problem of the functional representation of multiargument methods.

2.3.1 *What about functions of several arguments?*

In section 2.1.1, I said that there are no functions of several arguments. There are only functions of one tuple of arguments. The cardinality of a tuple may be whatever you need, and there are specific names for tuples with a few arguments: pair, triplet, quartet, and so on. Other possible names exist, and some prefer to call them tuple2, tuple3, tuple4, and so forth. But I also said that arguments can be applied one by one, each application of one argument returning a new function, except for the last one.

Let's try to define a function for adding two integers. You'll apply a function to the first argument, and this will return a function. The type will be as follows:

```
Function<Integer, Function<Integer, Integer>>
```

This may seem a bit complicated, particularly if you think that it could have been written like this:

```
Integer -> Integer -> Integer
```

Note that because of associativity, this is equivalent to

```
Integer -> (Integer -> Integer)
```

where the left `Integer` is the type of the argument, and the element between parentheses is the return type, which obviously is a function type. If you remove the word `Function` from `Function<Integer, Function<Integer, Integer>>`, you get this:

```
<Integer, <Integer, Integer>>
```

This is exactly the same. The Java way of writing function types is much more verbose but not more complex.

EXERCISE 2.3
Write a function to add two `Integers`.

SOLUTION 2.3
This function will take an `Integer` as its argument and return a function from `Integer` to `Integer`, so the type will be `Function<Integer, Function<Integer, Integer>>`. Let's give it the name `add`. It will be implemented using lambdas. The end result is shown here:

```
Function<Integer, Function<Integer, Integer>> add = x -> y -> x + y;
```

You can see that you'll soon have problems with the length of the lines! Java has no type aliases, but you can achieve the same result through inheritance. If you have many functions to define with the same type, you can extend it with a much shorter identifier, like this:

```
public interface BinaryOperator extends
                    Function<Integer, Function<Integer, Integer>> {}
BinaryOperator add = x -> y -> x + y;
BinaryOperator mult = x -> y -> x * y;
```

The number of arguments isn't limited. You can define functions with as many arguments as you need. As I said in the first part of this chapter, functions such as the `add` function or the `mult` function you just defined are said to be the *curried* form of the equivalent functions of tuples.

2.3.2   *Applying curried functions*

You've seen how to write curried function types and how to implement them. But how do you apply them? Well, just like any function. You apply the function to the first argument, and then apply the result to the next argument, and so on until the last one. For example, you can apply the `add` function to 3 and 5:

```
System.out.println(add.apply(3).apply(5));
```

```
8
```

Here, you're again missing some syntactic sugar. It would be great if you could apply a function just by writing its name followed by its argument. It would allow coding, as in Scala:

```
add(3)(5)
```

Or even better, as in Haskell:

```
add 3 5
```

Perhaps in a future version of Java?

2.3.3 *Higher-order functions*

In section 2.14, you wrote a method to compose functions. That method was a functional one, taking as its argument a tuple of two functions and returning a function. But instead of using a method, you could use a function! This special kind of function, taking functions as its arguments and returning functions, is called a *higher-order function* (HOF).

EXERCISE 2.4

Write a function to compose the two functions `square` and `triple` used in exercise 2.2.

SOLUTION 2.4

This exercise is easy if you follow the right procedure. The first thing to do is to write the type. This function will work on two arguments, so it'll be a curried function. The two arguments and the return type will be functions from `Integer` to `Integer`:

```
Function<Integer, Integer>
```

You can call this `T`. You want to create a function taking an argument of type `T` (the first argument) and returning a function from `T` (the second argument) to `T` (the return value). The type of the function is then as follows:

```
Function<T, Function<T, T>>
```

If you replace `T` with its value, you obtain the real type:

```
Function<Function<Integer, Integer>,
        Function<Function<Integer, Integer>,
                Function<Integer, Integer>>>
```

The main problem here is the line length! Let's now add the implementation, which is much easier than the type:

```
x -> y -> z -> x.apply(y.apply(z));
```

The complete code is shown here:

```
Function<Function<Integer, Integer>,
        Function<Function<Integer, Integer>,
                Function<Integer, Integer>>> compose =
                        x -> y -> z -> x.apply(y.apply(z));
```

You can write this code on a single line! Let's test this code with the `square` and `triple` functions:

```
Function<Integer, Integer> triple = x -> x * 3;
```

```
Function<Integer, Integer> square = x -> x * x;

Function<Integer, Integer> f = compose.apply(square).apply(triple);
```

In this code, you start by applying the first argument, which gives you a new function to apply to the second argument. The result is a function, which is the composition of the two function arguments. Applying this new function to (for example) 2 gives you the result of first applying triple to 2 and then applying square to the result (which corresponds to the definition of function composition):

```
System.out.println(f.apply(2));
```

36

Pay attention to the order of the parameters: triple is applied first, and then square is applied to the result returned by triple.

2.3.4   *Polymorphic higher-order functions*

Our compose function is fine, but it can compose only functions from Integer to Integer. It would be much more interesting if you could compose any types of functions, such as String to Double or Boolean to Long. But that's only the beginning. A fully polymorphic compose function would allow you to compose Function<Integer, Function<Integer, Integer>>, such as the add and mult you wrote in exercise 2.3. It should also allow you to compose functions of different types, provided that the return type of one is the same as the argument type of the other.

EXERCISE 2.5 (HARD)
Write a polymorphic version of the compose function.

HINT
You may face two problems in trying to solve this exercise. The first is the lack of polymorphic properties in Java. In Java, you can create polymorphic classes, interfaces, and methods, but you can't define polymorphic properties. The solution is to store the function in a method, class, or interface, instead of in a property.

The second problem is that Java doesn't handle variance, so you may find yourself trying to cast a Function<Integer, Integer> to a Function<Object, Object>, which will result in a compiler error. In this case, you'll have to help Java by specifying the type explicitly.

SOLUTION 2.5
The first step seems to be to "generify" the example of exercise 2.4:

```
<T, U, V> Function<Function<T, U>,
            Function<Function<V, T>,
                Function<V, U>>> higherCompose =
                    f -> g -> x -> f.apply(g.apply(x));
```

But this isn't possible, because Java doesn't allow standalone generic properties. To be generic, a property must be created in a scope defining the type parameters. Only

Variance

Variance describes how parameterized types behave in relation to subtyping. *Covariance* means that `Matcher<Red>` is considered a subtype of `Matcher<Color>` if Red is a subtype of `Color`. In such case, `Matcher<T>` is said to be covariant on T. If, on the contrary, `Matcher<Color>` is considered a subtype of `Matcher<Red>`, then `Matcher<T>` is said to be contravariant on T. In Java, although an `Integer` is a subtype of `Object`, a `List<Integer>` is not a subtype of `List<Object>`. You may find this strange, but a `List<Integer>` is an `Object`, but it is not a `List<Object>`. And a `Function<Integer, Integer>` is not a `Function<Object, Object>`. (This is much less surprising!)

In Java, all parameterized types are said to be invariant on their parameter.

classes, interfaces, and methods can define type parameters, so you have to define your property inside one of these elements. The most practical is a static method:

```
static <T, U, V> Function<Function<U, V>,
                        Function<Function<T, U>,
                                Function<T, V>>> higherCompose() {
  return f -> g -> x -> f.apply(g.apply(x));
}
```

Note that the method called `higherCompose()` takes no parameter and always returns the same value. It's a constant. The fact that it's defined as a method is irrelevant from this point of view. It isn't a method for composing functions. It's only a method returning a function to compose functions.

Beware of the order of the type parameters and how they correspond to the implementation lambda parameters, as shown in figure 2.3.

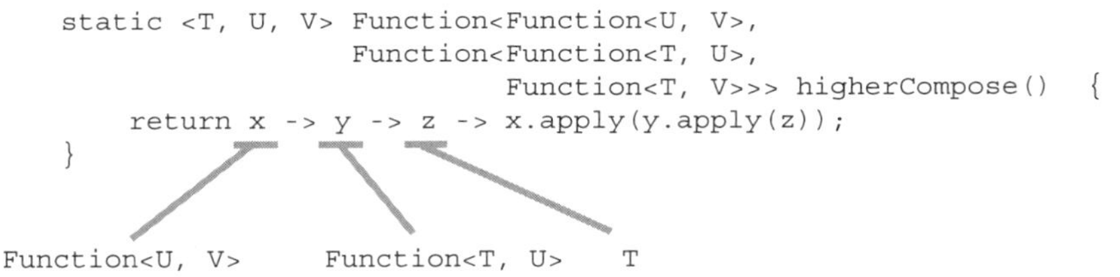

```
static <T, U, V> Function<Function<U, V>,
                Function<Function<T, U>,
                        Function<T, V>>> higherCompose() {
    return x -> y -> z -> x.apply(y.apply(z));
}
```

Function<U, V>   Function<T, U>   T

Figure 2.3 Pay attention to the order of type parameters.

You could give the lambda parameters more-meaningful names, such as uvFunction and tuFunction, or more simply uv and tu, but you should refrain from doing so. Names aren't reliable. They show the intention (of the programmer) and nothing else. You could easily switch the names without noticing any change:

```
static <T, U, V> Function<Function<U, V>,
                Function<Function<T, U>,
                        Function<T, V>>> higherCompose() {
```

```
    return tuFunc -> uvFunc -> t -> tuFunc.apply(uvFunc.apply(t));
}
```

In this example, tuFunc is a function from U to V, and uvFunc is a function from T to U.

If you need more information about the types, you can simply write them in front of each lambda parameter, enclosing the type and the parameter between parentheses:

```
static <T, U, V> Function<Function<U, V>,
                          Function<Function<T, U>,
                                   Function<T, V>>> higherCompose() {
  return (Function<U, V> f) -> (Function<T, U > g) -> (T x)
                                                    -> f.apply(g.apply(x));
}
```

Now you might want to use this function in the following way:

```
Integer x = Function.higherCompose().apply(square).apply(triple).apply(2);
```

But this doesn't compile, producing the following error:

```
Error:(39, 48) java: incompatible types: ...Function<java.lang.
  ➥Integer,java.lang.Integer> cannot be converted to ....Function<java.lang.
  ➥Object,java.lang.Object>
```

The compiler is saying that it couldn't infer the real types for the T, U, and V type parameters, so it used Object for all three. But the square and triple functions have types Function<Integer, Integer>. If you think that this is enough information to infer the T, U, and V types, then you're smarter than Java! Java tried to go the other way around, casting a Function<Integer, Integer> into a Function<Object, Object>. And although an Integer is an Object, a Function<Integer, Integer> isn't a Function <Object, Object>. These two types aren't related because types are invariant in Java. For the cast to work, the types should have been covariant, but Java doesn't know about variance.

The solution is to revert to the original problem and help the compiler by telling it what real types T, U, and V are. This can be done by inserting the type information between the dot and the method name:

```
Integer x = Function.<Integer, Integer, Integer>higherCompose().apply(....
```

This is somewhat impractical, but that isn't the main problem. More often, you'll group functions such as higherCompose in a library class, and you may wish to use static import to simplify the code:

```
import static com.fpinjava. ... .Function.*;
...
Integer x = <Integer, Integer, Integer>higherCompose().apply(...;
```

Unfortunately, this won't compile!

EXERCISE 2.6 (EASY NOW!)

Write the `higherAndThen` function that composes the functions the other way around, which means that `higherCompose(f, g)` is equivalent to `higherAndThen(g, f)`.

SOLUTION 2.6

```
public static <T, U, V> Function<Function<T, U>, Function<Function<U, V>,
                                              Function<T, V>>> higherAndThen() {
  return f -> g -> x -> g.apply(f.apply(x));
}
```

Testing function parameters

If you have any doubt concerning the order of the parameters, you should test these higher-order functions with functions of different types. Testing with functions from `Integer` to `Integer` will be ambiguous, because you'll be able to compose the functions in both orders, so an error will be difficult to detect. Here's a test using functions of different types:

```
public void TestHigherCompose() {

  Function<Double, Integer> f = a -> (int) (a * 3);
  Function<Long, Double> g = a -> a + 2.0;

  assertEquals(Integer.valueOf(9), f.apply((g.apply(1L))));
  assertEquals(Integer.valueOf(9),
    Function.<Long, Double, Integer>higherCompose().apply(f).apply(g).ap
           ply(1L));
}
```

Note that Java is unable to infer the types, so you have to provide them when calling the `higherCompose` function.

2.3.5 *Using anonymous functions*

Until now, you've been using named functions. These functions were implemented as anonymous classes, but the instances you created were named and had explicit types. Often you won't define names for functions, and you'll use them as anonymous instances. Let's look at an example.

Instead of writing

```
Function<Double, Double> f = x -> Math.PI / 2 - x;
Function<Double, Double> sin = Math::sin;
Double cos = Function.compose(f, sin).apply(2.0);
```

you can use anonymous functions:

```
Double cos = Function.compose(x -> Math.PI / 2 - x, Math::sin).apply(2.0);
```

Here, you use the `compose` method statically defined in the `Function` class. But this also applies to higher-order functions:

```
Double cos = Function.<Double, Double, Double>higherCompose()
                .apply(z -> Math.PI / 2 - z).apply(Math::sin).apply(2.0);
```

Method references

Beside lambdas, Java 8 also brings method references, which is a syntax that can be used to replace a lambda when the lambda implementation consists of a method call with a single argument. For example,

```
Function<Double, Double> sin = Math::sin;
```

is equivalent to this:

```
Function<Double, Double> sin = x -> Math.sin(x);
```

Here, `sin` is a static method in the `Math` class. If it was an instance method in the current class, you could have written the following:

```
Function<Double, Double> sin = this.sin(x);
```

This kind of code will be often used in this book to make a function out of a method.

WHEN TO USE ANONYMOUS AND WHEN TO USE NAMED FUNCTIONS

Apart from special cases when anonymous functions can't be used, it's up to you to choose between anonymous and named functions. As a general rule, functions that are used only once are defined as anonymous instances. But *used once* means that you write the function once. It doesn't mean that it's instantiated only once.

In the following example, you define a method to compute the cosine of a `Double` value. The method implementation uses two anonymous functions because you're using a lambda expression and a method reference:

```
Double cos(Double arg) {
  return Function.compose(z -> Math.PI / 2 - z, Math::sin).apply(arg);
}
```

Don't worry about the creation of anonymous instances. Java won't always create new objects each time the function is called. And anyway, instantiating such objects is cheap. Instead, you should decide whether to use anonymous or named functions by considering only the clarity and maintainability of your code. If you're concerned with performance and reusability, you should be using method references as often as possible.

TYPE INFERENCE

Type inference can also be an issue with anonymous functions. In the previous example, the types of the two anonymous functions can be inferred by the compiler because it knows that the `compose` methods take two functions as arguments:

```
static <T, U, V> Function<V, U> compose(Function<T, U> f, Function<V, T> g)
```

But this won't always work. If you replace the second argument with a lambda instead of a method reference,

```
Double cos(Double arg) {
  return Function.compose(z -> Math.PI / 2 - z,
                          a -> Math.sin(a)).apply(arg);
}
```

the compiler is lost and displays the following error message:

```
Error:(64, 63) java: incompatible types: java.lang.Object cannot be converted
      to double
Error:(64, 44) java: bad operand types for binary operator '-'
  first type: double
  second type: java.lang.Object
Error:(64, 72) java: incompatible types: java.lang.Object cannot be converted
      to java.lang.Double
```

The compiler is so confused that it even finds a nonexistent error in column 44! But the error in column 63 is real. As strange as it may seem, Java is unable to guess the type of the second argument. To make this code compile, you have to add type annotations:

```
Double cos(Double arg) {
  return Function.compose(z -> Math.PI / 2 - z,
                (Function<Double, Double>) (a) -> Math.sin(a)).apply(arg);
}
```

This is a good reason to prefer method references.

2.3.6 *Local functions*

You just saw that you can define functions locally in methods, but you can't define methods within methods.

On the other hand, functions can be defined inside functions without any problem through lambdas. The most frequent case you'll encounter is embedded lambdas, shown here:

```
public <T> Result<T> ifElse(List<Boolean> conditions, List<T> ifTrue) {
  return conditions.zip(ifTrue)
      .flatMap(x -> x.first(y -> y._1))
      .map(x -> x._2);
}
```

Don't worry if you don't understand what this code does. You'll learn about this kind of code in later chapters. Note, however, that the flatMap method takes a function as its argument (in the form of a lambda), and that the implementation of this function (the code after the ->) defines a new lambda, which corresponds to a locally embedded function.

Local functions aren't always anonymous. They're generally named when used as *helper functions*. In traditional Java, using helper methods is common practice. These methods allow you to simplify the code by abstracting portions of it. The same technique is used with functions, although you may not notice it because it's made implicit when using anonymous lambdas. But using explicitly declared local functions is always possible, as in the following example, which is nearly equivalent to the previous one:

```
public <T> Result<T> ifElse_(List<Boolean> conditions, List<T> ifTrue) {
  Function<Tuple<Boolean, T>, Boolean> f1 = y -> y._1;
  Function<List<Tuple<Boolean, T>>, Result<Tuple<Boolean, T>>> f2 =
                                                  x -> x.first(f1);
  Function<Tuple<Boolean, T>, T> f3 = x -> x._2;
  return conditions.zip(ifTrue)
      .flatMap(f2)
      .map(f3);
}
```

As mentioned previously, these two forms (with or without local named functions) have a little difference that can sometimes become important. When it comes to type inference, using named functions implies writing types explicitly, which can be necessary when the compiler can't infer types correctly.

It's not only useful to the compiler, but also a tremendous help to the programmer having trouble with types. Explicitly writing the expected types can help locate the exact place where expectations aren't met.

2.3.7 *Closures*

You've seen that pure functions must not depend on anything other than their arguments to evaluate their return values. Java methods often access class members, either to read or even write them. Methods may even access static members of other classes. I've said that *functional* methods are methods that respect referential transparency, which means they have no observable effects besides returning a value. The same is true for functions. Functions are pure if they don't have observable side effects.

But what about functions (and methods) with return values depending not only on their arguments, but on elements belonging to the enclosing scope? You've already seen this case, and these elements of the enclosing scope could be considered implicit parameters of the functions or methods using them.

Lambdas carry an additional requirement: a lambda can access a local variable only if it's final. This requirement isn't new to lambdas. It was already a requirement for anonymous classes prior to Java 8, and lambdas must respect the same condition, although it has been made a little less strict. Starting with Java 8, elements accessed from anonymous classes or lambdas can be implicitly final; they don't need to be declared final, provided they aren't modified. Let's look at an example:

```
public void aMethod() {

  double taxRate = 0.09;
  Function<Double, Double> addTax  = price -> price + price * taxRate;
  ...
}
```

In this example, the addTax function "closes" over the taxRate local variable. This will compile successfully as long as the taxRate variable is not modified, and there's no need to explicitly declare the variable final.

The following example won't compile because the taxRate variable is no longer implicitly final:

```
public void aMethod() {

  double taxRate = 0.09;
  Function<Double, Double> addTax  = price -> price + price * taxRate;
  ...
  taxRate = 0.13;
  ...
}
```

Note that this requirement only applies to local variables. The following will compile without a problem:

```
double taxRate = 0.09;

public void aMethod() {

  Function<Double, Double> addTax  = price -> price + price * taxRate;
  taxRate = 0.13;
  ...
}
```

It's important to note that, in this case, addTax is not a function of price, because it won't always give the same result for the same argument. It may, however, be seen as a function of the tuple (price, taxRate).

Closures are compatible with pure functions if you consider them as additional implicit arguments. They can, however, cause problems when refactoring the code, and also when functions are passed as parameters to other functions. This can result in programs that are difficult to read and maintain.

One way to make programs more modular is to use functions of tuples of arguments:

```
double taxRate = 0.09;

Function<Tuple<Double, Double>, Double> addTax
  = tuple -> tuple._2 + tuple._2 * tuple._1;

System.out.println(addTax.apply(new Tuple<>(taxRate, 12.0)));
```

But using tuples is cumbersome, because Java doesn't offer a simple syntax for this, except for function arguments, where the parentheses notation can be used. You'd have to define a special interface for a function of tuples, such as this:

```
interface Function2<T, U, V> {
  V apply(T t, U u);
}
```

This interface can be used in lambdas:

```
Function2<Double, Double, Double> addTax = (taxRate, price) -
    > price + price * taxRate;
double priceIncludingTax = addTax.apply(0.09, 12.0);
```

Note that the lambda is the only place where Java allows you to use the (x, y) notation for tuples. Unfortunately, it can't be used in any other cases, such as returning a tuple from a function.

You could also use the class BiFunction defined in Java 8, which simulates a function of a tuple of two arguments, or even BinaryOperator, which corresponds to a function of a tuple of two arguments of the same type, or even DoubleBinaryOperator, which is a function of a tuple of two double primitives. All these possibilities are fine, but what if you need three arguments or more? You could define Function3, Function4, and so on. But currying is a much better solution. That's why it's absolutely necessary to learn to use currying, which, as you already saw, is extremely simple:

```
double tax = 0.09;

Function<Double, Function<Double, Double>> addTax
  = taxRate -> price -> price + price * taxRate;

System.out.println(addTax.apply(tax).apply(12.00));
```

2.3.8 *Partial function application and automatic currying*

The closure and curried versions in the previous example give the same results and may be seen as equivalent. In fact, they are "semantically" different. As I've already said, the two parameters play totally different roles. The tax rate isn't supposed to change often, whereas the price is supposed to be different on each invocation. This appears clearly in the closure version. The function closes over a parameter that doesn't change (because it's final). In the curried version, both arguments may change on each invocation, although the tax rate won't change more often than in the closure version.

It's common to need a changing tax rate, such as when you have several tax rates for different categories of products or for different shipping destinations. In traditional Java, this could be accommodated by turning the class into a parameterized "tax computer":

```
public class TaxComputer {

  private final double rate;

  public TaxComputer(double rate) {
    this.rate = rate;
  }

  public double compute(double price) {
    return price * rate + price;
  }
}
```

This class allows you to instantiate several `TaxComputer` instances for several tax rates, and these instances can be reused as often as needed:

```
TaxComputer tc9 = new TaxComputer(0.09);
double price = tc9.compute(12);
```

The same thing can be achieved with a function by partially applying it:

```
Function<Double, Double> tc9 = addTax.apply(0.09);
double price = tc9.apply(12.0);
```

Here, the `addTax` function is the one from the end of section 2.3.7.

You can see that currying and partial application are closely related. Currying consists of replacing a function of a tuple with a new function that you can partially apply, one argument after the other. This is the main difference between a curried function and a function of a tuple. With a function of a tuple, all arguments are evaluated before the function is applied. With the curried version, all arguments must be known before the function is totally applied, but a single argument can be evaluated before the function is partially applied to it. You aren't obliged to totally curry the function. A function of three arguments can be curried into a function of a tuple that produces a function of a single argument.

In functional programming, currying and partially applying functions is done so often that it's useful to abstract these operations in order to be able to do this automatically. In the preceding sections, you used only curried functions and not functions of tuples. This presents a great advantage: partially applying this kind of function is absolutely straightforward.

EXERCISE 2.7 (VERY EASY)
Write a functional method to partially apply a curried function of two arguments to its first argument.

SOLUTION 2.7
You have nothing to do! The signature of this method is as follows:

```
<A, B, C> Function<B, C> partialA(A a, Function<A, Function<B, C>> f)
```

You can see immediately that partially applying the first argument is as simple as applying the second argument (a function) to the first one:

```
<A, B, C> Function<B, C> partialA(A a, Function<A, Function<B, C>> f) {
  return f.apply(a);
}
```

(If you'd like to see an example of how `partialA` may be used, please look at the unit test for this exercise, in the accompanying code.)

You may note that the original function was of type `Function<A, Function<B, C>>`, which means A → B → C. What if you want to partially apply this function to the second argument?

EXERCISE 2.8

Write a method to partially apply a curried function of two arguments to its second argument.

SOLUTION 2.8

With our previous function, the answer to the problem would be a method with the following signature:

```
<A, B, C> Function<A, C> partialB(B b, Function<A, Function<B, C>> f)
```

This exercise is slightly more difficult, but still simple if you carefully consider the types. Remember, you should always trust the types! They won't give you an immediate solution in all cases, but they will lead you to the solution. This function has only one possible implementation, so if you find an implementation that compiles, you can be sure it's correct!

What you know is you must return a function from A to C. So you can start the implementation by writing this:

```
<A, B, C> Function<A, C> partialB(B b, Function<A, Function<B, C>> f) {
  return a ->
```

Here, a is a variable of type A. After the right arrow, you must write an expression that's composed of the function f and the variables a and b, and it must evaluate to a function from A to C. The function f is a function from A to B -> C, so you can start by applying it to the A you have:

```
<A, B, C> Function<A, C> partialB(B b, Function<A, Function<B, C>> f) {
  return a -> f.apply(a)
```

This gives you a function from B to C. You need a C, and you already have a B, so once again, the answer is straightforward:

```
<A, B, C> Function<A, C> partialB(B b, Function<A, Function<B, C>> f) {
  return a -> f.apply(a).apply(b);
}
```

That's it! In fact, you had nearly nothing to do but to follow the types.

As I said, the most important thing is that you had a curried version of the function. You'll probably learn quickly how to write curried functions directly. One task that comes back frequently when starting to write functional Java programs is converting methods with several arguments into curried functions. This is extremely simple.

EXERCISE 2.9 (VERY EASY)

Convert the following method into a curried function:

```
<A, B, C, D> String func(A a, B b, C c, D d) {
  return String.format("%s, %s, %s, %s", a, b, c, d);
}
```

(I agree that this method is totally useless, but it's just an exercise.)

SOLUTION 2.9

Once again, you don't have much to do besides replacing the commas with right arrows. Remember, however, that you must define this function in a scope that accepts type parameters, which isn't the case for a property. You must then define it in a class, an interface, or a method with all needed type parameters.

You'll do it with a method. First, write the method type parameters:

```
<A,B,C,D>
```

Then, add the return type. It seems difficult at first, but it's only difficult to read. Just write the word Function< followed by the first parameter type and a comma:

```
<A,B,C,D> Function<A,
```

Then do the same thing with the second parameter type:

```
<A,B,C,D> Function<A, Function<B,
```

Then continue until no parameters are left:

```
<A,B,C,D> Function<A, Function<B, Function<C, Function<D,
```

Add the return type and close all opened brackets:

```
<A,B,C,D> Function<A, Function<B, Function<C, Function<D, String>>>>
```

Add the name of the function and the braces:

```
<A,B,C,D> Function<A, Function<B, Function<C, Function<D, String>>>> f() {
}
```

For the implementation, list as many parameters as needed, separating them with right arrows (ending with an arrow):

```
<A,B,C,D> Function<A, Function<B, Function<C, Function<D, E>>>> f() {
  return a -> b -> c -> d ->
}
```

Finally, add the implementation, which is the same as in the original method:

```
<A,B,C,D> Function<A, Function<B, Function<C, Function<D, String>>>> f() {
  return a -> b -> c -> d -> String.format("%s, %s, %s, %s", a, b, c, d);
}
```

The same principle can be applied to curry a function of a tuple.

EXERCISE 2.10

Write a method to curry a function of a Tuple<A, B> to C.

SOLUTION 2.10

Again, you just have to follow the types. You know the method will take a parameter of type Function<Tuple<A, B>, C> and will return Function<A, Function<B, C>>, so the signature is as follows:

```
<A, B, C> Function<A, Function<B, C>> curry(Function<Tuple<A, B>, C> f)
```

Now, for the implementation, you'll have to return a curried function of two arguments, so you can start with this:

```
<A, B, C> Function<A, Function<B, C>> curry(Function<Tuple<A, B>, C> f) {
  return a -> b ->
}
```

Eventually, you need to evaluate the return type. For this, you can use the function f and apply it to a new Tuple built with parameters a and b:

```
<A, B, C> Function<A, Function<B, C>> curry(Function<Tuple<A, B>, C> f) {
  return a -> b -> f.apply(new Tuple<>(a, b));
}
```

Once again, if it compiles, it can't be wrong. This certainty is one of the numerous benefits of functional programming! (This isn't always true, but you'll learn in the next chapter how to make this happen more often.)

2.3.9 *Switching arguments of partially applied functions*

If you have a function of two arguments, you might want to apply only the first argument to get a partially applied function. Let's say you have the following function:

```
Function<Double, Function<Double, Double>> addTax = x -> y -
    > y + y / 100 * x;
```

You might want to first apply the tax to get a new function of one argument that you can then apply to any price:

```
Function<Double, Double> add9percentTax = addTax.apply(9.0);
```

Then, when you want to add tax to a price, you can do this:

```
Double priceIncludingTax = add9percentTax.apply(price);
```

This is fine, but what if the initial function was as follows?

```
Function<Double, Function<Double, Double>> addTax = x -> y -
    > x + x / 100 * y;
```

In this case, the price is the first argument. Applying the price only is probably useless, but how can you apply the tax only? (You suppose you don't have access to the implementation.)

EXERCISE 2.11

Write a method to swap the arguments of a curried function.

SOLUTION 2.11

The following method returns a curried function with the arguments in reverse order. It could be generalized to any number of arguments and to any arrangement of them:

```
public static <T, U, V> Function<U, Function<T, V>> reverseArgs(Function<T,
  Function<U, V>> f) {
  return u -> t -> f.apply(t).apply(u);
}
```

Given this method, you can partially apply any of the two arguments. For example, if you have a function computing the monthly payment for a loan from an interest rate and an amount:

```
Function<Double, Function<Double, Double>> payment = amount -> rate -> ...
```

You can very easily create a function of one argument to compute the payment for a fixed amount and a varying rate, or a function computing the payment for a fixed rate and a varying amount.

2.3.10 *Recursive functions*

Recursive functions are a ubiquitous feature in most functional programming languages, although recursion and functional programming aren't connected. Some functional programmers even say that recursion is the goto feature of functional programming, and thus should be avoided as much as possible. Nevertheless, as functional programmers, you must master recursion, even if eventually you decide to avoid it.

As you may know, Java is limited in terms of recursion. Methods can call themselves recursively, but this implies that the state of the computation is pushed on the stack for each recursive call, until a terminal condition is reached, at which time all preceding states of the computation are popped out of the stack, one after the other, and evaluated. The size of the stack can be configured, but all threads will use the same size. The default size varies according to the implementation of Java, from 320 KB for a 32-bit version to 1,064 KB for a 64-bit implementation, both of which are very small compared to the size of the heap, where objects are stored. The end result is that the number of recursive steps is limited.

Determining how many recursive steps Java can handle is difficult, because it depends on the size of the data that's pushed on the stack, and also on the state of the stack when the recursive process starts. In general, Java can handle about 5,000 to 6,000 steps.

Pushing this limit artificially is possible because Java uses memoization internally. This technique consists of storing the results of functions or methods in memory to speed up future access. Instead of reevaluating a result, Java can retrieve it from memory if it has previously been stored. Besides speeding access, this can allow you to partly avoid recursion by finding a terminal state much quicker. We'll come back to this subject in chapter 4, where you'll learn how to create heap-based recursion in Java. For the rest of this section, you'll pretend Java's standard recursion isn't broken.

A recursive method is simple to define. The method factorial(int n) can be defined as returning 1 if its argument is 0, and n * factorial(n - 1) otherwise:

```
public int factorial(int n) {
  return n == 0 ? 1 : n * factorial(n - 1);
}
```

Recall that this will overflow the stack for n being somewhere between 5,000 and 6,000, so don't use this kind of code in production.

So writing recursive methods is easy. What about recursive functions?

EXERCISE 2.12

Write a recursive factorial function.

HINT

You shouldn't try to write an anonymous recursive function, because for the function to be able to call itself, it must have a name, and it must be defined under that name before calling itself. Because it should already be defined when it calls itself, that implies that it should be defined before you try to define it!

SOLUTION 2.12

Put aside this chicken-and-egg problem for the moment. Converting a single argument method into a function is straightforward. The type is Function<Integer, Integer>, and the implementation should be the same as for the method:

```
Function<Integer, Integer> factorial = n -
    > n <= 1 ? n : n * factorial.apply(n - 1);
```

Now for the tricky part. This code won't compile because the compiler will complain about an Illegal self reference. What does this mean? Simply that when the compiler reads this code, it's in the process of defining the factorial function. During this process, it encounters a call to the factorial function, which isn't yet defined.

As a consequence, defining a local recursive function isn't possible. But can you declare this function as a member variable or as a static variable? This wouldn't solve the self-reference problem, because it would be equivalent to defining a numeric variable such as this:

```
int x = x + 1;
```

This problem can be solved by first declaring the variable, and then changing its value, which can be done in the constructor or in any method but is much more convenient in an initializer, such as the following:

```
int x;
{
  x = x + 1;
}
```

This works because members are defined before initializers are executed, so the variable will first be initialized to the default value (0 for an int, null for a function). The fact that the variable is null for some time shouldn't be a real problem because initializers are executed before the constructor, so unless some other initializer uses this variable, you're safe. This trick can be used to define your function:

```
public Function<Integer, Integer> factorial;
{
  factorial = n -> n <= 1 ? n : n * factorial.apply(n - 1);
}
```

This can also be used for statically defined functions:

```
public static Function<Integer, Integer> factorial;

static {
  factorial = n -> n <= 1 ? n : n * factorial.apply(n - 1);
}
```

The only problem with this trick is that the field may not be declared final, which is annoying because functional programmers love immutability. Fortunately, another trick is available for this:

```
public final Function<Integer, Integer> factorial =
                n -> n <= 1 ? n : n * this.factorial.apply(n - 1);
```

By adding this. before the variable name, it's possible to self-reference it while making it final. For the static implementation, you just have to replace this with the name of the including class:

```
public static final Function<Integer, Integer> factorial =
        n -> n <= 1 ? n : n * FunctionExamples.factorial.apply(n - 1);
```

2.3.11 *The identity function*

You've seen that in functional programming, functions are treated as data. They can be passed as arguments to other functions, can be returned by functions, and can be used in operations, exactly like integers or doubles. In future programs, you'll apply operations to functions, and you'll need a neutral element, or identity element, for these operations. A neutral element will act as the 0 for addition, or 1 for multiplication, or the empty string for string concatenation.

The identity function can be added to the definition of our Function class in the form of a method named identity, returning the identity function:

```
static <T> Function<T, T> identity() {
  return t -> t;
}
```

With this additional method, our Function interface is now complete, as shown in the following listing.

Listing 2.2   The complete `Function` interface

```
public interface Function<T, U> {

  U apply(T arg);

  default <V> Function<V, U> compose(Function<V, T> f) {
    return x -> apply(f.apply(x));
  }

  default <V> Function<T, V> andThen(Function<U, V> f) {
    return x -> f.apply(apply(x));
  }

  static <T> Function<T, T> identity() {
    return t -> t;
  }

  static <T, U, V> Function<V, U> compose(Function<T, U> f,
                                          Function<V, T> g) {
    return x -> f.apply(g.apply(x));
  }

  static <T, U, V> Function<T, V> andThen(Function<T, U> f,
                                          Function<U, V> g) {
    return x -> g.apply(f.apply(x));
  }

  static <T, U, V> Function<Function<T, U>,
                    Function<Function<U, V>,
                             Function<T, V>>> compose() {
    return x -> y -> y.compose(x);
  }

  static <T, U, V> Function<Function<T, U>,
                    Function<Function<V, T>,
                             Function<V, U>>> andThen() {
    return x -> y -> y.andThen(x);
  }

  static <T, U, V> Function<Function<T, U>,
                    Function<Function<U, V>,
                             Function<T, V>>> higherAndThen() {
    return x -> y -> z -> y.apply(x.apply(z));
  }

  static <T, U, V> Function<Function<U, V>,
                    Function<Function<T, U>,
                             Function<T, V>>> higherCompose() {
    return (Function<U, V> x) ->
                  (Function<T, U> y) -> (T z) -> x.apply(y.apply(z));
  }
}
```

2.4   *Java 8 functional interfaces*

Lambdas are used in places where a specific interface is expected. This is how Java can determine which method to call. Java doesn't impose any constraints on naming, as may be the case in other languages. The only constraint is that the interface used must not be ambiguous, which generally means it should have only one abstract method. (In reality, it's a bit more complex, because some methods don't count.) Such interfaces are said to be *SAM type, for single abstract method*, and are called *functional interfaces*.

Note that lambdas aren't used only for functions. In standard Java 8, many functional interfaces are available, although they aren't all related to functions. The most important ones are listed here:

- `java.util.function.Function` is close to the `Function` developed in this chapter. It adds a wildcard to the method parameter types to make them more useful.
- `java.util.function.Supplier` is equivalent to a function with no argument. In functional programming, it's a constant, so it might not look useful at first, but it has two specific uses: First, if it's not referentially transparent (not a pure function), it can be used to supply variable data, such as time or random numbers. (We won't use such nonfunctional things!) The second use, much more interesting, is to allow lazy evaluation. We'll come back to this subject often in the next chapters.
- `java.util.function.Consumer` isn't at all for functions, but for effects. (Here, it's not a *side* effect, because the effect is the only result you get with a `Consumer`, since it doesn't return anything.)
- `java.lang.Runnable` can also be used for effects that don't take any parameters. It's often preferable to create a special interface for this, because `Runnable` is supposed to be used with threads, and most syntax-checking tools will complain if it's used in another context.

Java defines many other functional interfaces (43 in the `java.util.function` package) that are mostly useless for functional programming. Many of them deal with primitives and others with functions of two arguments, and there are special versions for operations (functions of two arguments of the same type).

In this book, I don't talk much about standard Java 8 functions. This is intentional. This isn't a book about Java 8. It's a book about functional programming, and it happens to use Java for the examples. You're learning how to construct things rather than to use provided components. After you master the concepts, it'll be up to you to choose between your own functions or the standard Java 8 ones. Our `Function` is similar to the Java 8 `Function`. It doesn't use a wildcard for its argument in order to simplify the code shown in the book. On the other hand, the Java 8 `Function` doesn't define `compose` and `andThen` as higher-order functions, but only as methods. Other than these differences, these `Function` implementations are interchangeable.

2.5 Debugging with lambdas

Using lambdas promotes a new style of code writing. Code that was once written in several short lines is often replaced with one-liners such as this:

```java
public <T> T ifElse(List<Boolean> conditions, List<T> ifTrue, T ifFalse) {
```

```
        return conditions.zip(ifTrue).flatMap(x -> x.first(y -> y._1))
                            .map(x -> x._2).getOrElse(ifFalse);
}
```

(Here, the implementation of the ifElse method is split over two lines because of the book margins, but in a code editor it could be on a single line.)

In Java 5 to 7, this code would be written without using lambdas, as shown in the following listing.

Listing 2.3 A one-liner lambda-based method converted to previous Java versions
---

```
public <T> T ifElse(List<Boolean> conditions, List<T> ifTrue, T ifFalse) {

    Function<Tuple<Boolean, T>, Boolean> f1 =
        new Function<Tuple<Boolean, T>, Boolean>() {
          public Boolean apply(Tuple<Boolean, T> y) {
            return y._1;
          }
        };

    Function<List<Tuple<Boolean, T>>, Result<Tuple<Boolean, T>>> f2 =
        new Function<List<Tuple<Boolean, T>>, Result<Tuple<Boolean, T>>>() {
          public Result<Tuple<Boolean, T>> apply(List<Tuple<Boolean, T>> x) {
            return x.first(f1);
          }
        };

    Function<Tuple<Boolean, T>, T> f3 =
        new Function<Tuple<Boolean, T>, T>() {
          public T apply(Tuple<Boolean, T> x) {
            return x._2;
          }
        };

    Result<List<Tuple<Boolean, T>>> temp1 = conditions.zip(ifTrue);
    Result<Tuple<Boolean, T>> temp2 = temp1.flatMap(f2);
    Result<T> temp3 = temp2.map(f3);
    T result = temp3.getOrElse(ifFalse);
    return result;
}
```

Obviously, reading and writing the lambda version is much easier. The pre-Java 8 versions were often considered too complicated to be acceptable. But when it comes to debugging, the lambda version is much more of a problem. If a single line is equivalent to 20 lines of traditional code, how can you put breakpoints in it to find potential errors? The problem is that not all debuggers are powerful enough to be used easily with lambdas. This will eventually change, but in the meantime you might have to find other solutions. One simple solution is to break the one-line version into several lines, such as this:

```
public <T> T ifElse(List<Boolean> conditions, List<T> ifTrue, T ifFalse) {
    return conditions.zip(ifTrue)
                    .flatMap(x -> x.first(y -> y._1))
```

```
            .map(x -> x._2)
            .getOrElse(ifFalse);
   }
```

This allows you to set breakpoints on each physical line. It's certainly useful and it makes the code easier to read (and easier to publish in books). But it doesn't solve our problem because each line still contains many elements that can't always be investigated through traditional debuggers.

To make this problem less crucial, it's important to extensively unit test each component, which means each method and each function passed as an argument to each method. Here, it's easy. The methods used are (in order of appearance) `List.zip`, `Option.flatMap`, `List.first`, `Option.map`, and `Option.getOrElse`. Whatever these methods are doing, they can be extensively tested. You don't know about them yet, but you'll build the `Option` and `List` components in the next chapters, and also write the implementations of the `map`, `flatMap`, `first`, `zip`, and `getOrElse` methods (as well as many others). As you'll see, these methods are purely functional. They can't throw any exceptions and they always return the intended result without doing anything else. So, after they're fully tested, nothing bad can happen.

Regarding the functions, the preceding example uses three of them:

- x → x.first
- y → y._1
- x → x._2

The first one can't throw any exceptions because x can't be `null` (you'll see why in chapter 5), and method `first` can't throw an exception either.

The second and third functions can't throw a `NullPointerException` because you've ensured that a `Tuple` couldn't be constructed with `null` arguments. (See chapter 1 for the code of the `Tuple` class.) Figure 2.4 shows these functions in their anonymous form.

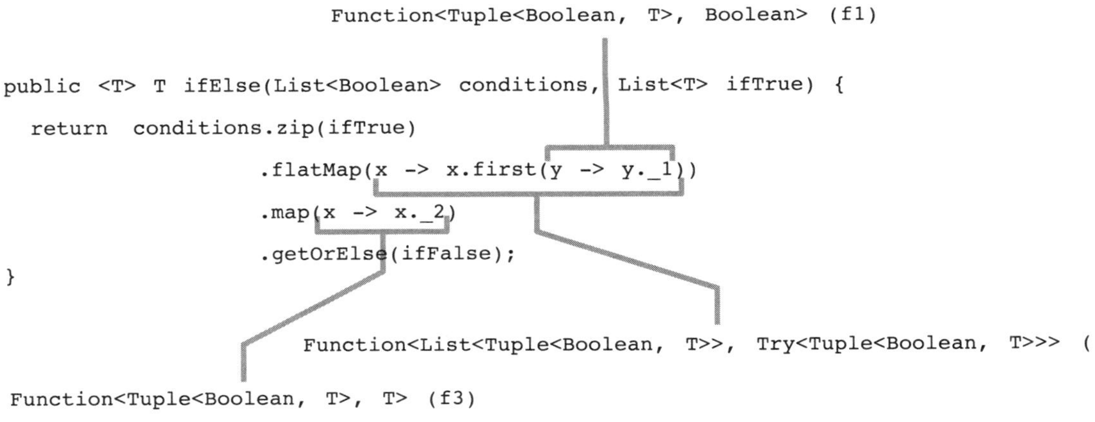

Figure 2.4   Functions in their anonymous form

This is one area where functional programming shines: if no components can break, the whole program can't either. In imperative programming, components might work fine in tests but break in production because of some nondeterministic behavior. If the behavior of a component depends on external conditions, you have no way to fully test it. And even if no component has any problem as a unit, the composition of several components could create conditions for the program to be ill-behaved. This can't happen with functional programming. If the components have a deterministic behavior, the whole composition will be deterministic too.

Many spots remain open for errors. The program might not do what is expected, because the components may be composed the wrong way. But implementation errors can't cause an unwanted crash. If this program crashes, it will be, for example, because a `null` reference has been passed to the `Tuple` constructor. You don't need a debugger to catch this kind of error.

So, yes, debugging functional programs that use lambdas extensively is somewhat more difficult than debugging imperative programs, but debugging is much less necessary, provided all the components have been validated. Keep in mind that this is true only if a thrown exception crashes the program. We'll come back to this in chapter 6. But for now, remember that by default, an exception or an error thrown will only crash the thread in which it happened, and not the whole application. Even an `OutOfMemoryError` might not crash the application, so you, as the programmer, have to handle this.

2.6   *Summary*

- A function is a relation between a source set and a target set. It establishes a correspondence between the elements of the source set (the domain) and the elements of the target set (the codomain).
- Pure functions have no visible effects beside returning a value.
- Functions have only one argument, which may be a tuple of several elements.
- Functions of tuples may be curried in order to apply them to one element of the tuple at a time.
- When a curried function is applied to only some of its arguments, we say that it's partially applied.
- In Java, functions may be represented by methods, lambdas, method references, or anonymous classes.
- Method references are the preferred representation for functions.
- Functions may be composed to create new functions.
- Functions can call themselves recursively, but the recursion depth is limited by the size of the stack.
- Lambdas and method references can be used in places where a functional interface is expected.

Making Java more functional

3

You now have all the types of functions you'll need. As you saw in the previous chapter, these functions don't require any exceptions to the traditional Java coding rules. Using methods as pure functions (a.k.a. functional methods) is perfectly in line with most so-called Java best practices. You haven't changed the rules or added any exotic constructs. You've just added some restrictions about what functional methods can do: they can return a value, and that's all. They can't mutate any objects or references in the enclosing scope, nor their arguments. In the first part of this chapter, you'll learn how to apply the same principles to Java control structures.

You've also learned how to create objects representing functions, so that these functions can be passed as arguments to methods and other functions. But for such functions to be useful, you must create the methods or functions that can manipulate them. In the second part of this chapter, you'll learn how to abstract collection operations and control structures to use the power of functions.

The last part of the chapter presents techniques that will allow you to get the most out of the type system when handling business problems.

3.1   *Making standard control structures functional*

Control structures are the main building blocks of imperative programming. No imperative Java programmer would believe it's possible to write programs without using if ... else, switch ... case, and for, while, and do loops. These structures are the essence of imperative programming. But in the following chapters, you'll learn how to write functional programs with absolutely no control structures. In this section, you'll be less adventurous—we'll only look at using the traditional control structures in a more functional style.

One point you learned in chapter 2 is that purely functional methods can't do anything but return a value. They can't mutate an object or reference in the enclosing scope. The value returned by a method can depend only on its arguments, although the method can read data in the enclosing scope. In such a case, the data is considered to be implicit arguments.

In imperative programming, control structures define a scope in which they generally do something, which means they have an effect. This effect might be visible only inside the scope of the control structure, or it might be visible in the enclosing scope. The control structures might also access the enclosing scope to read values. The following listing shows a basic example of email validation.

Listing 3.1   Simple email validation

```
final Pattern emailPattern =
    Pattern.compile("^[a-z0-9._%+-]+@[a-z0-9.-]+\\.[a-z]{2,4}$");

void testMail(String email) {
  if (emailPattern.matcher(email).matches()) {        ◁─────  ❶ The if condition
    sendVerificationMail(email);                       ◁──────    "closes" over the
  } else {                                                        emailPattern field.
    logError("email " + email + " is invalid.");       ◁──
  }
}                                                              ❷ If the condition is
                                                                 fulfilled, an email
void sendVerificationMail(String s) {                            is sent.
  System.out.println("Verification mail sent to " + s);
}                                                              If the condition
                                                              isn't fulfilled, an
private static void logError(String s) {                      error message is
  System.err.println("Error message logged: " + s);        ❸ logged.
}
```

Email ❹ sending is simulated.

Message ❺ logging is simulated.

In this example, the if ... else structure ❶ accesses the emailPattern variable from the enclosing scope. From the Java syntax point of view, there's no obligation for this variable to be final, but it's necessary if you want to make the testMail method functional.

Another solution would be to declare the pattern inside the method, but this would cause it to be compiled for each method call. If the pattern could change between calls, you should make it a second parameter of the method. If the condition is true, an effect ❷ is applied to this email variable. This effect consists of sending a verification email, probably to check whether the email address, besides being well formed, is a valid one. In this example, the effect is simulated ❹ by printing a message to standard output. If the condition is false, a different effect ❸ is applied to the variable by including it in an error message. This message is logged ❺, which once again is simulated by printing to *standard error.*

3.2 Abstracting control structures

The code in listing 3.1 is purely imperative. You'll never find such code in functional programming. Although the testMail method seems to be a pure effect because it doesn't return anything, it mixes data processing with effects. This is something you want to avoid, because it results in code that's impossible to test. Let's see how you can clean this up.

The first thing you may want to do is separate computation and effects so you can test the computation result. This could be done imperatively, but I prefer to use a function, as shown in the following listing.

Listing 3.2 Using a function to validate the email

```
final Pattern emailPattern =
    Pattern.compile("^[a-z0-9._%+-]+@[a-z0-9.-]+\\.[a-z]{2,4}$");
final Function<String, Boolean> emailChecker = s ->
                            emailPattern.matcher(s).matches();      <─┐

void testMail(String email) {                                         Declares emailChecker
  if (emailChecker.apply(email)) {              <─┐                    function in the
    sendVerificationMail(email);                                      enclosing scope
  } else {
    logError("email " + email + " is invalid.");    Applies emailChecker function
  }                                                  to the string to validate
}
```

Now you can test the data processing part of the program (validating the email string) because you've clearly separated it from the effects. But you still have many problems. One is that you handle only the case where the string doesn't validate. But if the string received is null, a NullPointerException (NPE) is thrown. Consider the following example:

```
testMail("john.doe@acme.com");
testMail(null);
testMail("paul.smith@acme.com");
```

The third line won't be executed, even though the email address is valid, because the NPE thrown by the second line kills the thread. It would be better to get a logged message indicating what happened, and to continue processing the next address.

Another problem appears if you receive an empty string:

```
testMail("");
```

This won't cause an error, but the address won't validate, and the following message will be logged:

```
email  is invalid.
```

The double space (between "email" and "is") indicates that the string was empty. A specific message would be better, such as this:

```
email must not be empty.
```

To handle these problems, you'll first define a special component to handle the result of the computation.

Listing 3.3   A component to manage the result of a computation

```
public interface Result {                          ◄─┐  The Result interface represents the
                                                        result of a computation.
  public class Success implements Result {}      ◄─┐  Success indicates a
                                                       successful computation.
  public class Failure implements Result {       ◄─
                                                       Failure indicates a failing
    private final String errorMessage;                 computation and is instantiated
                                                       with an error message.
    public Failure(String s) {
      this.errorMessage = s;
    }

    public String getMessage() {
      return errorMessage;
    }
  }
}
```

Now you can write your new version of the program.

Listing 3.4   The program with better error handling

```
import java.util.regex.Pattern;

public class EmailValidation {

  static Pattern emailPattern =
      Pattern.compile("^[a-z0-9._%+-]+@[a-z0-9.-]+\\.[a-z]{2,4}$");

  static Function<String, Result> emailChecker = s -> {
    if (s == null) {
      return new Result.Failure("email must not be null");
    } else if (s.length() == 0) {
      return new Result.Failure("email must not be empty");
    } else if (emailPattern.matcher(s).matches()) {
      return new Result.Success();
```

```
    } else {
      return new Result.Failure("email " + s + " is invalid.");
    }
  };
  public static void main(String... args) {
    validate("this.is@my.email");
    validate(null);
    validate("");
    validate("john.doe@acme.com");
  }
  private static void logError(String s) {
    System.err.println("Error message logged: " + s);
  }

  private static void sendVerificationMail(String s) {
    System.out.println("Mail sent to " + s);
  }
  static void validate(String s) {
    Result result = emailChecker.apply(s);
    if (result instanceof Result.Success) {
      sendVerificationMail(s);
    } else {
      logError(((Result.Failure) result).getMessage());
    }
  }
}
```

Running this program produces the expected output:

```
Error message logged: email this.is@my.email is invalid.
Mail sent to john.doe@acme.com
Error message logged: email must not be null
Error message logged: email must not be empty
```

But this still isn't satisfactory. Using instanceof to determine whether the result is a success is ugly. And using a cast to access the failure message is even more so. But worse than this is the fact that you have some program logic in the validate method that can't be tested. This is because the method is an effect, which means it doesn't return a value but mutates the outside world.

Is there a way to fix this? Yes. Instead of sending an email or logging a message, you could return a small program that does the same thing. Instead of executing

```
sendVerificationMail(s)
```

and

```
logError(((Result.Failure) result).getMessage());
```

you could return instructions that, when executed, will produce the same results. Thanks to lambdas, you can do this easily.

First, you need a functional interface representing an executable program:

```java
public interface Executable {
  void exec();
}
```

You could have used the standard `Runnable` interface, but most code verifiers raise a warning if this interface is used for something other than running a thread. So you'll use your own interface.

You can easily change your program, as shown in the following listing.

Listing 3.5   Returning executables

```java
public class EmailValidation {

  static Pattern emailPattern =
      Pattern.compile("^[a-z0-9._%+-]+@[a-z0-9.-]+\\.[a-z]{2,4}$");

  static Function<String, Result> emailChecker = s ->
      s == null
          ? new Result.Failure("email must not be null")
          : s.length() == 0
              ? new Result.Failure("email must not be empty")
              : emailPattern.matcher(s).matches()
                  ? new Result.Success()
                  : new Result.Failure("email " + s + " is invalid.");

  public static void main(String... args) {
    validate("this.is@my.email").exec();
    validate(null).exec();
    validate("").exec();
    validate("john.doe@acme.com").exec();
  }
```

❶ Executables are executed by calling exec()

```java
  private static void logError(String s) {
    System.err.println("Error message logged: " + s);
  }

  private static void sendVerificationMail(String s) {
    System.out.println("Mail sent to " + s);
  }
```

❷ Method validate now returns a value and has no side effect

```java
  static Executable validate(String s) {
    Result result = emailChecker.apply(s);
    return (result instanceof Result.Success)
        ? () -> sendVerificationMail(s)
        : () -> logError(((Result.Failure) result).getMessage());
  }
}
```

The `validate` method ❷ now returns `Executable` instead of `void`. It no longer has any side effect, and it's a pure function. When an `Executable` is returned ❶, it can be executed by calling its `exec` method.

Note that the `Executable` could also be passed to other methods or stored away to be executed later. In particular, it could be put in a data structure and executed in sequence after all computations are done. This allows you to separate the functional part of the program from the part that mutates the environment.

You've also replaced the if ... else control structure with the ternary operator. This is a matter of preference. The ternary operator is functional because it returns a value and has no side effect. In contrast, the if ... else structure can be made functional by making it mutate only local variables, but it can also have side effects. If you see imperative programs with many embedded if ... else structures, ask yourself how easy it would be to replace them with the ternary operator. This is often a good indication of how close to functional the design is. Note, however, that it's also possible to make the ternary operator nonfunctional by calling nonfunctional methods to get the resulting values.

3.2.1 *Cleaning up the code*

Your validate method is now functional, but it's dirty. Using the instanceof operator is almost always an indication of bad code. Another problem is that reusability is low. When the validate method returns a value, you have no choice besides executing it or not. What if you want to reuse the validation part but produce a different effect?

The validate method shouldn't have a dependency on sendVerificationMail or logError. It should only return a result expressing whether the email is valid, and you should be able to choose whatever effects you need for success or failure. Or you might prefer not to apply the effect but to compose the result with some other processing.

EXERCISE 3.1 (HARD)
Try to decouple the validation from the effects applied.

HINT
First, you'll need an interface with a single method to represent an effect. Second, because the emailChecker function returns a Result, the validate method could return this Result. In such a case, you'd no longer need the validate method. Third, you'll need to "bind" an effect to the Result. But because the result may be a success or a failure, it would be better to bind two effects and let the Result class choose which one to apply.

SOLUTION 3.1
The first thing to do is create the interface representing an effect, such as the following:

```
public interface Effect<T> {
  void apply(T t);
}
```

You may prefer the Consumer interface of Java 8. Although the name was badly chosen, it does the same job.

Then you'll need to make some changes to the Result interface, as shown in figure 3.1.

What's in a name?

Many great authors have written about names. Shakespeare wrote in *Romeo and Juliet*:[a]

> *What's in a name? that which we call a rose*
> *By any other name would smell as sweet;*

This says in two beautiful lines what Ferdinand de Saussure and other linguists have explained in hundreds of pages: the relationship between a name and what it names is arbitrary. The consequence is that a programmer should never trust names. Most often, names are chosen to reflect what objects are or do. But even when objects are able to do only one clear thing, there may be a mismatch.

Take the example of Java interfaces. They're supposed to be named either after what objects *are* (`Comparable`, `Clonable`, `Serializable`) or what they can *do* (`Listener`, `Supplier`, `Consumer`). Following this rule, a `Function` should be renamed `Applicable` and should have a method `apply`. A `Supplier` should define a method `supply`, and a `Consumer` should consume something and have a method named `consume`. But a `Consumer` defines an `accept` method, and it doesn't consume anything, because after having accepted an object, this object is still available.

Don't trust names. Trust types. Types don't lie. Types are your friends!

---

[a] William Shakespeare, *Romeo and Juliet* (1599), act 2, scene 2, http://shakespeare.mit.edu /romeo_juliet/romeo_juliet.2.2.html

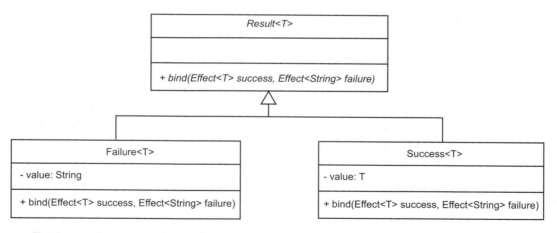

The abstract class `Result` has two implementations, `Success` and `Failure`. Note that whatever T is, the value held by `Failure` is always a `String`. In our example, T is `String`, but it could have been `Email`. The value of `Failure<Email>` would nonetheless have been a `String` holding the corresponding error message.

Figure 3.1 Changes to the `Result` interface

The following listing shows the modified version of the `Result` class.

Listing 3.6   A Result that can handle Effects

```java
public interface Result<T> {

  void bind(Effect<T> success, Effect<String> failure);

  public static <T> Result<T> failure(String message) {
    return new Failure<>(message);
  }

  public static <T> Result<T> success(T value) {
    return new Success<>(value);
  }

  public class Success<T> implements Result<T> {

    private final T value;

    private Success(T t) {
      value = t;
    }

    @Override
    public void bind(Effect<T> success, Effect<String> failure) {
      success.apply(value);
    }
  }

  public class Failure<T> implements Result<T> {

    private final String errorMessage;

    private Failure(String s) {
      this.errorMessage = s;
    }

    @Override
    public void bind(Effect<T> success, Effect<String> failure) {
      failure.apply(errorMessage);
    }
  }
}
```

The bind method handles Effects.

The success subclass is initialized with the successful value.

Success implements bind by applying the success effect to the value.

Failure implements bind by applying the failure effect to the error message.

You can choose whatever name you want for the `bind` method. You could call it `ifSuccess` or `forEach`. Only the type is important.

Now you can clean up the program by using the new `Effect` and `Result` interfaces, as shown in the following listing.

Listing 3.7   A cleaner version of the program

```java
public class EmailValidation {

  static Pattern emailPattern =
      Pattern.compile("^[a-z0-9._%+-]+@[a-z0-9.-]+\\.[a-z]{2,4}$");

  static Function<String, Result<String>> emailChecker = s -> {
    if (s == null) {
      return Result.failure("email must not be null");
    } else if (s.length() == 0) {
      return Result.failure("email must not be empty");
    } else if (emailPattern.matcher(s).matches()) {
      return Result.success(s);
    } else {
      return Result.failure("email " + s + " is invalid.");
    }
  };

  public static void main(String... args) {
    emailChecker.apply("this.is@my.email").bind(success, failure);
    emailChecker.apply(null).bind(success, failure);
    emailChecker.apply("").bind(success, failure);
    emailChecker.apply("john.doe@acme.com").bind(success, failure);
  }

  static Effect<String> success = s ->
                        System.out.println("Mail sent to " + s);

  static Effect<String> failure = s ->
                    System.err.println("Error message logged: " + s);
}
```

❶ Function emailChecker returns the new parameterized Result.

❷ Two Effects are bound to the result returned by the emailChecker function.

❸ You don't need the validate method anymore.

The `emailChecker` function now returns a parameterized `Result<String>` **❶**. It's irrelevant that `Result` is parameterized by the same type as the type of an error message. It could have been any type, such as `Result<Email>`. If you look at the `Result` implementation, you'll see that the value of `Failure` is always `String`, whatever the value of `Success` might be. The `Success` class holds a value of type `T`, and the `Failure` class holds a value of type `String`. In this example, it just so happens that `T` is `String`, but it could have been anything else. (You'll come back to this subject in the last section of this chapter.) The `validate` method has been removed, and two `Effect` instances are now defined **❸**: one for success and one for failure. These two effects are bound **❷** to the result of the `emailChecker` function.

3.2.2   *An alternative to if ... else*

You may wonder whether it's possible to completely remove conditional structures or operators. Can you write a program without any of these constructs? This may seem impossible, because many programmers have learned that decision-making is the basic building block of programming. But *decision-making* is an imperative programming notion. It's the notion of examining a value and deciding what to do next based on this observation. In functional programming, there's no "what to do next" question, but only functions returning values. The most basic `if` structure may be seen as the implementation of a function:

```
if (x > 0) {
  return x;
} else {
  return -x;
}
```

This is a function of x. It returns the absolute value of x. You could write this function as follows:

```
Function<Integer, Integer> abs = x -> {
  if (x > 0) {
    return x;
  } else {
    return -x;
  }
}
```

The difference with a function such as

```
Function<Integer, Integer> square = x -> x * x;
```

is that you have two implementations of the function and have to choose between the two depending on the value of the argument. This isn't a big problem, but what if you had many possible implementations? You'd end up with as many embedded `if ... else` structures as you have in listing 3.7, or as many embedded ternary operators as in listing 3.5. Can you do better?

EXERCISE 3.2

Write a `Case` class representing a condition and corresponding result. The condition will be represented by a `Supplier<Boolean>`, where `Supplier` is a functional interface such as this:

```
interface Supplier<T> {
  T get();
}
```

You can use the Java 8 implementation of `Supplier` or your own. The result corresponding to the condition will be represented by a `Supplier<Result<T>>`. To hold both, you can use a `Tuple<Supplier<Boolean>, Supplier<Result<T>>>`.

The `Case` class should define three methods:

```
public static <T> Case<T> mcase(Supplier<Boolean> condition,
                                Supplier<Result<T>> value)

public static <T> DefaultCase<T> mcase(Supplier<Result<T>> value)

public static <T> Result<T> match(DefaultCase<T> defaultCase,
                                  Case<T>... matchers)
```

I used the name *mcase* because *case* is a reserved word in Java; *m* stands for *match*. Of course, you can choose any other name.

The first mcase method defines a normal case, with a condition and a resulting value. The second mcase method defines a default case, represented by a subclass. The third method, match, selects a case. Because this method uses a vararg, the default case is to be put first, but will be the last to be used!

Additionally, the Case class should define the private DefaultCase subclass with the following signature:

```
private static class DefaultCase<T> extends Case<T>
```

SOLUTION 3.2

I said that the class must represent a Supplier<Boolean> for the condition and a Supplier<Result<T>>> for the resulting value. The simplest way to do this is to define it as follows:

```
public class Case<T> extends Tuple<Supplier<Boolean>, Supplier<Result<T>>>{
  private Case(Supplier<Boolean> booleanSupplier,
            Supplier<Result<T>> resultSupplier) {
    super(booleanSupplier, resultSupplier);
  }
}
```

The mcase methods are simple. The first one takes the two parameters and creates a new instance. The second receives only the second parameter (the Supplier for the value) and creates the default Supplier for the condition, which always returns true:

```
public static <T> Case<T> mcase(Supplier<Boolean> condition,
                                Supplier<Result<T>> value) {
  return new Case<>(condition, value);
}
public static <T> DefaultCase<T> mcase(Supplier<Result<T>> value) {
  return new DefaultCase<>(() -> true, value);
}
```

The DefaultCase class couldn't be simpler. It's only a marker class, so you only have to create a constructor calling super:

```
private static class DefaultCase<T> extends Case<T> {
  private DefaultCase(Supplier<Boolean> booleanSupplier,
                    Supplier<Result<T>> resultSupplier) {
    super(booleanSupplier, resultSupplier);
  }
}
```

The match method is more complex, but that's an overstatement because it has only three lines of code:

```
@SafeVarargs
public static <T> Result<T> match(DefaultCase<T> defaultCase,
                                  Case<T>... matchers) {
```

```
  for (Case<T> aCase : matchers) {
    if (aCase._1.get()) return aCase._2.get();
  }
  return defaultCase._2.get();
}
```

As I previously mentioned, the default case has to come first in the argument list because the second argument is a vararg, but this case is used last. You test all cases one by one by evaluating them through a call to the get method. If the result is true, you return the corresponding value after having evaluated it. If no case matches, the default case is used.

Note that *evaluation* means evaluation of the returned value. No effect is applied at this time. The following listing shows the complete class.

Listing 3.8 Matching conditions with the `Case` class

```
public class Case<T> extends Tuple<Supplier<Boolean>, Supplier<Result<T>>>{

  private Case(Supplier<Boolean> booleanSupplier,
               Supplier<Result<T>> resultSupplier) {
    super(booleanSupplier, resultSupplier);
  }

  public static <T> Case<T> mcase(Supplier<Boolean> condition,
                                  Supplier<Result<T>> value) {
    return new Case<>(condition, value);
  }

  public static <T> DefaultCase<T> mcase(Supplier<Result<T>> value) {
    return new DefaultCase<>(() -> true, value);
  }

  private static class DefaultCase<T> extends Case<T> {
    private DefaultCase(Supplier<Boolean> booleanSupplier,
                        Supplier<Result<T>> resultSupplier) {
      super(booleanSupplier, resultSupplier);
    }
  }

  @SafeVarargs
  public static <T> Result<T> match(DefaultCase<T> defaultCase,
                                    Case<T>... matchers) {
    for (Case<T> aCase : matchers) {
      if (aCase._1.get()) return aCase._2.get();
    }
    return defaultCase._2.get();
  }
}
```

() -> true is a lambda representing a Supplier<Boolean> that will always return true. In other words, it's a "lazy" true. Being lazy makes little sense for a literal value, but you must conform to the requirements of the DefaultCase constructor.

Now you can greatly simplify the code of your email validation application. As you can see in the following listing, it contains absolutely no control structures. (Note the use of static import for methods of `Case` and `Result`.)

> **Listing 3.9** **The email validation application with no control structures**

```
import java.util.regex.Pattern;
import static emailvalidation4.Case.*;
import static emailvalidation4.Result.*;

public class EmailValidation {

  static Pattern emailPattern =
      Pattern.compile("^[a-z0-9._%+-]+@[a-z0-9.-]+\\.[a-z]{2,4}$");

  static Effect<String> success = s ->
              System.out.println("Mail sent to " + s);

  static Effect<String> failure = s ->
              System.err.println("Error message logged: " + s);

  public static void main(String... args) {
    emailChecker.apply("this.is@my.email").bind(success, failure);
    emailChecker.apply(null).bind(success, failure);
    emailChecker.apply("").bind(success, failure);
    emailChecker.apply("john.doe@acme.com").bind(success, failure);
  }

  static Function<String, Result<String>> emailChecker = s -> match(
      mcase(() -> success(s)),
      mcase(() -> s == null, () -> failure("email must not be null")),
      mcase(() -> s.length() == 0, () ->
                                  failure("email must not be empty")),
      mcase(() -> !emailPattern.matcher(s).matches(), () ->
                                  failure("email " + s + " is invalid."))
  );
}
```

The default case →

But wait. There's a trick! You don't see any control structures because they're hidden in the `Case` class, which contains an `if` instruction and even a `for` loop. So are you cheating? Not really. First, you have a single clean loop and a single clean `if`. No more series of embedded `if` statements. Second, you've abstracted these structures. You can now write as many conditional applications as you want without having to write a single `if` or `for`. But most important, you're only at the beginning of your trip into functional programming. In chapter 5 you'll learn how to completely remove these two constructs.

In this chapter, you'll see how to generalize abstractions of all control structures. You've done this for conditional control structures such as embedded `if..else` statements (and `switch..case` is no different). Let's see how to do the same with loops.

3.3   *Abstracting iteration*

Loops are structures that iterate over lists. In Java, loops can also iterate over sets, or might even seem to iterate on nothing, such as indexed loops, but they always iterate on lists. Loops that seem to iterate on sets won't produce different results if executed twice, because an order is applied to the sets while iterating. And even if the order isn't the same on each iteration, it won't change during the course of one iteration. So iterating on a set turns it into a list from the iteration point of view.

An indexed loop isn't any different —it iterates over a list of the evaluated indexes. The loop could exit before evaluating all the arguments because index loops are lazy regarding their indexes. Loops are always lazy regarding their bodies, which means that if a loop exits, the remaining elements won't be processed. The if..else construct behaves similarly. The condition is always evaluated, so it's strict regarding the condition, but only one of the if and else parts is evaluated, depending on the condition, so if..else is lazy regarding its body too. Maybe you thought Java was a strict language, but this isn't true. Java is strict regarding method arguments, but fortunately it's also sometimes lazy.

Getting back to loops, their main use is to iterate over all elements of a list, as follows:

```
for(String email : emailList) {
  // Do something with email;
}
```

Each time you want to process a list, you use this construct, or other constructs such as while or do..while, which are no different. They're only syntactic sugar over iteration. Even the preceding for loop is syntactic sugar for the following:

```
for (int i = 0; i < emailList.size(); i++) {
  // do something with emailList.get(i)
}
```

The while loop is different because it's used to iterate as long as a condition is verified. It allows you to exit the loop on a condition that's applied before the first iteration. The do..while loop does the same, but only after the first iteration.

What's important is what's done inside the loop, so why should you have to write the loops again and again? Why can't you just say what you want done and have it be done without messing with the control structures, the conditions, and the indexes?

Take a simple example. Let's say you have a list of names, and you want to return comma-separated strings. Could you write the program on paper correctly the first time? If you're a good programmer, I guess you could. But many programmers have to write the code, run it, fix the bugs in the general case, run it again, fix the bugs in the marginal cases, and then run the program again until it's correct. The problem isn't difficult, but it's so boring that you often don't get it right on the first try. If you always write your programs correctly the first time, congratulations. You're a good programmer, and the remainder of this section might not be for you. But if you're an average programmer, keep reading.

Inside a loop, you might want to do several things:

- Transform each element into something else
- Aggregate elements into a single result
- Remove some elements according to a condition on the elements
- Remove some elements according to an external condition
- Group elements according to certain criteria

Various operations for which looping is needed can be applied to collections, such as concatenating, zipping, or unzipping. (*Zipping* means taking elements from two lists and creating a list of tuples. *Unzipping* is the inverse operation.)

All these operations could be abstracted. In chapter 5, you'll create functional data structures implementing all these abstractions. For now, you'll develop a library of these abstractions that you can apply to legacy Java collections.

3.3.1 Abstracting an operation on lists with mapping

Mapping, when applied to collections, means applying a transformation to each element of the collection. Here's how it's generally done in traditional imperative programming:

```
List<Double> newList = new ArrayList<>();
for (Integer value : integerList) {
  newList.add(value * 1.2);
}
```

In this example, an operation is applied to each element of an `Integer` list (`integer-List`) to increase it by 20%. The result of the operation is a double, so it's put in a new list that's created before the start of the loop. Although simple, this program raises some interesting questions.

The first point is that you could separate the iteration from the calculation. The following example does this with a method:

```
Double addTwentyPercent(Integer value) {
  return value * 1.2;
}

List<Double> newList = new ArrayList<>();
for (Integer value : integerList) {
  newList.add(addTwentyPercent(value));
}
```

This allows you to reuse the calculation, but it doesn't allow you to reuse the loop. To allow this, you can put the loop inside a method and pass it a function to apply the calculation:

```
Function<Integer, Double> addTwentyPercent = x -> x * 1.2;

List<Double> map(List<Integer> list, Function<Integer, Double> f) {
  List<Double> newList = new ArrayList<>();
  for (Integer value : list) {
    newList.add(f.apply(value));
```

```
  }
  return newList;
}
```

Now you can call the `map` method with an `Integer` list and a function from `Integer` to `Double` as arguments, and you'll get a new `Double` list in return. Plus, you can freely reuse the function and can call the `map` method with a different function.

You can greatly enhance reusability by using generics:

```
<T, U> List<U> map(List<T> list, Function<T, U> f) {
  List<U> newList = new ArrayList<>();
  for (T value : list) {
    newList.add(f.apply(value));
  }
  return newList;
}
```

You can include this method in a library where you'll define several methods, allowing you to abstract many list-related operations. You'll call this library `Collection-Utilities`.

3.3.2 Creating lists

Besides iterating, programmers need to repeat other basic operations again and again when working on lists. The most basic operation is creating lists. Java supports many ways to create lists, but they aren't consistent.

EXERCISE 3.3

Write methods that create an empty list, a list with one element, and a list from a collection of elements, as well as a vararg method that creates a list from a list of arguments. All these lists will be immutable.

SOLUTION 3.3

This is straightforward, as you can see in the following code:

```
public class CollectionUtilities {

  public static <T> List<T > list() {
    return Collections.emptyList();
  }

  public static <T> List<T > list(T t) {
    return Collections.singletonList(t);
  }

  public static <T> List<T > list(List<T> ts) {
    return Collections.unmodifiableList(new ArrayList<>(ts));
  }

  @SafeVarargs
  public static <T> List<T > list(T... t) {
    return Collections.unmodifiableList(Arrays.asList(Arrays.copyOf(t, t.length)));
  }
}
```

Note that the list(List<T> ts) method makes a copy of the argument list. This defensive copy is needed to ensure that the list won't be modified afterward by the caller of the list method. Also note that the vararg version may be called with an array as its argument. In such a case, the resulting list is backed by the original array. As a consequence, changing an element of the array would change the corresponding element of the resulting list. This is why you make a copy of the array argument.

Also note that the resulting lists aren't really immutable. They're immutable views of mutable lists, but this is sufficient because no one will have access to these mutable lists. They will only be mutable in the CollectionUtilities class.

3.3.3 *Using head and tail operations*

Functional operations on lists often access the *head* (or first element) of the list, as well as the *tail* (the list with its first element removed).

EXERCISE 3.4

Create two methods that return the head and the tail of a list, respectively. The list passed as an argument must not be modified. Because you'll need to make a copy of the list, also define a copy method. The list returned by tail should be immutable.

SOLUTION 3.4

The head() method is simple. If the list is empty, you throw an exception. Otherwise, you read the element at index 0 and return it.

The copy method is also basic. It's the same as the list-creation method, taking a list as its argument.

The tail method is slightly more complex. It must make a copy of its argument, remove the first element, and return the result:

```
public static <T> T head(List<T> list) {
  if (list.size() == 0) {
    throw new IllegalStateException("head of empty list");
  }
  return list.get(0);
}

private static <T> List<T > copy(List<T> ts) {
  return new ArrayList<>(ts);
}

public static <T> List<T> tail(List<T> list) {
  if (list.size() == 0) {
    throw new IllegalStateException("tail of empty list");
  }
  List<T> workList = copy(list);
  workList.remove(0);
  return Collections.unmodifiableList(workList);
}
```

Note that copy is private. It returns a mutable list. To make a copy from the outside, you can call list(List<T>), which returns an immutable list. Also note that this example throws exceptions when calling `head` or `tail` on an empty list. This isn't functional, because you should always catch exceptions but never throw them in order to be referentially transparent. It is, however, simpler at this stage. In chapter 5, when you look at functional lists, you'll see that the `head` and `tail` methods will be declared protected. This way, they'll be usable only inside the `List` class, and no exception will ever leak out of this class.

3.3.4 Functionally appending to a list

Appending an element to a Java list in an imperative program is a basic operation that's used again and again:

```
list.add(element);
```

But this operation isn't usable in functional programs because it mutates its argument and doesn't return the modified list. If you think it's functional because it doesn't mutate its element argument, remember what you learned in chapter 2: this is object notation. The list itself is an implicit argument to the method `add`, so it's equivalent to this:

```
add(list, element);
```

Transforming this method into a functional one is simple. You'll call it `append`:

```
public static <T> List<T> append(List<T> list, T t) {
  List<T> ts = copy(list);
  ts.add(t);
  return Collections.unmodifiableList(ts);
}
```

The append method makes a defensive copy of its first argument (through a call to the previously defined `copy` method), adds the second argument to it, and then returns the modified list wrapped in an immutable view. You'll soon have occasion to use this append method in places where it would be impossible to use `add`.

3.3.5 Reducing and folding lists

List *folding* transforms a list into a single value by using a specific operation. The resulting value may be of any type—it doesn't have to be of the same type as the elements of the list. Folding to a result that's the same type as the list elements is a specific case called *reducing*. Computing the sum of the elements of a list of integers is a simple case of reducing.

You can fold a list in two directions, from left to right or from right to left, depending on the operation used:

- If the operation is commutative, both ways of folding are equivalent.
- If the operation isn't commutative, the two ways of folding give different results.

Folding needs a starting value, which is the neutral element, or identity element, for the operation. This element is used as the starting value of the *accumulator*. When the computation is complete, the accumulator contains the result. Reducing, on the other hand, can be done without a starting element, with the condition that the list isn't empty, because the first (or last) element will be used as the starting element.

REDUCING LISTS OF NUMBERS WITH ADDITION

Suppose you have a list, (1, 2, 3, 4), and you want to compute the sum of the elements. The first way to do it is to put the accumulator on the left side of the operand:

```
(((0 + 1) + 2) + 3) + 4 = 10
```

You could also proceed from the other side:

```
1 + (2 + (3 + (4 + 0))) = 10
```

The results are identical. You could do the same thing with multiplication, but you'd have to use the identity element 1 as the starting value of the accumulator.

FOLDING LISTS OF CHARACTERS INTO STRINGS

Let's now do the same thing with a different operation applied to a list of characters, ('a', 'b', 'c'). The operation used here is as follows:

```
"x" + 'y' = "xy"
```

First, let's fold from the left:

```
(("" + 'a') + 'b') + 'c' = "abc"
```

Let's now try the same thing from the right:

```
'a' + ('b' + ('c' + "")) = "abc"
```

Folding from the right doesn't work because the left operand is a character, and the right one is a string. So you have to change the operation to the following:

```
'x' + "y" = "xy"
```

In this case, the character is prepended to the string instead of being appended. The first fold is called a *left fold*, which means that the accumulator is on the left side of the operation. When the accumulator is on the right side, it's a *right fold*.

UNDERSTANDING THE RELATIONSHIP BETWEEN LEFT AND RIGHT FOLDS

You might say that folding right can be defined in terms of folding left. Let's rewrite the right-folding operation by using a different form, called *corecursion*:

```
((0 + 3) + 2) + 1 = 6
```

In recursion as well as corecursion, evaluation of one step is dependent on the previous step. But a recursive definition starts with the last step and defines its relationship with the preceding one. In order to be able to conclude, it also has to define the base step. Corecursion, on the other hand, starts from the first step and defines its relationship to the next one. There's no need for a base step, because it's also the first step.

From this, it seems that right-folding a list is equivalent to left-folding the list after having reversed the order of the elements.

But wait. Addition is a commutative operation. If you use a noncommutative operation, you must change the operation as well. If you don't, you could end up with two different situations, depending on the types. If the operation has operands of different types, if won't compile. On the other hand, if the operation has operands of the same types but it isn't commutative, you'll get a wrong result with no error. So foldLeft and foldRight have the following relationship, where operation1 and operation2 give the same results with the same operands in reverse order:

```
foldLeft(list, acc, x -> y -> operation1)
```

is equivalent to

```
foldRight(reverse(list), acc, y -> x -> operation2)
```

If the operation is commutative, operation1 and operation2 are the same. Otherwise, if operation1 is x -> y -> compute(x, y), operation2 is x -> y -> compute(y, x).

Think about the reverse function used to reverse a list. Can you see how it could be expressed in terms of leftFold? This is part of the beauty of functional programming. Abstraction can be found everywhere. Now let's look at how you can apply this to legacy Java lists.

EXERCISE 3.5
Create a method to fold a list of integers that can be used, for example, to sum the elements of a list. This method will take a list of integers, an integer starting value, and a function as its parameters.

SOLUTION 3.5
The starting value is dependent on the operation applied. The value has to be the *neutral*, or *identity*, element of the operation. The operation is represented as a curried function, as you learned in the previous chapter:

```
public static Integer fold(List<Integer> is, Integer identity,
                           Function<Integer, Function<Integer, Integer>> f) {
  int result = identity;
  for (Integer i : is) {
    result = f.apply(result).apply(i);
  }
  return result;
}
```

After statically importing CollectionUtilities.*, this method can be called as follows:

```
List<Integer> list = list(1, 2, 3, 4, 5);
int result = fold(list, 0, x -> y -> x + y);
```

Here, `result` is equal to 15, which is the sum of 1, 2, 3, 4, and 5. Replacing + with *
and 0 with 1 (the identity element for multiplication) gives the result of 1 x 2 x 3 x 4 x
5 = 120.

LEFT-FOLDING EXAMPLE

The operation you just defined was named `fold` because folding left or right for integer addition or multiplication gives the same result. But if you want to use other functions, or if you want to make the folding method generic, you must distinguish
between right and left folds.

EXERCISE 3.6

Generalize the `fold` method to `foldLeft` so that it can be used to apply a left fold to a
list of elements of arbitrary types. To test that the method is correct, apply it to the following parameters,

```
List<Integer> list = list(1, 2, 3, 4, 5);
String identity = "0";
Function<String, Function<Integer, String>> f = x -> y -> addSI(x, y);
```

where method `addSI` is defined as follows:

```
String addSI(String s, Integer i) {
  return "(" + s + " + " + i + ")";
}
```

Verify that you get the following output:

```
(((((0 + 1) + 2) + 3) + 4) + 5)
```

Note that the `addSI` method allows you to verify that the arguments are in the correct
order. Using the `"(" + s + " + " + i + ")"` expression directly wouldn't allow this
verification because inverting the argument would change only the meaning of the +
signs without changing the result.

SOLUTION 3.6

The imperative implementation is quite simple:

```
public static <T, U> U foldLeft(List<T> ts, U identity,
                                Function<U, Function<T, U>> f) {
  U result = identity;
  for (T t : ts) {
    result = f.apply(result).apply(t);
  }
  return result;
}
```

This generic version can be used for integer operations, so the specific integer version
is useless.

RIGHT-FOLDING EXAMPLE

As you saw previously, folding left is a corecursive operation, so implementing it through an imperative loop is easy. On the other hand, folding right is a recursive operation. To test your tentative implementation, you can use the approach you used for folding left. You'll test the implementation against the following parameters,

```
List<Integer> list = list(1, 2, 3, 4, 5);
String identity = "0";
Function<Integer, Function<String, String>> f = x -> y -> addIS(x, y);
```

where the method addIS is defined as

```
private static String addIS(Integer i, String s) {
  return "(" + i + " " + " " + s + ")";
}
```

Verify that the output is as follows:

```
(1 + (2 + (3 + (4 + (5 + 0)))))
```

EXERCISE 3.7

Write an imperative version of the foldRight method.

SOLUTION 3.7

A right fold is a recursive operation. To implement it with an imperative loop, you have to process the list in reverse order:

```
public static <T, U> U foldRight(List<T> ts, U identity,
                                 Function<T, Function<U, U>> f) {
    U result = identity;
    for (int i = ts.size(); i > 0; i--) {
      result = f.apply(ts.get(i - 1)).apply(result);
    }
    return result;
  }
```

EXERCISE 3.8

Write a recursive version of foldRight. Beware that a naive recursive version won't fully work in Java because it uses the stack to accumulate intermediate calculations. In chapter 4, you'll learn how to make stack-safe recursion available.

HINT

You should apply the function to the head of the list and to the result of folding the tail.

SOLUTION 3.8

The naive version will work for at least 5,000 elements, which is enough for an exercise:

```
public static <T, U> U foldRight(List<T> ts, U identity,
                                 Function<T, Function<U, U>> f) {
  return ts.isEmpty()
      ? identity
      : f.apply(head(ts)).apply(foldRight(tail(ts), identity, f));
}
```

HEAP-BASED RECURSION   Solution 3.8 isn't tail recursive, so it can't be optimized to use the heap instead of the stack. We'll look at a heap-based implementation in chapter 5.

REVERSING A LIST

Reversing a list is sometimes useful, although this operation is generally not optimal in terms of performance. Finding other solutions that don't require reversing a list is preferable, but not always possible.

Defining a `reverse` method with an imperative implementation is easy by iterating backward over the list. You must be careful, though, not to mess with the indexes:

```
public static <T> List<T> reverse(List<T> list) {
  List<T> result = new ArrayList<T>();
  for(int i = list.size() - 1; i >= 0; i--) {
    result.add(list.get(i));
  }
  return Collections.unmodifiableList(result);
}
```

Many possible arrangements exist. For example, you could iterate from `list.size()` and use `i > 0` as the condition. You would then have to use `i - 1` as the index to the list.

EXERCISE 3.9 (HARD)

Define the reverse method without using a loop. Instead, use the methods you've developed to this point.

HINT

The methods to use are `foldLeft` and `append`. It might be useful to start defining a `prepend` method that adds an element in front of a list and is defined in terms of `append`.

SOLUTION 3.9

You can first define a `prepend` functional method that allows you to add an element in front of a list. This can be done by left-folding the list, using an accumulator containing the element to add instead of the empty list:

```
public static <T> List<T> prepend(T t, List<T> list) {
  return foldLeft(list, list(t), a -> b -> append(a, b));
}
```

Then you can define the reverse method as a left fold, starting with an empty list and using the `prepend` method as the operation:

```
public static <T> List<T> reverse(List<T> list) {
  return foldLeft(list, list(), x -> y -> prepend(y, x));
}
```

After you've done this, you can eventually replace the call to prepend with the corresponding implementation:

```
public static <T> List<T> reverse(List<T> list) {
  return foldLeft(list, list(), x -> y ->
                           foldLeft(x, list(y), a -> b -> append(a, b)));
}
```

> **WARNING** Don't use the solution 3.9 implementations of reverse and prepend in production code. Both imply traversing the whole list several times, so they're slow. In chapter 5, you'll learn how to create functional immutable lists that perform well on all occasions.

EXERCISE 3.10 (HARD)

In section 3.10 you defined a method to map a list by applying an operation to each element. This operation, as it was implemented, included a fold. Rewrite the map method in terms of foldLeft or foldRight.

HINT

To solve this problem, you should use the append or prepend method you just defined.

SOLUTION

To understand the problem, you have to consider that map consists of two operations: applying a function to each element, and then gathering all elements into a new list. This second operation is a fold, where the identity is the empty list (written as list() after a static import CollectionUtilities.*) and the operation is the addition of an element to a list.

Here's an implementation using the append and foldLeft methods:

```
public static <T, U> List<U> mapViaFoldLeft(List<T> list,
                                            Function<T, U> f) {
  return foldLeft(list, list(), x -> y -> append(x, f.apply(y)));
}
```

The following implementation uses foldRight and prepend:

```
public static <T, U> List<U> mapViaFoldRight(List<T> list,
                                             Function<T, U> f) {
  return foldRight(list, list(), x -> y -> prepend(f.apply(x), y));
}
```

Part of the beauty of functional programming is in finding every small element that can be abstracted and reused. After you get used to this way of thinking, you'll start seeing patterns everywhere and you'll want to abstract them.

You could define lots of other useful functions by composing the basic list functions you just wrote. But we'll delay their study until chapter 5, when you'll learn to replace the legacy Java lists with pure functional immutable lists that will offer many advantages, including much better performance for most of the functional operations.

3.3.6   *Composing mappings and mapping compositions*

It isn't unusual to apply several transformations to list elements. Imagine you have a list of prices, and you want to apply a 9% tax to all, and then add a fixed charge of $3.50 for shipping. You can do this by composing two mappings:

```
Function<Double, Double> addTax = x -> x * 1.09;
Function<Double, Double> addShipping = x -> x + 3.50;
List<Double> prices = list(10.10, 23.45, 32.07, 9.23);
List<Double> pricesIncludingTax = map(prices, addTax);
List<Double> pricesIncludingShipping =
                            map(pricesIncludingTax, addShipping);
System.out.println(pricesIncludingShipping);
```

This code prints the following:

```
[14.509, 29.0605, 38.456300000000006, 13.5607]
```

It works but it isn't efficient, because mapping is applied twice. You could obtain the same result with this:

```
System.out.println(map(map(prices,addTax),addShipping));
```

But this is still mapping twice. A much better solution is to compose the functions instead of composing mappings, or, in other words, to map the composition instead of composing mappings:

```
System.out.println(map(prices, addShipping.compose(addTax)));
```

Or if you prefer a more "natural" writing order:

```
System.out.println(map(prices, addTax.andThen(addShipping)));
```

3.3.7   *Applying effects to lists*

In the previous example, you printed the list in order to verify the result. In a real situation, you'd probably apply more-sophisticated effects to each element of the list. You could, for example, print each price after formatting it to display only two decimal digits. This could be done through iteration:

```
for (Double price : pricesIncludingShipping) {
  System.out.printf("%.2f", price);
  System.out.println();
}
```

But once again, you're mixing actions that could be abstracted. Iteration can be abstracted exactly as you did for mapping, and the effect applied to each element could be abstracted into something resembling a function, but with a side effect and no return value. This is exactly what the `Effect` interface you used in the solution to exercise 3.1 is for. So the example could be rewritten as follows:

```
Effect<Double> printWith2decimals = x -> {
  System.out.printf("%.2f", x);
```

```
    System.out.println();
};

public static <T> void forEach(Collection<T> ts, Effect<T> e) {
  for (T t : ts) e.apply(t);
}

forEach(pricesIncludingShipping, printWith2decimals);
```

This seems to be much more code, but the `Effect` interface and the `forEach` method can be written once and reused, so you can test each of them in isolation. Your business code is reduced to only one line.

3.3.8 *Approaching functional output*

With the `forEach` method, you can somewhat abstract side effects. You abstracted effect application so it can be isolated, but you could go much further. With the `forEach` method, one single effect is applied to each element of the list. It would be nice to be able to compose these effects into a single one. Think about it as a fold resulting in a single effect. If you could do this, your program could be a fully functional one with absolutely no side effects. It would produce a new program, with no control structures but a single list of effects that would be applied one after the other. Let's do this!

To represent the instructions of your program, you'll use the `Executable` interface you used in listing 3.5. Then you'll need a way to compose `Executable` instances, which can be done by a functional method or by a function. You're in a functional mood, so let's use a function:

```
Function<Executable, Function<Executable, Executable>> compose =
    x -> y -> () -> {
        x.exec();
        y.exec();
    };
```

Next you need a neutral element, or identity element, for the composition of `Executables`. This couldn't be simpler than an executable doing nothing. Let's call it `ez`:

```
Executable ez = () -> {};
```

The name `ez` stands for executable zero, which means the zero (or identity) element of the operation consisting of composing executables.

You can now write your purely functional program as follows:

```
Executable program = foldLeft(pricesIncludingShipping, ez,
    e -> d -> compose.apply(e).apply(() -> printWith2decimals.apply(d)));
```

It may seem a bit complicated, but it's simple. It's a `foldLeft` of the list `prices-IncludingShipping`, using `ez` as the initial value of the accumulator. The only part that's slightly more complex is the function. If you forget about the curried form and think about it as a function of two arguments, it takes an `Executable` (e) as its first argument and a `Double` (d) as its second argument, and it composes the first one with a new Executable consisting of applying the printWith2decimals method to the Double. As you see, it's just a matter of composing abstractions!

Note that you haven't applied any side effects. What you get is a new program (or rather a script) written in a new language. You can execute this program by calling exec() on it:

```
program.exec();
```

You get the following result:

```
14.51
29.06
38.46
13.56
```

This gives you a taste of how functional programming can produce output without using side effects. Deciding whether you should use this kind of technique in production is up to you. True functional languages give you no choice, but Java is in no way a functional language, so you have a choice. If you decide to program functionally, you may miss some facilities to help you in this domain, but it's important to know that everything remains possible.

3.3.9   *Building corecursive lists*

One thing programmers do again and again is build corecursive lists, and most of these are lists of integers. If you think you, as a Java programmer, don't do this too often, consider the following example:

```
for (int i = 0; i < limit; i++) {
  some processing...
}
```

This code is a composition of two abstractions: a corecursive list and some processing. The corecursive list is a list of integers from 0 (included) to limit (excluded). As we've already noted, functional programming is, among other things, about pushing abstraction to the limit. So let's abstract the construction of this corecursive list.

As I mentioned earlier, *corecursive* means that each element can be constructed by applying a function to the previous element, starting from the first one. This is what distinguishes corecursive from recursive constructs. (In recursive constructs, each element is a function of the previous one, starting with the last one.) We'll come back to this difference in chapter 4, but for now, this means that corecursive lists are easy to construct. Just start from the first element (int i = 0) and apply the chosen function (i -> i++).

You could have constructed the list first and then mapped it to a function corresponding to some processing ... or to a composition of functions, or an effect. Let's do this with a concrete limit:

```
for (int i = 0; i < 5; i++) {
  System.out.println(i);
}
```

This is nearly equivalent to the following:

```
list(0, 1, 2, 3, 4).forEach(System.out::println);
```

You've abstracted the list and the effect. But you can push abstraction further.

EXERCISE 3.11

Write a method to produce a list using a starting value, a limit, and the function `x -> x + 1`. You'll call this method range, and it will have the following signature:

```
List<Integer> range(int start, int end)
```

SOLUTION 3.11

You could use the `for` loop implementation to implement the `range` method. But you'll use a `while` loop to prepare for the next exercise:

```
public static List<Integer> range(int start, int end) {
  List<Integer> result = new ArrayList<>();
  int temp = start;
  while (temp < end) {
    result = CollectionUtilities.append(result, temp);
    temp = temp + 1;
  }
  return result;
}
```

I chose a `while` loop because it translates more easily into a generic method that can be applied to any type, given a function from this type to itself and a second function (called a `predicate`) from this type to a Boolean.

EXERCISE 3.12

Write a generic *range* method that will work for any type and any condition. Because the notion of range works mainly for numbers, let's call this method `unfold` and give it the following signature:

```
List<T> unfold(T seed, Function<T, T> f, Function<T, Boolean> p)
```

SOLUTION 3.12

Starting from the `range` method implementation, all you have to do is replace the specific parts with generic ones:

```
public static <T> List<T> unfold(T seed,
                                 Function<T, T> f,
                                 Function<T, Boolean> p) {
  List<T> result = new ArrayList<>();
  T temp = seed;
  while (p.apply(temp)) {
    result = append(result, temp);
    temp = f.apply(temp);
  }
  return result;
}
```

EXERCISE 3.13

Implement the range method in terms of unfold.

SOLUTION 3.13

There's nothing difficult here. You have to provide the seed, which is the start parameter of range; the function f, which is x -> x + 1; and the predicate p, which resolves to x -> x < end:

```
public static List<Integer> range(int start, int end) {
  return unfold(start, x -> x + 1, x -> x < end);
}
```

Corecursion and recursion have a dual relationship. One is the counterpart of the other, so it's always possible to change a recursive process into a corecursive one, and vice versa. This is the main subject of the next chapter, where you'll learn to change a recursive process into a corecursive one. For now, let's do the inverse process.

EXERCISE 3.14

Write a recursive version of range based on the functional method you've defined in previous sections.

HINT

The only method you need is prepend, although you can choose other implementations using different methods.

SOLUTION 3.14

Defining a recursive implementation is quite simple. You just have to prepend the start parameter to the same method, using the same end parameter and replacing the start parameter with the result of applying the f function to it. It's much easier to do than to verbalize:

```
public static List<Integer> range(Integer start, Integer end) {
    return end <= start
        ? CollectionUtilities.list()
        : CollectionUtilities.prepend(start, range(start + 1, end));
  }
```

Applying the range method to obtain the same result as the for loop you used earlier as an example is simple:

```
for (int i = 0; i < 5; i++) {
  System.out.println(i);
}
```

You can rewrite this as follows:

```
range(0, 5).forEach(System.out::println);
```

More interestingly, if the process applied inside the for loop is functional, the benefit is even more spectacular:

```
List<Integer> list = new ArrayList<>();
for (int i = 0; i < 5; i++) {
  list.add(i * i);
}
```

This can be replaced with the following (assuming the static import of `Collection-Utilities.*`):

```
mapViaFoldLeft(range(0, 5), x -> x * x);
```

Of course, in this example, `mapViaFoldRight` may also be used.

THE DANGER OF STACK-BASED RECURSION

Recursive implementations as developed in the previous examples shouldn't be used in production, because it's limited to somewhere between 6,000 and 7,000 steps. If you try to go further, the stack will overflow. Chapter 4 provides more information on this subject.

THE DANGER OF STRICTNESS

None of these versions (recursive and corecursive) are equivalent to the `for` loop. This is because, although Java is mostly a strict language (it's strict regarding method arguments), the `for` loop, like all Java control structures and some operators, is lazy. This means that in the `for` loop you used as an example, the order of evaluation will be index, computation, index, computation ..., although using the `range` method will first compute the complete list before mapping the function.

This problem arises because you shouldn't be using lists for this: lists are strict data structures. But you have to start somewhere. In chapter 9, you'll learn how to build lazy collections that will solve this problem.

In this section, you've learned how to abstract and encapsulate imperative operations that are unavoidable when using imperative data structures such as lists. In chapter 5, you'll learn how to completely replace these legacy data structures with purely functional ones, which will offer more freedom and better performance. In the meantime, you must look more closely at types.

3.4 *Using the right types*

In the previous examples, you've used standard types such as integers, doubles, and strings to represent business entities such as prices and email addresses. Although this is common practice in imperative programming, it causes problems that should be avoided. As I said, you should trust types more than names.

3.4.1 *Problems with standard types*

Let's examine a simplified problem and see how solving it by using standard types leads to problems. Imagine you have products with a name, a price, and a weight, and you have to create invoices representing product sales. These invoices have to mention the products, the quantities, the total price, and the total weight.

You could represent a `Product` with the following class:

```
public class Product {

  private final String name;
  private final double price;
  private final double weight;

  public Product(String name, double price, double weight) {
    this.name = name;
    this.price = price;
    this.weight = weight;
  }

  ... (getters)
}
```

Because properties are final, you need a constructor to initialize them and getters to read them, but we didn't represent the getters.

Next, you can use an `OrderLine` class to represent each line of an order. This class is shown in the following listing.

Listing 3.10   The component representing one line of an order

```
public class OrderLine {

  private Product product;
  private int count;

  public OrderLine(Product product, int count) {
    super();
    this.product = product;
    this.count = count;
  }

  public Product getProduct() {
    return product;
  }

  public void setProduct(Product product) {
    this.product = product;
  }

  public int getCount() {
    return count;
  }

  public void setCount(int count) {
    this.count = count;
  }

  public double getWeight() {
    return this.product.getWeight() * this.count;
  }

  public double getAmount() {
    return this.product.getPrice() * this.count;
  }
}
```

This looks like a good old Java object, initialized with a `Product` and an `int`, and representing one line of an order. It also has methods for computing the total price and the total weight for the line.

Continuing with the decision to use standard types, you'll use `List<OrderLine>` to represent an order. Listing 3.11 shows how you can handle orders. (If you aren't yet comfortable with functional style, you can compare this code to the imperative equivalent, `StoreImperative`, which you'll find on the book's website at https://github.com/fpinjava/fpinjava.)

Listing 3.11 Handling orders

```java
import java.util.List;
import static com.fpinjava.common.CollectionUtilities.*;

public class Store {

  public static void main(String[] args) {
    Product toothPaste = new Product("Tooth paste", 1.5, 0.5);
    Product toothBrush = new Product("Tooth brush", 3.5, 0.3);
    List<OrderLine> order = list(
        new OrderLine(toothPaste, 2),
        new OrderLine(toothBrush, 3));
    double weight = foldLeft(order, 0.0, x -> y -> x + y.getAmount());
    double price = foldLeft(order, 0.0, x -> y -> x + y.getWeight());
    System.out.println(String.format("Total price: %s", price));
    System.out.println(String.format("Total weight: %s", weight));
  }
}
```

Running this program displays the following result on the console:

```
Total price: 1.9
Total weight: 13.5
```

This is fine, but wrong! The problem is that the compiler didn't tell you anything about the error. The only way to catch this error is to test the program, but tests can't prove a program to be correct. They can only prove that you haven't been able to prove it incorrect through writing another program (which, by the way, could be incorrect too).

In case you didn't notice it (which is unlikely), the problem is in the following lines:

```java
double weight = foldLeft(order, 0.0, x -> y -> x + y.getAmount());
double price = foldLeft(order, 0.0, x -> y -> x + y.getWeight());
```

You've incorrectly mixed prices and weights, which the compiler couldn't notice because they're both doubles.

By the way, if you've learned about modeling, you might recall an old rule: classes shouldn't have several properties of the same type. Instead, they should have one property with a specific cardinality. Here, this would mean that a `Product` should have one property of type `double`, with cardinality 2. This is clearly not the right way to solve the problem, but it's a good rule to remember. If you find yourself modeling objects with several properties of the same type, you're probably doing it wrong.

What can you do to avoid such problems? First, you have to realize that prices and weights aren't numbers. They are quantities. Quantities may be numbers, but prices are quantities of money units, and weights are quantities of weight units. You should never be in the situation of adding pounds and dollars.

3.4.2 Defining value types

To avoid this problem, you should use *value types*. Value types are types representing values. You could define a value type to represent a price:

```java
public class Price {

  public final double value;

  public Price(double value) {
    this.value = value;
  }
}
```

You could do the same for the weight:

```java
public class Weight {

  public final double value;

  public Weight(double value) {
    this.value = value;
  }
}
```

But this doesn't solve your problem, because you could write this:

```java
weight += orderLine.getAmount().value;
price += orderLine.getWeight().value;
```

You need to define addition for `Price` and for `Weight`, and you could do that with a method:

```java
public class Price {

  ...

  public Price add(Price that) {
    return new Price(this.value + that.value);
  }
  ...
```

You also need multiplication, but multiplication is a bit different. Addition adds things of the same type, whereas multiplication multiplies things of one type by a number. So multiplication isn't commutative when it isn't applied just to numbers. Here's an example of multiplication for `Product`:

```java
public Price mult(int count) {
  return new Price(this.value * count);
}
```

In your program, you add prices and weights starting with zero. You can't do this any longer, so you need a zero for `Price` and a zero for `Weight`. This can be a singleton, so you'll use

```java
public static final Price ZERO = new Price(0.0);
```

in the `Price` class, and the same thing for the `Weight` class.

The `Product` class needs to be modified as follows:

```java
public class Product {

  public final String name;
  public final Price price;
  public final Weight weight;

  public Product(String name, Price price, Weight weight) {
    this.name = name;
    this.price = price;
    this.weight = weight;
  }
}
```

`OrderLine` needs to be modified too:

```java
public Weight getWeight() {
  return this.product.getWeight().mult(this.count);
}

public Price getAmount() {
  return this.product.price.mult(this.count);
}
```

You can now rewrite your program using these types and operations:

```java
import static com.fpinjava.common.CollectionUtilities.*;
import java.util.List;

public class Store {

  public static void main(String[] args) {

    Product toothPaste = new Product("Tooth paste", new Price(1.5), new Weigh
      t(0.5));
    Product toothBrush = new Product("Tooth brush", new Price(3.5), new Weigh
      t(0.3));

    List<OrderLine> order = list(
        new OrderLine(toothPaste, 2),
        new OrderLine(toothBrush, 3));

    Price price = Price.ZERO;
    Weight weight = Weight.ZERO;
```

```
    for (OrderLine orderLine : order) {
      price = price.add(orderLine.getAmount());
      weight = weight.add(orderLine.getWeight());
    }
  }
}
```

You can't mess with types anymore without the compiler warning you. But you can do far better than this. First, you can add validation to Price and Weight. Neither of them should be constructed with a zero value, except from inside the class itself, for the identity element. You can use a private constructor and a factory method. Here's how it goes for Price:

```
private Price(double value) {
  this.value = value;
}

public static Price price(double value) {
  if (value <= 0) {
    throw new IllegalArgumentException("Price must be greater than 0");
  } else {
    return new Price(value);
  }
}
```

But the main change you can make is to reuse the fold functions you developed in section 3.3. These functions take a function as their third parameter, so you first have to define a function for adding prices (in the Price class):

```
public static Function<Price, Function<OrderLine, Price>> sum =
                            x -> y -> x.add(y.getAmount());
```

You also need the same function in the Weight class in order to add weights:

```
public static Function<Weight, Function<OrderLine, Weight>> sum =
                            x -> y -> x.add(y.getWeight());
```

Finally, you'll add a toString method to Price and Weight in order to simplify testing:

```
public String toString() {
  return Double.toString(this.value);
}
```

Now you can modify your Store class to use folds:

```
Product toothPaste = new Product("Tooth paste", price(1.5), weight(0.5));
Product toothBrush = new Product("Tooth brush", price(3.5), weight(0.3));
List<OrderLine> order =
      list(new OrderLine(toothPaste, 2), new OrderLine(toothBrush, 3));
Price price = foldLeft(order, Price.ZERO, Price.sum);
Weight weight = foldLeft(order, Weight.ZERO, Weight.sum);
System.out.println(String.format("Total price: %s", price));
System.out.println(String.format("Total weight: %s", weight));
```

3.4.3   *The future of value types in Java*

Value types can be used for all business types to bring type safety to your programs. But value types as I've described them aren't real value types. Real value types are manipulated as if they were objects, but perform as if they were primitives. Other languages have built-in value types, but Java doesn't, although this might change; a proposal has been made to include value types in a future version of Java. If you're interested in the subject, you can read the proposal at http://cr.openjdk.java.net/~jrose/values/values-0.html.

3.5   *Summary*

- Java control structures can be made more functional by ensuring that no state mutation is visible from outside of the structures.
- Control structures can be abstracted from the effects they control.
- The `Result` interface may be used to represent the result of operations that may fail.
- Control structures like `if ... else` and `switch ... case` can be replaced with functions.
- Iteration can be abstracted into functions that may be used as a replacement for loops.
- Lists can be folded in two directions (right and left) to reduce them to a single object (which, by the way, may be a new list).
- Lists can be processed by recursion or corecursion.
- Functions can be mapped to lists to change the value and/or the type of its elements.
- Mapping can be implemented using folds.
- Effects can be bound to lists in order to be applied to each of their elements.
- Recursion and corecursion can also be used to construct lists.
- Recursion is limited in depth by the size of the Java stack.
- Value types can be used to make programs safer by allowing the compiler to detect type problems.

Recursion, corecursion, and memoization

The previous chapter introduced powerful methods and functions, but some shouldn't be used in production because they can overflow the stack and crash the application (or at least the thread in which they're called). These "dangerous" methods and functions are mainly explicitly recursive, but not always. You've seen that composing functions can also overflow the stack, and this can occur even with nonrecursive functions, although this isn't common.

In this chapter, you'll learn how to turn stack-based functions into heap-based functions. This is necessary because the stack is a limited memory area. For recursive functions to be safe, you have to implement them in such a way that they use the heap (the main memory area) instead of the limited stack space. To understand the problem completely, you must first understand the difference between recursion and corecursion.

4.1   *Understanding corecursion and recursion*

Corecursion is composing computing steps by using the output of one step as the input of the next one, starting with the first step. *Recursion* is the same operation, but starting with the last step. In recursion, you have to delay evaluation until you encounter a base condition (corresponding to the first step of corecursion).

Let's say you have only two instructions in your programming language: incrementation (adding 1 to a value) and decrementation (subtracting 1 from a value). As an example, you'll implement addition by composing these instructions.

4.1.1   *Exploring corecursive and recursive addition examples*

To add two numbers, x and y, you can do the following:

- If y = 0, return x.
- Otherwise, increment x, decrement y, and start again.

This can be written in Java as follows:

```
static int add(int x, int y) {
  while(y > 0) {
    x = ++x;
    y = --y;
  }
  return x;
}
```

Here's a simpler approach:

```
static int add(int x, int y) {
  while(y-- > 0) {
    x = ++x;
  }
  return x;
}
```

There's no problem with using the parameters x and y directly, because in Java, all parameters are passed by value. Also note that you use post-decrementation to simplify coding. You could have used pre-decrementation by slightly changing the condition, thus switching from iterating from y to 1, to iterating from y - 1 to 0:

```
static int add(int x, int y) {
  while(--y >= 0) {
    x = ++x;
  }
  return x;
}
```

The recursive version is trickier, but still simple:

```
static int addRec(int x, int y) {
  return y == 0
      ? x
      : addRec(++x, --y);
}
```

Both approaches seem to work, but if you try the recursive version with big numbers, you may have a surprise. Although this version,

```
addRec(10000, 3);
```

produces the expected result of 10,003, switching the parameters, like this,

```
addRec(3, 10000);
```

produces a `StackOverflowException`.

4.1.2   *Implementing recursion in Java*

To understand what's happening, you must look at how Java handles method calls. When a method is called, Java suspends what it's currently doing and pushes the environment on the stack to make a place for executing the called method. When this method returns, Java pops the stack to restore the environment and resume program execution. If you call one method after another, the stack always holds at most one of these method call environments.

But methods aren't composed only by calling them one after the other. Methods call methods. If `method1` calls `method2` as part of its implementation, Java again suspends the `method1` execution, pushes the current environment on the stack, and starts executing `method2`. When `method2` returns, Java pops the last pushed environment from the stack and resumes execution (of `method1` in this case). When `method1` completes, Java again pops the last environment from the stack and resumes what it was doing before calling this method.

Method calls may be deeply nested, and this nesting depth does have a limit, which is the size of the stack. In current situations, the limit is somewhere around a few thousand levels, and it's possible to increase this limit by configuring the stack size. But because the same stack size is used for all threads, increasing the stack size generally wastes space. The default stack size varies from 320 KB to 1024 KB, depending on the version of Java and the system used. For a 64-bit Java 8 program with minimal stack usage, the maximum number of nested method calls is about 7,000. Generally, you won't need more, except in specific cases. One such case is recursive method calls.

4.1.3   *Using tail call elimination*

Pushing the environment on the stack is typically necessary in order to resume computation after the called method returns, but not always. When the call to a method is the last thing the calling method does, there's nothing to resume when the method returns, so it should be OK to resume directly with the caller of the current method instead of the current method itself. A method call occurring in the last position, meaning it's the last thing to do before returning, is called a *tail call*. Avoiding pushing the environment to the stack to resume method processing after a tail call is an optimization technique known as *tail call elimination* (TCE). Unfortunately, Java doesn't use TCE.

Tail call elimination is sometimes called *tail call optimization* (TCO). TCE is generally an optimization, and you can live without it. But when it comes to recursive function calls, TCE is no longer an optimization. It's a necessary feature. That's why TCE is a better term than TCO when it comes to handling recursion.

4.1.4 Using tail recursive methods and functions

Most functional languages have TCE. But TCE isn't enough to make every recursive call possible. To be a candidate for TCE, the recursive call must be the last thing the method has to do.

Consider the following method, which is computing the sum of the elements of a list:

```
static Integer sum(List<Integer> list) {
    return list.isEmpty()
        ? 0
        : head(list) + sum(tail(list));
}
```

This method uses the `head` and `tail` methods from chapter 3. The recursive call to the `sum` method isn't the last thing the method has to do. The four last things the method does are as follows:

- Calls the `head` method
- Calls the `tail` method
- Calls the `sum` method
- Adds the result of `head` and the result of `sum`

Even if you had TCE, you wouldn't be able to use this method with lists of 10,000 elements. But you can rewrite this method in order to put the call to `sum` in the tail position:

```
static Integer sum(List<Integer> list) {
  return sumTail(list, 0);
}

static Integer sumTail(List<Integer> list, int acc) {
  return list.isEmpty()
      ? acc
      : sumTail(tail(list), acc + head(list));
}
```

Here, the `sumTail` method is tail recursive and can be optimized through TCE.

4.1.5 Abstracting recursion

So far, so good, but why bother with all this if Java doesn't have TCE? Well, Java doesn't have it, but you can do without it. All you need to do is the following:

- Represent unevaluated method calls
- Store them in a stack-like structure until you encounter a terminal condition
- Evaluate the calls in "last in, first out" (LIFO) order

Most examples of recursive methods use the factorial function. Other examples use the Fibonacci series. The factorial method presents no particular interest beside being recursive. The Fibonacci series is more interesting, and we'll come back to it later. To start with, you'll use the much simpler recursive addition method shown at the beginning of this chapter.

Recursive and corecursive functions are both functions where `f(n)` is a composition of `f(n - 1)`, `f(n - 2)`, `f(n - 3)`, and so on, until a terminal condition is encountered (generally `f(0)` or `f(1)`). Remember that in traditional programming, composing generally means composing the results of an evaluation. This means that composing function `f(a)` and `g(a)` consists of evaluating `g(a)` and then using the result as input to `f`. But it doesn't have to be done that way. In chapter 2, you developed a `compose` method to compose functions, and a `higherCompose` function to do the same thing. Neither evaluated the composed functions. They only produced another function that could be applied later.

Recursion and corecursion are similar, but there's a difference. You create a list of function calls instead of a list of functions. With corecursion, each step is terminal, so it may be evaluated in order to get the result and use it as input for the next step. With recursion, you start from the other end, so you have to put non-evaluated calls in the list until you find a terminal condition, from which you can process the list in reverse order. You stack the steps until the last one is found, and then you process the stack in reverse order (last in, first out), again evaluating each step and using the result as the input for the next (in fact, the previous) one.

The problem is that Java uses the thread stack for both recursion and corecursion, and its capacity is limited. Typically, the stack overflows after 6,000 to 7,000 steps. What you have to do is create a function or a method returning a non-evaluated step. To represent a step in the calculation, you'll use an abstract class called `TailCall` (because you want to represent a call to a method that appears in the tail position).

This `TailCall` abstract class has two subclasses. One represents an intermediate call, when the processing of one step is suspended to call the method again for evaluating the next step. This is represented by a subclass named `Suspend`. It's instantiated with `Supplier<TailCall>>`, which represents the next recursive call. This way, instead of putting all `TailCall`s in a list, you'll construct a linked list by linking each tail call to the next. The benefit of this approach is that such a linked list is a stack, offering constant time insertion as well as constant time access to the last inserted element, which is optimal for a LIFO structure.

The second subclass represents the last call, which is supposed to return the result, so you'll call it `Return`. It won't hold a link to the next `TailCall`, because there's nothing next, but it'll hold the result. Here's what you get:

```java
public abstract class TailCall<T> {
  public static class Return<T> extends TailCall<T> {
    private final T t;
    public Return(T t) {
      this.t = t;
```

```
    }
  }
  public static class Suspend<T> extends TailCall<T> {
    private final Supplier<TailCall<T>> resume;
    private Suspend(Supplier<TailCall<T>> resume) {
      this.resume = resume;
    }
  }
}
```

To handle these classes, you'll need some methods: one to return the result, one to return the next call, and one helper method to determine whether a TailCall is a Suspend or a Return. You could avoid this last method, but you'd have to use instanceof to do the job, which is ugly. The three methods are as follows:

```
public abstract TailCall<T> resume();
public abstract T eval();
public abstract boolean isSuspend();
```

The resume method has no implementation in Return and will throw a runtime exception. The user of your API shouldn't be in a situation to call this method, so if it's eventually called, it'll be a bug and you'll stop the application. In the Suspend class, this method will return the next TailCall.

The eval method returns the result stored in the Return class. In the first version, it'll throw a runtime exception if called on the Suspend class.

The isSuspend method returns true in Suspend, and false in Return. The following listing shows this first version.

> **Listing 4.1 The `TailCall` interface and its two implementations**

```
public abstract class TailCall<T> {

  public abstract TailCall<T> resume();
  public abstract T eval();
  public abstract boolean isSuspend();

  public static class Return<T> extends TailCall<T> {

    private final T t;

    public Return(T t) {
      this.t = t;
    }

    @Override
    public T eval() {
      return t;
    }

    @Override
    public boolean isSuspend() {
      return false;
    }
```

```
   @Override
   public TailCall<T> resume() {
     throw new IllegalStateException("Return has no resume");
   }
 }

 public static class Suspend<T> extends TailCall<T> {

   private final Supplier<TailCall<T>> resume;

   public Suspend(Supplier<TailCall<T>> resume) {
     this.resume = resume;
   }

   @Override
   public T eval() {
     throw new IllegalStateException("Suspend has no value");
   }

   @Override
   public boolean isSuspend() {
     return true;
   }

   @Override
   public TailCall<T> resume() {
     return resume.get();
   }
 }
}
```

To make the recursive method add work with any number of steps (within the limits of available memory!), you have a few changes to make. Starting with your original method,

```
static int add(int x, int y) {
  return y == 0
      ? x
      : add(++x, --y) ;
}
```

you need to make the modifications shown in the following listing.

Listing 4.2   The modified recursive method

```
static TailCall<Integer> add(int x, int y) {          ◁────      Method
  return y == 0                                                   returns
      ? new TailCall.Return<>(x)                ◁────        ❶    a TailCall
      : new TailCall.Suspend<>(() -> add(x + 1, y - 1));
}
```

In nonterminal condition,
❸ a Suspend is returned

In terminal condition,
a Return is returned ❷

This method returns a TailCall<Integer> instead of an int❶. This return value may be a Return<Integer> if you've reached a terminal condition ❷, or a Suspend

<Integer> if you haven't ❸. The Return is instantiated with the result of the computation (which is x, because y is 0), and the Suspend is instantiated with a Supplier <TailCall<Integer>>, which is the next step of the computation in terms of execution sequence, or the previous in terms of calling sequence. It's important to understand that Return corresponds to the last step in terms of the method call, but to the first step in terms of evaluation. Also note that we've slightly changed the evaluation, replacing ++x and --y with x + 1 and y - 1. This is necessary because we're using a closure, which works only if closed-over variables are effectively final. This is cheating, but not too much. We could have created and called two methods, dec and inc, using the original operators.

This method returns a chain of TailCall instances, all being Suspend instances except the last one, which is a Return.

So far, so good, but this method isn't a drop-in replacement for the original one. Not a big deal! The original method was used as follows:

```
System.out.println(add(x, y))
```

You can use the new method like this:

```
TailCall<Integer> tailCall = add(3, 100000000);
while(tailCall.isSuspend()) {
  tailCall = tailCall.resume();
}
System.out.println(tailCall.eval());
```

Doesn't it look nice? If you feel frustrated, I understand. You thought you would just use a new method in place of the old one in a transparent manner. You seem to be far from this. But you can make things much better with a little effort.

4.1.6 *Using a drop-in replacement for stack-based recursive methods*

In the beginning of the previous section, I said that the user of your recursive API would have no opportunity to mess with the TailCall instances by calling resume on a Return or eval on a Suspend. This is easy to achieve by putting the evaluation code in the eval method of the Suspend class:

```
public static class Suspend<T> extends TailCall<T> {

  ...

  @Override
  public T eval() {
    TailCall<T> tailRec = this;
    while(tailRec.isSuspend()) {
      tailRec = tailRec.resume();
    }
    return tailRec.eval();
  }
}
```

Now you can get the result of the recursive call in a much simpler and safer way:

```
add(3, 100000000).eval()
```

But this isn't what you want. You want to get rid of this call to the eval method. This can be done with a helper method:

```
public static int add(int x, int y) {
  return addRec(x, y).eval();
}

private static TailCall<Integer> addRec(int x, int y) {
  return y == 0
      ? ret(x)
      : sus(() -> addRec(x + 1, y - 1));
}
```

Now you can call the add method exactly as the original one. You can make your recursive API easier to use by providing static factory methods to instantiate Return and Suspend, which also allows you to make the Return and Suspend internal subclasses private:

```
public static <T> Return<T> ret(T t) {
  return new Return<>(t);
}

public static <T> Suspend<T> sus(Supplier<TailCall<T>> s) {
  return new Suspend<>(s);
}
```

The following listing shows the complete TailCall class. It adds a private no-args constructor to prevent extension by other classes.

Listing 4.3   The complete TailCall class

```
public abstract class TailCall<T> {

  public abstract TailCall<T> resume();
  public abstract T eval();
  public abstract boolean isSuspend();

  private TailCall() {}

  private static class Return<T> extends TailCall<T> {

    private final T t;

    private Return(T t) {
      this.t = t;
    }

    @Override
    public T eval() {
      return t;
    }

    @Override
    public boolean isSuspend() {
      return false;
    }
```

```
    @Override
    public TailCall<T> resume() {
      throw new IllegalStateException("Return has no resume");
    }
  }

  private static class Suspend<T> extends TailCall<T> {

    private final Supplier<TailCall<T>> resume;

    private Suspend(Supplier<TailCall<T>> resume) {
      this.resume = resume;
    }

    @Override
    public T eval() {
      TailCall<T> tailRec = this;
      while(tailRec.isSuspend()) {
        tailRec = tailRec.resume();
      }
      return tailRec.eval();
    }

    @Override
    public boolean isSuspend() {
      return true;
    }

    @Override
    public TailCall<T> resume() {
      return resume.get();
    }
  }

  public static <T> Return<T> ret(T t) {
    return new Return<>(t);
  }

  public static <T> Suspend<T> sus(Supplier<TailCall<T>> s) {
    return new Suspend<>(s);
  }
}
```

Now that you have a stack-safe tail recursive method, can you do the same thing with a function?

4.2 *Working with recursive functions*

In theory, recursive functions shouldn't be more difficult to create than methods, if functions are implemented as methods in an anonymous class. But lambdas aren't implemented as methods in anonymous classes.

The first problem is that, in theory, lambdas can't be recursive. But this is theory. In fact, you learned a trick to work around this problem in chapter 2. A statically defined recursive add function looks like this:

```
static Function<Integer, Function<Integer, TailCall<Integer>>> add =
    a -> b -> b == 0
```

```
        ? ret(a)
        : sus(() -> ContainingClass.add.apply(a + 1).apply(b - 1));
```

Here, ContainingClass stands for the name of the class in which the function is defined. Or you may prefer an instance function instead of a static one:

```
Function<Integer, Function<Integer, TailCall<Integer>>> add =
    a -> b -> b == 0
        ? ret(a)
        : sus(() -> this.add.apply(a + 1).apply(b - 1));
```

But here, you have the same problem you had with the add method. You must call eval on the result. You could use the same trick, with a helper method alongside the recursive implementation. But you should make the whole thing self-contained. In other languages, such as Scala, you can define helper functions locally, inside the main function. Can you do the same in Java?

4.2.1 Using locally defined functions

Defining a function inside a function isn't directly possible in Java. But a function written as a lambda is a class. Can you define a local function in that class? In fact, you can't. You can't use a static function, because a local class can't have static members, and anyway, they have no name. Can you use an instance function? No, because you need a reference to this. And one of the differences between lambdas and anonymous classes is the this reference. Instead of referring to the anonymous class instance, the this reference used in a lambda refers to the enclosing instance.

The solution is to declare a local class containing an instance function, as shown in the following listing.

Listing 4.4   A standalone tail recursive function

```
static Function<Integer, Function<Integer, Integer>> add = x -> y -> {
  class AddHelper {
    Function<Integer, Function<Integer, TailCall<Integer>>> addHelper =
        a -> b -> b == 0
            ? ret(a)
            : sus(() -> this.addHelper.apply(a + 1).apply(b - 1));    ⏴─────┐
  }                                                                         │
  return new AddHelper().addHelper.apply(x).apply(y).eval();               │
};
```
The this reference refers to the AddHelper class.

This function may be used as a normal function:

```
add.apply(3).apply(100000000)
```

4.2.2 Making functions tail recursive

Previously, I said that a simple recursive functional method computing the sum of elements in a list couldn't be handled safely because it isn't tail recursive:

```
static Integer sum(List<Integer> list) {
  return list.isEmpty()
      ? 0
      : head(list) + sum(tail(list));
}
```

You saw that you had to transform the method as follows:

```
static Integer sum(List<Integer> list) {
    return sumTail(list, 0);
}

static Integer sumTail(List<Integer> list, int acc) {
  return list.isEmpty()
      ? acc
      : sumTail(tail(list), acc + head(list));
}
```

The principle is quite simple, although it's sometimes tricky to apply. It consists of using an accumulator holding the result of the computation. This accumulator is added to the parameters of the method. Then the function is transformed into a helper method called by the original one with the initial value of the accumulator. It's important to make this process nearly instinctive, because you'll have to use it each time you want to write a recursive method or function.

It may be OK to change a method into two methods. After all, methods don't travel, so you only have to make the main method public and the helper method (the one doing the job) private. The same is true for functions, because the call to the helper function by the main function is a closure. The main reason to prefer a locally defined helper function over a private helper method is to avoid name clashes.

A current practice in languages that allow locally defined functions is to call all helper functions with a single name, such as go or process. This can't be done with nonlocal functions (unless you have only one function in each class). In the previous example, the helper function for sum was called sumTail. Another current practice is to call the helper function with the same name as the main function with an appended underscore, such as sum_. Whatever system you choose, it's useful to be consistent. In the rest of this book, I'll use the underscore to denote tail recursive helper functions.

4.2.3 *Doubly recursive functions: the Fibonacci example*

No book about recursive functions can avoid the Fibonacci series function. Although it's totally useless to most of us, it's ubiquitous and fun. Let's start with the requirements, in case you've never met this function.

The Fibonacci series is a suite of numbers, and each number is the sum of the two previous ones. This is a recursive definition. You need a terminal condition, so the full requirements are as follows:

- $f(0) = 0$
- $f(1) = 1$
- $f(n) = f(n-1) + f(n-2)$

This isn't the original Fibonacci series, in which the first two numbers are equal to 1. Each number is supposed to be a function of its position in the series, and that position starts at 1. In computing, you generally prefer to start at 0. Anyway, this doesn't change the problem.

Why is this function so interesting? Instead of answering this question right now, let's try a naive implementation:

```
public static int fibonacci(int number) {
  if (number == 0 || number == 1) {
    return number;
  }
  return fibonacci(number - 1) + fibonacci(number - 2);
}
```

Now let's write a simple program to test this method:

```
public static void main(String args[]) {
  int n = 10;
  for(int i = 0; i <= n; i++){
    System.out.print(fibonacci(i) +" ");
  }
}
```

If you run this test program, you'll get the first 10 (or 9, according to the original definition) Fibonacci numbers:

```
0 1 1 2 3 5 8 13 21 34 55
```

Based on what you know about naive recursion in Java, you may think that this method will succeed in calculating f(n) for n, up to 6,000 to 7,000 before overflowing the stack. Well, let's check it. Replace int n = 10 with int n = 6000 and see what happens. Launch the program and take a coffee break. When you return, you'll realize that the program is still running. It will have reached somewhere around 1,836,311,903 (your mileage may vary—you could get a negative number!), but it'll never finish. No stack overflow, no exception—just hanging in the wild. What's happening?

The problem is that each call to the function creates two recursive calls. So to calculate f(n), you need $2n$ recursive calls. Let's say your method needs 10 nanoseconds to execute. (Just guessing, but you'll see soon that it doesn't change anything.) Calculating f(5000) will take $2^{5000} \times 10$ nanoseconds. Do you have any idea how long this is? This program will never terminate because it would need longer than the expected duration of the solar system (if not the universe!).

To make a usable Fibonacci function, you have to change it to use a single tail recursive call. There's also another problem: the results are so big that you'll soon get an arithmetic overflow, resulting in negative numbers.

EXERCISE 4.1
Create a tail recursive version of the Fibonacci functional method.

HINT

The accumulator solution is the way to go. But there are two recursive calls, so you'll need two accumulators.

SOLUTION 4.1

Let's first write the signature of the helper method. It'll take two `BigInteger` instances as accumulators, and one for the original argument, and it'll return a `BigInteger`:

```
private static BigInteger fib_(BigInteger acc1, BigInteger acc2,
                               BigInteger x) {
```

You must deal with the terminal conditions. If the argument is 0, you return 0:

```
private static BigInteger fib_(BigInteger acc1, BigInteger acc2,
                               BigInteger x) {
  if (x.equals(BigInteger.ZERO)) {
    return BigInteger.ZERO;
```

If the argument is 1, you return the sum of the two accumulators:

```
private static BigInteger fib_(BigInteger acc1, BigInteger acc2,
                               BigInteger x) {
  if (x.equals(BigInteger.ZERO)) {
    return BigInteger.ZERO;
  } else if (x.equals(BigInteger.ONE)) {
    return acc1.add(acc2);
```

Eventually, you have to deal with recursion. You must do the following:

- Take accumulator 2 and make it accumulator 1.
- Create a new accumulator 2 by adding the two previous accumulators.
- Subtract 1 from the argument.
- Recursively call the function with the three computed values as its arguments.

Here's the transcription in code:

```
private static BigInteger fib_(BigInteger acc1, BigInteger acc2,
                               BigInteger x) {
  if (x.equals(BigInteger.ZERO)) {
    return BigInteger.ZERO;
  } else if (x.equals(BigInteger.ONE)) {
    return acc1.add(acc2);
  } else {
    return fib_(acc2, acc1.add(acc2), x.subtract(BigInteger.ONE));
  }
}
```

The last thing to do is to create the main method that calls this helper method with the initial values of the accumulators:

```
public static BigInteger fib(int x) {
  return fib_(BigInteger.ONE, BigInteger.ZERO, BigInteger.valueOf(x));
}
```

This is only one possible implementation. You may organize accumulators, initial values, and conditions in a slightly different manner, as long as it works. Now you can call fib(5000), and it'll give you the result in a couple of nanoseconds. Well, it'll take a few dozen milliseconds, but only because printing to the console is a slow operation. We'll come back to this shortly.

The result is impressive, whether it's the result of the computation (1,045 digits!) or the increase in speed due to the transformation of a dual recursive call into a single one. But you still can't use the method with values higher than 7,500.

EXERCISE 4.2

Turn this method into a stack-safe recursive one.

SOLUTION 4.2

This should be easy. The following code shows the needed changes:

```
BigInteger fib(int x) {
  return fib_(BigInteger.ONE, BigInteger.ZERO,
                            BigInteger.valueOf(x)).eval();
}

TailCall<BigInteger> fib_(BigInteger acc1, BigInteger acc2, BigInteger x) {
  if (x.equals(BigInteger.ZERO)) {
    return ret(BigInteger.ZERO);
  } else if (x.equals(BigInteger.ONE)) {
    return ret(acc1.add(acc2));
  } else {
    return sus(() -> fib_(acc2, acc1.add(acc2), x.subtract(BigInteger.ONE)));
  }
}
```

You may now compute fib(10000) and count the digits in the result!

4.2.4　Making the list methods stack-safe and recursive

In the previous chapter, you developed functional methods to work on lists. Some of these methods were naively recursive, so they couldn't be used in production. It's time to fix this.

EXERCISE 4.3

Create a stack-safe recursive version of the foldLeft method.

SOLUTION 4.3

The naively recursive version of the foldLeft method was tail recursive:

```
public static <T, U> U foldLeft(List<T> ts, U identity,
                                Function<U, Function<T, U>> f) {
  return ts.isEmpty()
      ? identity
      : foldLeft(tail(ts), f.apply(identity).apply(head(ts)), f);
}
```

Turning it into a fully recursive method is easy:

```
public static <T, U> U foldLeft(List<T> ts, U identity,
                                Function<U, Function<T, U>> f) {
  return foldLeft_(ts, identity, f).eval();
}

private static <T, U> TailCall<U> foldLeft_(List<T> ts, U identity,
                                Function<U, Function<T, U>> f) {
  return ts.isEmpty()
      ? ret(identity)
      : sus(() -> foldLeft_(tail(ts),
                      f.apply(identity).apply(head(ts)), f));
}
```

EXERCISE 4.4

Create a fully recursive version of the recursive range method.

HINT

Beware of the direction of list construction (append or prepend).

SOLUTION 4.4

The range method isn't tail recursive:

```
public static List<Integer> range(Integer start, Integer end) {
  return end <= start
      ? list()
      : prepend(start, range(start + 1, end));
}
```

You have to first create a tail recursive version, using an accumulator. Here, you need to return a list, so the accumulator will be a list, and you'll start with an empty list. But you must build the list in reverse order:

```
public static List<Integer> range(List<Integer> acc,
                                Integer start, Integer end) {
  return end <= start
      ? acc
      : range(append(acc, start), start + 1, end);
}
```

Then you must turn this method into a main method and a helper method by using true recursion:

```
public static List<Integer> range(Integer start, Integer end) {
  return range_(list(), start, end).eval();
}

private static TailCall<List<Integer>> range_(List<Integer> acc,
                                Integer start, Integer end) {
  return end <= start
      ? ret(acc)
      : sus(() -> range_(append(acc, start), start + 1, end));
}
```

The fact that you had to reverse the operation is important. Can you see why? If not, try the next exercise.

EXERCISE 4.5 (HARD)

Create a stack-safe recursive version of the `foldRight` method.

SOLUTION 4.5

The stack-based recursive version of the `foldRight` method is as follows:

```
public static <T, U> U foldRight(List<T> ts, U identity,
                                  Function<T, Function<U, U>> f) {
  return ts.isEmpty()
       ? identity
       : f.apply(head(ts)).apply(foldRight(tail(ts), identity, f));
}
```

This method isn't tail recursive, so let's first create a tail recursive version. You might end up with this:

```
public static <T, U> U foldRight(U acc, List<T> ts, U identity,
                                  Function<T, Function<U, U>> f) {
  return ts.isEmpty()
       ? acc
       : foldRight(f.apply(head(ts)).apply(acc), tail(ts), identity, f);
}
```

Unfortunately, this doesn't work! Can you see why? If not, test this version and compare the result with the standard version. You can compare the two versions by using the test designed in the previous chapter:

```
public static String addIS(Integer i, String s) {
  return "(" + i + " + " + s + ")";
}

List<Integer> list = list(1, 2, 3, 4, 5);
System.out.println(foldRight(list, "0", x -> y -> addIS(x, y)));
System.out.println(foldRightTail("0", list, "0", x -> y -> addIS(x, y)));
```

You'll get the following result:

```
(1 + (2 + (3 + (4 + (5 + 0)))))
(5 + (4 + (3 + (2 + (1 + 0)))))
```

This shows that the list is processed in reverse order. One easy solution is to reverse the list in the main method before calling the helper method. If you apply this trick while making the method stack-safe and recursive, you'll get this:

```
public static <T, U> U foldRight(List<T> ts, U identity,
                                  Function<T, Function<U, U>> f) {
  return foldRight_(identity, reverse(ts), f).eval();
}

private static <T, U> TailCall<U> foldRight_(U acc, List<T> ts,
                                  Function<T, Function<U, U>> f) {
```

```
    return ts.isEmpty()
        ? ret(acc)
        : sus(() -> foldRight_(f.apply(head(ts)).apply(acc), tail(ts), f));
}
```

In chapter 5, you'll develop the process of reversing the list by implementing fold-Left in terms of `foldRight`, and `foldRight` in terms of `foldLeft`. But this shows that the recursive implementation of `foldRight` won't be optimal because reverse is an O(*n*) operation: the time needed to execute it is proportional to the number of elements in the list, because you must traverse the list. By using reverse, you double this time by traversing the list twice. The conclusion is that when considering using fold-Right, you should do one of the following:

- Not care about performance
- Change the function (if possible) and use `foldLeft`
- Use `foldRight` only with small lists
- Use an imperative implementation

4.3 *Composing a huge number of functions*

In chapter 2, you saw that you'll overflow the stack if you try to compose a huge number of functions. The reason is the same as for recursion: because composing functions results in methods calling methods.

Having to compose more than 7,000 functions may be something you don't expect to do soon. On the other hand, there's no reason not to make it possible. If it's possible, someone will eventually find something useful to do with it. And if it's not useful, someone will certainly find something fun to do with it.

Exercise 4.6

Write a function, `composeAll`, taking as its argument a list of functions from T to T and returning the result of composing all the functions in the list.

Solution 4.6

To get the result you want, you can use a right fold, taking as its arguments the list of functions, the `identity` function (obtained by a call to the statically imported `Function` `.identity()` method), and the `compose` method written in chapter 2:

```
static <T> Function<T, T> composeAll(List<Function<T, T>> list) {
  return foldRight(list, identity(), x -> y -> x.compose(y));
}
```

To test this method, you can statically import all the methods from your `Collection-Utilities` class (developed in chapter 3) and write the following:

```
Function<Integer, Integer> add = y -> y + 1;
System.out.println(composeAll(map(range(0, 500), x -> add)).apply(0));
```

If you don't feel comfortable with this kind of code, it's equivalent to, but much more readable than, this:

```
List<Function<Integer, Integer>> list = new ArrayList<>();
for (int i = 0; i < 500; i++) {
  list.add(x -> x + 1);
}

int result = composeAll(list).apply(0);
System.out.println(result);
```

Running this code displays 500, as it's the result of composing 500 functions incrementing their argument by 1. What happens if you replace 500 with 10,000? You'll get a StackOverflowException. The reason should be obvious.

By the way, on the machine I used for this test, the program breaks for a list of 2,856 functions.

EXERCISE 4.7

Fix this problem so you can compose an (almost) unlimited number of functions.

SOLUTION 4.7

The solution to this problem is simple. Instead of composing the functions by nesting them, you have to compose their results, always staying at the higher level. This means that between each call to a function, you'll return to the original caller. If this isn't clear, imagine the imperative way to do this:

```
T y = identity;

for (Function<T, T> f : list) {
  y = f.apply(y);
}
```

Here, identity means the identity element of the given function. This isn't composing functions, but composing function applications. At the end of the loop, you'll get a T and not a Function<T, T>. But this is easy to fix. You create a function from T to T, which has the following implementation:

```
static <T> Function<T, T> composeAll(List<Function<T, T>> list) {
  return x -> {
    T y = x;                                  ◁──────   A copy of x is made; you
    for (Function<T, T> f : list) {                     can't modify x because it
      y = f.apply(y);                                   must be effectively final.
    }
    return y;
  };
}
```

You can't use x directly, because it would create a closure, so it should be effectively final. That's why you make a copy of it. This code works fine, except for two things.

The first is that it doesn't look functional. This can be fixed easily by using a fold. It can be either a left fold or a right fold:

```
<T> Function<T, T> composeAllViaFoldLeft(List<Function<T, T>> list) {
  return x -> foldLeft(list, x, a -> b -> b.apply(a));
}

<T> Function<T, T> composeAllViaFoldRight(List<Function<T, T>> list) {
  return x -> foldRight(list, x, a -> a::apply);
}
```

You're using a method reference for the `composeAllViaFoldRight` implementation. This is equivalent to the following:

```
<T> Function<T, T> composeAllViaFoldRight(List<Function<T, T>> list) {
  return x -> FoldRight.foldRight(list, x, a -> b -> a.apply(b));
}
```

If you have trouble understanding how it works, think about the analogy with `sum`. When you defined `sum`, the list was a list of integers. The initial value (x here) was `0`; a and b were the two parameters to add; and the addition was defined as a + b. Here, the list is a list of functions; the initial value is the identity function; a and b are functions; and the implementation is defined as `b.apply(a)` or `a.apply(b)`. In the `foldLeft` version, b is the function coming from the list, and a is the current result. In the `foldRight` version, a is the function coming from the list, and b is the current result.

To see this in action, refer to the unit tests in the code available from the book's site (https://github.com/fpinjava/fpinjava).

Exercise 4.8

The code has two problems, and you fixed only one. Can you see another problem and fix it?

Hint

The second problem isn't visible in the result because the functions you're composing are specific. They are, in fact, a single function from integer to integer. The order in which they're composed is irrelevant. Try to use the `composeAll` method with the following function list:

```
Function<String, String> f1 = x -> "(a" + x + ")";
Function<String, String> f2 = x -> "{b" + x + "}";
Function<String, String> f3 = x -> "[c" + x + "]";
System.out.println(composeAllViaFoldLeft(list(f1, f2, f3)).apply("x"));
System.out.println(composeAllViaFoldRight(list(f1, f2, f3)).apply("x"));
```

Solution 4.8

We've implemented `andThenAll` rather than `composeAll`! To get the correct result, you first have to reverse the list:

```
<T> Function<T, T> composeAllViaFoldLeft(List<Function<T, T>> list) {
  return x -> foldLeft(reverse(list), x, a -> b -> b.apply(a));
}
```

```
<T> Function<T, T> composeAllViaFoldRight(List<Function<T, T>> list) {
  return x -> foldRight(list, x, a -> a::apply);
}

<T> Function<T, T> andThenAllViaFoldLeft(List<Function<T, T>> list) {
  return x -> foldLeft(list, x, a -> b -> b.apply(a));
}

<T> Function<T, T> andThenAllViaFoldRight(List<Function<T, T>> list) {
  return x -> foldRight(reverse(list), x, a -> a::apply);
}
```

4.4 Using memoization

In section 4.2.3, you implemented a function to display a series of Fibonacci numbers. One problem with this implementation of the Fibonacci series is that you want to print the string representing the series up to f(n), which means you have to compute f(1), f(2), and so on, until f(n). But to compute f(n), you have to recursively compute the function for all preceding values. Eventually, to create the series up to n, you'll have computed f(1) n times, f(2) n - 1 times, and so on. The total number of computations will then be the sum of the integers 1 to *n*. Can you do better? Could you possibly keep the computed values in memory so you don't have to compute them again if they're needed several times?

4.4.1 Memoization in imperative programming

In imperative programming, you wouldn't even have this problem, because the obvious way to proceed would be as follows:

```
public static void main(String args[]) {
  System.out.println(fibo(10));
}

public static String fibo(int limit) {
  switch(limit) {
    case 0:
      return "0";
    case 1:
      return "0, 1";
    case 2:
      return "0, 1, 1";
    default:
      BigInteger fibo1 = BigInteger.ONE;
      BigInteger fibo2 = BigInteger.ONE;
      BigInteger fibonacci;
      StringBuilder builder = new StringBuilder("0, 1, 1");
      for (int i = 3; i <= limit; i++) {
        fibonacci = fibo1.add(fibo2);
        builder.append(", ").append(fibonacci);    ⊣ Stores f(n – 1) for
        fibo1 = fibo2;                        ◁─────┘   the next pass
        fibo2 = fibonacci;         ◁─┐ Stores f(n) for the
      }                             │ next pass
      return builder.toString();
  }
}
```

Although this program concentrates most of the problems that FP is supposed to avoid or to solve, it works and is much more efficient than your functional version. The reason is memoization.

Memoization is a technique that keeps in memory the result of a computation so it can be returned immediately if you have to redo the same computation in the future. Applied to functions, memoization makes the functions memorize the results of previous calls, so they can return the results much faster if they're called again with the same arguments.

This might seem incompatible with functional principles, because a memoized function maintains a state. But it isn't, because the result of the function is the same when it's called with the same argument. (You could even argue that it's more the same, because it isn't computed again!) The side effect of storing the results must not be visible from outside the function.

In imperative programming, this might not even be noticed. Maintaining state is the universal way of computing results, so memoization isn't even noticed.

4.4.2 Memoization in recursive functions

Recursive functions often use memoization implicitly. In your example of the recursive Fibonacci function, you wanted to return the series, so you calculated each number in the series, leading to unnecessary recalculations. A simple solution is to rewrite the function in order to directly return the string representing the series.

EXERCISE 4.9

Write a stack-safe tail recursive function taking an integer n as its argument and returning a string representing the values of the Fibonacci numbers from 0 to n, separated by a comma and a space.

HINT

One solution is to use `StringBuilder` as the accumulator. `StringBuilder` isn't a functional structure because it's mutable, but this mutation won't be visible from the outside. Another solution is to return a list of numbers and then transform it into a `String`. This solution is easier, because you can abstract the problem of the separators by first returning a list and then writing a function to turn the list into a comma-separated string.

SOLUTION 4.9

The following listing shows the solution using `List` as the accumulator.

Listing 4.5 Recursive Fibonacci with implicit memoization

Calls the fibo_ helper method to get the list of Fibonacci numbers

```
public static String fibo(int number) {
  List<BigInteger> list = fibo_(list(BigInteger.ZERO),
      BigInteger.ONE, BigInteger.ZERO, BigInteger.valueOf(number)).eval();
  return makeString(list, ", ");
}
```

```
private static <T> TailCall<List<BigInteger>> fibo_(List<BigInteger> acc,
                    BigInteger acc1, BigInteger acc2, BigInteger x) {
  return x.equals(BigInteger.ZERO)
      ? ret(acc)
      : x.equals(BigInteger.ONE)
          ? ret(append(acc, acc1.add(acc2)))
          : sus(() -> fibo_(append(acc, acc1.add(acc2)),
                    acc2, acc1.add(acc2), x.subtract(BigInteger.ONE)));
}

public static <T> String makeString(List<T> list, String separator) {
  return list.isEmpty()
      ? ""
      : tail(list).isEmpty()
          ? head(list).toString()
          : head(list) + foldLeft(tail(list), "",
                    x -> y -> x + separator + y);
}
```

Formats the list into a comma-separated string through a call to the makeString method

RECURSION OR CORECURSION?

This example demonstrates the use of implicit memoization. Don't conclude that this is the best way to solve the problem. Many problems are much easier to solve when twisted. So let's twist this one.

Instead of a suite of numbers, you could see the Fibonacci series as a suite of pairs (tuples). Instead of trying to generate this,

```
0, 1, 1, 2, 3, 5, 8, 13, 21, ...
```

you could try to produce this:

```
(0, 1), (1, 1), (1, 2), (2, 3), (3, 5), (5, 8), (8, 13), (13, 21), ...
```

In this series, each tuple can be constructed from the previous one. The second element of tuple n becomes the first element of tuple n + 1. The second element of tuple n + 1 is equal to the sum of the two elements of tuple n. In Java, you can write a function for this:

```
x -> new Tuple<>(x._2, x._1.add(x._2));
```

You can now replace the recursive method with a corecursive one:

```
public static String fiboCorecursive(int number) {
  Tuple<BigInteger, BigInteger> seed =
                    new Tuple<>(BigInteger.ZERO, BigInteger.ONE);
  Function<Tuple<BigInteger, BigInteger>,Tuple<BigInteger, BigInteger>> f =
                    x -> new Tuple<>(x._2, x._1.add(x._2));
  List<BigInteger> list = map(List.iterate(seed, f, number + 1), x -> x._1);
  return makeString(list, ", ");
}
```

The `iterate` method takes a seed, a function, and a number *n*, and creates a list of length *n* by applying the function to each element to compute the next one. Here's its signature:

```
public static <B> List<B> iterate(B seed, Function<B, B> f, int n)
```

This method is available in the `fpinjava-common` module.

4.4.3 *Automatic memoization*

Memoization isn't mainly used for recursive functions. It can be used to speed up any function. Think about how you perform multiplication. If you need to multiply 234 by 686, you'll probably need a pen and some paper, or a calculator. But if you're asked to multiply 9 by 7, you can answer immediately, without doing any computation. This is because you use a memoized multiplication. A memoized function works the same way, although it needs to make the computation only once to retain the result.

Imagine you have a functional method `doubleValue` that multiplies its argument by 2:

```
Integer doubleValue(Integer x) {
  return x * 2;
}
```

You could memoize this method by storing the result into a map:

```
Map<Integer, Integer> cache = new ConcurrentHashMap<>();    ⊲──┐ Map is used to
Integer doubleValue(Integer x) {                               └── store the results
  if (cache.containsKey(x)) {       ⊲──────── Looks in the map to see if the
    return cache.get(x);                       result has already been computed
  } else {
    Integer result = x * 2;         ⊲──── If not found, computes the result
    cache.put(x, result) ;          ⊲──── Puts the result in the map
    return result;                  ⊲──── Returns the result
  }
}
```

If found, returns the result (annotation pointing to `return cache.get(x);`)

In Java 8, this can be made much shorter:

```
Map<Integer, Integer> cache = new ConcurrentHashMap<>();

Integer doubleValue(Integer x) {
  return cache.computeIfAbsent(x, y -> y * 2);
}
```

If you prefer using functions (which is likely, given the subject of this book), you can apply the same principle:

```
Function<Integer, Integer> doubleValue =
                  x -> cache.computeIfAbsent(x, y -> y * 2);
```

But two problems arise:

- You have to repeat this modification for all functions you want to memoize.
- The map you use is exposed to the outside.

The second problem is easy to address. You can put the method or the function in a separate class, including the map, with private access. Here's an example in the case of a method:

```
public class Doubler {

  private static Map<Integer, Integer> cache = new ConcurrentHashMap<>();

  public static Integer doubleValue(Integer x) {
    return cache.computeIfAbsent(x, y -> y * 2);
  }
}
```

You can then instantiate that class and use it each time you want to compute a value:

```
Integer y = Doubler.doubleValue(x);
```

With this solution, the map is no longer accessible from the outside. You can't do the same for functions, because functions can't have static members. One possibility is to pass the map to the function as an additional argument. This can be done through a closure:

```
class Doubler {
  private static Map<Integer, Integer> cache = new ConcurrentHashMap<>();

  public static Function<Integer, Integer> doubleValue =
                        x -> cache.computeIfAbsent(x, y -> y * 2);
}
```

You can use this function as follows:

```
Integer y = Doubler.doubleValue.apply(x);
```

This gives no advantage compared to the method solution. But you can also use this function in more idiomatic examples, such as this:

```
map(range(1, 10), Doubler.doubleValue);
```

This is equivalent to using the method version with the following syntax:

```
map(range(1, 10), Doubler::doubleValue);
```

THE REQUIREMENTS

What you need is a way to do the following:

```
Function<Integer, Integer> f = x -> x * 2;
Function<Integer, Integer> g = Memoizer.memoize(f);
```

Then you can use the memoized function as a drop-in replacement for the original one. All values returned by function g will be calculated through the original function f the first time, and returned from the cache for all subsequent accesses. By contrast, if you create a third function,

```
Function<Integer, Integer> f = x -> x * 2;
Function<Integer, Integer> g = Memoizer.memoize(f);
Function<Integer, Integer> h = Memoizer.memoize(f);
```

the values cached by g won't be returned by h; g and h will use separate caches.

IMPLEMENTATION

The Memoizer class is simple and is shown in the following listing.

Listing 4.6   The Memoizer class

```
public class Memoizer<T, U> {

  private final Map<T, U> cache = new ConcurrentHashMap<>();

  private Memoizer() {}

  public static <T, U> Function<T, U> memoize(Function<T, U> function) {
    return new Memoizer<T, U>().doMemoize(function);
  }

  private Function<T, U> doMemoize(Function<T, U> function) {
    return input -> cache.computeIfAbsent(input, function::apply);
  }
}
```

The memoized method returns a memoized version of its function argument.

The doMemoize method handles the computation, calling the original function if necessary.

The following listing shows how this class can be used. The program simulates a long computation to show the result of memoizing the function.

Listing 4.7   Demonstrating the memoizer

```
private static Integer longCalculation(Integer x) {
  try {
    Thread.sleep(1_000);
  } catch (InterruptedException ignored) {}
  return x * 2;
}

private static Function<Integer, Integer> f =
                            MemoizerDemo::longCalculation;

private static Function<Integer, Integer> g = Memoizer.memoize(f);

public static void automaticMemoizationExample() {
  long startTime = System.currentTimeMillis();
  Integer result1 = g.apply(1);
  long time1 = System.currentTimeMillis() - startTime;
  startTime = System.currentTimeMillis();
```

Simulates a long computation

The function to memoize

The memoized function

```
    Integer result2 = g.apply(1);
    long time2 = System.currentTimeMillis() - startTime;
    System.out.println(result1);
    System.out.println(result2);
    System.out.println(time1);
    System.out.println(time2);
  }
```

Running the `automaticMemoizationExample` method on my computer produces the following result:

```
2
2
1000
0
```

Note that the exact result will depend on the speed of your computer.

You can now make memoized functions out of ordinary ones by calling a single method, but to use this technique in production, you'd have to handle potential memory problems. This code is acceptable if the number of possible inputs is low, so you can keep all results in memory without causing memory overflow. Otherwise, you can use soft references or weak references to store memoized values.

MEMOIZATION OF "MULTIARGUMENT" FUNCTIONS

As I said before, there's no such thing in this world as a function with several arguments. Functions are applications of one set (the source set) to another set (the target set). They can't have several arguments. Functions that appear to have several arguments are one of these:

- Functions of tuples
- Functions returning functions returning functions ... returning a result

In either case, you're concerned only with functions of one argument, so you can easily use your `Memoizer` class.

Using functions of tuples is probably the simplest choice. You could use the `Tuple` class written in previous chapters, but to store tuples in maps, you'd have to implement `equals` and `hashcode`. Besides this, you'd have to define tuples for two elements (pairs), tuples for three elements, and so on. Who knows where to stop?

The second option is much easier. You have to use the curried version of the functions, as you did in previous chapters. Memoizing curried functions is easy, although you can't use the same simple form as previously. You have to memoize each function:

```
Function<Integer, Function<Integer, Integer>> mhc =
                    Memoizer.memoize(x ->
                            Memoizer.memoize(y -> x + y));
```

You can use the same technique to memoize a function of three arguments:

```
Function<Integer, Function<Integer, Function<Integer, Integer>>> f3 =
                            x -> y -> z -> x + y - z;
```

```
Function<Integer, Function<Integer, Function<Integer, Integer>>> f3m =
            Memoizer.memoize(x ->
                    Memoizer.memoize(y ->
                            Memoizer.memoize(z -> x + y - z)));
```

The following listing shows an example of using this memoized function of three arguments.

Listing 4.8 Testing a memoized function of three arguments for performance

```
Function<Integer, Function<Integer, Function<Integer, Integer>>> f3m =
        Memoizer.memoize(x ->
                Memoizer.memoize(y ->
                        Memoizer.memoize(z ->
        longCalculation(x) + longCalculation(y) - longCalculation(z))));

    public void automaticMemoizationExample2() {
        long startTime = System.currentTimeMillis();
        Integer result1 = f3m.apply(2).apply(3).apply(4);
        long time1 = System.currentTimeMillis() - startTime;
        startTime = System.currentTimeMillis();
        Integer result2 = f3m.apply(2).apply(3).apply(4);
        long time2 = System.currentTimeMillis() - startTime;
        System.out.println(result1);
        System.out.println(result2);
        System.out.println(time1);
        System.out.println(time2);
    }
```

This program produces the following output:

```
2
2
3002
0
```

This shows that the first access to the `longCalculation` method has taken 3,000 milliseconds, and the second has returned immediately.

On the other hand, using a function of a tuple may seem easier after you have the `Tuple` class defined. The following listing shows an example of `Tuple3`.

Listing 4.9 An implementation of `Tuple3`

```
public class Tuple3<T, U, V> {

    public final T _1;
    public final U _2;
    public final V _3;

    public Tuple3(T t, U u, V v) {
        _1 = Objects.requireNonNull(t);
        _2 = Objects.requireNonNull(u);
        _3 = Objects.requireNonNull(v);
    }
```

```
@Override
public boolean equals(Object o) {
  if (!(o instanceof Tuple3)) return false;
  else {
    Tuple3 that = (Tuple3) o;
    return _1.equals(that._1) && _2.equals(that._2)
                                      && _3.equals(that._3);
  }
}

@Override
public int hashCode() {
  final int prime = 31;
  int result = 1;
  result = prime * result + _1.hashCode();
  result = prime * result + _2.hashCode();
  result = prime * result + _3.hashCode();
  return result;
}
}
```

The following listing shows an example of testing a memoized function taking `Tuple3` as its argument.

> ### Listing 4.10　A memoized function of `Tuple3`

```
Function<Tuple3<Integer, Integer, Integer>, Integer> ft =
                  x -> longCalculation(x._1)
                              + longCalculation(x._2)
                                    - longCalculation(x._3);
Function<Tuple3<Integer, Integer, Integer>, Integer> ftm =
                                    Memoizer.memoize(ft);

public void automaticMemoizationExample3() {
  long startTime = System.currentTimeMillis();
  Integer result1 = ftm.apply(new Tuple3<>(2, 3, 4));
  long time1 = System.currentTimeMillis() - startTime;
  startTime = System.currentTimeMillis();
  Integer result2 = ftm.apply(new Tuple3<>(2, 3, 4));
  long time2 = System.currentTimeMillis() - startTime;
  System.out.println(result1);
  System.out.println(result2);
  System.out.println(time1);
  System.out.println(time2);
}
```

ARE MEMOIZED FUNCTIONS PURE?

Memoizing is about maintaining state between function calls. A memoized function is a function whose behavior is dependent on the current state. But it'll always return the same value for the same argument. Only the time needed to return the value will be different. So the memoized function is still a pure function if the original function is pure.

A variation in time may be a problem. A function like the original Fibonacci function needing many years to complete may be called *nonterminating*, so an increase in time may create a problem. On the other hand, making a function faster shouldn't be a problem. If it is, there's a much bigger problem somewhere else!

4.5   Summary

- A recursive function is a function that's defined by referencing itself.
- In Java, recursive methods push the current computation state onto the stack before recursively calling themselves.
- The Java default stack size is limited. It can be configured to a larger size, but this generally wastes space because all threads use the same stack size.
- Tail recursive functions are functions in which the recursive call is in the last (tail) position.
- In some languages, recursive functions are optimized using tail call elimination (TCE).
- Java doesn't implement TCE, but it's possible to emulate it.
- Lambdas may be made recursive.
- Memoization allows functions to remember their computed values in order to speed up later accesses.
- Memoization can be made automatic.

Data handling with lists

Data structures are among the most important concepts in programming, as well as in everyday life. The world as we see it is itself a huge data structure composed of simpler data structures, which are in turn composed of simpler structures. Each time we try to model something, be it objects or facts, we end up with data structures.

There are many types of data structures. In computing, data structures are generally represented as a whole by the term *collections*. A collection is a group of data items that have some relation to each other. In the simplest form, this relation is the fact that they belong to the same group.

124

5.1 How to classify data collections

Data collections can be classified from many different points of view. You can classify data collections as linear, associative, and graph:

- Linear collections are collections in which elements are related along a single dimension. In such a collection, each element has a relation to the next element. The most common example of a linear collection is the list.

- Associative collections are collections that can be viewed as a function. Given an object o, a function f(o) will return `true` or `false` according to whether this object belongs to the collection or not. Unlike in linear collections, there's no relation between the elements of the collection. These collections aren't ordered, although it is possible to define an order on the elements. The most common examples of associative collections are the set and the associative array (which is also called a map or dictionary). We'll study a functional implementation of maps in chapter 11.

- Graphs are collections in which each element is in relationships with multiple other elements. A particular example is the tree, and more specifically the binary tree, where each element is related to two other elements. You'll learn more about trees from a functional perspective in chapter 10.

5.1.1 Different types of lists

In this chapter, we'll focus on the most common type of linear collections, the list. The list is the most used data structure in functional programming, so it's generally used to teach functional programming concepts. Be aware, however, that what you'll learn in this chapter is not specific to lists but is shared by many other data structures (which may not be collections).

Lists can be further classified based on several different aspects, including the following:

- *Access*—Some lists will be accessed from one end only, and others will be accessed from both ends. Some will be written from one end and read from the other end. Finally, some lists may allow access to any element using its position in the list; the position of an element is also called its *index*.

- *Type of ordering*—In some lists, the elements will be read in the same order in which they were inserted. This kind of structure is said to be FIFO (first in, first out). In others, the order of retrieval will be the inverse of the order of insertion (LIFO, or last in, first out). Finally, some lists will allow you to retrieve the elements in a completely different order.

- *Implementation*—Access type and ordering are concepts strongly related to the implementation you choose for the list. If you choose to represent the list by linking each element to the next, you'll get a completely different result, from the access point of view, than from an implementation based on an indexed array. Or if you choose to link each element to the next as well as to the previous element, you'll get a list that can be accessed from both ends.

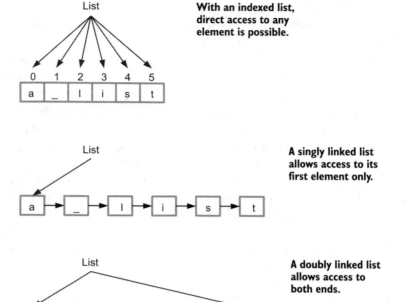

With an indexed list, direct access to any element is possible.

A singly linked list allows access to its first element only.

A doubly linked list allows access to both ends.

Figure 5.1   **Different types of lists offer different types of access to their elements.**

Figure 5.1 shows different types of lists offering different kinds of access. Note that this figure shows the principle behind each type of list, but not the way the lists are implemented.

5.1.2   *Relative expected list performance*

One very important criterion when choosing a type of list is the expected performance for various kinds of operations. Performance is often expressed in Big O notation. This notation is mainly used in mathematics, but when used in computing, it indicates the way the complexity of an algorithm changes when responding to a change of input size. When used to characterize the performance of list operations, this notation shows how the performance varies as a function of the length of the list. For example, consider the following performances:

- $O(1)$—This means that the time needed for an operation will be constant. (You may think of it as meaning that the time for one element will be multiplied by 1 for n elements.)
- $O(\log(n))$—This means that the time for an operation on n elements will be the time for one element multiplied by $\log(n)$.
- $O(n)$—The time for n elements will be the time for one element multiplied by n.
- $O(n^2)$—The time for n elements will be the time for one element multiplied by n^2.

It would be ideal to create a data structure with O(1) performance for all types of operations. Unfortunately, this has not been found possible yet. Each type of list offers different performance for different operations. Indexed lists offer O(1) performance for data retrieval and near to O(1) for insertion. The singly linked list offers O(1) performance for insertion and retrieval on one end, and O(n) for the other end.

Choosing the best structure is a compromise. Most often, you'll seek O(1) performance for the most frequent operations, and you'll have to accept O(log(n)) or even O(n) for some operations that don't occur very often.

Be aware that this way of measuring performance has a real meaning for structures that can be scaled infinitely. This is not the case for the data structures we manipulate, because your structures are limited in size by the available memory. A structure with O(n) access time might always be faster than another one with O(1) due to this size limit. If the time for one element is much smaller for the first structure, its memory limitation may prevent the second from showing its benefits. It's often better to have O(n) performance with an access time of 1 nanosecond to one element than O(1) with an access time of 1 millisecond. (The latter will be faster than the former only for sizes over 1,000,000 elements.)

5.1.3   *Trading time against memory space, and time against complexity*

You just saw that choosing an implementation for a data structure is generally a question of trading time against time. You'll choose an implementation that's faster on some operations, but slower on others, based on which operations are the most frequent. But there are other trading decisions to make.

Imagine you want a structure from which elements can be retrieved in sorted order, the smallest first. You might choose to sort the elements on insertion, or you might prefer to store them as they arrive and search for the smallest on retrieval only. One important criterion for making the decision would be whether the retrieved element is systematically removed from the structure. If not, it might be accessed several times without removal, so it would probably be better to sort the elements at insertion time, in order to avoid sorting them several times on retrieval. This use case corresponds to what's called a *priority queue*, in which you're waiting for a given element. You might test the queue many times until the expected element is returned. Such a use case requires that elements be sorted at insertion time.

But what if you want to access elements by several different sort orders? For example, you might want to access elements in the same order they were inserted, or in reverse order. The result might correspond to the doubly linked list of figure 5.1. It seems that in such a case, elements should be sorted at retrieval time. You might favor one order, leading to O(1) access time from one end and O(n) from the other end, or you might invent a different structure, perhaps giving O(log(n)) access time from both ends. Another solution would be to store two lists, one in insertion order and one in reverse order. This way, you'd have a slower insertion time, but O(1) retrieval from both ends. One drawback is that this approach would probably use more memory.

Thus you can see that choosing the right structure might also be a question of trading time against memory space.

But you might also invent some structure minimizing both insertion time and retrieval time from both ends. These types of structures have already been invented, and you'd only have to implement them, but such structures are much more complex than the simplest ones, so you'd be trading time against complexity.

5.1.4   *In-place mutation*

Most data structures change over time because elements are inserted and removed. Basically, there are two ways to handle such operations. The first one is *update in place*.

Update in place consists of changing the elements of the data structure by mutating the structure itself. It would have been considered a good idea when all programs were single threaded, although it wasn't. It's much worse now that all programs are multithreaded. This doesn't only concern replacing elements. It's the same for adding or removing, sorting, and all operations that mutate the structure. If programs are allowed to mutate data structures, these structures simply can't be shared without sophisticated protections that are rarely done right the first time, leading to deadlock, livelock, thread starving, stale data, and all those sorts of troubles.

So what's the solution? Simply use immutable data structures. Many imperative programmers are shocked when they first read this. How can you do useful things with data structures if you can't mutate them? After all, you often start with empty structures and want to add data to them. How can you possibly do this if they're immutable?

Update in place

In a 1981 article titled "The transaction concept: virtues and limitations," Jim Gray wrote this:[a]

> Update in place: a poison apple?
>
> When bookkeeping was done with clay tablets or paper and ink, accountants developed some clear rules about good accounting practices. One of the cardinal rules is double-entry bookkeeping so that calculations are self checking, thereby making them fail-fast. A second rule is that one never alters the books; if an error is made, it is annotated and a new compensating entry is made in the books. The books are thus a complete history of the transactions of the business...
>
> Update-in-place strikes many systems designers as a cardinal sin: it violates traditional accounting practices which have been observed for hundreds of years.

---

[a]   Jim Gray, "The transaction concept: virtues and limitations" (Tandem Computers, Technical Report 81.3, June 1981), http://www.hpl.hp.com/techreports/tandem/TR-81.3.pdf.

The answer is simple. As with double-entry accounting, instead of changing what existed previously, you create new data to represent the new state. Instead of adding an element to an existing list, you create a new list with the added element. The main benefit is that if another thread was manipulating the list at insertion time, it's not affected by the change because it doesn't see it.

Generally, this conception immediately raises two protests:

- If the other thread doesn't see the change, it's manipulating stale data.
- Making a new copy of the list with the added element is a time- and memory-consuming process, so immutable data structures lead to very poor performance.

Both arguments are fallacious. The thread manipulating the "stale data" is in fact manipulating the data as it was when it started reading it. If inserting an element occurs after the manipulation is finished, there's no concurrency problem. But if the insertion occurs while the manipulation is going on, what would occur with a mutable data structure? Either it wouldn't be protected against concurrent access, and the data might be corrupted or the result false (or both), or some protection mechanism would lock the data, delaying the insertion until after the manipulation by the first thread is completed. In the second case, the end result would be exactly the same as with an immutable structure.

5.1.5 *Persistent data structures*

As you saw in the previous section, making a copy (sometimes called a *defensive copy*) of the data structure before inserting an element is often considered a time-consuming operation that leads to poor performance. This isn't the case if you use data sharing, which is possible because immutable data structures are persistent. Figure 5.2 shows how elements could be removed and added to create a new, immutable, singly linked list with optimal performance.

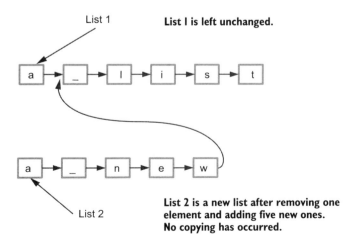

List 1

List I is left unchanged.

List 2

List 2 is a new list after removing one element and adding five new ones. No copying has occurred.

Figure 5.2   Removing and adding elements without mutation or copying

As you can see, no copying occurs at all. The result is that such a list might be more performant for removing and inserting elements than a mutable list. So functional data structures (immutable and persistent) are not always slower than mutable ones. They're often even faster (although they might be slower on some operations). In any case, they're much safer.

5.2   *An immutable, persistent, singly linked list implementation*

The structure of the singly linked list shown in figures 5.1 and 5.2 is theoretical. The list can't be implemented that way, because elements can't be linked to one another. They'd have to be special elements to allow linking, and you want your lists to be able to store any elements. The solution is to devise a recursive list structure composed of the following:

- An element that will be the first element of the list, also called the *head*.
- The rest of the list, which is a list by itself and is called the *tail*.

Note that you already encountered a generic element that's composed of two elements of different types: the `Tuple`. A singly linked list of elements of type `A` is in fact a `Tuple<A, List<A>>`. You could then define a list as

```
class List<A> extends Tuple<A, List<A>>
```

But as I explained in chapter 4, you need a terminal case, as you do in every recursive definition. By convention, this terminal case is called `Nil` and corresponds to the empty list. And because `Nil` has no head nor tail, it's not a `Tuple`. Your new definition of a list is either

- An empty list (`Nil`)
- A tuple of an element and a list

Instead of using a `Tuple` with properties `_1` and `_2`, you'll create a specific `List` class with two properties: `head` and `tail`. This will simplify the handling of the `Nil` case. Figure 5.3 shows the structure of your list implementation.

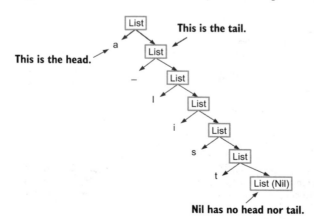

Figure 5.3   The representation of the singly linked list implementation

Listing 5.1 shows the basic implementation of this list.

Listing 5.1   Singly linked lists

```
public abstract class List<A> {                    ◁——  The List is implemented as an abstract class,
                                                         parameterized by the type of its elements,
  public abstract A head();                              represented by the type variable A.
  public abstract List<A> tail();
  public abstract boolean isEmpty();
  @SuppressWarnings("rawtypes")                          A singleton instance
  public static final List NIL = new Nil();      ◁——     representing the empty list

  private List() {}
                                                         The Nil (not in list) subclass
  private static class Nil<A> extends List<A> {   ◁——    represents the empty list.

    private Nil() {}                                  ◁——  The Nil subclass as a private
                                                           no-args constructor
    public A head() {
      throw new IllegalStateException("head called en empty list");
    }

    public List<A> tail() {
      throw new IllegalStateException("tail called en empty list");
    }

    public boolean isEmpty() {
      return true;
    }
  }
                                                    ◁——  The Cons (construct)
  private static class Cons<A> extends List<A> {          subclass represents
                                                          non-empty lists.
    private final A head;
    private final List<A> tail;

    private Cons(A head, List<A> tail) {        ◁——  The Cons subclass as a private
      this.head = head;                              constructor taking as
      this.tail = tail;                              parameters an A (the head)
    }                                                and a List<A> (the tail)

    public A head() {
      return head;
    }

    public List<A> tail() {
      return tail;
    }

    public boolean isEmpty() {
      return false;
    }
  }
                                                    A static factory method for
  @SuppressWarnings("unchecked")                    constructing an empty List
  public static <A> List<A> list() {         ◁——
    return NIL;
  }
```

```
@SafeVarargs
public static <A> List<A> list(A... a) {
  List<A> n = list();
  for (int i = a.length - 1; i >= 0; i--) {
    n = new Cons<>(a[i], n);
  }
  return n;
}
}
```

A static factory method for constructing a non-empty List

Processes the indices in reverse order because the last element must be inserted first. From the accessibility point of view, singly linked lists are in fact stacks.

The list class is implemented as an abstract class. The List class contains two private static subclasses to represent the two possible forms a List can take: Nil for an empty list, and Cons for a non-empty one.

The List class defines three abstract methods: head(), which will return the first element of the list; tail(), which will return the rest of the list (without the first element); and isEmpty(), which will return true if the list is empty and false otherwise. The List class is parameterized with type parameter A, which represents the type of the list elements.

Subclasses have been made private, so you construct lists through calls to the static factory methods. These methods can be statically imported:

```
import static fpinjava.datastructures.List.*;
```

They can then be used without referencing the enclosing class, as follows:

```
List<Integer> ex1 = list();
List<Integer> ex2 = list(1);
List<Integer> ex3 = list(1, 2);
```

Note that the empty list has no type parameter. In other words, it's a raw type that can be used to represent an empty list of elements of any types. As such, creating or using an empty list will generate a warning by the compiler. The advantage is that you can use a singleton for the empty list. Another solution would have been to use a parameterized empty list, but this would have caused much trouble. You'd have had to create a different empty list for each type parameter. To solve this problem, you use a singleton empty list with no parameter type. This generates a compiler warning. In order to restrict this warning to the List class and not let it leak to the List users, you don't give direct access to the singleton. That's why there's a (parameterized) static method to access the singleton, and a @SuppressWarnings("rawtypes") on the NIL property, as well as a @SuppressWarnings("unchecked") on the list() method.

Note that the list(A ... a) method is annotated with @SafeVarargs to indicate that the method doesn't do anything that could lead to heap pollution. This method uses an imperative implementation based on a for loop. This isn't very "functional," but it's a trade-off for simplicity and performance. If you insist on implementing it in a functional way, you can do so. All you need is a function taking an array as its argument and returning its last element, and another one to return the array without its last element. Here's one possible solution:

```
@SafeVarargs
public static <A> List<A> list(A... as) {
  return list_(list(), as).eval();
}

public static <A> TailCall<List<A>> list_(List<A> acc, A[] as) {
  return as.length == 0
      ? ret(acc)
      : sus(() -> list_(new Cons<>(as[as.length -1], acc),
          Arrays.copyOfRange(as, 0, as.length - 1)));
}
```

Be sure, however, not to use this implementation, because it's 10,000 times slower than the imperative one. This is a good example of when not to be blindly functional. The imperative version has a functional interface, and this is what you need. Note that recursion isn't the problem. Recursion using `TailCall` is nearly as fast as iteration. The problem here is the `copyOfRange` method, which is very slow.

5.3 *Data sharing in list operations*

One of the huge benefits of immutable persistent data structures like the singly linked list is the performance boost provided by data sharing. You can already see that accessing the first element of the list is immediate. It's just a matter of calling the `head()` method, which is a simple accessor for the `head` property.

Removing the first element is equally fast. Just call the `tail()` method, which will return the `tail` property. Now let's see how to get a new list with an additional element.

EXERCISE 5.1
Implement the instance functional method cons, adding an element at the beginning of a list. (Remember *cons* stands for *construct*.)

SOLUTION 5.1
This instance method has the same implementation for the `Nil` and `Cons` subclasses:

```
public List<A> cons(A a) {
  return new Cons<>(a, this);
}
```

EXERCISE 5.2
Implement `setHead`, an instance method for replacing the first element of a `List` with a new value.

SOLUTION 5.2
You might think of implementing a static method for this, but you'd have to test for an empty list:

```
public static <A> List<A> setHead(List<A> list, A h) {
  if (list.isEmpty()) {
    throw new IllegalStateException("setHead called on an empty list");
  } else {
```

```
        return new Cons<>(h, list.tail());
    }
}
```

This makes little sense. As a general rule, if you find yourself forced to use an if ...
else structure, you're probably on the wrong path. Think of how you'd implement
instance methods calling this static one.

A much better solution is to add an abstract method to the List class:

```
public abstract List<A> setHead(A h);
```

Implementation in the Nil subclass is straightforward. Just throw an exception,
because trying to access the head of an empty list is considered a bug:

```
public List<A> setHead(A h) {
    throw new IllegalStateException("setHead called on empty list");
}
```

The Cons implementation corresponds to the else clause of the static method:

```
public List<A> setHead(A h) {
    return new Cons<>(h, tail());
}
```

And if you need a static method, it can simply call the instance implementation:

```
public static <A> List<A> setHead(List<A> list, A h) {
    return list.setHead(h);
}
```

EXERCISE 5.3

Write a toString method to display the content of a list. An empty list will be displayed as " [NIL] ", and a list containing the integers from 1 to 3 will be displayed as
" [1, 2, 3, NIL] ". For a list of arbitrary objects, the toString method will be called
to display each object.

SOLUTION 5.3

The Nil implementation is very simple:

```
public String toString() {
    return "[NIL]";
}
```

The cons method is recursive and uses a StringBuilder as the accumulator. Note that
the StringBuilder, although it's a mutable object, has a functional-friendly append
method, because it returns the mutated StringBuilder instance.

```
public String toString() {
    return String.format("[%sNIL]",
                         toString(new StringBuilder(), this).eval());
}
```

```
private TailCall<StringBuilder> toString(StringBuilder acc, List<A> list) {
  return list.isEmpty()
      ? ret(acc)
      : sus(() -> toString(acc.append(list.head()).append(", "),
                           list.tail()));
}
```

If you have problems remembering how the `TailCall` class is used to make recursion work from the heap rather than from the stack, please refer to chapter 4.

5.3.1 More list operations

You can rely on data sharing to implement various other operations in a very efficient way—often more efficiently than what can be done with mutable lists. In the rest of this section, you'll add functionality to the linked list based on data sharing.

EXERCISE 5.4

The `tail` method, although it doesn't mutate the list in any way, has the same effect as removing the first element. Write a more general method, `drop`, that removes the first n elements from a list. Of course, this method won't remove the element, but will return a new list corresponding to the intended result. This "new" list won't be anything new, because data sharing will be used, so nothing will be created. Figure 5.4 shows how you should proceed.

The signature of the method will be

```
public List<A> drop(int n);
```

HINT

You should use recursion to implement the `drop` method. And don't forget to consider every special case, such as an empty list, or n being higher than the list length.

SOLUTION 5.4

Here, you have the choice to implement a static method or instance methods. Instance methods are needed if you want to use object notation, which is much easier to read. For example, if you want to drop two elements of a list of integers and then replace the first element of the result with 0, you could use static methods:

```
List<Integer> newList = setHead(drop(list, 2), 0);
```

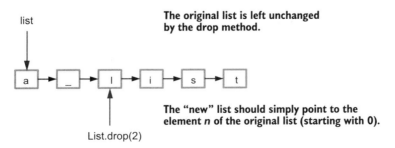

Figure 5.4 Dropping the *n* first elements of a list while not mutating or creating anything.

```
l1 = drop(list, 2)
l2 = setHead(l1, 0)
```

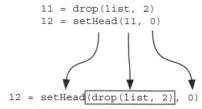

```
l2 = setHead(drop(list, 2), 0)
```

Figure 5.5 Without object notation, composed functions may be difficult to read. Using object notation results in much more readable code.

Each time you add a method to the process, the method name is added to the left, and the additional arguments, besides the list itself, are added to the right, as shown in figure 5.5.

Using object notation makes the code much easier to read:

```
List<Integer> newList = drop(list, 2).setHead(0);
```

The implementation of the drop method in the Nil class simply returns this:

```
public List<A> drop(int n) {
  return this;
}
```

In the Cons class, you use a private helper method to implement recursion in the same way you learned in chapter 4. This code assumes that the methods TailCall.ret and TailCall.sus are imported statically:

```
public List<A> drop(int n) {
  return n <= 0
      ? this
      : drop_(this, n).eval();
}
private TailCall<List<A>> drop_(List<A> list, int n) {
  return n <= 0 || list.isEmpty()
      ? ret(list)
      : sus(() -> drop_(list.tail(), n - 1));
}
```

Note that you have to test for an empty list parameter. This wouldn't be necessary if the drop method were recursive. But only the drop_ helper method is recursive, and this method isn't defined for Nil. Forgetting to test for the empty list would result in an exception being thrown while calling list.tail(). Of course, you'd need a better way to handle this case. After all, dropping four elements of a list of three makes little sense. You could throw an exception, but it would be better to use more-functional techniques that you'll learn in the next chapter.

EXERCISE 5.5

Implement a dropWhile method to remove elements from the head of the List as long as a condition holds true. Here's the signature to add to the List abstract class:

```
public abstract List<A> dropWhile(Function<A, Boolean> f);
```

Solution 5.5

We won't look at the `Nil` implementation because it will only return `this`. The implementation for the `Cons` class is recursive:

```
@Override
public List<A> dropWhile(Function<A, Boolean> f) {
  return dropWhile_(this, f).eval();
}

private TailCall<List<A>> dropWhile_(List<A> list,
                                     Function<A, Boolean> f) {
  return !list.isEmpty() && f.apply(list.head())
      ? sus(() -> dropWhile_(list.tail(), f))
      : ret(list);
}
```

Note that when calling `dropWhile` on an empty list, you may face a problem. The following code, for example, won't compile:

```
list().dropWhile(f)
```

The reason for this is that Java is unable to infer the type of the list from the function you pass to the `dropWhile` method. Let's say you're dealing with a list of integers. You can then use either this solution:

```
List<Integer> list = list();
list.dropWhile(f);
```

or this one:

```
List.<Integer>list().dropWhile(f);
```

CONCATENATING LISTS

A very common operation on lists consists of "adding" one list to another to form a new list that contains all elements of both original lists. It would be nice to be able to simply link both lists, but this isn't possible. The solution is to add all elements of one list to the other list. But elements can only be added to the front (head) of the list, so if you want to concatenate `list1` to `list2`, you must start by adding the last element of `list1` to the front of `list2`, as indicated in figure 5.6.

One way to proceed is to first reverse `list1`, producing a new list, and then add each element to `list2`, this time starting from the head of the reversed list. But you haven't yet defined a reverse method. Can you still define `concat`? Yes you can. Just consider how you could define this method:

- If `list1` is empty, return `list2`.
- Else return the addition of the first element (`list1.head`) of `list1` to the concatenation of the rest of `list1` (`list1.tail`) to `list2`.

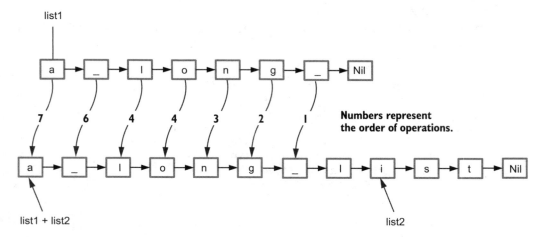

Figure 5.6 Sharing data by concatenation. You can see that both lists are preserved and that `list2` is shared by the resulting list. But you can also see that you can't proceed exactly as is indicated in the figure, because you'd have to access the last element of `list1` first, which isn't possible due to the structure of the list.

This recursive definition can be translated into code as follows:

```java
public static List<A> concat(List<A> list1, List<A> list2) {
    return list1.isEmpty()
        ? list2
        : new Cons<>(list1.head(), concat(list1.tail(), list2));
}
```

The beauty of this solution (for some readers) is that you don't need a figure to expose how it works, because it isn't "working." It's just a mathematical definition translated into code.

The main drawback of this definition (for other readers) is that, for the same reason, you can't easily represent it in a figure. This may sound like humor, but it's not. Both solutions represent exactly the same "operation," but one represents the process (from which you can see the result) and the other expresses the result directly. Whichever is better is a matter of choice. But functional programming most often involves thinking in terms of what the intended result is, rather than how to obtain it. Functional code is a direct translation of the definition into code.

Obviously, this code will overflow the stack if `list1` is too long, although you'll never have a stack problem with the length of `list2`. The consequence is that you won't have to worry if you're careful to only add small lists to the front end of lists of any length.

An important point to note is that what you're actually doing is adding elements of the first list, in reverse order, to the front of the second list. This is obviously different from the common sense understanding of concatenation: adding the second list to the tail of the first one. This is definitely not how it works with the singly linked list.

If you need to concatenate lists of arbitrary length, you can just apply what you learned in chapter 4 to make the `concat` method stack-safe.

If you ponder what you've done, you might guess that there's much room left for abstraction here. What if the `concat` method were only a specific application of a much more general operation? Maybe you could abstract this operation, make it stack-safe, and then reuse it to implement many other operations? Wait and see!

You may have noticed that the complexity of this operation (and hence the time it'll take to be executed by Java) is proportional to the length of the first list. In other words, if you concatenate `list1` and `list2`, of length n1 and n2, the complexity is O($n1$), which means it's independent of n2. In other words, depending on n2, this operation may be more efficient than concatenating two mutable lists in imperative Java.

DROPPING FROM THE END OF THE LIST

It's sometimes necessary to remove elements from the end of a list. Although the singly linked list is not the ideal data structure for this kind of operation, you must still be able to implement it.

EXERCISE 5.6

Write a method to remove the last element from a list. This method should return the resulting list. Implement it as an instance method with the following signature:

```
List<A> init()
```

HINT

There might be a way to express this function in terms of another one, and one we've already spoken about. Maybe now would be the right time to create this helper function.

SOLUTION 5.6

To remove the last element, you have to traverse the list (from front to back) and build up the new list (from back to front, because the "last" element in a list must be `Nil`). This is a consequence of the way lists are created with `Cons` objects. This results in a list with the elements in reverse order, so the resulting list must be reversed. That means you only have to implement a `reverse` method:

```
public List<A> reverse() {
  return reverse_(list(), this).eval();
}
private TailCall<List<A>> reverse_(List<A> acc, List<A> list) {
  return list.isEmpty()
      ? ret(acc)
      : sus(() -> reverse_(new Cons<>(list.head(), acc), list.tail()));
}
```

With the `reverse` method, you can implement `init` very easily:

```
public List<A> init() {
  return reverse().tail().reverse();
}
```

Of course, these are the implementations for the Cons class. In the Nil class, the reverse method returns this, and the init method throws an exception.

5.4   *Using recursion to fold lists with higher-order functions*

In chapter 3, you learned how to fold lists, and folding applies to immutable lists as well. But with mutable lists, you had the choice to implement these operations through iteration or recursively. In chapter 3, you implemented folds iteratively because you were using mutable lists, where adding and removing elements was done in place by nonfunctional methods. The add method returned nothing, and the remove method returned only the removed element, while modifying the list argument. Because immutable lists are recursive data structures, you can very easily use recursion to implement folding operations.

Let's consider common folding operations on lists of numbers.

EXERCISE 5.7

Write a functional method to compute the sum of all elements of a list of integers using simple stack-based recursion.

SOLUTION 5.7

The recursive definition of the sum of all elements of a list is

- For an empty list: 0
- For a non-empty list: head plus the sum of the tail

This translates nearly word-for-word into Java code:

```
public static Integer sum(List<Integer> ints) {
  return ints.isEmpty()
      ? 0
      : ints.head() + sum(ints.tail());
}
```

Don't forget that this implementation will overflow the stack for long lists, so don't use this kind of code in production.

EXERCISE 5.8

Write a functional method to compute the product of all elements of a list of doubles using simple stack-based recursion.

SOLUTION 5.8

The recursive definition of the product of all elements of a non-empty list is

```
head * product of tail
```

But what should it return for an empty list? Of course, if you remember your math courses, you'll know the answer. If you don't, you may find the answer in the requirement for a non-empty list shown in solution 5.7.

Consider what will happen when you've applied the recursive formula to all elements. You'll end up with a result that will have to be multiplied by the product of all elements of an empty list. Because you want to eventually get this result, you have no choice but to say that the product of all elements of an empty list is 1. This is the same situation as with the sum example, when you use 0 as the sum of all elements of an empty list. The identity element, or neutral element, for the sum operation is 0, and the identity or neutral element for the product is 1. So your `product` method could be written as follows:

```
public static Double product(List<Double> ds) {
  return ds.isEmpty()
      ? 1.0
      : ds.head() * product(ds.tail());
}
```

Note that the product operation is different from the sum operation in one important way. It has an *absorbing element*, which is an element that satisfies the following condition:

$$a \times absorbing\ element = absorbing\ element \times a = absorbing\ element$$

The absorbing element for multiplication is 0. By analogy, the absorbing element of any operation (if it exists) is also called the *zero element*. The existence of a zero element allows you to escape the computation, also called *short circuiting*:

```
public static Double product(List<Double> ds) {
  return ds.isEmpty()
      ? 1.0
      : ds.head() == 0.0
          ? 0.0
          : ds.head() * product(ds.tail());
}
```

But forget about this optimized version and look at the definitions for sum and `product`. Can you detect a pattern that could be abstracted? Let's look at them side by side (after having changed the parameter name):

```
public static Integer sum(List<Integer> list) {
  return list.isEmpty()
      ? 0
      : list.head() + sum(list.tail());
}
public static Double product(List<Double> list) {
  return list.isEmpty()
      ? 1
      : list.head() * product(list .tail());
}
```

Now let's remove the differences and replace them with a common notation:

```
public static Type operation(List<Type> list) {
  return list.isEmpty()
```

```
            ? identity
            : list.head() operator operation(list .tail());
    }
public static Type operation(List<Type> list) {
    return list.isEmpty()
            ? identity
            : list.head() operator operation(list .tail());
    }
```

The two operations are nearly the same. If you can find a way to abstract the common parts, you'll just have to provide the variable information (Type, operation, identity, and operator) to implement both operations without repeating yourself. This common operation is what we call a *fold*, which you studied in chapter 3. In that chapter, you learned that there are two kinds of folds—right fold and left fold—as well as a relation between these two operations.

Listing 5.2 shows the common parts of the sum and product operations abstracted into a method called foldRight, taking as its parameters the list to fold, an identity element, and a higher-order function representing the operation used to fold the list. The identity element is obviously the identity for the given operation, and the function is in curried form. (See chapter 2 if you don't remember what this means.) This function represents the operator portion of your code.

Listing 5.2   Implementing foldRight and using it for sum and product

```
public static <A, B> B foldRight(List<A> list,       ◁——— A and B represent the Type.
                                 B n,                 ◁——— n is the identity.
                                 Function<A, Function<B, B>> f ) {   ◁——┐
    return list.isEmpty()
        ? n                                                          │
        : f.apply(list.head()).apply(foldRight(list.tail(), n, f));  │
}                                                            f is a function and
                                                                    represents
public static Integer sum(List<Integer> list) {    ◁—┐          the operator.
    return foldRight(list, 0, x -> y -> x + y);        │
}                                                      │   sum and product are the
                                                       │   names of the operations.
public static Double product(List<Double> list) {  ◁—┘
    return foldRight(list, 1.0, x -> y -> x * y);
}
```

Note that the Type variable part has been replaced with two types here, A and B. This is because the result of folding isn't always of the same type as the elements of the list. Here, it's abstracted a bit more than is needed for the sum and product operations, but this will be useful soon.

The operation variable part is, of course, the names of the two methods.

The fold operation isn't specific to arithmetic computations. You can use a fold to transform a list of characters into a string. In such a case, A and B are two different types: Char and String. But you can also use a fold to transform a list of strings into a single string. Can you see now how you could implement concat?

By the way, `foldRight` is very similar to the singly linked list itself. If you think of the list 1, 2, 3 as

```
Cons(1, Cons(2, Cons(3, Nil)
```

you can see immediately that it's very similar to a right fold:

```
f(1, f(2, f(3, identity)
```

But perhaps you've already realized that `Nil` is the identity for adding elements to lists. This make sense: if you want to transform a list of characters into a string, you have to start with an empty list. (By the way, `Nil` is also the identity for list concatenation, although you could do without it, provided the list of lists to be concatenated isn't empty. In such a case, it's called a *reduce* rather than a *fold*. But this is possible only because the result is of the same type as the elements.)

This can be put in practice by passing `Nil` and `cons` to `foldRight` as the identity and the function that are used to fold:

```
List.foldRight(list(1, 2, 3), list(), x -> y -> y.cons(x))
```

This simply produces a new list with the same elements in the same order, as you can see by running the following code:

```
System.out.println(List.foldRight(list(1, 2, 3), list(),
                                        x -> y -> y.cons(x)));
```

This code produces the following output:

```
[1, 2, 3, NIL]
```

Here's a trace of what's happening at each step:

```
foldRight(list(1, 2, 3), list(), x -> y -> y.cons(x));
foldRight(list(1, 2), list(3), x -> y -> y.cons(x));
foldRight(list(1), list(2, 3), x -> y -> y.cons(x));
foldRight(list(), list(1, 2, 3), x -> y -> y.cons(x));
```

EXERCISE 5.9

Write a method to compute the length of a list. This method will use the `foldRight` method.

SOLUTION 5.9

The `Nil` implementation is obvious and returns 0. The `Cons` implementation may be written as

```
public int length() {
  return foldRight(this, 0, x -> y -> y + 1);
}
```

Note that this implementation, beside being stack-based recursive, has very poor performance. Even if transformed to heap-based, it's still O(n), meaning the time needed to return the length is proportional to the length of the list. In following chapters, you'll see how to get the length of a linked list in constant time.

EXERCISE 5.10

The foldRight method uses recursion, but it's not tail recursive, so it will rapidly overflow the stack. How rapidly depends on several factors, the most important of which is the size of the stack. In Java, the size of the stack is configurable through the -Xss command-line parameter, but the major drawback is that the same size is used for all threads. Using a bigger stack would be a waste of memory for most threads.

Instead of using foldRight, create a foldLeft method that's tail recursive and can be made stack-safe. Here's its signature:

```
public abstract <B> B foldLeft(B identity, Function<B, Function<A, B>> f);
```

HINT

If you don't remember the difference between foldLeft and foldRight, refer to section 3.3.5.

SOLUTION 5.10

The Nil implementation will obviously return identity. For the Cons implementation, start with defining a front-end method foldLeft calling a stack-based tail recursive helper method foldLeft_ with an accumulator acc initialized to identity and a reference to this:

```
public <B> B foldLeft(B identity, Function<B, Function<A, B>> f) {
  return foldLeft_(identity, this, f);
}

private <B> B foldLeft_(B acc, List<A> list,
                                       Function<B, Function<A, B>> f) {
  return list.isEmpty()
      ? acc
      : foldLeft_(f.apply(acc).apply(list.head()), list.tail(), f);
}
```

Then make the following changes so you can use the TailCall interface you defined in chapter 4 (the ret and sus methods are imported statically):

```
public <B> B foldLeft(B identity, Function<B, Function<A, B>> f) {
  return foldLeft_(identity, this, f).eval();
}

private <B> TailCall<B> foldLeft_(B acc, List<A> list,
                                       Function<B, Function<A, B>> f) {
  return list.isEmpty()
      ? ret(acc)
      : sus(() -> foldLeft_(f.apply(acc).apply(list.head()),
                                           list.tail(), f));
}
```

EXERCISE 5.11

Use your new `foldLeft` method to create new stack-safe versions of `sum`, `product`, and `length`.

SOLUTION 5.11

This is the `sumViaFoldLeft` method:

```
public static Integer sumViaFoldLeft(List<Integer> list) {
  return list.foldLeft(0, x -> y -> x + y);
}
```

The `productViaFoldLeft` method is as follows:

```
public static Double productViaFoldLeft(List<Double> list) {
  return list.foldLeft(1.0, x -> y -> x * y);
}
```

And here's the `lengthViaFoldLeft` method:

```
public static <A> Integer lengthViaFoldLeft(List<A> list) {
  return list.foldLeft(0, x -> ignore -> x + 1);
}
```

Note that once again, the second parameter of method `length` (representing each element of the list on each recursive call of the method) is ignored. This method is as inefficient as the previous one and shouldn't be used in production code.

EXERCISE 5.12

Use `foldLeft` to write a static functional method for reversing a list.

SOLUTION 5.12

Reversing a list via a left fold is very simple, starting from an empty list as the accumulator and cons-ing each element of the first list to this accumulator:

```
public static <A> List<A> reverseViaFoldLeft(List<A> list) {
  return list.foldLeft(list(), x -> x::cons);
}
```

This example uses a method reference instead of a lambda, as explained in chapter 2. If you prefer to use a lambda, it's equivalent to the following:

```
public static <A> List<A> reverseViaFoldLeft(List<A> list) {
  return list.foldLeft(list(), x -> a -> x.cons(a));
}
```

EXERCISE 5.13 (HARD)

Write `foldRight` in terms of `foldLeft`.

SOLUTION 5.13

This implementation can be useful for getting a stack-safe version of `foldRight`:

```
public static <A, B> B foldRightViaFoldLeft(List<A> list,
                        B identity, Function<A, Function<B, B>> f) {
  return list.reverse().foldLeft(identity, x -> y -> f.apply(y).apply(x));
}
```

Note that you can also define `foldLeft` in terms of `foldRight`, although this is much less useful:

```
public static <A, B> B foldLeftViaFoldRight(List<A> list,
                        B identity, Function<B, Function<A, B>> f) {
  return List.foldRight(list.reverse(),identity, x -> y ->
                                          f.apply(y).apply(x));
}
```

Again, note that the `foldLeft` method you use is an instance method of `List`. In contrast, `foldRight` is a static method. (We'll define an instance `foldRight` method soon.)

5.4.1   *Heap-based recursive version of foldRight*

As I said, the recursive `foldRight` implementation is only for demonstrating these concepts, because it's stack-based and thus shouldn't be used in production code. Also note that this is a static implementation. An instance implementation would be much easier to use, allowing you to chain method calls with the object notation.

EXERCISE 5.14

Use what you learned in chapter 4 to write a heap-based recursive instance version of the `foldRight` method.

HINT

The method can be defined in the parent `List` class. Write a tail recursive stack-based version of the `foldRight` method (using a helper method). Then change the helper method to a heap-based recursive implementation using the `TailCall` interface you developed in chapter 4.

SOLUTION 5.14

First, let's write the stack-based tail recursive helper method. All you have to do is write a helper method that takes an accumulator as an additional parameter. The accumulator has the same type as the function return type, and its initial value is equal to the `identity` element (which, by the way, is used twice).

```
public <B> B foldRight_(B acc, List<A> ts, B identity,
                        Function<A, Function<B, B>> f) {
  return ts.isEmpty()
      ? acc
      : foldRight_(f.apply(ts.head()).apply(acc), ts.tail(), identity, f);
}
```

Then write the main method that calls this helper method:

```
public <B> B foldRight(B identity, Function<A, Function<B, B>> f) {
  return foldRight_(identity, this.reverse(), identity, f);
}
```

Now change both methods to use `TailCall` heap-based recursion:

```
public <B> B foldRight(B identity, Function<A, Function<B, B>> f) {
  return foldRight_(identity, this.reverse(), identity, f).eval();
}

private <B> TailCall<B> foldRight_(B acc, List<A> ts, B identity,
                                  Function<A, Function<B, B>> f) {
  return ts.isEmpty()
      ? ret(acc)
      : sus(() -> foldRight_(f.apply(ts.head()).apply(acc),
                                          ts.tail(), identity, f));
}
```

Of course, you should also write the `Nil` implementation, which is really simple.

You can make this much shorter by reusing your implementation of `foldRightVia-FoldLeft`:

```
public <B> B foldRight(B identity, Function<A, Function<B, B>> f) {
  return reverse().foldLeft(identity, x -> y -> f.apply(y).apply(x));
}
```

EXERCISE 5.15
Implement concat in terms of either `foldLeft` or `foldRight`.

SOLUTION 5.15
The concat method can be implemented easily using a right fold:

```
public static <A> List<A> concat(List<A> list1, List<A> list2) {
  return foldRight(list1, list2, x -> y -> new Cons<>(x, y));
}
```

Another solution is to use a left fold. In this case, the implementation will be the same as `reverseViaFoldLeft` applied to the reversed first list, using the second list as the accumulator:

```
public static <A> List<A> concat(List<A> list1, List<A> list2) {
  return list1.reverse().foldLeft(list2, x -> x::cons);
}
```

This implementation (based on `foldLeft`) may seem less efficient because it must first reverse the first list. In fact, it's not, because your implementation of `foldRight` is based on folding left the reversed list. (If this isn't clear, refer to the implementations of reverse [exercise 5.6], `foldLeft` [exercise 5.10], and `foldRight` [listing 5.2].)

EXERCISE 5.16
Write a method for flattening a list of lists into a list containing all elements of each contained list.

HINT
This operation consists of a series of concatenations. In other words, it's similar to adding all elements of a list of integers, although integers are replaced with lists, and

addition is replaced with concatenation. Other than this, it's exactly the same as the sum method.

SOLUTION 5.16

In this solution, you can use a method reference instead of a lambda to represent the second part of the function: `x -> x::concat` is equivalent to `x -> y -> x.concat(y)`.

```
public static <A> List<A> flatten(List<List<A>> list) {
  return foldRight(list, List.<A>list(), x -> y -> concat(x,y));
}
```

5.4.2   *Mapping and filtering lists*

You can define many useful abstractions for working on lists. One abstraction consists of changing all the elements of a list by applying a common function to them.

EXERCISE 5.17

Write a functional method that takes a list of integers and multiplies each of them by 3.

HINT

Try using the methods you've defined up to now. Don't use recursion explicitly. The goal is to abstract stack-safe recursion once and for all so you can put it to work without having to reimplement it each time.

SOLUTION 5.17

```
public static List<Integer> triple(List<Integer> list) {
  return List.foldRight(list, List.<Integer>list(), h -> t ->
                                          t.cons(h * 3));
}
```

EXERCISE 5.18

Write a function that turns each value in a `List<Double>` into a `String`.

SOLUTION 5.18

This operation can be seen as concatenating an empty list of the expected type (`List<String>`) with the original list, with each element being transformed before being cons-ed to the accumulator. As a result, the implementation is very similar to what you did in the `concat` method:

```
public static List<String> doubleToString(List<Double> list) {    ⟵─┐ Starting with
  return List.foldRight(list, List.<String>list(),                   │ an empty list
                  h -> t -> t.cons(Double.toString(h)));    ⟵─┐
}
```
Consing the transformed element

EXERCISE 5.19

Write a general functional method `map` that allows you to modify each element of a list by applying a specified function to it. This time, make it an instance method of `List`. Add the following declaration in the `List` class:

```
public abstract <B> List<B> map(Function<A, B> f);
```

HINT

Use the stack-safe instance version of the `foldRight` method.

SOLUTION 5.19

The `map` method may be implemented in the parent `List` class:

```
public <B> List<B> map(Function<A, B> f) {
  return foldRight(list(), h -> t -> new Cons<>(f.apply(h),t));
}
```

EXERCISE 5.20

Write a `filter` method that removes from a list the elements that don't satisfy a given predicate. Once again, implement this as an instance method with the following signature:

```
public List<A> filter(Function<A, Boolean> f)
```

SOLUTION 5.20

Here's an implementation in the parent `List` class, using `foldRight`. Don't forget to use the stack-safe version of this method.

```
public List<A> filter(Function<A, Boolean> f) {
  return foldRight(list(), h -> t -> f.apply(h) ? new Cons<>(h,t) : t);
}
```

EXERCISE 5.21

Write a `flatMap` method that applies to each element of `List<A>` a function from `A` to `List<B>`, and returns a `List<B>`. Its signature will be

```
public <B> List<B> flatMap(Function<A, List<B>> f);
```

For example, `List.list(1,2,3).flatMap(i -> List.list(i, -i))` should return `list(1,-1,2,-2,3,-3)`.

SOLUTION 5.21

Once again, it can be implemented in the parent `List` class, using `foldRight`:

```
public <B> List<B> flatMap(Function<A, List<B>> f) {
  return foldRight(list(), h -> t -> concat(f.apply(h), t));
}
```

EXERCISE 5.22

Create a new version of `filter` based on `flatMap`.

SOLUTION 5.22

Here's a static implementation:

```
public static <A> List<A> filterViaFlatMap(List<A> list,
                                           Function<A, Boolean> p) {
  return list.flatMap(a -> p.apply(a) ? List.list(a) : List.list());
}
```

Notice that there's a strong relation between map, flatten, and flatMap. If you map a function returning a list to a list, you get a list of lists. You can then apply flatten to get a single list containing all the elements of the enclosed lists. You'd get exactly the same result by directly applying flatMap.

One consequence of this relation is that you can redefine flatten in terms of flatMap:

```
public static <A> List<A> flatten(List<List<A>> list) {
  return list.flatMap(x -> x);
}
```

This isn't surprising, because the call to concat has been abstracted into flatMap.

5.5 Summary

- Data structures are among the most important concepts in programming.
- The singly linked list is the most often used data structure in functional programming.
- Using immutable and persistent lists brings thread-safety.
- Using data sharing allows for very high performance for most operations, although not for all.
- You can create other data structures to get good performance for specific use cases.
- You can fold lists by recursively applying functions.
- You can use heap-based recursion to fold lists without the risk of overflowing the stack.
- Once you've defined foldRight and foldLeft, you shouldn't need to use recursion again to handle lists. foldRight and foldLeft abstract recursion for you.

Dealing with optional data

Representing optional data in computer programs has always been a problem. The concept of optional data is very simple in everyday life. Representing the absence of something when this something is contained in a container is easy—whatever it is, it can be represented by an empty container. An absence of apples can be represented by an empty apple basket. The absence of gasoline in a car can be visualized as an empty gas tank.

Representing the absence of data in computer programs is more difficult. Most data is represented as a reference pointing to it, so the most obvious way to represent the absence of data is to use a pointer to nothing. This is what a null pointer is.

In Java, a variable is a pointer to a value. Variables may be created `null` (static and instance variables are created `null` by default), and they may then be changed to point to values. They can even be changed again to point to `null` if data is removed.

To handle optional data, Java 8 introduced the `Optional` type. However, in this chapter, you'll develop your own type, which you'll call `Option`. The goal is to learn how this kind of structure works. After completing this chapter, you should feel free to use the standard Java 8 library version `Optional`, but you'll see in the upcoming chapters that it's much less powerful than the type you'll create in this chapter.

6.1   *Problems with the null pointer*

One of the most frequent bugs in imperative programs is the `NullPointerException`. This error is raised when an identifier is dereferenced and found to be pointing to nothing. In other words, some data is expected but is found missing. Such an identifier is said to be pointing to `null`.

The `null` reference was invented in 1965 by Tony Hoare while he was designing the ALGOL object-oriented language. Here's what he said 44 years later:[1]

> I call it my billion-dollar mistake ... My goal was to ensure that all use of references should be absolutely safe, with checking performed automatically by the compiler. But I couldn't resist the temptation to put in a null reference, simply because it was so easy to implement. This has led to innumerable errors, vulnerabilities, and system crashes, which have probably caused a billion dollars of pain and damage in the last forty years.

Although it should be well known nowadays that `null` references should be avoided, that's far from being the case. The Java standard library contains methods and constructors taking optional parameters that must be set to `null` if they're unused. Take, for example, the `java.net.Socket` class. This class defines the following constructor:

```
public Socket(String address,
              int port,
              InetAddress localAddr,
              int localPort throws IOException
```

According to the documentation,

> If the specified local address is `null`, it is the equivalent of specifying the address as the AnyLocal address.

Here, the `null` reference is a valid parameter. This is sometimes called a *business null*. Note that this way of handling the absence of data isn't specific to objects. The port may also be absent, but it can't be `null` because it's a primitive:

> *A local port number of zero will let the system pick up a free port in the bind operation.*

This kind of value is sometimes called a *sentinel value*. It's not used for the value itself (it doesn't mean port 0) but to specify the absence of a port value.

There are many other examples of handling the absence of data in the Java library. This is really dangerous because the fact that the local address is `null` could be unintentional and due to a previous error. But this won't cause an exception. The program will continue working, although not as intended.

---

[1]   Tony Hoare, "Null References: The Billion Dollar Mistake" (QCon, August 25, 2009), http://mng.bz/l2MC.

There are other cases of business nulls. If you try to retrieve a value from a `HashMap` using a key that's not in the map, you'll get a `null`. Is this an error? You don't know. It might be that the key is valid but has not been registered in the map; or it might be that the key is supposedly valid and should be in the map, but there was a previous error while computing the key. For example, the key could be `null`, whether intentionally or due to an error, and this wouldn't raise an exception. It could even return a non-null value because the `null` key is allowed in a `HashMap`. This situation is a complete mess.

Of course, you know what to do about this. You know that you should never use a reference without checking whether it's `null` or not. (You do this for each object parameter received by a method, don't you?) And you know that you should never get a value from a map without first testing whether the map contains the corresponding key. And you know that you should never try to get an element from a list without verifying first that the list is not empty and that it has enough elements if you're accessing the element through its index. And you do this all the time, so you never get a `Null-PointerException` or an `IndexOutOfBoundsException`.

If you're this kind of perfect programmer, you can live with `null` references. But for the rest of us, an easier and safer way of dealing with the absence of a value, whether intentional or resulting from an error, is necessary. In this chapter, you'll learn how to deal with absent values that aren't the result of an error. This kind of data is called *optional data*.

Tricks for dealing with optional data have always been around. One of the best known and most often used is the list. When a method is supposed to return either a value or nothing, some programmers use a list as the return value. The list may contain zero or one element. Although this works perfectly, it has several important drawbacks:

- There's no way to ensure that the list contains at most one element. What should you do if you receive a list of several elements?
- How can you distinguish between a list that's supposed to hold at most one element and a regular list?
- The `List` class defines many methods and functions to deal with the fact that lists may contain several elements. These methods are useless for our use case.
- Functional lists are recursive structures, and you don't need this. A much simpler implementation is sufficient.

6.2 Alternatives to null references

It looks like our goal is to avoid the `NullPointerException`, but this isn't exactly the case. The `NullPointerException` should always indicate a bug. As such, you should apply the "fail fast" principle: if there's an error, the program should fail as fast as possible. Totally removing business nulls won't allow you to get rid of the `NullPointer-Exception`. It will just ensure that `null` references will only be caused by bugs in the program and not by optional data.

The following code is an example of a method returning optional data:

```
static Function<List<Integer>, Double> mean = xs -> {
  if (xs.isEmpty()) {
    ???;
  } else {
    return xs.foldLeft(0.0, x -> y -> x + y) / xs.length();
  }
};
```

The `mean` function is an example of a *partial function*, as you saw in chapter 2: it's defined for all lists except the empty list. How should you handle the empty list case?

One possibility is to return a sentinel value. What value should you choose? Because the type is `Double`, you can use a value that's defined in the `Double` class:

```
static Function<List<Integer>, Double> mean = xs -> {
  if (xs.isEmpty()) {
    return Double.NaN;
  } else {
    return xs.foldLeft(0.0, x -> y -> x + y) / xs.length();
  }
};
```

This works because `Double.NaN` (Not a Number) is actually a *double value* (note the lowercase *d*). `Double.NaN` is a primitive!

So far so good, but you have three problems:

- What if you want to apply the same principle to a function returning an `Integer`? There's no equivalent to the `NaN` value in the integer class.
- How can you signal to the user of your function that it could return a sentinel value?
- How can you handle a parametric function, such as

  ```
  static <A, B> Function<List<A>, B> f = xs -> {
    if (xs.isEmpty()) {
      ???;
    } else {
      return ...;
    };
  ```

Another solution is to throw an exception:

```
static Function<List<Integer>, Double> mean = xs -> {
  if (xs.isEmpty()) {
    throw new MeanOfEmptyListException();
  } else {
    return xs.foldLeft(0.0, x -> y -> x + y) / xs.length();
  }
};
```

But this solution is ugly and creates more trouble than it solves:

- Exceptions are generally used for erroneous results, but here there's no error. There's simply no result, and that's because there was no input data! Or should you consider calling the function with an empty list a bug?
- What exception should you throw? A custom one (like in the example)? Or a standard one?
- Should you use a checked or unchecked exception? Moreover, your function is no longer a pure function. It's no longer referentially transparent, which leads to the numerous problems I talked about in chapter 2. Also, your function is no longer composable.

You could also return `null` and let the caller deal with it:

```
static Function<List<Integer>, Double> mean = xs -> {
  if (xs.isEmpty()) {
    return null;
  } else {
    return xs.foldLeft(0.0, x -> y -> x + y) / xs.length();
  }
};
```

Returning `null` is the worst possible solution:

- It forces (ideally) the caller to test the result for `null` and act accordingly.
- It will crash if boxing is used.
- As with the exception solution, the function is no longer composable.
- It allows the potential problem to be propagated far from its origin. If the caller forgets to test for a `null` result, a `NullPointerException` could be thrown from anywhere in the code.

A better solution would be to ask the user to provide a special value that will be returned if no data is available. For example, this function computes the maximum value of a list:

```
static <A, B> Function<B, Function<List<A>, B>> max = x0 -> xs -> {
  return xs.isEmpty()
    ? x0
    : ...;
```

Here's how you could define a max function:

```
static <A extends Comparable<A>> Function<A, Function<List<A>, A>> max() {
  return x0 -> xs -> xs.isEmpty()
    ? x0
    : xs.tail().foldLeft(xs.head(), x -> y -> x.compareTo(y) < 0 ? x : y);
}
```

Remember that you must use a method that returns the function because there's no way to parameterize a property.

If you find this too complex, here's a functional method version:

```
static <A extends Comparable<A>> A max(A x0, List<A> xs) {
  return xs.isEmpty()
    ? x0
    : xs.tail().foldLeft(xs.head(), x -> y -> x.compareTo(y) < 0 ? x : y);
}
```

This works, but it's overcomplicated. The simplest solution would be to return a list:

```
public static <A extends Comparable<A>> Function<List<A>, List<A>> max() {
  return xs -> xs.isEmpty()
    ? List.list()
    : List.list(xs.foldLeft(xs.head(), x -> y -> x.compareTo(y) < 0
                                                    ? x : y));
}
```

Although this solution works perfectly, it's a bit ugly because the argument type and the return type of the function are the same, although they don't represent the same thing. To solve this problem, you could simply create a new type, similar to `List` but with a different name indicating what it's supposed to mean. And while you're at it, you could select a more suitable implementation ensuring that this "list" will have at most one element.

6.3   *The Option data type*

The `Option` data type you'll create in this chapter will be very similar to the `List` data type. Using an `Option` type for optional data allows you to compose functions even when the data is absent (see figure 6.1). It will be implemented as an abstract class, `Option`, containing two private subclasses representing the presence and the absence of data. The subclass representing the absence of data will be called `None`, and the subclass representing the presence of data will be called `Some`. A `Some` will contain the corresponding data value.

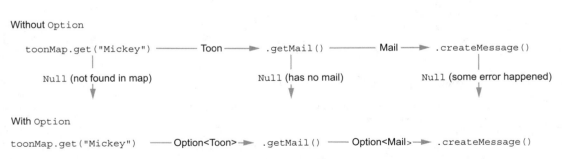

Figure 6.1   Without the `Option` type, composing functions wouldn't produce a function because the resulting program would potentially throw a `NullPointerException`.

The following listing shows the code for these three classes.

Listing 6.1 The `Option` data type

```
package optionaldata;

public abstract class Option<A> {

  @SuppressWarnings("rawtypes")
  private static Option none = new None();
  public abstract A getOrThrow();

  private static class None<A> extends Option<A> {

    private None() {}

    @Override
    public A getOrThrow() {
      throw new IllegalStateException("get called on None");
    }

    @Override
    public String toString() {
      return "None";
    }
  }

  private static class Some<A> extends Option<A> {

    private final A value;

    private Some(A a) {
      value = a;
    }

    @Override
    public A getOrThrow() {
      return this.value;
    }

    @Override
    public String toString() {
      return String.format("Some(%s)", this.value);
    }
  }

  public static <A> Option<A> some(A a) {
    return new Some<>(a);
  }

  @SuppressWarnings("unchecked")
  public static <A> Option<A> none() {
    return none;
  }
}
```

A singleton instance of None will be used for all types.

getOrThrow() allows you to retrieve the value from an Option.

The None subclass represents the absence of value.

Constructors are private.

In the None class, getOrThrow() throws an exception.

toString() returns a human-readable representation of an Option.

Constructors are private.

toString() returns a human-readable representation of an Option

The some factory method allows you to create an Option from a value.

The none factory method returns the none singleton.

In this listing, you can see how close `Option` is to `List`. They're both abstract classes with two private implementations. The `None` subclass corresponds to `Nil` and the `Some` subclass to `Cons`. The `getOrThrow` method is similar to the `head` method in `List`.

You can use `Option` for your definition of the `max` function, as shown here:

```
static <A extends Comparable<A>> Function<List<A>, Option<A>> max() {
  return xs -> xs.isEmpty()
      ? Option.none()
      : Option.some(xs.foldLeft(xs.head(),
                  x -> y -> x.compareTo(y) > 0 ? x : y));
}
```

Now your function is a total function, which means it has a value for all lists, including the empty one. Note how similar this code is to the version returning a list. Although the implementation of `Option` is different from the `List` implementation, its usage is nearly the same. As you'll see soon, the similarity extends much further.

But as it is, the `Option` class isn't very useful. The only way to use an `Option` would be to test the actual class to see if it's a `Some` or a `None`, and call the `getOrThrow` method to obtain the value in the former case. And this method will throw an exception if there's no data, which isn't very functional. To make it a powerful tool, you'll need to add some methods, in the same way you did for `List`.

6.3.1 *Getting a value from an Option*

Many methods that you created for `List` will also be useful for `Option`. In fact, only methods related to multiple values, such as folds, may be useless here. But before you create these methods, let's start with some `Option`-specific usage.

To avoid testing for the subclass of an `Option`, you need to define methods that, unlike `getOrThrow`, may be useful in both subclasses, so you can call them from the `Option` parent class. The first thing you'll need is a way to retrieve the value in an `Option`. One frequent use case when data is missing is to use a default value.

EXERCISE 6.1

Implement a `getOrElse` method that will return either the contained value if it exists, or a provided default one otherwise. Here's the method signature:

```
A getOrElse(A defaultValue)
```

SOLUTION 6.1

This method will be implemented as an instance method declared in the abstract `Option` class as follows:

```
public abstract A getOrElse(A defaultValue);
```

The `Some` implementation is obvious and will simply return the value it contains:

```
public A getOrElse(A defaultValue) {
  return this.value;
}
```

The `None` implementation will return the default value:

```
public A getOrElse(A defaultValue) {
  return defaultValue;
}
```

So far so good. You can now define methods that return options and use the returned value transparently, as follows:

```
int max1 = max().apply(List.<Integer>list(3, 5, 7, 2, 1)).getOrElse(0);
int max2 = max().apply(List.list()).getOrElse(0);
```

Here, max1 will be equal to 7 (the maximum value in the list), and max2 will be set to 0 (the default value).

But you might be having a problem. Look at the following example:

```
int max1 = max().apply(List.list(3, 5, 7, 2, 1)).getOrElse(getDefault());
System.out.println(max1);
int max2 = max().apply(List.<Integer>list()).getOrElse(getDefault());
System.out.println(max2);

int getDefault() {
  throw new RuntimeException();
}
```

Of course, this example is a bit contrived. The getDefault method isn't functional at all. This is only to show you what's happening. What will this example print? If you think it will print 7 and then throw an exception, think again.

This example will print nothing and will directly throw an exception because Java is a strict language. Method parameters are evaluated before the method is actually executed, whether they're needed or not. The getOrElse method parameter is thus evaluated in any case, whether it's called on a Some or a None. The fact that the method parameter isn't needed for a Some is irrelevant. This makes no difference when the parameter is a literal, but it makes a huge difference when it's a method call. The getDefault method will be called in any case, so the first line will throw an exception and nothing will be displayed. This is generally not what you want.

EXERCISE 6.2

Fix the previous problem by using lazy evaluation for the getOrElse method parameter.

HINT

Use the Supplier class you defined in chapter 3 (exercise 3.2).

SOLUTION 6.2

The signature of the method will be changed to

```
public abstract A getOrElse(Supplier<A> defaultValue);
```

The Some implementation doesn't change, except for the method signature, because the parameter isn't used:

```
@Override
public A getOrElse(Supplier<A> defaultValue) {
  return this.value;
}
```

The most important change is in the None class:

```
@Override
public A getOrElse(Supplier<A> defaultValue) {
  return defaultValue.get();
}
```

In the absence of a value, the parameter is evaluated through a call to the Supplier .get() method. The max example can now be rewritten as follows:

```
int max1 = max().apply(List.list(3, 5, 7, 2, 1))
                .getOrElse(() -> getDefault());

System.out.println(max1);
int max2 = max().apply(List.<Integer>list()).getOrElse(() -> getDefault());
System.out.println(max2);
int getDefault() {
  throw new RuntimeException();
}
```

This program prints 7 to the console before throwing an exception.

Now that you have the getOrElse method, you don't need the getOrThrow method any longer. But it might be useful when developing other methods for the Option class, so we'll keep it and make it protected.

6.3.2 Applying functions to optional values

One very important method in List is the map method, which allows you to apply a function from A to B to each element of a list of A, producing a list of B. Considering that an Option is like a list containing at most one element, you can apply the same principle.

EXERCISE 6.3

Create a map method to change an Option<A> into an Option<B> by applying a function from A to B.

HINT

Define an abstract method in the Option class with one implementation in each subclass. The method signature in Option will be

```
public abstract <B> Option<B> map(Function<A, B> f)
```

SOLUTION 6.3

The None implementation is simple. You just have to return a None instance. As I said earlier, the Option class contains a None singleton that can be used for this:

```
public <B> Option<B> map(Function<A, B> f) {
  return none();
}
```

Note that although `this` and `none` refer to the same object, you can't return `this` because it's parameterized with `A`. The `none` reference points to the same object, but with a raw type (no parameter). This is why you annotate `none` with `@SuppressWarnings` (`"rawtypes"`) in order to keep compiler warnings from leaking to the caller. In the same manner, you use a call to the `none()` factory method instead of directly accessing the `none` instance in order to avoid the "Unchecked assignment warning" that you already avoided in the `none()` method by using the `@SuppressWarnings` (`"unchecked"`) annotation.

The `Some` implementation isn't much more complex. All you need to do is get the value, apply the function to it, and wrap the result in a new `Some`:

```
public <B> Option<B> map(Function<A, B> f) {
  return new Some<>(f.apply(this.value));
}
```

6.3.3 *Dealing with Option composition*

As you'll soon realize, functions from `A` to `B` aren't the most common ones in functional programming. At first you may have trouble getting acquainted with functions returning optional values. After all, it seems to involve extra work to wrap values in `Some` instances and later retrieve these values. But with further practice, you'll see that these operations occur only rarely. When chaining functions to build a complex computation, you'll often start with a value that's returned by some previous computation and pass the result to a new function without seeing the intermediate result. In other words, you'll more often use functions from `A` to `Option<B>` than functions from `A` to `B`.

Think about the `List` class. Does this ring a bell? Yes, it leads to the `flatMap` method.

EXERCISE 6.4

Create a `flatMap` instance method that takes as an argument a function from `A` to `Option<B>` and returns an `Option<B>`.

HINT

You can define different implementations in both subclasses; but you should try to devise a unique implementation that works for both subclasses and put it in the `Option` class. Its signature will be

```
<B> Option<B> flatMap(Function<A, Option<B>> f)
```

Try using some of the methods you already have (`map` and `getOrElse`).

SOLUTION 6.4

The trivial solution would be to define an abstract method in the `Option` class, return `none()` in the `None` class, and return `f.apply(this.value)` in the `Some` class. This is probably the most efficient implementation. But a more elegant solution is to map the `f` function, giving an `Option<Option<B>>`, and then use the `getOrElse` method to extract the value (`Option<B>`), providing `None` as the default value:

```
public <B> Option<B> flatMap(Function<A, Option<B>> f) {
  return map(f).getOrElse(Option::none);
}
```

EXERCISE 6.5

Just as you needed a way to map a function that returns an Option (leading to flat-Map), you'll need a version of getOrElse for Option default values. Create the orElse method with the following signature:

```
Option<A> orElse(Supplier<Option<A>> defaultValue)
```

HINT

As you might guess from the name, there's no need to "get" the value in order to implement this method. This is how Option is mostly used: through Option composition rather than wrapping and getting values. One consequence is that the same implementation will work for both subclasses.

SOLUTION 6.5

The solution consists in mapping the function x -> this, which results in an Option<Option<A>>, and then using getOrElse on this result with the provided default value:

```
public Option<A> orElse(Supplier<Option<A>> defaultValue) {
  return map(x -> this).getOrElse(defaultValue);
}
```

EXERCISE 6.6

In chapter 5, you created a filter method to remove from a list all elements that didn't satisfy a condition expressed in the form of a predicate (in other words, it was a function returning a Boolean). Create the same method for Option. Here's its signature:

```
Option<A> filter(Function<A, Boolean> f)
```

HINT

Because an Option is like a List with at most one element, the implementation seems trivial. In the None subclass, you simply return none(). In the Some class, you return the original Option if the condition holds, and none() otherwise. But try to devise a smarter implementation that fits in the Option parent class.

SOLUTION 6.6

The solution is to flatMap the function used in the Some case:

```
public Option<A> filter(Function<A, Boolean> f) {
  return flatMap(x -> f.apply(x)
      ? this
      : none());
}
```

6.3.4 *Option use cases*

If you already know about the Java 8 Optional class, you may have remarked that Optional contains an isPresent() method allowing you to test whether the Optional contains a value or not. (Optional has a different implementation that's not based on two different subclasses.) You can easily implement such a method, although you'll call it isSome() because it will test whether the object is a Some or a None. You could also call it isNone(), which might seem more logical because it would be the equivalent of the List.isEmpty() method.

Although the isSome() method is sometimes useful, it's not the best way to use the Option class. If you were to test an Option through the isSome() method before calling getOrThrow() to get the value, it wouldn't be much different from testing a reference for null before dereferencing it. The only difference would be in the case where you forget to test first: you'd risk seeing an IllegalStateException instead of a Null-PointerException.

The best way to use Option is through composition. To do this, you must create all the necessary methods for all use cases. These use cases correspond to what you'd do with the value after testing that it's not null. You could do one of the following:

- Use the value as the input to another function
- Apply an effect to the value
- Use the value if it's not null, or use a default value to apply a function or an effect

The first and third use cases have already been made possible through the methods you've already created. Applying an effect can be done in different ways that you'll learn about in chapter 13.

As an example, look at how the Option class can be used to change the way you use a map. Listing 6.2 shows the implementation of a functional Map. This is not a functional implementation, but only a wrapper around a legacy ConcurrentHashMap to give it a functional interface.

Listing 6.2 Using Option in a functional Map

```
import com.fpinjava.optionaldata.exercise06_05.Option;
import java.util.concurrent.ConcurrentHashMap;
import java.util.concurrent.ConcurrentMap;

public class Map<T, U> {

  private final ConcurrentMap<T, U> map = new ConcurrentHashMap<>();

  public static <T, U> Map<T, U> empty() {
    return new Map<>();
  }

  public static <T, U> Map<T, U> add(Map<T, U> m, T t, U u) {
    m.map.put(t, u);
    return m;
  }
```

```
  public Option<U> get(final T t) {
    return this.map.containsKey(t)
        ? Option.some(this.map.get(t))
        : Option.none();
  }

  public Map<T, U> put(T t, U u) {
    return add(this, t, u);
  }

  public Map<T, U> removeKey(T t) {
    this.map.remove(t);
    return this;
  }
}
```

> This version of map encapsulates the "check before use" pattern to avoid returning null references.

As you can see, `Option` allows you to encapsulate into the map implementation the pattern for querying the map with `containsKey` before calling `get`. The following listing shows how this is intended to be used.

Listing 6.3   Putting `Option` to work

```
import com.fpinjava.optionaldata.exercise06_06.Option;
import com.fpinjava.optionaldata.listing06_02.Map;

public class UseMap {

  public static void main(String[] args) {

    Map<String, Toon> toons = new Map<String, Toon>()
        .put("Mickey", new Toon("Mickey", "Mouse", "mickey@disney.com"))
        .put("Minnie", new Toon("Minnie", "Mouse"))
        .put("Donald", new Toon("Donald", "Duck", "donald@disney.com"));

    Option<String> mickey = toons.get("Mickey").flatMap(Toon::getEmail);
    Option<String> minnie = toons.get("Minnie").flatMap(Toon::getEmail);
    Option<String> goofy = toons.get("Goofy").flatMap(Toon::getEmail);

    System.out.println(mickey.getOrElse(() -> "No data"));
    System.out.println(minnie.getOrElse(() -> "No data"));
    System.out.println(goofy.getOrElse(() -> "No data"));
  }

  static class Toon {

    private final String firstName;
    private final String lastName;
    private final Option<String> email;

    Toon(String firstName, String lastName) {
      this.firstName = firstName;
      this.lastName = lastName;
      this.email = Option.none();
    }

    Toon(String firstName, String lastName, String email) {
      this.firstName = firstName;
      this.lastName = lastName;
      this.email = Option.some(email);
    }
```

> Option composition through flatMap

```
    public Option<String> getEmail() {
      return email;
    }
  }
}
```

In this (very simplified) program, you can see how various functions returning `Option` can be composed. You don't have to test for anything, and you don't risk a `NullPointer-Exception`, although you may be asking for the email of a `Toon` that doesn't have one, or even for a `Toon` that doesn't exist in the map.

But there's a little problem. This program prints

```
mickey@disney.com
No data
No data
```

The first line is Mickey's email. The second line says "No data" because Minnie has no email. The third line says "No data" because Goofy isn't in the map. Clearly, you'd need a way to distinguish these two cases. The `Option` class doesn't allow you to distinguish the two. You'll see in the next chapter how you can solve this problem.

EXERCISE 6.7

Implement the `variance` function in terms of `flatMap`. The variance of a series of values represents how those values are distributed around the mean. If all values are very near to the mean, the variance is low. A variance of 0 is obtained when all values are equal to the mean. The variance of a series is the mean of `Math.pow(x - m, 2)` for each element x in the series, m being the mean of the series. Here's the signature of the function:

```
Function<List<Double>, Option<Double>> variance = ...
```

HINT

To implement this function, you must first implement a function to compute the sum of a `List<Double>`. Then you should create a `mean` function like the one you created previously in this chapter, but working on doubles. If you have trouble defining these functions, refer to chapters 4 and 5 or use the following functions:

```
static Function<List<Double>, Double> sum =
                         ds -> ds.foldLeft(0.0, a -> b -> a + b);

static Function<List<Double>, Option<Double>> mean =
      ds -> ds.isEmpty()
          ? Option.none()
          : Option.some(sum.apply(ds) / ds.length());
```

SOLUTION 6.7

Once you've defined the `sum` and `mean` functions, the `variance` function is quite simple:

```
static Function<List<Double>, Option<Double>> variance =
      ds -> mean.apply(ds)
```

```
        .flatMap(m -> mean.apply(ds.map(x -> Math.pow(x - m, 2))));
```

Note that using functions isn't mandatory. You must use functions if you need to pass them as arguments to higher-order functions, but when you only need to apply them, functional methods may be simpler to use.

If you prefer to use methods when possible, you may arrive at the following solution:

```java
public static Double sum(List<Double> ds) {
  return sum_(0.0, ds).eval();
}

public static TailCall<Double> sum_(Double acc, List<Double> ds) {
  return ds.isEmpty()
      ? ret(acc)
      : sus(() -> sum_(acc + ds.head(), ds.tail()));
}

public static Option<Double> mean(List<Double> ds) {
  return ds.isEmpty()
      ? Option.none()
      : Option.some(sum(ds) / ds.length());
}

public static Option<Double> variance(List<Double> ds) {
  return mean(ds).flatMap(m -> mean(ds.map(x -> Math.pow(x - m, 2))));
}
```

As you can see, functional methods are simpler to use for two reasons. First, you don't need to write `.apply` between the name of the function and the argument. Second, the types are shorter because you don't need to write the word `Function`. For this reason, you'll use functional methods instead of functions as often as possible.

But remember that it's very easy to switch from one to the other. Given this method,

```java
B aToBmethod(A a) {
  return ...
}
```

you can create an equivalent function by writing this:

```java
Function<A, B> aToBfunction = a -> aToBmethod(a);
```

Or you can use a method reference:

```java
Function<A, B> aToBfunction = this::aToBmethod;
```

Conversely, you can create a method from the preceding function:

```java
B aToBmethod2(A a) {
  return aToBfunction.apply(a)
}
```

As the implementation of variance demonstrates, with flatMap you can construct a computation with multiple stages, any of which may fail, and the computation will abort as soon as the first failure is encountered, because None.flatMap(f) will immediately return None without applying f.

6.3.5 *Other ways to combine options*

Deciding to use Option may seem to have huge consequences. In particular, some developers may believe that their legacy code will be made obsolete. What can you do now that you need a function from Option<A> to Option<B>, and you only have an API with methods for converting an A into a B? Do you need to rewrite all your libraries? Not at all. You can easily adapt them.

EXERCISE 6.8

Define a lift method that takes a function from A to B as its argument and returns a function from Option<A> to Option<B>. As usual, use the methods you've defined already. Figure 6.2 shows that the lift method works.

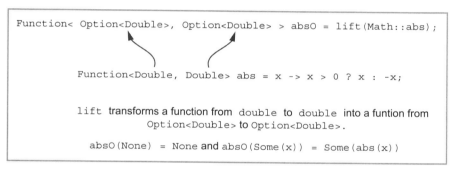

Figure 6.2   Lifting a function

HINT

Use the map method to create a static method in the Option class.

SOLUTION 6.8

The solution is pretty simple:

```
static <A, B> Function<Option<A>, Option<B>> lift(Function<A, B> f) {
  return x -> x.map(f);
}
```

Of course, most of your existing libraries won't contain functions but methods. Converting a method that takes an A as its argument and returns a B into a function from Option<A> to Option<B> is easy. For example, lifting the method String.toUpperCase can be done this way:

```
Function<Option<String>, Option<String>> upperOption =
                                lift(x -> x.toUpperCase());
```

Or you can use a method reference:

```
Function<Option<String>, Option<String>> upperOption =
                                    lift(String::toUpperCase);
```

EXERCISE 6.9
Such solutions are useless for methods that throw exceptions. Write a `lift` method that works with methods that throw exceptions.

SOLUTION 6.9
All you have to do is wrap the implementation of the function returned by `lift` in a `try ... catch` block, returning `None` if an exception is thrown:

```
static <A, B> Function<Option<A>, Option<B>> lift(Function<A, B> f) {
  return x -> {
    try {
      return x.map(f);
    } catch (Exception e) {
      return Option.none();
    }
  };
}
```

You might also need to transform a function from `A` to `B` into a function from `A` to `Option<B>`. You can apply the same technique:

```
static <A, B> Function<A, Option<B>> hlift(Function<A, B> f) {
  return x -> {
    try {
      return Option.some(x).map(f);
    } catch (Exception e) {
      return Option.none();
    }
  };
}
```

Note, however, that this is not very useful, because the exception is lost. In the next chapter, you'll learn how to solve this problem.

What if you want to use a legacy method taking two arguments? Let's say you want to use the `Integer.parseInt(String s, int radix)` with an `Option<String>` and an `Option<Integer>`. How can you do this?

The first step is to create a function from this method. That's simple:

```
Function<Integer, Function<String, Integer>> parseWithRadix =
                 radix -> string -> Integer.parseInt(string, radix);
```

Note that I've inverted the arguments here to create a curried function. This makes sense because applying the radix only would give us a useful function that can parse all strings with a given radix:

```
Function<String, Integer> parseHex = parseWithRadix.apply(16);
```

The inverse (applying a `String` first) would make much less sense.

EXERCISE 6.10

Write a method `map2` taking as its arguments an `Option<A>`, an `Option<B>`, and a function from `(A, B)` to `C` in curried form, and returning an `Option<C>`.

HINT

Use the `flatMap` and possibly the `map` methods.

SOLUTION 6.10

Here's the solution using `flatMap` and `map`. This pattern is very important to understand, and you'll come across it often. We'll come back to this in chapter 8.

```
<A, B, C> Option<C> map2(Option<A> a,
                         Option<B> b,
                         Function<A, Function<B, C>> f) {
  return a.flatMap(ax -> b.map(bx -> f.apply(ax).apply(bx)));
}
```

With `map2`, you can now use any two-argument method as if it had been created for manipulating `Option`.

What about methods with more arguments? Here's an example of a `map3` method:

```
<A, B, C, D> Option<D> map3(Option<A> a,
                            Option<B> b,
                            Option<C> c,
                            Function<A, Function<B, Function<C, D>>> f) {
  return a.flatMap(ax -> b.flatMap(bx -> c.map(cx ->
                                 f.apply(ax).apply(bx).apply(cx))));
}
```

Do you see the pattern?

6.3.6 *Composing List with Option*

Composing `Option` instances is not all you need. Each new type you define must be, at some point, composable with any other. In the previous chapter, you defined the `List` type. To write useful programs, you need to be able to compose `List` and `Option`.

The most common operation is converting a `List<Option<A>>` into an `Option<List<A>>`. A `List<Option<A>>` is what you get when mapping a `List<B>` with a function from `B` to `Option<A>`. Usually, what you'll need for the result is a `Some<List<A>>` if all elements are `Some<A>`, and a `None<List<A>>` if at least one element is a `None<A>`.

EXERCISE 6.11

Write a function `sequence` that combines a `List<Option<T>>` into an `Option<List<T>>`. It will be a `Some<List<T>>` if all values in the original list were `Some` instances, or a `None<List<T>>` otherwise. Here's its signature:

```
Option<List<A>> sequence(List<Option<A>> list)
```

HINT

To find your way, you can test the list to see whether it's empty or not and make a recursive call to sequence if not. Then, remembering that foldRight and foldLeft abstract recursion, you could use one of those methods to implement sequence.

SOLUTION 6.11

Here's an explicitly recursive version that could be used if list.head() and list.tail() were made public:

```
<A> Option<List<A>> sequence(List<Option<A>> list) {
  return list.isEmpty()
      ? some(List.list())
      : list.head()
            .flatMap(hh -> sequence(list.tail()).map(x -> x.cons(hh)));
}
```

But list.head() and list.tail() should be usable only inside the List class, because these methods may throw exceptions. Fortunately, the sequence method can also be implemented using foldRight and map2. This is even better, because fold-Right uses heap-based recursion.

```
<A> Option<List<A>> sequence(List<Option<A>> list) {
  return list.foldRight(some(List.list()),
                        x -> y -> map2(x, y, a -> b -> b.cons(a)));
}
```

Consider the following example:

```
Function<Integer, Function<String, Integer>> parseWithRadix =
                    radix -> string -> Integer.parseInt(string, radix);
Function<String, Option<Integer>> parse16 =
                              Option.hlift(parseWithRadix.apply(16));
List<String> list = List.list("4", "5", "6", "7", "8", "9");
Option<List<Integer> result = Option.sequence(list.map(parse16));
```

This produces the intended result but is somewhat inefficient, because the map method and the sequence method will both invoke foldRight.

EXERCISE 6.12

Define a traverse method that produces the same result but invokes foldRight only once. Here's its signature:

```
Option<List<B>> traverse(List<A> list, Function<A, Option<B>> f)
```

HINT

You need to implement sequence in terms of traverse. Don't use recursion. Prefer the foldRight method that abstracts recursion for you.

SOLUTION 6.12

First define the traverse method:

```
<A, B> Option<List<B>> traverse(List<A> list,
                               Function<A, Option<B>> f) {
  return list.foldRight(some(List.list()),
             x -> y -> map2(f.apply(x), y, a -> b -> b.cons(a)));
}
```

Then you can redefine the sequence method in terms of `traverse`:

```
<A> Option<List<A>> sequence(List<Option<A>> list) {
  return traverse(list, x -> x);
}
```

6.4   *Miscellaneous utilities for Option*

In order to make `Option` as useful as possible, you need to add some utility methods. Some of these methods are a must, and others are questionable because their use is not in the spirit of functional programming. You nevertheless must consider adding them. You may need a method to test whether an `Option` is a `None` or a `Some`. You may also need an `equals` method for comparing options, in which case you mustn't forget to define a compatible `hashCode` method.

6.4.1   *Testing for Some or None*

Until now, you haven't needed to test an option to know whether it was a `Some` or a `None`. Ideally, you should never have to do this. In practice, though, there are times when it's simpler to use this trick than to resort to real functional techniques.

For example, you defined the `map2` method as

```
<A, B, C> Option<C> map2(Option<A> a,
                         Option<B> b,
                         Function<A, Function<B, C>> f) {
  return a.flatMap(ax -> b.map(bx -> f.apply(ax).apply(bx)));
}
```

This is very smart, and because you want to look smart, you might prefer this solution. But some may find the following version simpler to understand:

```
<A, B, C> Option<C> map2(Option<A> a,
                         Option<B> b,
                         Function<A, Function<B, C>> f) {
  return a.isSome() && b.isSome()
      ? some(f.apply(a.get()).apply(b.getOrThrow()))
      : none();
}
```

> **TESTING THE CODE**   If you want to test this code, you'll have to define the `isSome` method first, but this is not to encourage you to use this nonfunctional technique. You should always prefer the first form, but you should also understand fully the relation between the two forms. Besides, you'll probably find yourself needing the `isSome` method someday.

6.4.2   *equals and hashcode*

Much more important are the definitions of the equals and hashcode methods. As you know, these methods are strongly related and must be consistently defined. If equals is true for two instances of Option, their hashcode methods should return the same value. (The inverse is not true. Objects having the same hashcode may not always be equal.)

Here are the implementations of equals and hashcode for Some:

```
@Override
public boolean equals(Object o) {
  return (this == o || o instanceof Some)
                        && this.value.equals(((Some<?>) o).value);
}

@Override
public int hashCode() {
  return Objects.hashCode(value);
}
```

And here are the corresponding implementations for None:

```
@Override
public boolean equals(Object o) {
  return this == o || o instanceof None;
}

@Override
public int hashCode() {
  return 0;
}
```

6.5   *How and when to use Option*

As you may know, Java 8 has introduced the Optional class that may be seen by some as identical to your Option, although it's not implemented in the same way at all, and it lacks most of the functional methods you've put into Option. There's much controversy about whether the new features of Java 8 are a move toward functional programming. They certainly are, although this is not official. The official position is that Optional is not a functional feature.

Here's how Brian Goetz, Java language architect at Oracle, answered a question about this subject on Stack Overflow. The question was "Should Java 8 getters return optional types?" Here is Brian Goetz's answer:[2]

> Of course, people will do what they want. But we did have a clear intention when adding this feature, and it was not to be a general purpose Maybe or Some type, as much as many people would have liked us to do so. Our intention was to provide a limited mechanism for library method return types where there needed to be a clear way to represent "no result" and using null for such was overwhelmingly likely to cause errors.

---

[2] The full discussion may be read at http://mng.bz/Rkk1.

For example, you probably should never use it for something that returns an array of results, or a list of results; instead return an empty array or list. You should almost never use it as a field of something or a method parameter.

I think routinely using it as a return value for getters would definitely be over-use.

There's nothing wrong with `Optional` that it should be avoided, it's just not what many people wish it were, and accordingly we were fairly concerned about the risk of zealous over-use.

(Public service announcement: NEVER call `Optional.get` unless you can prove it will never be `null`; instead use one of the safe methods like `orElse` or `ifPresent`. In retrospect, we should have called get something like getOrElse-ThrowNoSuchElementException or something that made it far clearer that this was a highly dangerous method that undermined the whole purpose of `Optional` in the first place. Lesson learned.)

This is a very important answer that deserves some reflection. First of all, and this might be the most important part, "people will do what they want." Nothing to add here. Just do what *you* want. This doesn't mean you should do whatever you want without thinking. But feel free to try every solution that comes to mind. You shouldn't refrain from using `Optional` in a particular way just because it wasn't intended to be used that way. Imagine the first man who ever thought about grabbing a stone to hit something with more strength. He had two options (pun intended!): refraining from doing it because stones had obviously not been intended to be used as hammers, or just trying it.

Second, Goetz says that `get` shouldn't be called unless you can prove it will never be `null`. Doing this would completely ruin any benefit of using `Option`. But you don't need to give `get` a very long name. `getOrThrow` would do the job. Note that returning an empty list to indicate the absence of a result doesn't by itself solve the problem. Forgetting to test whether the list is empty will produce an `IndexOutOfBoundException` instead of a `NullPointerException`. Not much better!

When to use getOrThrow

The correct advice is to avoid `getOrThrow` as much as possible. As a rule of thumb, each time you find yourself using this method outside of the `Option` class, you should consider whether there's another way to go. Using `getOrThrow` is exiting the functional safety of the `Option` class.

The same thing is true for the `head` and `tail` methods of the `List` class. If possible, these methods shouldn't be used outside of the `List` class. Directly accessing the value(s) contained in classes like `List` or `Option` always brings the risk of a `NullPointerException` if this is done on the `None` or `Nil` subclasses. It may not be possible to avoid in library classes, but it should be avoided in business classes. That's why the best solution is to make this method protected, so that it can only be called from inside the `Option` class.

But the most important point is the original question: should getters return Option (or Optional)? Generally, they shouldn't, because properties should be final and initialized at declaration or in constructors, so there's absolutely no need for getters to return Option. (I must admit, however, that initializing fields in constructors doesn't guarantee that access to properties is impossible before they're initialized. This is a marginal problem that's easily solved by making classes final, if possible.)

But some properties might be optional. For example, a person will always have a first name and a last name, but they might have no email. How can you represent this? By storing the property as an Option. In such cases, the getter will have to return an Option. Saying that "routinely using it as a return value for getters would definitely be over-use" is like saying that a property without a value should be set to null, and the corresponding getter should return null. This completely destroys the benefit of having Option.

What about methods that take Option as their argument? In general, this should not occur. To compose methods returning Option, you shouldn't use methods that take Option as their argument. For example, to compose the three following methods, you don't need to change the methods to make them accept Option as their argument:

```
Option<String> getName () {
   ...
}

Option<String> validate(String name) {
   ...
}

Option<Toon> getToon(String name) {
   ...
}
```

Given that the validate method is a static method of class Validate, and toonMap is an instance of Map with the get instance method, the functional way to compose these methods is as follows:

```
Option<Toon> toon = getName()
                  .flatMap(Validate::validate)
                  .flatMap(toonMap::get)
```

So there's little use for methods taking Option as parameters in business code.

There's another reason why Option (or Optional) should probably be used rarely (if ever). Generally, the absence of data is the result of errors that you should often handle by throwing an exception in imperative Java. As I said previously, returning Option.None instead of throwing an exception is like catching an exception and swallowing it silently. Usually it's not a billion-dollar mistake, but it's still a big one. You'll learn in the next chapter how to deal with this situation. After that, you'll hardly ever need the Option data type again. But don't worry. All you've learned in this chapter will still be extremely useful.

The Option type is the simplest form of a kind of data type that you'll use again and again. It's a parameterized type, it has a method to make an Option<A> from an A, and it has a flatMap method that can be used to compose Option instances. Although it's not very useful by itself, it has acquainted you with very fundamental concepts of functional programming.

6.6 Summary

- You need a way to represent optional data, which means data that may or may not be present.
- The null pointer is the most impractical and dangerous way to represent the absence of data.
- Sentinel values and empty lists are other possible ways to represent the absence of data, but they don't compose well.
- The Option data type is a much better way to represent optional data. The Some subtype represents data, and the None subtype represents the absence of data.
- Functions can be applied to Option through the map and flatMap methods, allowing for easy Option composition.
- Functions operating on values may be lifted to operate on Option instances.
- List can be composed with Option. A List<Option> can be turned into an Option<List> using the sequence method.
- Option instances can be compared for equality. Instances of subtype Some are equal if their wrapped values are equal. Because there's only one instance of None, all instances of None are equal.
- Although Option may represent the result of a computation producing an exception, all information about the occurring exception is lost. In the next chapter, you'll learn how to deal with this problem.

Handling errors
and exceptions

7

This chapter covers

- Holding information about errors with the `Either` type
- Easier error handling with the biased `Result` type
- Accessing the data inside a `Result`
- Applying effects to `Result` data
- Lifting functions to operate on `Result`

In chapter 6, you learned how to deal with optional data without having to manipulate `null` references by using the `Option` data type. As you saw, this data type is perfect for dealing with the absence of data when this isn't the result of an error. But it's not an efficient way to handle errors, because, although it allows you to cleanly report the absence of data, it swallows the cause of this absence. All missing data is thus treated the same way, and it's up to the caller to try to figure out what happened, which is generally impossible.

7.1 The problems to be solved

Most of the time, the absence of data is the result of an error, either in the input data or in the computation. These are two very different cases, but they end with the same result: data is absent, and it was meant to be present.

In classical imperative programming, when a function or a method takes an object parameter, most programmers know that they should test this parameter for null. What they should do if the parameter is null is often undefined. Remember the example from listing 6.3 in chapter 6:

```
Option<String> goofy = toons.get("Goofy").flatMap(Toon::getEmail);

System.out.println(goofy.getOrElse(() -> "No data"));
```

In this example, output of "No data" was obtained because the "Goofy" key was not in the map. This could be considered a normal case. But take a look at this one:

```
Option<String> toon = getName()
                    .flatMap(toons::get)
                    .flatMap(Toon::getEmail);

System.out.println(toon.getOrElse(() -> "No data"));

Option<String> getName() {
  String name = // retrieve the name from the user interface
  return name;
}
```

If the user enters an empty string, what should you do? An obvious solution would be to validate the input and return an Option<String>. In the absence of a valid string, you could return None. But although you haven't yet learned how to functionally let the user input a string, you can be sure that such an operation could throw an exception. The program would look like this:

```
Option<String> toon = getName()
                    .flatMap(Example::validate)
                    .flatMap(toons::get)
                    .flatMap(Toon::getEmail);

System.out.println(toon.getOrElse(() -> "No data"));

Option<String> getName() {
  try {
    String name = // retrieve the name from the user interface
    return Option.some(name);
  } catch (Exception e) {
    return Option.none();
  }
}

Option<String> validate(String name) {
  return name.length() > 0 ? Option.some(name) : Option.none();
}
```

Now think about what could happen:

- Everything goes well, and you get an email printed to the console.
- An IOException is thrown, and you get "No data" printed to the console.
- The name entered by the user doesn't validate, and you get "No data."
- The name validates but isn't found in the map. You get "No data."
- The name is found in the map, but the corresponding toon has no email. You get "No data."

What you need is different messages printed to the console to indicate what's happening in each case.

If you wanted to use the types you already know, you could use a Tuple<Option<T>, Option<String>> as the return type of each method, but this is a bit complicated. Tuple is a product type, which means that the number of elements that can be represented by a Tuple<T, U> is the number of possible T multiplied by the number of possible U. You don't need that because every time you have a value for T, you'll have None for U. In the same way, each time U is Some, T will be None. What you need is a sum type, which means a type E<T, U> that will hold either a T *or* a U, but not a T *and* a U.

7.2 The Either type

Designing a type that can hold either a T or a U is easy. You just have to slightly modify the Option type by changing the None type to make it hold a value. You'll also change the names. The two private subclasses of the Either type will be called Left and Right.

Listing 7.1 The Either type

```
public abstract class Either<T, U> {

  private static class Left<T, U> extends Either<T, U> {

    private final T value;

    private Left(T value) {
      this.value = value;
    }

    @Override
    public String toString() {
      return String.format("Left(%s)", value);
    }
  }

  private static class Right<T, U> extends Either<T, U> {

    private final U value;

    private Right(U value) {
      this.value = value;
    }
```

```
    @Override
    public String toString() {
      return String.format("Right(%s)", value);
    }
  }

  public static <T, U> Either<T, U> left(T value) {
    return new Left<>(value);
  }

  public static <T, U> Either<T, U> right(U value) {
    return new Right<>(value);
  }
}
```

Now you can easily use `Either` instead of `Option` to represent values that could be absent due to errors. You have to parameterize `Either` with the type of your data and the type of the error. By convention, you'll use the `Right` subclass to represent success (which is "right") and the `Left` to represent error. But you won't call the subclass `Wrong` because the `Either` type may be used to represent data that can be represented by one type or another, both being valid.

Of course, you have to choose what type will represent the error. You can choose `String` in order to carry an error message, or you can choose `Exception`. For example, the `max` function you defined in chapter 6 could be modified as follows:

```
<A extends Comparable<A>> Function<List<A>, Either<String, A>> max() {
  return xs -> xs.isEmpty()
      ? Either.left("max called on an empty list")
      : Either.right(xs.foldLeft(xs.head(), x -> y -> x.compareTo(y) < 0 ?
                                                          x : y));
}
```

7.2.1 Composing Either

To compose methods or functions returning `Either`, you need to define the same methods you defined on the `Option` class.

EXERCISE 7.1

Define a `map` method to change an `Either<E, A>` into an `Either<E, B>`, given a function from A to B. The signature of the `map` method is as follows:

```
public abstract <B> Either<E, B> map(Function<A, B> f);
```

HINT

I've used type parameters E and A to make clear which side you should map, E standing for *error*. But it would be possible to define two `map` methods (call them `mapLeft` and `mapRight`) to map one or the other side of an `Either` instance. In other words, you're developing a "biased" version of `Either` that will be mappable on one side only.

SOLUTION 7.1

The `Left` implementation is a bit more complex than the `None` implementation for `Option` because you have to construct a new `Either` holding the same (error) value as the original:

```
public <B> Either<E, B> map(Function<A, B> f) {
  return new Left<>(value);
}
```

The `Right` implementation is exactly like the one in `Some`:

```
public <B> Either<E, B> map(Function<A, B> f) {
  return new Right<>(f.apply(value));
}
```

EXERCISE 7.2

Define a `flatMap` method to change an `Either<E, A>` into an `Either<E, B>`, given a function from `A` to `Either<E, B>`. The signature of the `flatMap` method is as follows:

```
public abstract <B> Either<E, B> flatMap(Function<A, Either<E, B>> f);
```

SOLUTION 7.2

The `Left` implementation is exactly the same as for the `map` method:

```
public <B> Either<E, B> flatMap(Function<A, Either<E, B>> f) {
  return new Left<>(value);
}
```

The `Right` implementation is the same as the `Option.flatMap` method:

```
public <B> Either<E, B> flatMap(Function<A, Either<E, B>> f) {
  return f.apply(value);
}
```

EXERCISE 7.3

Define methods `getOrElse` and `orElse` with the following signatures:

```
A getOrElse(Supplier<A> defaultValue)

Either<E, A> orElse(Supplier<Either<E, A>> defaultValue)
```

HINT

Not all exercises have a satisfying solution!

SOLUTION 7.3

The `orElse` method can be defined in the `Either` class, because the same implementation works for both subclasses:

```
public Either<E, A> orElse(Supplier<Either<E, A>> defaultValue) {
  return map(x -> this).getOrElse(defaultValue);
}
```

Solutions for the `getOrElse` methods are straightforward. In the `Right` subclass, you just have to return the contained value:

```
public A getOrElse(Supplier<A> defaultValue) {
  return value;
}
```

In the `Left` subclass, just return the default value:

```
public A getOrElse(Supplier<A> defaultValue) {
  return defaultValue.get();
}
```

This method works, but it's far from ideal. The problem is that you don't know what has happened if no value was available. You simply get the default value, not even knowing if it's the result of a computation or the result of an error. To handle error cases correctly, you'd need a biased version of `Either`, where the left type is known. Rather than using `Either` (which, by the way, has many other interesting uses), you can create a specialized version using a known fixed type for the `Left` class.

The first question you might ask is, "What type should I use?" Obviously, two different types come to mind: `String` and `RuntimeException`. A string can hold an error message, as an exception does, but many error situations will produce an exception. Using a `String` as the type carried by the `Left` value will force you to ignore the relevant information in the exception and use only the included message. It's thus better to use `RuntimeException` as the `Left` value. That way, if you only have a message, you can wrap it into an exception.

7.3 The Result type

Because the new type will generally represent the result of a computation that might have failed, you'll call it `Result`. It's very similar to the `Option` type, with the difference that the subclasses are named `Success` and `Failure`, as shown in the following listing.

> **Listing 7.2 The `Result` class**

```
import java.io.Serializable;

public abstract class Result<V> implements Serializable {    ◁──── The Result class takes only one type parameter, corresponding to the success value.

  private Result() {
  }

  private static class Failure<V> extends Result<V> {    ◁──── The Failure subclass contains a RuntimeException.

    private final RuntimeException exception;

    private Failure(String message) {
      super();
```

Constructors are private. If a Failure is constructed with a message, it's wrapped into a RuntimeException (more specifically, the IllegalStateException subclass).

If constructed with a RuntimeException, it's stored as is.

```
        this.exception = new IllegalStateException(message);
    }
    private Failure(RuntimeException e) {
      super();
      this.exception = e;
    }
    private Failure(Exception e) {
      super();
      this.exception = new IllegalStateException(e.getMessage(), e);
    }

    @Override
    public String toString() {
      return String.format("Failure(%s)", exception.getMessage());
    }
  }

  private static class Success<V> extends Result<V> {

    private final V value;

    private Success(V value) {
      super();
      this.value = value;
    }

    @Override
    public String toString() {
      return String.format("Success(%s)", value.toString());
    }
  }

  public static <V> Result<V> failure(String message) {
    return new Failure<>(message);
  }

  public static <V> Result<V> failure(Exception e) {
    return new Failure<V>(e);
  }

  public static <V> Result<V> failure(RuntimeException e) {
    return new Failure<V>(e);
  }

  public static <V> Result<V> success(V value) {
    return new Success<>(value);
  }
}
```

If constructed with a checked exception, it's wrapped into a RuntimeException.

The Success subclass stores the successful value.

Result instances are created using factory methods.

This class is much like the Option class, with the additional stored exception.

7.3.1 Adding methods to the Result class

You'll need the same methods in the `Result` class that you defined in the `Option` and `Either` classes, with small differences.

EXERCISE 7.4

Define `map`, `flatMap`, `getOrElse`, and `orElse` for the `Result` class. For `getOrElse`, you can define two methods: one taking a value as its argument, and one taking a `Supplier`. Here are the signatures:

```
public abstract V getOrElse(final V defaultValue);
public abstract V getOrElse(final Supplier<V> defaultValue);
public abstract <U> Result<U> map(Function<V, U> f);
public abstract <U> Result<U> flatMap(Function<V, Result<U>> f);
public Result<V> orElse(Supplier<Result<V>> defaultValue)
```

The first version of `getOrElse` is useful when the default value is a literal because it's already evaluated. In that case, you don't need to use lazy evaluation.

SOLUTION 7.4

This time, you'll have no problem with `getOrElse`, because you just have to throw the exception contained in a `Failure`. All other methods are very similar to those of the `Either` class. Here are the implementations for the `Success` class:

```
public V getOrElse(V defaultValue) {
  return value;
}

public V getOrElse(Supplier<V> defaultValue) {
  return value;
}

public <U> Result<U> map(Function<V, U> f) {
  try {
    return success(f.apply(successValue()));
  } catch (Exception e) {
    return failure(e.getMessage(), e);
  }
}

public <U> Result<U> flatMap(Function<V, Result<U>> f) {
  try {
    return f.apply(successValue());
  } catch (Exception e) {
    return failure(e.getMessage());
  }
}
```

And here are the implementations for the `Failure` class:

```
public V getOrElse(V defaultValue) {
  return defaultValue;
}

public V getOrElse(Supplier<V> defaultValue) {
```

```
    return defaultValue.get();
}

public <U> Result<U> map(Function<V, U> f) {
  return failure(exception);
}

public <U> Result<U> flatMap(Function<V, Result<U>> f) {
  return failure(exception);
}
```

As in `Option`, `map` and `flatMap` can't return `this` in the `Failure` class because the type would be invalid.

Finally, you can define the `orElse` method in the parent class because the implementation is valid for both subclasses:

```
public Result<V> orElse(Supplier<Result<V>> defaultValue) {
  return map(x -> this).getOrElse(defaultValue);
}
```

7.4   *Result patterns*

The `Result` class can now be used in a functional way, which means through composing methods representing computations that may succeed or fail. This is important because `Result` and similar types are often described as containers that may or may not contain a value. This description is partly wrong. `Result` is a computational context for a value that may or may not be present. The way to use it is not by retrieving the value, but by composing instances of `Result` using its specific methods.

You can, for example, modify the previous `ToonMail` example to use this class. First you have to modify the `Map` and `Toon` classes as shown in listings 7.3 and 7.4.

Listing 7.3   The modified `Map` class with the `get` method returning a `Result`

```
import java.util.concurrent.ConcurrentHashMap;
import java.util.concurrent.ConcurrentMap;

public class Map<T, U> {

  private final ConcurrentMap<T, U> map = new ConcurrentHashMap<>();

  public static <T, U> Map<T, U> empty() {
    return new Map<>();
  }

  public static <T, U> Map<T, U> add(Map<T, U> m, T t, U u) {
    m.map.put(t, u);
    return m;
  }

  public Result<U> get(final T t) {
    return this.map.containsKey(t)
      ? Result.success(this.map.get(t))
      : Result.failure(String.format("Key %s not found in map", t));
  }
}
```

If the key is contained in the map, return a Success containing the retrieved object.

Otherwise, return a Failure containing an error message.

```
  public Map<T, U> put(T t, U u) {
    return add(this, t, u);
  }

  public Map<T, U> removeKey(T t) {
    this.map.remove(t);
    return this;
  }
}
```

Listing 7.4   The modified `Toon` class with the modified `mail` property

```
public class Toon {

  private final String firstName;
  private final String lastName;
  private final Result<String> email;                          If no mail is provided,
                                                                store a Failure.
  Toon(String firstName, String lastName) {
    this.firstName = firstName;
    this.lastName = lastName;
    this.email = Result.failure(String.format("%s %s has no mail",
                                        firstName, lastName));   ◁
  }

  Toon(String firstName, String lastName, String email) {      If the object is
    this.firstName = firstName;                                 constructed with an
    this.lastName = lastName;                                   email, it's wrapped
    this.email = Result.success(email);            ◁           in a Success.
  }

  public Result<String> getEmail() {        ◁
    return email;                                  The getEmail method returns a Result
  }                                                (which is either a Success or a Failure).
}
```

Now you can modify the ToonMail program as follows.

Listing 7.5   The modified program, using `Result`

```
import java.io.IOException;
                                                   Methods returning Result are
public class ToonMail {                            composed through flatMap.

  public static void main(String[] args) {
    Map<String, Toon> toons = new Map<String, Toon>()
        .put("Mickey", new Toon("Mickey", "Mouse", "mickey@disney.com"))
        .put("Minnie", new Toon("Minnie", "Mouse"))
        .put("Donald", new Toon("Donald", "Duck", "donald@disney.com"));
    Result<String> result =
            getName().flatMap(toons::get).flatMap(Toon::getEmail);   ◁
    System.out.println(result);
  }

  public static Result<String> getName() {     ◁     The getName method
    return Result.success("Mickey");                 simulates an input that
  }                                                   may result in a Failure.
}
```

The program in listing 7.5 uses the `getName` method to simulate an input operation that may throw an exception. To represent an exception being thrown, you just have to return a `Failure` wrapping the exception.

Note how the various operations returning a `Result` are composed. You don't need to access the value contained in the `Result` (which may be an exception). The `flatMap` method is used for such composition.

Try to run this program with various implementations of the `getName` method, such as these:

```
return Result.success("Mickey");
return Result.failure(new IOException("Input error"));
return Result.success("Minnie");
return Result.success("Goofy");
```

Here's what the program prints in each case:

```
Success(mickey@disney.com)
Failure(Input error)
Failure(Minnie Mouse has no mail)
Failure(Key Goofy not found in map)
```

This result may seem good, but it's not. The problem is that Minnie, having no email, and Goofy, not being in the map, are reported as failures. They might be failures, but they might alternatively be normal cases. After all, if having no email was a failure, you wouldn't have allowed a `Toon` instance to be created without one. Obviously this is not a failure, but only optional data. The same is true for the map. It might be an error if a key isn't in the map (assuming it was supposed to be there), but from the map point of view, it's just optional data.

You might think this isn't a problem because you already have a type for this: the `Option` type you developed in chapter 6. But look at the way you've composed your functions:

```
getName().flatMap(toons::get).flatMap(Toon::getEmail);
```

This was only possible because `getName`, `Map.get`, and `Toon.getEmail` all return a `Result`. If `Map.get` and `Toon.getMail` were to return `Options`, they'd no longer compose with `getName`.

It would still be possible to convert a `Result` to and from an `Option`. For example, you could add a `toOption` method in `Result`:

```
public abstract Option<V> toOption()
```

The `Success` implementation would be

```
public Option<V> toOption() {
  return Option.some(value);
}
```

The `Failure` implementation would be

```
public Option<V> toOption() {
  return Option.none();
}
```

You could then use it as follows:

```
Option<String> result =
    getName().toOption().flatMap(toons::get).flatMap(Toon::getEmail);
```

Of course, this would require you to use the version of `Map` you defined in chapter 6 (listing 6.2) and a specific version of the `Toon` class:

```
public class Toon {
  private final String firstName;
  private final String lastName;
  private final Option<String> email;

  Toon(String firstName, String lastName) {
    this.firstName = firstName;
    this.lastName = lastName;
    this.email = Option.none();
  }

  Toon(String firstName, String lastName, String email) {
    this.firstName = firstName;
    this.lastName = lastName;
    this.email = Option.some(email);
  }

  public Option<String> getEmail() {
    return email;
  }
}
```

But you would have lost all the benefit of using `Result`! Now if an exception is thrown inside the `getName` method, it's still wrapped in a `Failure`, but the exception is lost in the `toOption` method, and the program simply prints

```
none
```

You may think you should go the other way and convert an `Option` into a `Result`. This would work (although, in your example, you should call the new `toResult` method on both `Option` instances returned by `Map.get` and `Toon.getMail`), but it would be tedious, and because you'll usually have to convert `Option` to `Result`, a much better way would be to cast this conversion into the `Result` class. All you have to do is create a new subclass corresponding to the `None` case, because the `Some` case doesn't need conversion, apart from changing its name for `Success`. Listing 7.6 shows the new `Result` class with the new subclass called `Empty`.

Listing 7.6   The new `Result` class handling errors and optional data

```java
public abstract class Result<V> implements Serializable {

  @SuppressWarnings("rawtypes")
  private static Result empty = new Empty();

    . . .

  private static class Empty<V> extends Result<V> {

    public Empty() {
      super();
    }

    @Override
    public V getOrElse(final V defaultValue) {
      return defaultValue;
    }

    @Override
    public <U> Result<U> map(Function<V, U> f) {
      return empty();
    }

    @Override
    public <U> Result<U> flatMap(Function<V, Result<U>> f) {
      return empty();
    }

    @Override
    public String toString() {
      return "Empty()";
    }

    @Override
    public V getOrElse(Supplier<V> defaultValue) {
      return defaultValue.get();
    }
  }

  private static class Failure<V> extends Empty<V> {

    private final RuntimeException exception;

    private Failure(String message) {
      super();
      this.exception = new IllegalStateException(message);
    }

    private Failure(RuntimeException e) {
      super();
      this.exception = e;
    }

    private Failure(Exception e) {
      super();
      this.exception = new IllegalStateException(e.getMessage(), e);
    }

    @Override
```

Like the None instance in Option, Result contains a singleton instance of Empty, which is a raw type.

The Failure class extends the Empty class in order not to redefine the getOrElse and OrElse methods that have the same implementations.

```
  public String toString() {
    return String.format("Failure(%s)", exception.getMessage());
  }

  @Override
  public <U> Result<U> map(Function<V, U> f) {
    return failure(exception);
  }

  @Override
  public <U> Result<U> flatMap(Function<V, Result<U>> f) {
    return failure(exception);
  }
}

. . .

  @SuppressWarnings("unchecked")
  public static <V> Result<V> empty() {
    return empty;
  }
}
```

The Failure class overrides the map and flatMap methods of Empty in order to use the contained exception.

Like the none method in Option, the empty method returns the Empty singleton.

Now you can again modify your ToonMail application, as shown in listings 7.7 through 7.9.

Listing 7.7   The Map class using the new Result.Empty class for optional data

```
public class Map<T, U> {

  private final ConcurrentMap<T, U> map = new ConcurrentHashMap<>();

  public static <T, U> Map<T, U> empty() {
    return new Map<>();
  }

  public static <T, U> Map<T, U> add(Map<T, U> m, T t, U u) {
    m.map.put(t, u);
    return m;
  }

  public Result<U> get(final T t) {
    return this.map.containsKey(t)
        ? Result.success(this.map.get(t))
        : Result.empty();
  }

  public Map<T, U> put(T t, U u) {
    return add(this, t, u);
  }

  public Map<T, U> removeKey(T t) {
    this.map.remove(t);
    return this;
  }
}
```

The get method now returns Result.empty() if the key isn't found in the map.

Listing 7.8   The `Toon` class using `Result.Empty` for optional data

```java
public class Toon {

  private final String firstName;
  private final String lastName;
  private final Result<String> email;

  Toon(String firstName, String lastName) {
    this.firstName = firstName;
    this.lastName = lastName;
    this.email = Result.empty();
  }

  Toon(String firstName, String lastName, String email) {
    this.firstName = firstName;
    this.lastName = lastName;
    this.email = Result.success(email);
  }

  public Result<String> getEmail() {
    return email;
  }
}
```

If you construct the instance without an email, the property is set to Result.empty().

Listing 7.9   The `ToonMail` application handling optional data correctly

```java
public class ToonMail {

  public static void main(String[] args) {
    Map<String, Toon> toons = new Map<String, Toon>()
        .put("Mickey", new Toon("Mickey", "Mouse", "mickey@disney.com"))
        .put("Minnie", new Toon("Minnie", "Mouse"))
        .put("Donald", new Toon("Donald", "Duck", "donald@disney.com"));
    Result<String> result =
            getName().flatMap(toons::get).flatMap(Toon::getEmail);
    System.out.println(result);
  }

  public static Result<String> getName() {
    return Result.success("Mickey");
    //return Result.failure(new IOException("Input error"));
    //return Result.success("Minnie");
    //return Result.success("Goofy");
  }
}
```

The methods are composed through flatMap as in listing 7.5.

The various implementations, to test all cases

Now your programs print the following results for each implementation of the get-
Name method (commented out in listing 7.9):

```
Success(mickey@disney.com)
Failure(Input error)
Empty()
Empty()
```

You may think that something is missing because you can't distinguish between the two different empty cases, but this isn't the case. Error messages aren't needed for optional data, so if you think you need a message, the data isn't optional. The success result is optional, but in that case a message is mandatory, so you should be using a `Failure`. This will create an exception, but nothing forces you to throw it!

7.5 *Advanced Result handling*

So far, you've seen a very limited use of `Result`. `Result` should never be used for directly accessing the wrapped value (if it exists). The way you used `Result` in the previous example corresponds to the simpler specific composition use case: get the result of one computation and use it for the input of the next computation. More specific use cases exist. You could choose to use the result only if it matches some predicate (which means some condition). You could also use the failure case, for which you'd need to map the failure to something else, or transform the failure into a success of exception (`Success<Exception>`). You might also need to use several `Result`s as the input for a single computation. You'd probably benefit from some helper methods that create `Result` from computations, in order to deal with legacy code. Finally, you'll sometimes need to apply effects to `Result`s.

7.5.1 *Applying predicates*

Applying a predicate to a `Result` is something that you'll often have to do. This is something that can easily be abstracted, so that you can write it only once.

EXERCISE 7.5

Write a method `filter` taking a condition that's represented by a function from `T` to `Boolean`, and returning a `Result<T>`, which will be a `Success` or a `Failure` depending on whether the condition holds for the wrapped value. The signature will be

```
filter(Function<T, Boolean> f);
```

Create a second method taking a condition as its first argument and a `String` as a second argument, and using the string argument for the potential `Failure` case.

HINT

Although it's possible to define abstract methods in the `Result` class and implement them in subclasses, try not to do so. Instead use one or more methods you've previously defined to create a single implementation in the `Result` class.

SOLUTION 7.5

You have to create a function that takes the wrapped value as a parameter, applies the function to it, and returns the same `Result` if the condition holds or `Empty` (or `Failure`) otherwise. Then all you have to do is `flatMap` this function:

```
public Result<T> filter(Function<T, Boolean> p) {
  return flatMap(x -> p.apply(x)
      ? this
      : failure("Condition not matched"));
}
```

```
public Result<T> filter(Function<T, Boolean> p, String message) {
  return flatMap(x -> p.apply(x)
      ? this
      : failure(message));
}
```

EXERCISE 7.6

Define an `exists` method that takes a function from `T` to `Boolean` and returns `true` if the wrapped value matches the condition, or `false` otherwise. Here's the method signature:

```
boolean exists(Function<T, Boolean> p);
```

HINT

Once again, try not to define an implementation in each subclass. Instead, create a single implementation in the parent class using the methods you have at your disposal.

SOLUTION 7.6

The solution is simply to `map` the function to `Result<T>`, giving a `Result<Boolean>`, and then to use `getOrElse` with `false` as the default value. You don't need to use a `Supplier` because the default value is a literal:

```
public boolean exists(Function<T, Boolean> p) {
  return map(p).getOrElse(false);
}
```

Using `exists` as the name of this method may seem questionable. But it's the same method that could be applied to a list, returning `true` if at least one element satisfies the condition, so it makes sense to use the same name. Some might argue that this implementation would also work for a `forAll` method that returns `true` if all elements in the list fulfill the condition. It's up to you either to choose another name or to define a `forAll` method in the `Result` class with the same implementation. The important point is understanding what makes `List` and `Result` similar and what makes them different.

7.5.2   Mapping failures

It's sometimes useful to change a `Failure` into a different one, as in the following example.

Listing 7.10   A memory monitor

```
package com.fpinjava.handlingerrors.listing07_10;

import com.fpinjava.common.List;
import com.fpinjava.common.Result;
import javax.management.Notification;
import javax.management.NotificationEmitter;
import javax.management.NotificationListener;
import java.lang.management.ManagementFactory;
import java.lang.management.MemoryNotificationInfo;
```

```java
import java.lang.management.MemoryPoolMXBean;

public class MemoryMonitor {

  public static void monitorMemory(double threshold) {
    findPSOldGenPool().forEachOrThrow(poolMxBean ->
            poolMxBean.setCollectionUsageThreshold((int) Math.floor(poolMxBean
                .getUsage().getMax() * threshold)));
    NotificationEmitter emitter = (NotificationEmitter) ManagementFactory.getM
      emoryMXBean();
    emitter.addNotificationListener(notificationListener, null, null);
  }

  private static NotificationListener notificationListener =
                        (Notification notification, Object handBack) -> {
    if (notification.getType().equals(MemoryNotificationInfo
                        .MEMORY_COLLECTION_THRESHOLD_EXCEEDED)) {
      // cleanly shutdown the application;
    }
  };

  private static Result<MemoryPoolMXBean> findPSOldGenPool() {
    return List.fromCollection(ManagementFactory.getMemoryPoolMXBeans())
            .first(x -> x.getName().equals("PS Old Gen"));
  }
}
```

The first method returns a Result. In the case of an error, it will be a Failure with a useless error message. This should be replaced with a meaningful message.

In multithreaded Java programs, an OutOfMemoryError (OOME) will often crash a thread but not the application, leaving it in an indeterminate state. To solve this problem, you have to catch the error and cleanly stop the application.

Catching an OOME is generally done with the help of an UncaughtException-Handler. This approach allows you to put the handler in a low-level library and to continue asking business developers not to catch OOMEs. But when an OOME is caught, there's sometimes not enough memory left to run the handler, leading to the application's erratic behavior. One way to solve this problem is to monitor memory with MemoryPoolMXBean. This solution allows you to register a notification handler that will be called automatically after garbage collection if it results in not enough memory being freed.

In the example, if you call the monitorMemory method with 0.8 as the parameter value, the notification listener will be called if more than 80% of the heap is still occupied immediately after a garbage collection. At this time, you hope to have enough memory left to cleanly log the problem and stop the application.

This program works fine (although the code is horrible, mostly due to how the Java library is written, with methods taking null as parameters, forcing you to cast the MemoryPoolMXBean into a NotificationEmitter, but that's another story).

Note that this program makes use of the first method on List, which you haven't defined yet. This method is very similar to the filter method, although it returns a Result, possibly wrapping the first element satisfying the condition.

Although the program works, you have a problem: if for any reason the find-PSOldGenPool method returns a Failure, whether because you misspelled "PS Old Gen" or because you're using a new version of Java in which the name has changed, you'll get the following error message in the Failure:

```
No element satisfying function com.fpinjava.handlingerrors
                               .listing07_10.MemoryMonitor$
$Lambda$3/1096979270@7b23ec81 in list
[sun.management.MemoryPoolImpl@3feba861,
sun.management.MemoryPoolImpl@5b480cf9,
sun.management.MemoryPoolImpl@6f496d9f,
sun.management.MemoryPoolImpl@723279cf,
sun.management.MemoryPoolImpl@10f87f48,
sun.management.MemoryPoolImpl@b4c966a, NIL]
```

EXERCISE 7.7

Define a mapFailure method that takes a String as its argument and transforms a Failure into another Failure using the string as its error message. If the Result is Empty or Success, this method should do nothing.

HINT

Define an abstract method in the parent class.

SOLUTION 7.7

Here's the abstract method in the parent class:

```
public abstract Result<T> mapFailure(String s);
```

The Empty and Success implementations just return this:

```
public Result<T> mapFailure(String s) {
  return this;
}
```

The Failure implementation wraps the existing exception into a new one created with the given message. It then creates a new Failure by calling the corresponding static factory method:

```
public Result<T> mapFailure(String s) {
  return failure(new IllegalStateException(s, exception));
}
```

You could choose RuntimeException as the exception type, or a more specific custom subtype of RuntimeException. Note that some other methods of the same kind might be useful, such as these:

```
public abstract Result<T> mapFailure(String s, Exception e);
public abstract Result<T> mapFailure(Exception e);
```

Another useful method would be one that maps an Empty to a Failure, given a String message.

7.5.3 *Adding factory methods*

You've seen how Success and Failure can be created from a value. Some other use cases are so frequent that they deserve to be abstracted into supplemental static factory methods. To adapt legacy libraries, you'll probably often create Result from a value that could possibly be null. To do this, you could use a static factory method with the following signatures:

```
public static <T> Result<T> of(T value)
public static <T> Result<T> of(T value, String message)
```

A method creating a Result from a function from T to Boolean and an instance of T might also be useful:

```
public static <T> Result<T> of(Function<T, Boolean> predicate, T value)
public static <T> Result<T> of(Function<T, Boolean> predicate,
                                        T value, String message)
```

EXERCISE 7.8
Define these static factory methods.

HINT
You have to make a choice about what to return in each case.

SOLUTION 7.8
There are no difficulties in this exercise. Here are possible implementations, based on the choice to return Empty when no error message is used, and a Failure otherwise:

```
public static <T> Result<T> of(T value) {
  return value != null
      ? success(value)
      : Result.failure("Null value");
}

public static <T> Result<T> of(T value, String message) {
  return value != null
      ? success(value)
      : failure(message);
}

public static <T> Result<T> of(Function<T, Boolean> predicate, T value) {
  try {
    return predicate.apply(value)
        ? success(value)
        : empty();
  } catch (Exception e) {
    String errMessage =
        String.format("Exception while evaluating predicate: %s", value);
    return Result.failure(new IllegalStateException(errMessage, e));
  }
}

public static <T> Result<T> of(Function<T, Boolean> predicate,
                               T value, String message) {
```

```
  try {
    return predicate.apply(value)
        ? Result.success(value)
        : Result.failure(String.format(message, value));
  } catch (Exception e) {
    String errMessage =
          String.format("Exception while evaluating predicate: %s",
                                String.format(message, value));
    return Result.failure(new IllegalStateException(errMessage, e));
  }
}
```

Note that you should handle the possibility that the message parameter may be `null`. Not doing so would throw an NPE, so a `null` message would be considered a bug. Instead, you could check the parameter and use a default value in the case of `null`. This is up to you. In any case, consistently checking parameters for `null` should be abstracted, as you'll see in chapter 15.

7.5.4   *Applying effects*

So far, you haven't applied any effects to values wrapped in `Result`, other than by getting these values (through `getOrElse`). This isn't satisfying because it destroys the advantage of using `Result`. On the other hand, you haven't yet learned the necessary techniques to apply effects functionally. Effects include anything that modifies something in the outside world, such as writing to the console, to a file, to a database, or to a field in a mutable component, or sending a message locally or over a network.

The technique I'll show you now isn't functional, but it is an interesting abstraction that allows you to use `Result` without knowing the functional techniques involved. You can use the technique shown here until we look at the functional versions, or you may even find that this is powerful enough to be used on a regular basis.

> **NOTE**   The technique discussed in this section is the approach taken by the functional constructs of Java 8, which isn't surprising, because Java isn't a functional programming language.

To apply an effect, use the `Effect` interface you developed in chapter 3. This is a very simple functional interface:

```
public interface Effect<T> {
  void apply(T t);
}
```

You could name this interface `Consumer` and define an `accept` method instead, as is the case in Java 8. I've already said that this name was very badly chosen, because a `Consumer` should have a consume method. But, in fact, a `Consumer` doesn't consume anything—after applying an effect to a value, the value is left unchanged and is still available for further computations or effects.

EXERCISE 7.9

Define a `forEach` method that takes an `Effect` as its parameter and applies it to the wrapped value.

HINT

Define an abstract method in the `Result` class with an implementation in each subclass.

SOLUTION 7.9

Here's the abstract method declaration in `Result`:

```
public abstract void forEach(Effect<T> ef)
```

The `Empty` and `Failure` implementations do nothing. As a result, you only need to implement the method in `Empty`, because `Failure` extends this class:

```
public void forEach(Effect<T> ef) {
  // Empty. Do nothing.
}
```

The `Success` implementation is straightforward. You just have to apply the effect to the value:

```
public void forEach(Effect<T> ef) {
  ef.apply(value);
}
```

This `forEach` method would be perfect for the `Option` class you created in chapter 6. But that's not the case for `Result`. Generally, you want to take special actions on a failure. One simple way to handle failure is to throw the exception.

EXERCISE 7.10

Define the `forEachOrThrow` method to handle this use case. Here's its signature in the Result class:

```
public abstract void forEachOrThrow(Effect<T> ef)
```

HINT

You have a choice to make for the `Empty` case.

SOLUTION 7.10

The `Success` implementation is identical to that of the `forEach` method. The `Failure` implementation just throws the wrapped exception:

```
public void forEachOrThrow(Effect<T> ef) {
  throw exception;
}
```

The `Empty` implementation is more of a problem. You can choose to do nothing, considering that `Empty` isn't an error. Or you can decide that calling `forEachOrThrow` means that you want to convert the absence of data into an error. This is a tough decision to make. Empty is not an error by itself. And if you need to make it an error, you can use one of the mapFailure methods, so it's probably better to implement forEachOrThrow in Empty as a do-nothing method.

EXERCISE 7.11

The more general use case when applying an effect to Result is applying the effect if it's a Success, and handling the exception in some way if it's a Failure. The forEachOrThrow method is fine for throwing, but sometimes you just want to log the error and continue. Rather than defining a method for logging, define a forEachOrException method that will apply an effect if a value is present and return a Result. This Result will be Empty if the original Result was a Success, or Empty and Success <RuntimeException> if it was a Failure.

SOLUTION 7.11

The method is declared as abstract in the Result parent class:

```
public abstract Result<RuntimeException> forEachOrException(Effect<T> ef)
```

The Empty implementation returns Empty:

```
public Result<RuntimeException> forEachOrException(Effect<T> ef) {
  return empty();
}
```

The Success implementation applies the effect to the wrapped value and returns Empty:

```
public Result<RuntimeException> forEachOrException(Effect<T> ef) {
  ef.apply(value);
  return empty();
}
```

The Failure implementation returns a Success<RuntimeException> holding the original exception, so that you can act on it:

```
public Result<RuntimeException> forEachOrException(Effect<T> ef) {
  return success(exception);
}
```

The typical use case for this method is as follows (using a hypothetical Logger type with a log method):

```
Result<Integer> result = getComputation();

result.forEachOrException(System.out::println).forEach(Logger::log);
```

Remember that these methods aren't functional, but they are a good and simple way to use Result. If you prefer to apply effects functionally, you'll have to wait until chapter 13.

7.5.5 *Advanced result composition*

Use cases for Result are more or less the same as for Option. In the previous chapter, you defined a lift method for composing Options by transforming a function from A to B into a function from Option<A> to Option<B>. You can do the same for Result.

EXERCISE 7.12

Write a lift method for Result. This will be a static method in the Result class with the following signature:

```
static <A, B> Function<Result<A>, Result<B>> lift(final Function<A, B> f)
```

SOLUTION 7.12

Here's the very simple solution:

```
public static <A, B> Function<Result<A>, Result<B>> lift(final Function<A,
                                                            B> f) {
  return x -> {
    try {
      return x.map(f);
    } catch (Exception e) {
      return failure(e);
    }
  };
}
```

EXERCISE 7.13

Define lift2 for lifting a function from A to B to C, and lift3 for functions from A to B to C to D, with the following signatures:

```
public static <A, B, C> Function<Result<A>, Function<Result<B>,
                        Result<C>>> lift2(Function<A, Function<B, C>> f)
public static <A, B, C, D> Function<Result<A>,
              Function<Result<B>, Function<Result<C>,
              Result<D>>>> lift3(Function<A, Function<B, Function<C, D>>> f)
```

SOLUTION 7.13

Here are the solutions:

```
public static <A, B, C> Function<Result<A>, Function<Result<B>,
                        Result<C>>> lift2(Function<A, Function<B, C>> f) {
  return a -> b -> a.map(f).flatMap(b::map);
}

public static <A, B, C, D> Function<Result<A>,
              Function<Result<B>, Function<Result<C>,
              Result<D>>>> lift3(Function<A, Function<B, Function<C, D>>> f) {
  return a -> b -> c -> a.map(f).flatMap(b::map).flatMap(c::map);
}
```

I guess you can see the pattern. You could define lift for any number of parameters that way.

EXERCISE 7.14

In chapter 6, you defined a `map2` method, taking as its arguments an `Option<A>`, an `Option<B>`, and a function from A to B to C, and returning an `Option<C>`. Define a `map2` method for `Result`.

HINT

Don't use the method you defined for `Option`. Instead, use the `lift2` method.

SOLUTION 7.14

The solution defined for `Option` was

```
<A, B, C> Option<C> map2(Option<A> a,
                         Option<B> b,
                         Function<A, Function<B, C>> f) {
  return a.flatMap(ax -> b.map(bx -> f.apply(ax).apply(bx)));
}
```

This is the same pattern you used for `lift2`. So the `map2` method will look like this:

```
public static <A, B, C> Result<C> map2(Result<A> a,
                                        Result<B> b,
                                        Function<A, Function<B, C>> f) {
  return lift2(f).apply(a).apply(b);
}
```

A common use case for such functions is calling methods or constructors with arguments of type `Result` returned by other functions or methods. Take the previous `ToonMail` example. To populate the `Toon` map, you could construct toons by asking the user to input the first name, last name, and mail on the console, using the following methods:

```
static Result<String> getFirstName() {
  return success("Mickey");
}

static Result<String> getLastName() {
  return success("Mickey");
}

static Result<String> getMail() {
  return success("mickey@disney.com");
}
```

The real implementation will be different, but you still have to learn how to functionally get input from the console. For now, you'll use these mock implementations.

Using these implementations, you could create a `Toon` as follows:

```
Function<String, Function<String, Function<String, Toon>>> createPerson =
                                  x -> y -> z -> new Toon(x, y, z);
Result<Toon> toon2 = lift3(createPerson)
    .apply(getFirstName())
    .apply(getLastName())
    .apply(getMail());
```

But you're reaching the limits of abstraction. You might have to call methods or constructors with more than three arguments. In such a case, you could use the following pattern:

```
Result<Toon> toon = getFirstName()
        .flatMap(firstName -> getLastName()
            .flatMap(lastName -> getMail()
                .map(mail -> new Toon(firstName, lastName, mail))));
```

This pattern has two advantages:

- You can use any number of arguments.
- You don't need to define a function.

Note that you could use lift3 without defining the function separately, but you'd have to specify the types because of the poor type inference capacities of Java:

```
Result<Toon> toon2 =
        lift3((String x) -> (String y) -> (String z) -> new Toon(x, y, z))
            .apply(getFirstName())
            .apply(getLastName())
            .apply(getMail());
```

Your new pattern is sometimes called *comprehension*. Some languages have syntactic sugar for such constructs, roughly equivalent to this:

```
for {
  firstName in getFirstName(),
  lastName in getLastName(),
  mail in getMain()
} return new Toon(firstName, lastName, mail)
```

Java doesn't have this kind of syntactic sugar, but it's easy to do without it. Just notice that the calls to flatMap or map are nested. Start with a call to the first method (or start from a Result instance), flatMap each new call, and end by mapping the call to the constructor or method you intend to use. For example, to call a method taking five parameters when you only have five Result instances, use the following approach:

```
Result<Integer> result1 = success(1);
  Result<Integer> result2 = success(2);
  Result<Integer> result3 = success(3);
  Result<Integer> result4 = success(4);
  Result<Integer> result5 = success(5);

  Result<Integer> result = result1
      .flatMap(p1 -> result2
          .flatMap(p2 -> result3
              .flatMap(p3 -> result4
                  .flatMap(p4 -> result5
                      .map(p5 -> compute(p1, p2, p3, p4, p5))))));
  private int compute(int p1, int p2, int p3, int p4, int p5) {
    return p1 + p2 + p3 + p4 + p5;
  }
```

This example is a bit contrived, but it shows you how the pattern can be extended. The fact that the last call (the most deeply nested) is to `map` instead of `flatMap`, however, is not inherent to the pattern. That's only because the last method (`compute`) returns a raw value. If it returned a `Result`, you'd have to use `flatMap` instead of `map`. But because this last method is often a constructor, and constructors always return raw values, you'll often find yourself using `map` as the last method call.

7.6   *Summary*

- Representing the absence of data due to an error is necessary. The `Option` type doesn't allow this.
- The `Either` type allows you to represent data of either one type (`Right`) or another (`Left`).
- `Either` can be mapped or flat-mapped like `Option`, but it can be on both sides (right or left).
- `Either` can be biased by making one side (`Left`) always represent the same type (`RuntimeException`). You call this biased `Either` type `Result`. Success is represented by a `Success` subtype and failure by a `Failure` subtype.
- One way to use the `Result` type is to get the wrapped value if it's present or to use a provided default type otherwise.
- The default type, if not a literal, must be lazily evaluated.
- Composing `Option` (representing optional data) with `Result` (representing data or an error) is tedious. This use case is made easier by adding an `Empty` subtype to `Result`, making the `Option` type useless.
- Failures can be mapped if needed, such as to make error messages more explicit.
- Several static factory methods simplify `Result` creation from various situations like using nullable data, or conditional data, which is represented by data and a condition that must be fulfilled.
- Effects can be applied to `Result` (although in a nonfunctional way) through the `forEach` method.
- The `forEachOrThrow` method handles the specific cases where an effect must be applied if data is present or an exception thrown otherwise.
- The `forEach` and `forEachOrThrow` methods are specific cases of the more general `forEachOrException`. This method applies an effect (if a value is present) and returns either `Empty` (if the effect could be applied) or `Success<RuntimeException>` (if data was missing).
- You can lift functions from A to B (using the `lift` method) to operate from `Result<A>` to `Result<B>`. You can lift functions from A to B to C (through the `lift2` method) to a function from `Result<A>` to `Result<B>` to `Result<C>`.
- You can use the comprehension pattern to compose any number of `Result`s.

Advanced list handling

This chapter covers
- Speeding list processing with memoization
- Composing `List` and `Result`
- Implementing indexed access on lists
- Unfolding lists
- Automatic parallel list processing

In chapter 5, you created your first data structure, the singly linked list. At that point, you didn't have at your disposal all the techniques needed to make it a complete tool for data handling. One particularly useful tool you were missing was some way to represent operations producing optional data, or operations that can produce an error. In chapters 6 and 7, you learned how to represent optional data and errors. In this chapter, you'll learn how to compose operations that produce optional data or errors with lists.

You also developed some functions that were far from optimal, such as `length`, and I said that you'd eventually learn more-efficient techniques for these operations. In this chapter, you'll learn how to implement these techniques. You'll also learn how to automatically parallelize some list operations in order to benefit from the multicore architecture of today's computers.

8.1   *The problem with length*

Folding a list involves starting with a value and composing it successively with each element of the list. This obviously takes an amount of time proportional to the length of the list. Is there any way to make this operation faster? Or, at least, is there a way to make it appear faster?

As an example of a fold application, you created a `length` method in `List` in exercise 5.9 with the following implementation:

```
public int length() {
  return foldRight(this, 0, x -> y -> y + 1);
}
```

In this implementation, the list is folded using an operation that consists of adding 1 to the result. The starting value is `0`, and the value of each element of the list is simply ignored. This is what allows you to use the same definition for all lists. Because the list elements are ignored, the list element's type is irrelevant.

You can compare the preceding operation with one that computes the sum of a list of integers:

```
public static Integer sum(List<Integer> list) {
  return list.foldRight(0, x -> y -> x + y);
}
```

The main difference here is that the `sum` method can only work with integers, whereas the `length` method works for any type. Notice that `foldRight` is only a way to abstract recursion. The length of a list can be defined as 0 for an empty list and 1 plus the length of the tail for a non-empty list. In the same way, the sum of a list of integers can be defined recursively as 0 for an empty list, and head plus the sum of the tail for a non-empty one.

There are other operations that can be applied to lists in this way, and, among them, several for which the type of the list elements is irrelevant:

- The hash code of a list can be computed by simply adding the hash codes of its elements. Because the hash code is an integer (at least for Java objects), this operation doesn't depend on the object's type.
- The string representation of a list, as returned by the `toString` method, can be computed by composing the `toString` representation of the list elements. Once again, the actual type of the elements is irrelevant.

Some operations may depend on some characteristics of the element's type, but not on the specific type itself. For example, a `max` method that returns the maximum element of a list will only need the type to be `Comparable` or a `Comparator`.

8.1.1   *The performance problem*

All these methods can be implemented using a fold, but such implementations have a major drawback: the time needed to compute the result is proportional to the length of the list. Imagine you have a list of about a million elements, and you want to check the length. Counting the elements may seem the only way to go (this is what the fold-based `length` method does). But if you were adding elements to the list until it reaches a million, you surely wouldn't count the elements after adding each one.

In such a situation, you'd keep a count of the elements somewhere, and add one to this count each time you added an element to the list. Maybe you'd have to count once if you were starting with a non-empty list, but that's it. This technique is what you learned in chapter 4: memoization. The question is, where can you store the memoized value? The answer is obvious: in the list itself.

8.1.2 The benefit of memoization

Maintaining a count of the elements in a list will take some time, so adding an element to a list will be slightly slower than if you didn't keep the count. It might look like you're trading time against time. If you build a list of 1,000,000 elements, you'll lose 1,000,000 times the amount of time needed to add one to the count. In compensation, however, the time needed to get the length of the list will be near 0 (and obviously constant). Maybe the total time lost in incrementing the count will equal the gain when calling `length`. But as soon as you call `length` more than once, the gain is absolutely obvious.

8.1.3 The drawbacks of memoization

Memoization can turn a function that works in $O(n)$ time (time proportional to the number of elements) into $O(1)$ time (constant time). This is a huge benefit, although it has a time cost, because it makes the insertion of elements slightly slower. But slowing insertion is generally not a big problem.

A much more important problem is the increase in memory space. Data structures implementing in-place mutation don't have this problem. In a mutable list, nothing keeps you from memoizing the list length as a mutable integer, which takes only 32 bits. But with an immutable list, you have to memoize the length in each element. It's difficult to know the exact increase in size, but if the size of a singly linked list is around 40 bytes per node (for the nodes themselves), plus two 32-bit references for the head and the tail (on a 32-bit JVM), this would result in about 100 bytes per element. In this case, adding the length would cause an increase of slightly over 30%. The result would be the same if the memoized values were references, such as memoizing the `max` or `min` of a list of `Comparable` objects. On a 64-bit JVM, it's even more difficult to calculate due to some optimization in the size of the references, but you get the idea.

> **SIZES OF OBJECT REFERENCES** For more information about the size of object references in Java 7 and Java 8, see Oracle's documentation on compressed oops (http://mng.bz/TjY9) and JVM performance enhancements (http://mng.bz/8X0o).

It's up to you to decide whether you want to use memoization in your data structures. It may be a valid option for functions that are often called and don't create new objects for their results. For example, the `length` and `hashCode` functions return integers, and the `max` and `min` functions return references to already existing objects, so they may be good candidates. On the other hand, the `toString` function creates new strings that would have to be memoized, so that would probably be a huge waste of memory space. The other factor to take into consideration is how often the function is used. The `length` function may be used more often than `hashCode`, because using lists as map keys is not a common practice.

EXERCISE 8.1

Create a memoized version of the `length` method. Its signature in the `List` class will be

```
public abstract int lengthMemoized();
```

SOLUTION 8.1

The implementation in the `Nil` class is exactly the same as for the nonmemoized `length` method:

```
public int lengthMemoized() {
  return 0;
}
```

To implement the `Cons` version, you must first add the memoizing field to the class and initialize it in the constructor:

```
private final int length;
private Cons(A head, List<A> tail) {
  this.head = head;
  this.tail = tail;
  this.length = tail.length() + 1;
}
```

Then you can implement the `lengthMemoized` method to simply return the length:

```
public int lengthMemoized() {
  return length;
}
```

This version will be much faster than the original one. One interesting thing to note is the relationship between the `length` and `isEmpty` methods. You might tend to think that `isEmpty` is equivalent to `length == 0`, but although this is true from the logical point of view, there can be a huge difference in implementation, and thus in performance.

Note that memoizing the maximum or minimum value in a list of `Comparable` could be done the same way (although with a static method), but it wouldn't help in the case where you want to remove the max or min value from the list. Min or max elements are often accessed to retrieve elements by priority. In that case, the elements' `compareTo` method would compare their priorities. Memoizing priority would let you know immediately which element has the maximum priority, but it wouldn't help much because what you often need is to remove the corresponding element. For such use cases, you'll need a different data structure, which you'll learn to create in chapter 11.

8.1.4 *Actual performance*

As I said, it's up to you to decide if you should memoize some functions of the `List` class. A few experiments should help you make your decision. Measuring the available memory size just before and after the creation of a list of 1,000,000 integers shows a very small increase when using memoization. Although this measurement method isn't very precise, the average decrease in available memory is about 22 MB in both cases (with or without memoization), varying between 20 MB and 25 MB. This shows that the theoretical increase of 4 MB (1,000,000 x 4 bytes) isn't as significant as you'd expected. On the other hand, the increase in performance is huge. Asking for the length ten times might cost more than 200 milliseconds without memoization. With memoization, the time is 0 (too short a time to be measured in milliseconds).

Note that although adding an element increases the cost (adding one to the tail length and storing the result), removing an element has zero cost, because the tail length is already memoized.

Another way to go, if memoization isn't desirable, is to optimize the `length` method. Instead of using a fold, you can resort to imperative style, with a loop and a local mutable variable. Here's the `length` implementation borrowed from the Scala `List` class:

```
public int length() {
  List<A> these = this;
  int len = 0;
  while (!these.isEmpty()) {
    len += 1;
    these = these.tail();
  }
  return len;
}
```

Although it doesn't look very functional in style, this implementation is perfectly compatible with the definition of functional programming. It's a pure function without any observable effect from the outside world. The main problem is that it's only five times faster than the fold-based implementation, where the memoized implementation can be millions of times faster for very large lists.

8.2 *Composing List and Result*

In the previous chapter, you saw that `Result` and `List` are very similar data structures, mainly differing in their cardinality but sharing some of their most important methods, such as `map`, `flatMap`, and even `foldLeft` and `foldRight`.

You saw how lists could be composed with lists, and results with results. Now, you're going to see how results can be composed with lists.

8.2.1   *Methods on List returning Result*

At this point, you've noticed that I try to avoid accessing the elements of results and lists directly. Accessing the head or the tail of a list will throw an exception if the list is Nil, and throwing an exception is one of the worst things that can happen in functional programming. But you saw that you could safely access the value in a Result by providing a default value to be used in the case of a failure or empty result. Can you do the same when accessing the head of a list? Not exactly, but you can return a Result.

EXERCISE 8.2

Implement a headOption method in List<A> that will return a Result<A>.

HINT

Use the following abstract method declaration in List, and implement it in each subclass:

```
public abstract Result<A> headOption();
```

Note that the method is called headOption to indicate that a value is optional, although you'll use Result for the type.

SOLUTION 8.2

The implementation of the Nil class returns Empty:

```
public Result<A> headOption() {
  return Result.empty();
}
```

The Cons implementation returns a Success holding the head value:

```
public Result<A> headOption() {
  return Result.success(head);
}
```

EXERCISE 8.3

Create a lastOption method returning a Result of the last element in the list.

HINT

Don't use explicit recursion, but try to build on the methods you developed in chapter 5. You should be able to define a single method in the List class.

SOLUTION 8.3

A trivial solution is to use explicit recursion:

```
public Result<A> lastOption() {
  return isEmpty()
      ? Result.empty()
      : tail().isEmpty()
          ? Result.success(head())
          : tail().lastOption();
}
```

This solution has several problems. It's stack-based recursive, so you should transform it to make it heap-based, plus you have to handle the case of the empty list, where `tail().lastOption()` would throw an NPE.

But you can simply use a fold, which abstracts recursion for you! All you need to do is create the right function for folding. You need to always keep the last value if it exists. This might be the function to use:

```
Function<Result<A>, Function<A, Result<A>>> f =
                              x -> y -> Result.success(y);
```

Or use a method reference:

```
Function<Result<A>, Function<A, Result<A>>> f =
                              x -> Result::success;
```

Then you just have to `foldLeft` the list using `Result.Empty` as the identity:

```
public Result<A> lastOption() {
  return foldLeft(Result.empty(), x -> Result::success);
}
```

EXERCISE 8.4

Can you replace the `headOption` method with a single implementation in the `List` class? What would be the benefits and drawbacks of such an implementation?

SOLUTION 8.4

It's possible to create such an implementation:

```
public Result<A> headOption() {
  return foldRight(Result.empty(), x -> y -> Result.success(x));
}
```

The only benefit is that it's more fun if you like it that way. When devising the `last-Option` implementation, you knew you had to traverse the list in order to find the last element. To find the first element, you don't need to traverse the list. Using `fold-Right` here is exactly the same as reversing the list and then traversing the result to find the last element (which is the first element of the original list). Not very efficient! And by the way, this is exactly what the `lastOption` method does to find the last element: reverses the list and takes the first element of the result. So except for the fun, there's really no reason to use this implementation.

8.2.2   *Converting from List<Result> to Result<List>*

When a list contains the results of some computations, it will often be a `List<Result>`. For example, mapping a function from `T` to `Result<U>` on a list of `T` will produce a list of `Result<U>`. Such values will often have to be composed with functions taking a `List<T>` as their argument. This means you'll need a way to convert the resulting `List<Result<U>>` into a `List<U>`, which is the same kind of flattening involved in the flatMap method, with the huge difference that two different data types are involved: List and Result. You can apply several strategies to this conversion:

- Throw away all failures or empty results and produce a list of U from the remaining list of successes. If there's no success in the list, the result could simply contain an empty List.
- Throw away all failures or empty results and produce a list of U from the remaining list of successes. If there's no success in the list, the result would be a Failure.
- Decide that all elements must be successes for the whole operation to succeed. Construct a list of U with the values if all are successes and return it as a Success <List<U>>, or return a Failure<List<U>> otherwise.

The first solution would correspond to a list of results where all results are optional. The second solution means that there should be at least one success in the list for the result to be a success. The third solution corresponds to the case where all results are mandatory.

EXERCISE 8.5

Write a method called flattenResult that takes a List<Result<A>> as its argument and returns a List<A> containing all the success values in the original list, ignoring the failures and empty values. This will be a static method in List with the following signature:

```
public static <A> List<A> flattenResult(List<Result<A>> list)
```

Try not to use explicit recursion but to compose methods from the List and Result classes.

HINT

The name chosen for the method is an indication of what you have to do.

SOLUTION 8.5

To solve this exercise, you can use the foldRight method to fold the list with a function producing a list of lists. Each Success will be transformed into a list of one element containing the value, whereas each Failure or Empty will be transformed into an empty list. Here's the function:

```
Function<Result<A>, Function<List<List<A>>, List<List<A>>>> f =
                    x -> y -> y.cons(x.map(List::list).getOrElse(list()));
```

Once you have this function, you can use it to fold the list to the right, producing a list of lists of values, with some elements being empty lists:

```
list.foldRight(list(), f)
```

All that's left to do is to flatten the result. The complete method is as follows:

```
public static <A> List<A> flattenResult(List<Result<A>> list) {
```

```
    return flatten(list.foldRight(list(), x -> y ->
                  y.cons(x.map(List::list).getOrElse(list()))));
}
```

Please note that this is not the most efficient way to do it. Take this mostly as an exercise.

EXERCISE 8.6

Write a sequence function that combines a List<Result<T>> into a Result<List<T>>. It will be a Success<List<T>> if all values in the original list were Success instances, or a Failure<List<T>> otherwise. Here's its signature:

```
public static <A> Result<List<A>> sequence(List<Result<A>> list)
```

HINT

Once again, use the foldRight method and not explicit recursion. You'll also need the map2 method you defined in the Result class.

SOLUTION 8.6

Here's the implementation using foldRight and map2:

```
public static <A> Result<List<A>> sequence(List<Result<A>> list) {
  return list.foldRight(Result.success(List.list()),
                  x -> y -> Result.map2(x, y, a -> b -> b.cons(a)));
}
```

Note that this implementation handles an empty Result as if it were a Failure and returns the first failing case it encounters, which can be a Failure or an Empty. This may or may not be what you need. To stick with the idea that Empty means optional data, you'd need to first filter the list to remove the Empty elements:

```
public static <A> Result<List<A>> sequence2(List<Result<A>> list) {
  return list.filter(a -> a.isSuccess() || a.isFailure())
      .foldRight(Result.success(List.list()),
                  x -> y -> Result.map2(x, y, a -> b -> b.cons(a)));
}
```

Ultimately you should abstract the removal of empty elements into a separate method in the List class. But for the rest of this book, we'll continue considering Empty as a Failure in the context of the sequence method.

EXERCISE 8.7

Define a more generic traverse method that traverses a list of A while applying a function from A to Result<B> and producing a Result<List<B>>. Here's its signature:

```
public static <A, B> Result<List<B>> traverse(List<A> list,
                                  Function<A, Result<B>> f)
```

Then define a new version of sequence in terms of traverse.

HINT

Don't use recursion. Prefer the foldRight method, which abstracts recursion for you.

SOLUTION 8.7

First define the traverse method:

```
public static <A, B> Result<List<B>> traverse(List<A> list,
                                        Function<A, Result<B>> f) {
  return list.foldRight(Result.success(List.list()),
      x -> y -> Result.map2(f.apply(x), y, a -> b -> b.cons(a)));
}
```

Then you can redefine the sequence method in terms of traverse:

```
public static <A> Result<List<A>> sequence(List<Result<A>> list) {
  return traverse(list, x -> x);
}
```

8.3   *Abstracting common List use cases*

Many common use cases of the List data type deserve to be abstracted so you don't have to repeat the same code again and again. You'll regularly find yourself discovering new use cases that can be implemented by combining basic functions. You should never hesitate to incorporate these use cases as new functions in the List class. The following exercises show several of the most common use cases.

8.3.1   *Zipping and unzipping lists*

Zipping is the process of assembling two lists into one by combining the elements of the same index. Unzipping is the reverse procedure, consisting of making two lists out of one by "deconstructing" the elements, such as producing two lists of x and y coordinates from one list of points.

EXERCISE 8.8

Write a zipWith method that combines the elements of two lists of different types to produce a new list, given a function argument. Here's the signature:

```
public static <A, B, C> List<C> zipWith(List<A> list1, List<B> list2,
                                  Function<A, Function<B, C>> f)
```

This method takes a List<A> and a List<B> and produces a List<C> with the help of a function from A to B to C.

HINT

The zipping should be limited to the length of the shortest list.

SOLUTION 8.8

For this exercise, you must use explicit recursion because recursion must be done on both lists simultaneously. You don't have any abstraction at your disposal for this. Here's the solution:

```
public static <A, B, C> List<C> zipWith(List<A> list1, List<B> list2,
                                  Function<A, Function<B, C>> f) {
  return zipWith_(list(), list1, list2, f).eval().reverse();
}
```

```
private static <A, B, C> TailCall<List<C>> zipWith_(List<C> acc,
        List<A> list1, List<B> list2, Function<A, Function<B, C>> f) {
  return list1.isEmpty() || list2.isEmpty()
      ? ret(acc)
      : sus(() -> zipWith_(
          new Cons<>(f.apply(list1.head()).apply(list2.head()), acc),
          list1.tail(), list2.tail(), f));
}
```

The `zipWith_` helper method is called with an empty list as the starting accumulator. If one of the two argument lists is empty, recursion is stopped and the current accumulator is returned. Otherwise, a new value is computed by applying the function to the head value of both lists, and the helper function is called recursively with the tails of both argument lists.

EXERCISE 8.9

The previous exercise consisted of creating a list by matching elements of both lists by their indexes. Write a `product` method that will produce a list of all possible combinations of elements taken from both lists. In other words, given the two lists `list("a", "b", "c")` and `list("d", "e", "f")` and string concatenation, the product of the two lists should be `List("ad", "ae", "af", "bd", "be", "bf", "cd", "ce", "cf")`.

HINT

For this exercise, you don't need to use explicit recursion.

SOLUTION 8.9

The solution is similar to the comprehension pattern you used to compose `Result` in chapter 7. The only difference here is that it produces as many combinations as the product of the number of elements in the lists, whereas for combining `Result`, the number of combinations was always limited to one.

```
public static <A, B, C> List<C> product(List<A> list1, List<B> list2,
                                Function<A, Function<B, C>> f) {
  return list1.flatMap(a -> list2.map(b -> f.apply(a).apply(b)));
}
```

Note that it's possible to compose more than two lists this way. The only problem is that the number of combinations will grow exponentially.

One of the common use cases for `product` and `zipWith` is to use a constructor for the combination function. Here's an example using the `Tuple` constructor:

```
List.product(List.list(1, 2, 3), List.list(4, 5, 6),
                                x -> y -> new Tuple<>(x, y));
List.zipWith(List.list(1, 2, 3), List.list(4, 5, 6),
                                x -> y -> new Tuple<>(x, y));
```

The first line will produce a list of all possible tuples constructed from the elements of both lists:

```
[(1,4), (1,5), (1,6), (2,4), (2,5), (2,6), (3,4), (3,5), (3,6), NIL]
```

The second line will only produce the list of tuples built from elements with the same index:

```
[(1,4), (2,5), (3,6), NIL]
```

Of course, you may use any constructor of any class. (Java objects are in fact tuples with special names.)

EXERCISE 8.10

Write an `unzip` static method to transform a list of tuples into a tuple of lists. Here's its signature:

```
<A, B> Tuple<List<A>, List<B>> unzip(List<Tuple<A, B>> list)
```

HINT

Don't use explicit recursion. A simple call to `foldRight` should do the job.

SOLUTION 8.10

You need to `foldRight` the list using a tuple of two empty lists as the identity:

```
public static <A,B> Tuple<List<A>, List<B>> unzip(List<Tuple<A, B>> list) {
  return list.foldRight(new Tuple<>(list(), list()),
              t -> tl -> new Tuple<>(tl._1.cons(t._1), tl._2.cons(t._2)));
}
```

EXERCISE 8.11

Generalize the `unzip` function so it can transform a list of any type into a tuple of lists, given a function that takes an object of the list type as its argument, and produces a tuple. For example, given a list of `Payment` instances, you should be able to produce a tuple of lists: one containing the credit cards used to make the payments, and the other containing payment amounts. Implement this method as an instance method in `List` with the following signature:

```
<A1, A2> Tuple<List<A1>, List<A2>> unzip(Function<A, Tuple<A1, A2>> f)
```

HINT

The solution is pretty much the same as for exercise 8.10.

SOLUTION 8.11

One important thing is that the result of the function is to be used twice. In order not to apply the function twice, you must use a multiline lambda:

```
public <A1, A2> Tuple<List<A1>, List<A2>> unzip(Function<A,
                                        Tuple<A1, A2>> f) {
  return this.foldRight(new Tuple<>(list(), list()), a -> tl -> {
    Tuple<A1, A2> t = f.apply(a);
    return new Tuple<>(tl._1.cons(t._1), tl._2.cons(t._2));
  });
}
```

8.3.2 *Accessing elements by their index*

The singly linked list isn't the best structure for indexed access to its elements, but sometimes it's necessary to use indexed access. As usual, you should abstract such a procedure into List methods.

EXERCISE 8.12

Write a getAt method that takes an index as its argument and returns the corresponding element. The method should not throw an exception in the case of the index being out of bounds.

HINT

This time, start with an explicitly recursive version. Then try to answer the following questions:

- Is it possible to do it with a fold? Right or left?
- Why is the explicit recursive version better?
- Can you see a way to solve the problem?

SOLUTION 8.12

The explicitly recursive solution is easy:

```
public Result<A> getAt(int index) {
  return index < 0 || index >= length()
      ? Result.failure("Index out of bound")
      : getAt_(this, index).eval();
}

private static <A> TailCall<Result<A>> getAt_(List<A> list, int index) {
    return index == 0
              ? TailCall.ret(Result.success(list.head()))
              : TailCall.sus(() -> getAt_(list.tail(), index - 1));
}
```

First, you can check the index to see if it's positive and less than the list length. If it isn't, just return a Failure. Otherwise, call the helper method to process the list recursively. This method checks whether the index is 0. If it is, it returns the head of the list. Otherwise, it calls itself recursively on the tail of the list with a decremented index.

This looks like the best possible recursive solution. Is it possible to use a fold? Yes, it is, and it should be a left fold. But the solution is tricky:

```
public Result<A> getAt(int index) {
  Tuple<Result<A>, Integer> identity =
              new Tuple<>(Result.failure("Index out of bound"), index);

  Tuple<Result<A>, Integer> rt = index < 0 || index >= length()
      ? identity
      : foldLeft(identity, ta -> a -> ta._2 < 0
          ? ta
          : new Tuple<>(Result.success(a), ta._2 - 1));
  return rt._1;
}
```

First you have to define the identity value. Because this value must hold both the result and the index, it will be a `Tuple` holding the `Failure` case. Then you can check the index for validity. If it's found invalid, make the temporary result (`rt`) equal to `identity`. Otherwise, fold to the left with a function returning either the already computed result (`ta`) if the index is less than 0, or a new `Success` otherwise.

This solution might seem smarter, but it's not, for three reasons:

- It's far less legible. This may be subjective, so it's up to you to decide.
- You have to use an intermediate result (`rt`) because Java can't infer the right type. Try replacing `rt` with its value in the last line if you don't believe me.
- It's less efficient because it will continue folding the whole list even after it finds the searched-for value.

EXERCISE 8.13 (HARD AND OPTIONAL)

Find a solution that makes the fold-based version terminate as soon as the result is found.

HINT

You'll need a special version of `foldLeft` for this, and also a special version of `Tuple`.

SOLUTION 8.13

First, you need a special version of `foldLeft` in which you can escape the fold when the absorbing element (or "zero" element) of the folding operation is found. Think of a list of integers that you want to fold by multiplying them. The absorbing element for the multiplication is 0. Here's the declaration of a short-circuiting (or escaping) version of `foldLeft` in the `List` class:

```
public abstract <B> B foldLeft(B identity, B zero,
                                    Function<B, Function<A, B>> f);
```

THE ZERO ELEMENT   It's by analogy that the absorbing element of any operation is sometimes called "zero," but remember that it's not always equal to 0. The 0 value is only the absorbing element for multiplication. For the addition of positive integers, it would be infinity.

And here's the `Cons` implementation:

```
@Override
public <B> B foldLeft(B identity, B zero, Function<B, Function<A, B>> f) {
  return foldLeft(identity, zero, this, f).eval();
}

private <B> TailCall<B> foldLeft(B acc, B zero, List<A> list,
                                    Function<B, Function<A, B>> f) {
  return list.isEmpty() || acc.equals(zero)
      ? ret(acc)
      : sus(() -> foldLeft(f.apply(acc).apply(list.head()),
                                    zero, list.tail(), f));
}
```

As you can see, the only difference is that if the accumulator value is found to be "zero," recursion is stopped and the accumulator is returned.

Now you need a zero value for your fold. The zero value is a `Tuple<Result<A, Integer>` with the `Integer` value equal to `-1` (the first value smaller than 0). Can you use a standard `Tuple` for this? No, you can't, because it must have a special equals method, returning `true` when the integer values are equal, whatever the `Result<A>` is. The complete method is as follows:

```
public Result<A> getAt(int index) {

  class Tuple<T, U> {

    public final T _1;
    public final U _2;

    public Tuple(T t, U u) {
      this._1 = Objects.requireNonNull(t);
      this._2 = Objects.requireNonNull(u);
    }

    @Override
    public boolean equals(Object o) {
      if (!(o.getClass() == this.getClass()))
        return false;
      else {
        @SuppressWarnings("rawtypes")
        Tuple that = (Tuple) o;
        return _2.equals(that._2);
      }
    }
  }

  Tuple<Result<A>, Integer> zero =
              new Tuple<>(Result.failure("Index out of bound"), -1);
  Tuple<Result<A>, Integer> identity =
              new Tuple<>(Result.failure("Index out of bound"), index);
  Tuple<Result<A>, Integer> rt = index < 0 || index >= length()
      ? identity
      : foldLeft(identity, zero, ta -> a -> ta._2 < 0
                  ? ta
                  : new Tuple<>(Result.success(a), ta._2 - 1));
  return rt._1;
}
```

Note that I've omitted the `hashCode` and `toString` methods to make the code shorter.

Now the fold will automatically stop as soon as the searched-for element is found. Of course, you can use the new `foldLeft` method for escaping any computation with a zero element. (Remember: zero, not 0.)

8.3.3 Splitting lists

Sometimes you need to split a list into two parts at a specific position. Although the singly linked list is far from ideal for this kind of operation, it's relatively simple to implement. Splitting a list has several useful applications, among which is processing its parts in parallel using several threads.

EXERCISE 8.14

Write a `splitAt` method that takes an `int` as its parameter and returns two lists by splitting the list at the given position. There shouldn't be any `IndexOutOfBound-Exceptions`. Instead, an index below 0 should be treated as 0, and an index above max should be treated as the maximum value for the index.

HINT

Make the method explicitly recursive.

SOLUTION

An explicitly recursive solution is easy to design:

```
public Tuple<List<A>, List<A>> splitAt(int index) {
  return index < 0
      ? splitAt(0)
      : index > length()
          ? splitAt(length())
          : splitAt(list(), this.reverse(), this.length() - index).eval();
}

private TailCall<Tuple<List<A>, List<A>>> splitAt(List<A> acc,
                                                 List<A> list, int i) {
  return i == 0 || list.isEmpty()
      ? ret(new Tuple<>(list.reverse(), acc))
      : sus(() -> splitAt(acc.cons(list.head()), list.tail(), i - 1));
}
```

Note that the first method uses recursion to adjust the value of the index. There's no need for using `TailCall`, however, because this method will recurse at most once. The second method is very similar to the `getAt` method, with the difference that the list is first reversed. The method accumulates the elements until the index position is reached, so the accumulated list is in the correct order, but the remaining list has to be reversed back.

EXERCISE 8.15 (NOT SO HARD IF YOU'VE DONE EXERCISE 8.13)

Can you think of an implementation using a fold instead of explicit recursion?

HINT

An implementation traversing the whole list is easy. An implementation traversing the list only until the index is found is much more difficult and will need a new special version of `foldLeft` with escape, returning both the escaped value and the rest of the list.

SOLUTION 8.15

A solution traversing the whole list could be as follows:

```
public Tuple<List<A>, List<A>> splitAt(int index) {
  int ii = index < 0 ? 0 : index >= length() ? length() : index;
```

```
Tuple3<List<A>, List<A>, Integer> identity =
                        new Tuple3<>(List.list(), List.list(), ii);
Tuple3<List<A>, List<A>, Integer> rt =
        foldLeft(identity, ta -> a -> ta._3 == 0
                ? new Tuple3<>(ta._1, ta._2.cons(a), ta._3)
                : new Tuple3<>(ta._1.cons(a), ta._2, ta._3 - 1));
    return new Tuple<>(rt._1.reverse(), rt._2.reverse());
}
```

The result of the fold is accumulated in the first list accumulator until the index is reached (after the index value has been adjusted to avoid index out of bounds). Once the index is found, the list traversal continues, but the remaining values are accumulated in the second list accumulator.

One problem with this implementation is that by accumulating the remaining values in the second list accumulator, you reverse this part of the list. Not only should you not need to traverse the remainder of the list, but it's done twice here: once for accumulating in reverse order, and once for eventually reversing the result. To avoid this, you should modify the special "escaping" version of foldLeft so it will return not only the escaped result (the absorbing, or zero element), but also the rest of the list, untouched. To achieve this, you must change the signature to return a Tuple:

```
public abstract <B> Tuple<B, List<A>> foldLeft(B identity, B zero,
                                        Function<B, Function<A, B>> f);
```

Then you need to change the implementation in the Nil class:

```
@Override
public <B> Tuple<B, List<A>> foldLeft(B identity, B zero,
                                        Function<B, Function<A, B>> f) {
    return new Tuple<>(identity, list());
}
```

Finally, you must change the Cons implementation to return the remainder of the list:

```
@Override
public <B> Tuple<B, List<A>> foldLeft(B identity, B zero,
                                        Function<B, Function<A, B>> f) {
    return foldLeft(identity, zero, this, f).eval();
}

private <B> TailCall<Tuple<B, List<A>>> foldLeft(B acc, B zero,
                        List<A> list, Function<B, Function<A, B>> f) {
    return list.isEmpty() || acc.equals(zero)
        ? ret(new Tuple<>(acc, list))
        : sus(() -> foldLeft(f.apply(acc).apply(list.head()),
                                        zero, list.tail(), f));
}
```

Now you can rewrite the splitAt method using this special foldLeft method:

```
public Tuple<List<A>, List<A>> splitAt(int index) {

    class Tuple3<T, U, V> {
```

```
    public final T _1;
    public final U _2;
    public final V _3;

    public Tuple3(T t, U u, V v) {
      this._1 = Objects.requireNonNull(t);
      this._2 = Objects.requireNonNull(u);
      this._3 = Objects.requireNonNull(v);
    }

    @Override
    public boolean equals(Object o) {
      if (!(o.getClass() == this.getClass()))
        return false;
      else {
        @SuppressWarnings("rawtypes")
        Tuple3 that = (Tuple3) o;
        return _3.equals(that._3);
      }
    }
  }
}

Tuple3<List<A>, List<A>, Integer> zero =
                              new Tuple3<>(list(), list(), 0);
Tuple3<List<A>, List<A>, Integer> identity =
                              new Tuple3<>(list(), list(), index);
Tuple<Tuple3<List<A>, List<A>, Integer>, List<A>> rt = index <= 0
      ? new Tuple<>(identity, this)
      : foldLeft(identity, zero, ta -> a -> ta._3 < 0
              ? ta
              : new Tuple3<>(ta._1.cons(a), ta._2, ta._3 - 1));
return new Tuple<>(rt._1._1.reverse(), rt._2);
}
```

Here, you again need a specific Tuple3 class with a special equals method returning true when the third elements are equal, not taking into account the two first elements. Note that the second resulting list doesn't need to be reversed.

When not to use folds

Just because it's possible to use a fold doesn't mean you should do so. The preceding exercises are just that: exercises. As a functional library designer, you need to choose the most efficient implementation.

A functional library must have a functional interface and must respect the functional programming requirements, which means all functions must be true functions with no side effects, and all must respect referential transparency. What happens inside the library is irrelevant. A functional library in an imperative-oriented language like Java can be compared to a compiler for a functional-oriented language. The compiled code will always be imperative because this is what the computer understands. A functional library gives more choice. Some functions may be implemented in functional style and others in imperative style; it doesn't matter. Splitting a singly linked list or finding an element by its index is much easier and much faster when it's implemented imperatively than functionally because the singly linked list isn't adapted for such an operation.

The most functional way to go is probably not to implement these functions based on folds, but to avoid implementing them at all. If you need structures with functional implementations of these functions, the best thing to do is to create specific structures, as you'll see in chapter 10.

8.3.4 Searching for sublists

One common use case for lists is searching to find out whether a list is contained in another (longer) list. In other words, you want to know whether a list is a sublist of another list.

EXERCISE 8.16

Implement a hasSubList method to check whether a list is a sublist of another. For example, the list (3, 4, 5) is a sublist of (1, 2, 3, 4, 5) but not of (1, 2, 4, 5, 6). Implement it as a static method with the following signature:

```
public static <A> boolean hasSubsequence(List<A> list, List<A> sub)
```

HINT

You'll first have to implement a startsWith method to determine whether a list starts with a sublist. Once this is done, you'll test this method recursively, starting from each element of the list.

SOLUTION 8.16

An explicitly recursive startsWith method can be implemented as follows:

```
public static <A> Boolean startsWith(List<A> list, List<A> sub) {
  return sub.isEmpty()
      ? true
      : list.isEmpty()
          ? false
          : list.head().equals(sub.head())
              ? startsWith(list.tail(), sub.tail())
              : false;
}
```

This is a stack-based version that can be transformed into a heap-based one using TailCall:

```
public static <A> Boolean startsWith(List<A> list, List<A> sub) {
  return startsWith_(list, sub).eval();
}
public static <A> TailCall<Boolean> startsWith_(List<A> list,
                                                List<A> sub) {
  return sub.isEmpty()
      ? ret(Boolean.TRUE)
```

```
        : list.isEmpty()
            ? ret(Boolean.FALSE)
            : list.head().equals(sub.head())
                ? sus(() -> startsWith_(list.tail(), sub.tail()))
                : ret(Boolean.FALSE);
}
```

From there, implementing hasSubList is straightforward:

```
public static <A> boolean hasSubList(List<A> list, List<A> sub) {
  return hasSubList_(list, sub).eval();
}

public static <A> TailCall<Boolean> hasSubList_(List<A> list, List<A> sub){
  return list.isEmpty()
      ? ret(sub.isEmpty())
      : startsWith(list, sub)
          ? ret(true)
          : sus(() -> hasSubList_(list.tail(), sub));
}
```

8.3.5   *Miscellaneous functions for working with lists*

Many other useful functions can be developed to work with lists. The following exercises will give you some practice in this domain. Note that the proposed solutions are certainly not the only ones. Feel free to invent your own.

EXERCISE 8.17

Create a groupBy method taking a function from A to B as a parameter and returning a Map, where keys are the result of the function applied to each element of the list and values are lists of elements corresponding to each key. In other words, given a list of Payments such as these,

```
public class Payment {

  public final String name;
  public final int amount;

  public Payment(String name, int amount) {
    this.name = name;
    this.amount = amount;
  }
}
```

the following code should create a Map containing (key/value) pairs where each key is a name and the corresponding value is the list of Payments made by the corresponding person:

```
Map<String, List<Payment>> map = list.groupBy(x -> x.name);
```

HINT

Use the functional Map wrapper from previous chapters. This time, try to create an imperative version first. Then create a functional version based on a fold. Which one do you prefer?

SOLUTION 8.17

Here's an imperative version. There's not much to say about it, because it's just traditional imperative code with a local mutable state:

```
public <B> Map<B, List<A>> groupByImperative(Function<A, B> f) {
  List<A> workList = this;
  Map<B, List<A>> m = Map.empty();
  while (!workList.isEmpty()) {
    final B k = f.apply(workList.head());
    List<A> rt = m.get(k).getOrElse(list()).cons(workList.head());
    m = m.put(k, rt);
    workList = workList.tail();
  }
  return m;
}
```

Note that this implementation is perfectly functional because no state mutation is visible from outside the method. But the style is quite imperative, with a `while` loop and local variables.

Here's a version in a more functional style, using a fold:

```
public <B> Map<B, List<A>> groupBy(Function<A, B> f) {
  return foldRight(Map.empty(), t -> mt -> {
    final B k = f.apply(t);
    return mt.put(k, mt.get(k).getOrElse(list()).cons(t));
  });
}
```

It's up to you to choose the style you prefer. Obviously, the second version is more compact. But the main advantage is that it better expresses the intent. `groupBy` is a fold. Choosing the imperative style is re-implementing the fold, whereas choosing the functional style is reusing the abstraction.

EXERCISE 8.18

Write an `unfold` method that takes a starting element `S` and a function `f` from `S` to `Result<Tuple<A, S>>` and produces a `List<A>` by successively applying `f` to the `S` value as long as the result is a `Success`. In other words, the following code should produce a list of integers from 0 to 9:

```
List.unfold(0, i -> i < 10
    ? Result.success(new Tuple<>(i, i + 1))
    : Result.empty());
```

SOLUTION 8.18

A simple non-stack-safe recursive version is easy to implement:

```
public static <A, S> List<A> unfold_(S z,
                                    Function<S, Result<Tuple<A, S>>> f) {
    return f.apply(z).map(x ->
                  unfold_(x._2, f).cons(x._1)).getOrElse(list());
}
```

Unfortunately, although this solution is smart, it will blow the stack for a little more than 1,000 recursion steps. To solve this problem, you can create a tail recursive version and use the `TailCall` class to make recursion happen on the heap:

```
public static <A, S> List<A> unfold(S z,
                                    Function<S, Result<Tuple<A, S>>> f) {
  return unfold(list(), z, f).eval().reverse();
}

private static <A, S> TailCall<List<A>> unfold(List<A> acc, S z,
                                    Function<S, Result<Tuple<A, S>>> f) {
    Result<Tuple<A, S>> r = f.apply(z);
    Result<TailCall<List<A>>> result =
            r.map(rt -> sus(() -> unfold(acc.cons(rt._1), rt._2, f)));
    return result.getOrElse(ret(acc));
}
```

Note, however, that this reverses the list. This might not be a big problem for small lists, but it could be for huge ones. In such cases, reverting to imperative style might be an option.

EXERCISE 8.19

Write a range method that takes two integers as its parameters and produces a list of all integers greater than or equal to the first and less than the second.

HINT

Of course, you should use methods you've already defined.

SOLUTION 8.19

This is very simple if you reuse the method from exercise 8.18:

```
public static List<Integer> range(int start, int end) {
  return List.unfold(start, i -> i < end
        ? Result.success(new Tuple<>(i, i + 1))
        : Result.empty());
}
```

EXERCISE 8.20

Create an exists method that takes a function from A to Boolean representing a condition, and that returns true if the list contains at least one element satisfying this condition. Don't use explicit recursion, but try to build on the methods you've already defined.

HINT

There's no need to evaluate the condition for all elements of the list. The method should return as soon as the first element satisfying the condition is found.

SOLUTION 8.20

A recursive solution could be defined as follows:

```
public boolean exists(Function<A, Boolean> p) {
  return p.apply(head()) || tail().exists(p);
}
```

Because the || operator lazily evaluates its second argument, the recursive process will stop as soon as an element is found that satisfies the condition expressed by the predicate p. But this is a non-tail-recursive stack-based method, and it will blow the stack if the list is long and no satisfying element is found in the first 1,000 or 2,000 elements. Incidentally, it will also throw an exception if the list is empty, so you'd have to define an abstract method in the List class with a specific implementation for the Nil subclass.

A much better solution consists of reusing the foldLeft method with a zero parameter:

```
public boolean exists(Function<A, Boolean> p) {
  return foldLeft(false, true, x -> y -> x || p.apply(y))._1;
}
```

EXERCISE 8.21

Create a forAll method that takes a function from A to Boolean representing a condition, and that returns true if all the elements in the list satisfy this condition.

HINT

Don't use explicit recursion. And once again, you don't always need to evaluate the condition for all elements of the list. The forAll method will be very similar to the exists method.

SOLUTION 8.21

The solution is very close to the exists method with two differences: the identity and zero values are inverted, and the Boolean operator is && instead of ||:

```
public boolean forAll(Function<A, Boolean> p) {
  return foldLeft(true, false, x -> y -> x && p.apply(y))._1;
}
```

Note that another possibility is to reuse the exists method:

```
public boolean forAll(Function<A, Boolean> p) {
  return !exists(x -> !p.apply(x));
}
```

This methods checks whether an element exists that doesn't meet the inverse of the condition.

8.4 *Automatic parallel processing of lists*

Most computations that are applied to lists resort to folds. A fold involves applying an operation as many times as there are elements in the list. For very long lists and long-lasting operations, a fold can take a considerable amount of time. Because most computers are now equipped with multicore processors (if not multiple processors), you may be tempted to find a way to make the computer process a list in parallel.

In order to parallelize a fold, you need only one thing (beside a multicore processor, of course): an additional operation allowing you to recompose the results of each parallel computation.

8.4.1   Not all computations can be parallelized

Take the example of a list of integers. Finding the mean of all integers isn't something you can directly parallelize. You could break the list into four pieces (if you have a computer with four processors) and compute the mean of each sublist. But you wouldn't be able to compute the mean of the list from the means of the sublists.

On the other hand, computing the mean of a list implies computing the sum of all elements and then dividing it by the number of elements. And computing the sum is something that can be easily parallelized by computing the sums of the sublists, and then computing the sum of the sublist sums.

This is a very particular example, where the operation used for the fold (the addition) is the same as the operation used to assemble the sublist results. This isn't always the case. Take the example of a list of characters that's folded by adding a character to a `String`. To assemble the intermediate results, you need a different operation: string concatenation.

8.4.2   Breaking the list into sublists

First, you must break the list into sublists, and you must do this automatically. One important question is how many sublists you should obtain. At first glance, you might think that one sublist for each available processor would be ideal, but this isn't exactly the case. The number of processors (or, more precisely, the number of logical cores) isn't the most important factor. There's a more crucial question: will all sublist computations take the same amount of time? Probably not, but this depends on the type of computation. If you were to divide the list into four sublists because you decided to dedicate four threads to parallel processing, some threads might finish very quickly, while others might have to make a much longer computation. This would ruin the benefit of parallelization, because it might result in most of the computing task being handled by a single thread.

A better solution is to divide the list into a large number of sublists, and then submit each sublist to a pool of threads. This way, as soon as a thread finishes processing a sublist, it's handed a new one to process. So the first task is to create a method that will divide a list into sublists.

EXERCISE 8.22

Write a `divide(int depth)` method that will divide a list into a number of sublists. The list will be divided in two, and each sublist recursively divided in two, with the `depth` parameter representing the number of recursion steps. This method will be implemented in the `List` parent class with the following signature:

```
List<List<A>> divide(int depth)
```

HINT

You'll first define a new version of the `splitAt` method that returns a list of lists instead of a `Tuple<List, List>`. Let's call this method `splitListAt` and give it the following signature:

```
List<List<A>> splitListAt(int i)
```

SOLUTION 8.22

The `splitListAt` method is an explicitly recursive method made stack-safe through the use of the `TailCall` class:

```
public List<List<A>> splitListAt(int i) {
  return splitListAt(list(), this.reverse(), i).eval();
}

private TailCall<List<List<A>>> splitListAt(List<A> acc,
                                            List<A> list, int i) {
  return i == 0 || list.isEmpty()
      ? ret(List.list(list.reverse(), acc))
      : sus(() -> splitListAt(acc.cons(list.head()), list.tail(), i - 1));
}
```

This method will, of course, always return a list of two lists. Then you can define the divide method as follows:

```
public List<List<A>> divide(int depth) {
  return this.isEmpty()
      ? list(this)
      : divide(list(this), depth);
}

private List<List<A>> divide(List<List<A>> list, int depth) {
  return list.head().length() < depth || depth < 2
      ? list
      : divide(list.flatMap(x -> x.splitListAt(x.length() / 2)), depth / 2);
}
```

Note that you don't need to make this method stack-safe because the number of recursion steps will only be log(length). In other words, you'll never have enough heap memory to hold a list long enough to cause a stack overflow.

8.4.3 *Processing sublists in parallel*

To process the sublists in parallel, you'll need a special version of the method to execute, which will take as an additional parameter an `ExecutorService` configured with the number of threads you want to use in parallel.

EXERCISE 8.23

Create a `parFoldLeft` method in `List<A>` that will take the same parameters as `fold-Left` plus an `ExecutorService` and a function from B to B to B and that will return a

`Result<List<B>>`. The additional function will be used to assemble the results from the sublists. Here's the signature of the method:

```
public<B> Result<B> parFoldLeft(ExecutorService es, B identity,
            Function<B, Function<A, B>> f, Function<B, Function<B, B>> m)
```

SOLUTION 8.23

First, you must define the number of sublists you want to use and divide the list accordingly:

```
final int chunks = 1024;
final List<List<A>> dList = divide(chunks);
```

Then, you'll map the list of sublists with a function that will submit a task to the `ExecutorService`. This task consists of folding each sublist and returning a `Future` instance. The list of `Future` instances is mapped to a function calling `get` on each `Future` to produce a list of results (one for each sublist). Note that you must catch the potential exceptions.

Eventually, the list of results is folded with the second function, and the result is returned in a `Result.Success`. In the case of an exception, a `Failure` is returned.

```
try {
  List<B> result = dList.map(x -> es.submit(() -> x.foldLeft(identity,
                                                      f))).map(x -> {
    try {
      return x.get();
    } catch (InterruptedException | ExecutionException e) {
      throw new RuntimeException(e);
    }
  });
  return Result.success(result.foldLeft(identity, m));
} catch (Exception e) {
  return Result.failure(e);
}
```

You'll find an example benchmark of this method in the accompanying code (https://github.com/fpinjava/fpinjava). The benchmark consists of computing 10 times the Fibonacci value of 35,000 random numbers between 1 and 30 with a very slow algorithm. On a four-core Macintosh, the parallel version executes in 22 seconds, whereas the serial version needs 83 seconds.

EXERCISE 8.24

Although mapping can be implemented through a fold (and thus can benefit from automatic parallelization), it can also be implemented in parallel without using a fold. This is probably the simplest automatic parallelization that can be implemented on a list. Create a `parMap` method that will automatically apply a given function to all elements of a list in parallel. Here's the method signature:

```
public <B> Result<List<B>> parMap(ExecutorService es, Function<A, B> g)
```

HINT

In fact, there's nearly nothing to do in this exercise. Just submit each function application to the ExecutorService, and get the results from each corresponding Callable.

SOLUTION 8.24

Here's the solution:

```
public <B> Result<List<B>> parMap(ExecutorService es, Function<A, B> g) {
  try {
    return Result.success(this.map(x -> es.submit(() -> g.apply(x)))
                                                      .map(x -> {
      try {
        return x.get();
      } catch (InterruptedException | ExecutionException e) {
        throw new RuntimeException(e);
      }
    }));
  } catch (Exception e) {
    return Result.failure(e);
  }
}
```

The benchmark available in the code accompanying this book will allow you to measure the increase in performance. This increase may, of course, vary depending on the machine running the program.

8.5   *Summary*

- List processing can be made faster through the use of memoization.
- You can convert a List of Result instances into a Result of List.
- You can assemble two lists by zipping them. You can also unzip lists of tuples to produce a Tuple of lists.
- You can implement indexed access to list elements using explicit recursion.
- You can implement a special version of foldLeft to escape the fold when a "zero" result is obtained.
- You can create lists by unfolding with a function and a terminal condition.
- Lists can be automatically split, which allows automatic processing of sublists in parallel.

Working with laziness

This chapter covers

- Understanding the importance of laziness
- Implementing laziness in Java
- Creating a lazy list data structure: the `Stream`
- Optimizing lazy lists by memoizing evaluated values
- Handling infinite streams

Some languages are said to be *lazy*, while others are not. Does this mean that some languages work harder than others? Not at all. Laziness is opposed to strictness. It has nothing to do with how hard a language can work, although you could sometimes think of lazy languages as languages that don't require the programmer to work as hard as they must with strict ones.

Laziness, as you'll see, has many advantages for some specific problems, such as composing infinite data structures and evaluating error conditions.

9.1   Understanding strictness and laziness

When applied to method arguments, strictness means that arguments are evaluated as soon as they're received by the method. Laziness means that arguments are evaluated only when they're needed.

Of course, strictness and laziness apply not only to method arguments, but to everything. For example, consider the following declaration:

```
int x = 2 + 3;
```

Here, x is immediately evaluated to 5 because Java is a strict language; it performs the addition immediately. Let's look at another example:

```
int x = getValue();
```

In Java, as soon as the x variable is declared, the `getValue` method is called to provide the corresponding value. On the other hand, with a lazy language, the `getValue` method is only called if and when the x variable is to be used. This can make a huge difference.

For example, look at the following Java program:

```
public static void main(String... args) {
  int x = getValue();
}

public static int getValue() {
  System.out.println("Returning 5");
  return 5;
}
```

This program will print `Returning 5` on the console because the `getValue` method will be called, although the returned value will never be used. In a lazy language, nothing would be evaluated, so nothing would be printed on the console.

9.1.1 *Java is a strict language*

Java, in principle, has no option concerning laziness. Java is strict. Everything is evaluated immediately. Method arguments are said to be passed *by value*, which means first they're evaluated, and then the evaluated value is passed. On the other hand, in lazy languages, arguments are said to be passed *by name*, which means *unevaluated*. Don't be confused by the fact that method arguments in Java are often references. References are addresses, and these addresses are passed by value.

Some languages are strict (like Java); others are lazy; some are strict by default and are optionally lazy; and others are lazy by default and are optionally strict.

Java, however, isn't always strict. These are some lazy constructs in Java:

- Boolean operators `||` and `&&`
- Ternary operator `?:`
- `if ... else`
- `for` loop
- `while` loop
- Java 8 streams

If you think about it, you'll soon realize that not much could be done if Java weren't sometimes lazy. Can you imagine an `if ... else` structure where both branches were systematically evaluated? Or can you imagine a loop from which it was impossible to escape? All languages have to be lazy sometimes. This said, standard Java is often not lazy enough for functional programming.

9.1.2 *The problem with strictness*

Strictness is so fundamental in languages like Java that it's seen by many programmers as the only possibility for evaluating expressions, even if, in reality, nothing would be possible with a totally strict language. Moreover, Java's documentation doesn't use the words *non-strict* or *lazy* when describing lazy constructs. For example, the Boolean operators `||` and `&&` aren't called *lazy*, but *short-circuiting*. But the simple reality is that these operators are non-strict regarding their arguments. We can easily show how this is different from a "strict" evaluation of method arguments.

Imagine that you wanted to simulate Boolean operators with a function. The following listing shows what you could do.

> **Listing 9.1   The and and or logical methods**

```
public class BooleanMethods {

  public static void main(String[] args) {
    System.out.println(or(true, true));
    System.out.println(or(true, false));
    System.out.println(or(false, true));
    System.out.println(or(false, false));

    System.out.println(and(true, true));
    System.out.println(and(true, false));
    System.out.println(and(false, true));
    System.out.println(and(false, false));
  }

  public static boolean or(boolean a, boolean b) {
    return a ? true : b ? true : false;
  }

  public static boolean and(boolean a, boolean b) {
    return a ? b ? true : false : false;
  }
}
```

There are, of course, simpler ways to do this using the Boolean operators, but your goal here is to avoid these operators. Are you done? Running this program will display the following result on the console:

```
true
true
true
false
true
```

```
false
false
false
```

So far, so good. But now try running the following program.

Listing 9.2 The problem with strictness

```java
public class BooleanMethods {

  public static void main(String[] args) {
    System.out.println(getFirst() || getSecond());
    System.out.println(or(getFirst(), getSecond()));
  }

  public static boolean getFirst() {
    return true;
  }

  public static boolean getSecond() {
    throw new IllegalStateException();
  }

  public static boolean or(boolean a, boolean b) {
    return a ? true : b ? true : false;
  }

  public static boolean and(boolean a, boolean b) {
    return a ? b ? true : false : false;
  }
}
```

This programs prints the following:

```
true
Exception in thread "main" java.lang.IllegalStateException
```

Obviously, the or method isn't equivalent to the || operator. The difference is that ||
evaluates its operand lazily, which means the second operand isn't evaluated if the first
one is true, because it's not necessary for computing the result. But the or method
evaluates its arguments strictly, which means that the second argument is evaluated
even if its value isn't needed, so the IllegalStateException is always thrown.

In chapters 6 and 7 you encountered this problem with the getOrElse method
because its argument was always evaluated, even if the computation was successful.

9.2 *Implementing laziness*

Laziness is necessary on many occasions. Java does in fact use laziness for constructs
like if ... else, loops, and try ... catch blocks. Without laziness, a catch block,
for example, would be evaluated even in the absence of an exception. Implementing
laziness is a must when it comes to providing behavior for errors, as well as when you
need to manipulate infinite data structures.

Implementing laziness in Java isn't fully possible, but you can produce a good approximation using the `Supplier` class you used in previous chapters:

```
public interface Supplier<T> {
  T get();
}
```

Note that you created your own class, but Java 8 also offers a `Supplier` class. Which one you use is up to you. They are completely equivalent.

Using the `Supplier` class, you can rewrite the `BooleanMethods` example as follows.

Listing 9.3   Using laziness to emulate Boolean operators

```
public class BooleanMethods {
  public static void main(String[] args) {
    System.out.println(getFirst() || getSecond());
    System.out.println(or(() -> getFirst(), () -> getSecond()));
  }

  public static boolean getFirst() {
    return true;
  }

  public static boolean getSecond() {
    throw new IllegalStateException();
  }

  public static boolean or(Supplier<Boolean> a, Supplier<Boolean> b) {
    return a.get() ? true : b.get() ? true : false;
  }

  public static boolean and(Supplier<Boolean> a, Supplier<Boolean> b) {
    return a.get() ? b.get() ? true : false : false;
  }
}
```

This programs prints out the following:

```
true
true
```

The problem of laziness is nearly solved, although you've been forced to change the signature of your method. This is a low price to pay for using laziness. Of course, it might be overkill if the parameters are very quick to evaluate, or if they're already evaluated, such as when using literal values. But it may save a great deal of time when evaluation requires a long computation. And if that evaluation isn't free of side effects, it may completely change the outcome of the program.

9.3   *Things you can't do without laziness*

So far, it may seem that the absence of laziness in evaluating expressions in Java isn't a big deal. After all, why should you bother rewriting Boolean methods when you can use Boolean operators? There are, however, other cases where laziness would be useful.

There are even several algorithms that can't be implemented without resorting to laziness. I've already talked about how useless a strict version of if ... else would be. Think about the following algorithm:

1 Take the list of positive integers.
2 Filter the primes.
3 Return the list of the first ten results.

This is an algorithm for finding the first ten primes, but this algorithm can't be implemented without laziness. If you don't believe me, just try it. Start with the first line. If you're strict, you'll first evaluate the list of positive integers. You'll never have the opportunity to go to the second line, because the list of integers is infinite, and you'll exhaust available memory before reaching the (nonexistent) end.

Clearly, this algorithm can't be implemented without laziness, but you know how to replace it with a different algorithm. The preceding algorithm was functional. If you want to find the result without resorting to laziness, you'll have to replace it with an imperative algorithm, like this:

1 Take the first integer.
2 Check whether it's a prime.
3 If it is, store it in a list.
4 Check whether this resulting list has ten elements.
5 If it has ten elements, return it as the result.
6 If not, increment the integer by 1.
7 Go to line 2.

Sure, it works. But what a mess! First, it's a bad recipe. Shouldn't you increment the tested integer by 2 rather than by 1, in order to not test even numbers? And why test multiples of 3, 5, and so on? But more importantly, it doesn't express the nature of the problem. It's only a recipe for computing the result.

This isn't to say that the implementation details (such as not testing even numbers) aren't important for getting good performance. But these implementation details should be clearly separated from the problem definition. The imperative description isn't a description of the problem—it's a description of another problem giving the same result.

In functional programming, you generally solve this kind of problem with a special structure: the lazy list, called Stream.

9.4 Why not use the Java 8 Stream?

Java 8 introduced a new structure called Stream. Can you use it for this type of computation? Well, you could, but there are several reasons not to do this:

- Defining your own structure is far more rewarding. In doing so, you'll learn and understand many things that you wouldn't even have thought of if you were using Java 8 streams.

- Java streams are a very powerful tool, but not the tool you need. Java 8 streams were designed with the idea of automatic parallelization in mind. To allow for automatic parallelization, many compromises were made. Many functional methods are missing because they would have made automatic parallelization more difficult.
- Java 8 streams are stateful. Once they've been used for some operations, they will have changed their state and are no longer usable.
- Folding Java 8 streams is a strict operation that causes the evaluation of all elements.

For all these reasons, you'll define your own streams in this chapter. After you've finished this chapter, you may prefer to use the Java 8 streams, but you'll do so fully understanding what's missing in the Java 8 implementation.

9.5   *Creating a lazy list data structure*

Now that you know how to represent non-evaluated data as instances of `Supplier`, you can easily define a lazy list data structure. It will be called `Stream` and will be very similar to the singly linked list you developed in chapter 5, with some subtle but very important differences. The following listing shows the starting point of your `Stream` data type.

Listing 9.4   The `Stream` data type

```java
import com.fpinjava.common.Supplier;

public abstract class Stream<A> {

  private static Stream EMPTY = new Empty();          ◁── The empty stream is represented by a nonparameterized singleton.
  public abstract A head();
  public abstract Stream<A> tail();
  public abstract Boolean isEmpty();
  private Stream() {}                                  ◁── The constructor of the Stream class is private to prevent direct instantiation.

  private static class Empty<A> extends Stream<A> {    ◁── The Empty subclass is exactly the same as the List.Nil subclass.

    @Override
    public Stream<A> tail() {
      throw new IllegalStateException("tail called on empty");
    }

    @Override
    public A head() {
      throw new IllegalStateException("head called on empty");
    }

    @Override
    public Boolean isEmpty() {
      return true;
    }
  }

  private static class Cons<A> extends Stream<A> {     ◁── A non-empty stream is represented by the Stream subclass.

    private final Supplier<A> head;
```

The head is non-evaluated, taking the form of a `Supplier<T>`.

```
    private final Supplier<Stream<A>> tail;

    private Cons(Supplier<A> h, Supplier<Stream<A>> t) {
      head = h;
      tail = t;
    }

    @Override
    public A head() {
      return head.get();
    }

    @Override
    public Stream<A> tail() {
      return tail.get();
    }

    @Override
    public Boolean isEmpty() {
      return false;
    }
  }

  static <A> Stream<A> cons(Supplier<A> hd, Supplier<Stream<A>> tl) {
    return new Cons<>(hd, tl);
  }

  @SuppressWarnings("unchecked")
  public static <A> Stream<A> empty() {
    return EMPTY;
  }

  public static Stream<Integer> from(int i) {
    return cons(() -> i, () -> from(i + 1));
  }
}
```

Similarly, the tail is represented by a **Supplier<Stream<T>>**, which is evaluated by calling the corresponding get method.

The head method evaluates the head before returning the evaluated value.

The tail method evaluates the tail before returning the evaluated value.

The cons factory method constructs a **Stream** by calling the private Cons constructor.

The empty factory method returns the EMPTY singleton.

The from factory method returns an infinite stream of integers, starting from the given value.

Here's an example of how to use this `Stream` type:

```
Stream<Integer> stream = Stream.from(1);
System.out.println(stream.head());
System.out.println(stream.tail().head());
System.out.println(stream.tail().tail().head());
```

This program prints the following:

```
1
2
3
```

This probably doesn't seem very useful. To make `Stream` a valuable tool, you'll need to add some methods to it. But first you must optimize it slightly.

9.5.1 *Memoizing evaluated values*

The idea behind laziness is that you can save time by evaluating data only when it's needed. This implies that you must evaluate data when it's first accessed. But reevaluating it on subsequent accesses is a waste of time. Because you're writing functional programs, multiple evaluation won't harm anything, but it will slow the program. One solution is to memoize the evaluated value.

To do this, you'll have to add fields for evaluated values in the Cons class:

```
private final Supplier<A> head;
private A h;
private final Supplier<Stream<A>> tail;
private Stream<A> t;
```

Then change the getters as follows:

```
public A head() {
  if (h == null) {
    h = head.get();
  }
  return h;
}

public Stream<A> tail() {
  if (t == null) {
    t = tail.get();
  }
  return t;
}
```

This well-known technique isn't specific to functional programming. It's sometimes called *evaluation on demand*, or *evaluation as needed*, or *lazy evaluation*. When the value is asked for the first time, the evaluated field is null, so the value is evaluated. On subsequent access, the value won't be evaluated again, and the previously evaluated value will be returned.

Some languages offer lazy evaluation as a standard feature, whether by default or optionally. With such languages, you don't need to resort to null references and mutable fields. Unfortunately, Java isn't one of these languages. In Java, the most frequent approach when a value is to be initialized later is to first assign it the null reference if it's an object type, or a sentinel value if it's a primitive. This is risky because there's no guarantee that the value will indeed be initialized to a significant value when needed. A null reference will probably cause a NullPointerException to be thrown, which at least will be noticed if exception handling has been implemented correctly, but a zero value could be an acceptable business value, leading to a program silently using this acceptable but incorrect value.

Alternatively, you could use a Result<A> to represent the value. This would avoid the use of the null reference, but you'd still have to use mutable fields. Because all this stuff is private, it's acceptable to use null. But if you prefer, you can use a Result (or an Option) to represent the h and t fields.

Note that although the h and t fields must be mutable, they don't need synchronization. The worst thing that may happen is that one thread will test the field and find it null, and then a second thread might also test the field before it has been initialized by the first one. The end result is that the field will have been initialized twice with potentially different (although equal) values. By itself, this isn't a big problem; writing references is atomic, so the data can't be corrupted. However, this could cause two instances of the corresponding object to coexist in memory. This won't be a problem if you only test objects for equality, but it could be if you test them for identity (which, of course, you never do).

Also note that it's possible to completely avoid `null` references and mutable fields at the cost of slight modifications in other places. Try to figure out how to do this. If you don't know how, keep this idea in mind. We'll come back to it near the end of this chapter.

The following listing shows the complete `Stream` class with lazy evaluation of the head and `tail`.

Listing 9.5   The complete `Stream` class

```java
abstract class Stream<A> {

  private static Stream EMPTY = new Empty();
  public abstract A head();
  public abstract Stream<A> tail();
  public abstract Boolean isEmpty();
  private Stream() {}

  private static class Empty<A> extends Stream<A> {

    @Override
    public Stream<A> tail() {
      throw new IllegalStateException("tail called on empty");
    }

    @Override
    public A head() {
      throw new IllegalStateException("head called on empty");
    }

    @Override
    public Boolean isEmpty() {
      return true;
    }
  }

  private static class Cons<A> extends Stream<A> {

    private final Supplier<A> head;
    private A h;
    private final Supplier<Stream<A>> tail;
    private Stream<A> t;

    private Cons(Supplier<A> h, Supplier<Stream<A>> t) {
      head = h;
      tail = t;
    }

    @Override
    public A head() {                      // The method for memoizing
      if (h == null) {                     // the evaluated head
        h = head.get();
```

```
      }
      return h;
    }

    @Override
    public Stream<A> tail() {
      if (t == null) {
        t = tail.get();
      }
      return t;
    }

    @Override
    public Boolean isEmpty() {
      return false;
    }
  }

  static <A> Stream<A> cons(Supplier<A> hd, Supplier<Stream<A>> tl) {
    return new Cons<>(hd, tl);
  }

  static <A> Stream<A> cons(Supplier<A> hd, Stream<A> tl) {
    return new Cons<>(hd, () -> tl);
  }

  @SuppressWarnings("unchecked")
  public static <A> Stream<A> empty() {
    return EMPTY;
  }

  public static Stream<Integer> from(int i) {
    return cons(() -> i, () -> from(i + 1));
  }
}
```

A convenience method to simplify stream creation

EXERCISE 9.1

Write a `headOption` method that returns the evaluated `head` of the stream. This method will be declared in the `Stream` parent class with the following signature:

```
public abstract Result<A> headOption();
```

SOLUTION 9.2

The `Empty` implementation returns an empty `Result`:

```
@Override
public Result<A> headOption() {
  return Result.empty();
}
```

The `Cons` implementation returns a `Success` of the evaluated `head`:

```
@Override
public Result<A> headOption() {
  return Result.success(head());
}
```

9.5.2 *Manipulating streams*

In the remainder of this chapter, you'll learn how to compose streams while making the most of the fact that the data is unevaluated. But in order to look at the streams, you'll need a method to evaluate them. Evaluating all the elements of a stream can be done by converting it to a List. Or you can process a stream by evaluating only the first *n* elements, or by evaluating elements as long as a condition is met.

EXERCISE 9.2

Create a toList method to convert a Stream into a List.

HINT

You can implement an explicitly recursive method in the Stream class.

SOLUTION 9.2

A recursive version will simply cons the head of the stream to the result of the toList method applied to the tail. Of course, you'll need to make this process tail recursive in order to use TailCall to get a stack-safe implementation:

```
public List<A> toList() {
  return toList(this, List.list()).eval().reverse();
}

private TailCall<List<A>> toList(Stream<A> s, List<A> acc) {
  return s.isEmpty()
      ? ret(acc)
      : sus(() -> toList(s.tail(), List.cons(s.head(), acc)));
}
```

Note that the static imports of TailCall.ret() and TailCall.sus() aren't shown here.

Beware that calling toList on an infinite stream, such as the stream created by Stream.from(1), will create an infinite list. Unlike the stream, the list is eagerly evaluated, so it will result, in theory, in a never-ending program. (In reality, it will end with an OutOfMemoryError.) Be sure to create a condition that will truncate the list before running the program, as you'll see in the next exercise.

EXERCISE 9.3

Write a take(n) method that returns the first n elements of a stream, and a drop(n) method that returns the remaining stream after removing the first n elements. Note that you have to ensure that no evaluation occurs while calling these methods. Here are the signatures in the Stream parent class:

```
public abstract Stream<A> take(int n);
public abstract Stream<A> drop(int n);
```

SOLUTION 9.3

Both implementations in the Empty class return this. For the take method in the Cons class, you need to create a new Stream<A> by calling the cons method with the non-evaluated head of the stream (which means a reference to the head field and not a call to the head() method) and making a recursive call to take(n - 1) on the tail of the stream until n == 1. The drop method is even simpler. You just have to call drop(n - 1) recursively on the tail while n > 0. Note that the take method doesn't need to be made stack-safe, because the recursive call to take is already lazy.

```
public Stream<A> take(int n) {
  return n <= 0
      ? empty()
      : cons(head, () -> tail().take(n - 1));
}
```

The take method allows you to work on an infinite stream by truncating it after a number of elements. Beware, however, that this method must be called on the stream before converting it to a list:

```
List<Integer> list = Stream.from(1).take(10).toList();
```

Calling the equivalent method on the resulting list will instead hang until memory is exhausted, causing an OutOfMemoryError:

```
List<Integer> list = Stream.from(1).toList().takeAtMost(10);
```

By contrast, the drop method must be made stack-safe:

```
public Stream<A> drop(int n) {
  return drop(this, n).eval();
}
public TailCall<Stream<A>> drop(Stream<A> acc, int n) {
  return n <= 0
      ? ret(acc)
      : sus(() -> drop(acc.tail(), n - 1));
}
```

EXERCISE 9.4

Write a takeWhile method that will return a Stream containing all starting elements as long as a condition is matched. Here's the method signature in the Stream parent class:

```
public abstract Stream<A> takeWhile(Function<A, Boolean> p)
```

HINT

Be aware that, unlike take and drop, this method will evaluate one element, because it will have to test the first element to verify whether it fulfills the condition expressed by the predicate. You should verify that only the first element of the stream is evaluated.

SOLUTION 9.4

This method is very similar to the take method. The main difference is that the terminal condition is no longer n <= 0 but the provided function returning false:

```
public Stream<A> takeWhile(Function<A, Boolean> f) {
  return f.apply(head())
      ? cons(head, () -> tail().takeWhile(f))
      : empty();
}
```

Once again, you don't need to make the method stack-safe because the recursive call is unevaluated. The `Empty` implementation returns `this`.

EXERCISE 9.5

Write a `dropWhile` method that returns a stream with the front elements removed as long as they satisfy a condition. Here's the signature in the `Stream` parent class:

```
public Stream<A> dropWhile(Function<A, Boolean> p);
```

HINT

You'll need to write a tail recursive version of this method in order to make it stack-safe.

SOLUTION 9.5

As in previous recursive methods, the solution will include a main method calling a stack-safe recursive helper method and evaluating its result:

```
public Stream<A> dropWhile(Function<A, Boolean> p) {
  return dropWhile(this, p).eval();
}

private TailCall<Stream<A>> dropWhile(Stream<A> acc,
                                      Function<A, Boolean> p) {
  return acc.isEmpty()
      ? ret(acc)
      : p.apply(acc.head())
          ? sus(() -> dropWhile(acc.tail(), p))
          : ret(acc);
}
```

Because this method uses a helper method, it can be implemented in the `Stream` parent class.

9.6 *The true essence of laziness*

Laziness is often perceived as evaluating expressions only when (and if) needed. In fact, this is only an application of laziness.

> ### What laziness really means
>
> The real difference between strictness and laziness is that strictness is about *doing things*, and laziness is about *noting things to do*. Lazy evaluation of data notes that data must be evaluated sometime in the future. But laziness isn't limited to evaluating data.

> **(continued)**
> Printing to the console in Java is strict, and it's incompatible with functional programming because it's an effect. But noting that you should print to the console sometime in the future (which could be called "lazy printing") is different. This lazy effect is just producing data that could be returned as the result of the program. More on this subject in chapter 13.

Take the example of a very simple imperative program:

```
List<String> names = ...
for(String name : names) {
  System.out.println(String.format("Hello, %s!", name));
}
```

This program applies strictness, because for each name in the list it executes what it has to do. A lazy version of the program might look like this:

```
List<String> names = ...
names.map(name -> (Runnable) () -> System.out.println(name));
```

Instead of printing each name, this program produces a list of instructions for printing the names. In other words, this program writes a program that can be executed later. What's important to understand is that the two programs aren't equivalent, because if you run them, they won't produce the same results. But the output of the second program is equivalent to the first program itself, because if you run the output of the second program, you'll get exactly the same result as you would by running the first program.

Of course, to run the output of the second program, you'd need some sort of interpreter. You'll learn how to do this in chapter 13 (although you probably already have a good idea about what's involved).

One huge advantage of this approach is that you could produce a description of a program producing an error, and then decide not to execute it based on some condition. Or you could produce an infinite expression, and then apply some means of reducing it to a finite one.

You already saw an example of the first case when you wrote a method to simulate the laziness of Boolean operators. For an example of the second case, imagine you have a list of all the positive integers. In imperative programming, this could be written as follows:

```
for (int i = 0;; i++) {}
```

Such a program will never terminate, although it doesn't do anything. But if you want to find the first integer for which the Fibonacci value is greater than 500, you could write this:

```
for (int i = 0;; i++) {
  if (fibo(i) > 500) return i;
}
```

Now your program terminates because the list of integers will stop being evaluated after the answer is found. This is because the for loop is a lazy structure. Although `for (int i = 0;; i++)` represents an infinite sequence of integers, it will only be evaluated as needed.

In chapter 8, you created the following `exists` method in the `List` class:

```
public Boolean exists(Function<T, Boolean> p) {
  return p.apply(head()) || tail().exists(p);
}
```

This method traversed the list until an element was found satisfying the predicate p. The rest of the list wasn't examined because the `||` operator is lazy and doesn't evaluate its second argument if the first one evaluates to `true`.

EXERCISE 9.6

Create an `exists` method for `Stream`. The method should cause elements to be evaluated only until the condition is met. If the condition is never met, all elements will be evaluated.

SOLUTION 9.6

A simple solution could be very similar to the `exists` method in `List`:

```
public boolean exists(Function<A, Boolean> p) {
  return p.apply(head()) || tail().exists(p);
}
```

Of course, you should make it stack-safe. In order to write a stack-safe implementation, you must first make it tail recursive, and then use the `TailCall` class:

```
public boolean exists(Function<A, Boolean> p) {
  return exists(this, p).eval();
}

private TailCall<Boolean> exists(Stream<A> s, Function<A, Boolean> p) {
  return s.isEmpty()
      ? ret(false)
      : p.apply(s.head())
          ? ret(true)
          : sus(() -> exists(s.tail(), p));
}
```

This version works for both subclasses, so it can be put in the `Stream` parent class.

9.6.1 Folding streams

In chapter 5 you saw how to abstract recursion into fold methods, and you learned how to fold lists right or left. Folding streams is a bit different. Although the principle is the same, the main difference is that streams are unevaluated. A recursive operation could overflow the stack and cause a `StackOverflowException` to be thrown, but a description of a recursive operation will not. The consequence is that a `foldRight`, which can't be made stack-safe in `List`, will in many cases not overflow the stack. It will overflow if it implies evaluating each operation, such as adding the elements of a `Stream<Integer>`, but it won't if, instead of evaluating an operation, it constructs a description of an unevaluated one.

On the other hand, the `List` implementation of `foldRight` based on `foldLeft` (which can be made stack-safe) can't be used with streams, because it would require reversing the stream, which would cause the evaluation of all elements; it might even be impossible in the case of an infinite stream. And the stack-safe version of `foldLeft` can't be used either, because it inverts the direction of the computation.

EXERCISE 9.7

Create a `foldRight` method for streams. This method will be similar to the `List.fold-Right` method, but you should take care of laziness.

HINT

Laziness is expressed by the elements being `Supplier<T>` instead of `T`. The signature of the method in the `Stream` parent class will be

```
public abstract <B> B foldRight(Supplier<B> z,
                          Function<A, Function<Supplier<B>, B>> f);
```

SOLUTION 9.7

The implementation in the `Empty` class is obvious:

```
public <B> B foldRight(Supplier<B> z,
                    Function<A, Function<Supplier<B>, B>> f) {
  return z.get();
}
```

And here's the `Cons` implementation:

```
public <B> B foldRight(Supplier<B> z,
                    Function<A, Function<Supplier<B>, B>> f) {
  return f.apply(head()).apply(() -> tail().foldRight(z, f));
}
```

Note that this method isn't stack-safe, so it shouldn't be used for such computations as the sum of a list of more than about a thousand integers. You'll see, however, that it has many interesting use cases.

EXERCISE 9.8

Implement the `takeWhile` method in terms of `foldRight`. Verify how it behaves on long lists.

SOLUTION 9.8

The starting value is a `Supplier` of an empty stream. This could be written `()  ->  empty()`, but you can also use the method reference version, `Stream::empty`. The function tests the current element (`f.apply(a)`). If the result is `true` (meaning that the element fulfills the condition expressed by the predicate p), a stream is returned by cons-ing a `Supplier` of a to the current stream.

```
public Stream<A> takeWhile(Function<A, Boolean> p) {
  return foldRight(Stream::empty, a -> b -> p.apply(a)
      ? cons(() -> a, b)
      : empty());
}
```

As you can verify by running the tests provided in the code accompanying this book (https://github.com/fpinjava/fpinjava), this method won't overflow the stack, even for streams longer than one million elements. This is because `foldRight` doesn't evaluate the result by itself. Evaluation depends on the function used to make the fold. If this function constructs a new stream (as it does in the case of `takeWhile`), this stream isn't evaluated.

EXERCISE 9.9

Implement `headOption` using `foldRight`.

SOLUTION 9.9

The starting element will be a non-evaluated empty stream (`Result::empty` or `()  -> Result.empty()`). This will be the returned value if the stream is empty. The function used to fold the stream will simply ignore the second argument, so the first time it's applied (to the head element), it returns `Result.success(a)`, and this result will never change.

```
public Result<A> headOptionViaFoldRight() {
  return foldRight(Result::empty, a -> ignore -> Result.success(a));
}
```

EXERCISE 9.10

Implement `map` in terms of `foldRight`. Verify that this method doesn't evaluate any of the stream elements.

SOLUTION 9.10

Start with a `Supplier` of an empty stream. The function used to make the fold will cons a non-evaluated application of the function on the current element with the current result.

```
public <B> Stream<B> map(Function<A, B> f) {
  return foldRight(Stream::empty, a -> b -> cons(() -> f.apply(a), b));
}
```

EXERCISE 9.11

Implement `filter` in terms of `foldRight`. Verify that this method doesn't evaluate more stream elements than needed.

SOLUTION 9.11

Again, start with a non-evaluated empty stream. The function used to fold applies the filter to the current argument. If the result is `true`, the element is used to create a new stream by `cons`-ing it with the current stream result. Otherwise, the current stream result is left unchanged. (Calling `get` on `b` doesn't evaluate any elements.)

```
public Stream<A> filter(Function<A, Boolean> p) {
  return foldRight(Stream::empty, a -> b -> p.apply(a)
      ? cons(() -> a, b)
      : b.get());
}
```

Note that this method evaluates the stream elements until the first match is found. See the corresponding tests in the accompanying code for details.

EXERCISE 9.12

Implement `append` in terms of `foldRight`. The `append` method should be non-strict in its argument.

SOLUTION 9.12

The starting element is the (non-evaluated) stream you want to append. The folding function simply creates a new stream by `cons`-ing the current element on the current result.

```
public Stream<A> append(Supplier<Stream<A>> s) {
  return foldRight(s, a -> b -> cons(() -> a, b));
}
```

EXERCISE 9.13

Implement `flatMap` in terms of `foldRight`.

SOLUTION 9.13

Again, you start with an unevaluated empty stream. The function is applied to the current element, producing a stream to which the current result is appended. This has the effect of flattening the result (transforming a `Stream<Stream<B>>` into a `Stream<B>`).

```
public <B> Stream<B> flatMap(Function<A, Stream<B>> f) {
  return foldRight(Stream::empty, a -> b -> f.apply(a).append(b));
}
```

TRACING EVALUATION AND FUNCTION APPLICATION

It's important to notice the consequence of laziness. With strict collections, like lists, applying successively a `map`, a `filter`, and a new `map` would imply iterating over the list three times:

```
private static Function<Integer, Integer> f = x -> {
  System.out.println("Mapping " + x);
  return x * 3;
};

private static Function<Integer, Boolean> p = x -> {
  System.out.println("Filtering " + x);
  return x % 2 == 0;
};

public static void main(String... args) {
  List<Integer> list = List.list(1, 2, 3, 4, 5).map(f).filter(p);
  System.out.println(list);
}
```

As you can see, functions f and p aren't true functions because they log to the console. This isn't very functional, but it will help you understand what's happening. You could have easily implemented a functional version of this test by returning a tuple of the result and a list of logging strings. (You can do this as an extra exercise if you like.) This program prints the following:

```
Mapping 5
Mapping 4
Mapping 3
Mapping 2
Mapping 1
Filtering 15
Filtering 12
Filtering 9
Filtering 6
Filtering 3
[6, 12, NIL]
```

This shows that all elements are processed by function f, implying a full traversal of the list. Then all elements are processed by function p, implying a second full traversal of the list that results from the first map.

By contrast, look at the following program, which uses a Stream instead of a List:

```
private static Stream<Integer> stream =
    Stream.cons(() -> 1,
        Stream.cons(() -> 2,
            Stream.cons(() -> 3,
                Stream.cons(() -> 4,
                    Stream.cons(() -> 5, Stream.<Integer>empty()))))));

private static Function<Integer, Integer> f = x -> {
  System.out.println("Mapping " + x);
  return x * 3;
};

private static Function<Integer, Boolean> p = x -> {
  System.out.println("Filtering " + x);
  return x % 2 == 0;
};
```

```
public static void main(String... args) {
  Stream<Integer> result = stream.map(f).filter(p);
  System.out.println(result.toList());
}
```

This is the output:

```
Mapping 1
Filtering 3
Mapping 2
Filtering 6
Mapping 3
Filtering 9
Mapping 4
Filtering 12
Mapping 5
Filtering 15
[6, 12, NIL]
```

You can see that the stream traversal occurs only once. First the element 1 is mapped with f, giving 3. Then 3 is filtered (and discarded because it's not even). Then 2 is mapped with f, giving 6, which is filtered and kept for the result.

As you can see, the laziness of streams allows you to compose the descriptions of the computations rather than their results. Note that the evaluation of elements is reduced to a minimum.

The following result is obtained if you use unevaluated values to construct the stream and an evaluating method with logging, while removing the printing of the result:

```
Evaluating 1
Mapping 1
Filtering 3
Evaluating 2
Mapping 2
Filtering 6
```

You can see that only the first two elements are evaluated. The rest of the evaluations were the result of the final printing.

EXERCISE 9.14
Write a find method that takes a predicate (a function from A to Boolean) as a parameter and returns a Result<A>. This will be a Success if an element is found to match the predicate, or an Empty otherwise.

HINT
You should have nearly nothing to write. Just combine two of the methods you've written in the previous sections.

SOLUTION 9.14
Just compose the filter method with headOption:

```
public Result<A> find(Function<A, Boolean> p) {
    return filter(p).headOption();
}
```

9.7   Handling infinite streams

Because a stream is unevaluated, it can be made infinite while still being composable in computations. A simple example is the `from` method that you've already seen:

```
public static Stream<Integer> from(int i) {
    return cons(() -> i, () -> from(i + 1));
}
```

This method returns an infinite stream of integers, starting from `i` and adding one to each new element. This is a very convenient way to create a finite stream of increasing integers:

```
Stream<Integer> stream = from(0).take(10000);
```

This code will create a stream of 10,000 integers, from 0 to 9,999, without evaluating anything.

EXERCISE 9.15

Write a `repeat` method that takes an object as its parameter and returns an infinite stream of the same object.

SOLUTION 9.15

This method is very similar to the `from` method:

```
public static <A> Stream<A> repeat(A a) {
    return cons(() -> a, () -> repeat(a));
}
```

EXERCISE 9.16

Generalize the `from` and `repeat` methods by writing an `iterate` method that takes two parameters: a seed, which will be used for the first value, and a function that will compute the next one. Here's its signature:

```
public static <A> Stream<A> iterate(A seed, Function<A, A> f)
```

Then rewrite the `from` and `repeat` methods based on `iterate`.

SOLUTION 9.16

The `iterate` method has exactly the same structure as `from` and `repeat`, with the difference that the starting value and the function have been parameterized:

```
public static <A> Stream<A> iterate(A seed, Function<A, A> f) {
    return cons(() -> seed, () -> iterate(f.apply(seed), f));
}

public static <A> Stream<A> repeat(A a) {
    return iterate(a, x -> x);
}
```

```
public static Stream<Integer> from(int i) {
  return iterate(i, x -> x + 1);
}
```

Note that because the seed is passed as a method parameter, it's evaluated before being used to create an "unevaluated" value (a `Supplier`). It is, of course, very easy to create a version of `iterate` that takes an unevaluated seed:

```
public static <A> Stream<A> iterate(Supplier<A> seed, Function<A, A> f) {
  return cons(seed, () -> iterate(f.apply(seed.get()), f));
}
```

EXERCISE 9.17

Write a `fibs` function that generates the infinite stream of Fibonacci numbers: 0, 1, 1, 2, 3, 5, 8, and so on.

HINT

Consider producing an intermediate stream of tuples of integers using the `iterate` method.

SOLUTION 9.17

The solution consists in creating a stream of tuples (x, y) with x and y being two successive Fibonacci numbers. Once this stream is produced, you just have to map it with a function from a tuple to its first element:

```
public static Stream<Integer> fibs() {
  return iterate(new Tuple<>(0, 1),
                 x -> new Tuple<>(x._2, x._1 + x._2)).map(x -> x._1);
}
```

EXERCISE 9.18

The `iterate` method can be further generalized. Write an `unfold` method that takes as its parameters a starting state of type `S` and a function from `S` to `Result<Tuple<A, S>>`, and returns a stream of `A`. Returning a `Result` makes it possible to indicate whether the stream should stop or continue.

Using a state `S` means that the source of data generation doesn't have to be of the same type as the generated data. To apply this new method, write new versions of `fibs` and `from` in terms of the `unfold` method. Here's the `unfold` signature:

```
public static <A, S> Stream<A> unfold(S z,
                                      Function<S, Result<Tuple<A, S>>> f)
```

SOLUTION 9.18

To start with, apply the `f` function to the initial state `z`. This produces a `Result<Tuple<A, S>>`. Then map this result with a function from a `Tuple<A, S>`, producing a stream by `cons`-ing the left member of the tuple (the `A` value) with a (non-evaluated) recursive call to `unfold`, and using the right member of the tuple as the initial state. The result of this mapping is either Success(stream) or Empty. Then use getOrElse to return either the contained stream or a default empty stream:

```
public static <A, S> Stream<A> unfold(S z,
                                Function<S, Result<Tuple<A, S>>> f) {
    return f.apply(z).map(x -> cons(() -> x._1,
                        () -> unfold(x._2, f))).getOrElse(empty());
}
```

The new version of from uses the integer seed as the initial state, and a function from Integer to Tuple<Integer, Integer>. Here, the state is of the same type as the value:

```
public static Stream<Integer> from(int n) {
    return unfold(n, x -> Result.success(new Tuple<>(x, x + 1)));
}
```

The fibs method makes more complete use of the unfold method. The state is a Tuple<Integer, Integer>, and the function produces a Tuple<Integer, Tuple<Integer, Integer>>:

```
public static Stream<Integer> fibs() {
    return unfold(new Tuple<>(1, 1),
        x -
        > Result.success(new Tuple<>(x._1, new Tuple<>(x._2, x._1 + x._2))));
}
```

You can see how compact and elegant these method implementations are!

9.8   *Avoiding null references and mutable fields*

In section 9.5.1, I said it was easy to modify your Stream class to memoize the head and tail without resorting to null references and mutable fields. Did you find a solution? In fact, memoization of the tail reference isn't really necessary because the tail itself is a lazy structure (a Stream), so evaluating the reference won't take a noticeable amount of time. You'll only memoize the head.

Avoiding null references is easy: you can use Result.Empty instead of null as long as the value is non-evaluated, and use Result.Success to hold the evaluated value. To avoid using mutable fields, you need to produce a new Stream when the value is evaluated. To do so, you'll use two constructors: one with the non-evaluated head and one with the evaluated one:

```
private final Supplier<A> head;
private final Result<A> h;
private final Supplier<Stream<A>> tail;

private Cons(Supplier<A> h, Supplier<Stream<A>> t) {
    head = h;
    tail = t;
    this.h = Result.empty();
}

private Cons(A h, Supplier<Stream<A>> t) {
```

```
    head = () -> h;
    tail = t;
    this.h = Result.success(h);
}
```

Because evaluation occurs in the head method, you need a new implementation of it. But you also need to return the new Stream with the head value. You can make the head method return a Tuple<A, Stream<A>>:

```
public Tuple<A, Stream<A>> head() {
  A a = h.getOrElse(head.get());
  return h.isEmpty()
      ? new Tuple<>(a, new Cons<>(a, tail))
      : new Tuple<>(a, this);
}
```

Of course, all methods using head() must now use head()._1 instead. And if a reference to the stream was held, it must be replaced with the new stream (head()._2). Note that so far this has never occurred inside the Stream class!

The headOption method must also be modified to return a tuple. You'll find the complete Stream class in the listing09_06 package in the code accompanying this book (https://github.com/fpinjava/fpinjava).

EXERCISE 9.19

Using foldRight to implement various methods is a smart technique. Unfortunately, it doesn't really work for filter. If you test this method with a predicate that's not matched by more than 1,000 or 2,000 consecutive elements, it will overflow the stack. Using the new Stream class without null or mutable fields, write a stack-safe filter method.

HINT

The problem comes from long sequences of elements for which the predicate returns false. Try to think of a way to get rid of these elements.

SOLUTION 9.19

The solution is to remove the long series of elements that return false by using the dropWhile method. To do this, you must reverse the condition (!p.apply(x)) and then test the resulting stream for emptiness. If the stream is empty, return it. (Any empty stream will do, because the empty stream is a singleton. It just needs to be of the right type.) If the stream isn't empty, create a new stream by cons-ing the head with the filtered tail.

Note that the head method returns a tuple, so you must use the left (first) element of this tuple as the head element of the stream. In theory, you should use the right (second) element of the tuple for any further access. Not doing so would cause a new evaluation of the head. But because you don't access the head a second time, but only the tail, you can use stream.getTail() instead. This allows you to avoid the use of a local variable to reference the result of stream.head().

```
public Stream<A> filter(Function<A, Boolean> p) {
  Stream<A> stream = this.dropWhile(x -> !p.apply(x));
  return stream.isEmpty()
      ? stream
      : cons(() -> stream.head()._1,
             () -> stream.tail().filter(p));
}
```

Another possibility is to use the `headOption` method. This method returns a `Tuple` holding a `Result<A>` that can be mapped to produce the new stream through a recursive call. In the end, this produces a `Result<Stream<A>>` that will be empty if no elements satisfy the predicate. All that remains to be done is to call `getOrElse` on this `Result`, passing an empty stream as the default value.

```
public Stream<A> filter(Function<A, Boolean> p) {
  Stream<A> stream = this.dropWhile(x -> !p.apply(x));
  return stream.headOption()._1.map(a -> cons(() -> a,
                    () -> stream.tail().filter(p))).getOrElse(empty());
}
```

9.9   *Summary*

- Strict evaluation means evaluating values as soon as they're referenced.
- Lazy evaluation means evaluating values only if and when they're needed.
- Some languages are strict, and others are lazy. Some are lazy by default and optionally strict; others are strict by default and optionally lazy.
- Java is a strict language. It's strict regarding method arguments.
- Although Java isn't lazy, you can use the `Supplier` interface to implement laziness.
- Laziness allows you to manipulate and compose infinite data structures.
- A `Stream` is a non-evaluated, possibly infinite, list.
- You can use memoization to avoid evaluating the same values several times.
- Right folds don't cause stream evaluation. Only some functions used for folding do.
- Using folds, you can compose several iterating operations without resulting in multiple iterations.
- You can easily define and compose infinite streams.

More data handling with trees

10

This chapter covers

- Understanding the relationships between size, height, and depth in a tree structure
- Understanding the relationship between insertion order and the binary search tree structure
- Traversing trees in various orders
- Implementing the binary search tree
- Merging, folding, and balancing trees

In chapter 5, you learned about the singly linked list, which is probably the most widely used data structure in functional programming. Although the list is a very efficient data structure for many operations, it has some limitations, the main one being that the complexity of accessing elements grows proportionally with the number of elements. For example, searching for a particular element may necessitate examining all elements if it happens that the searched-for element is the last in the list. Among other less efficient operations are sorting, accessing elements by their index, and finding the maximal or minimal element. Obviously, to find the maximal (or minimal) element in a list, one has to traverse the whole list. In this chapter, you'll learn about a data structure that solves these problems: binary trees.

10.1 The binary tree

Data trees are structures in which, unlike lists, each element is linked to more than one element. In some trees, an element (sometimes called a *node*) may be linked to a variable number of other elements. Most often, though, elements are linked to a fixed number of elements. In binary trees, as the same suggests, each element is linked to two elements. Those links are called *branches*. In binary trees, we talk about left and right branches. Figure 10.1 shows an example of a binary tree.

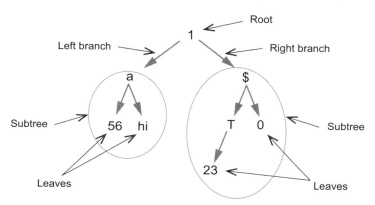

Figure 10.1   A binary tree is a recursive structure composed of a root and two branches. The left branch is a link to the left subtree, and the right branch is a link to the right subtree. Terminal elements have empty branches (not represented in the figure) and are called leaves.

The tree represented in figure 10.1 isn't very common because its elements are of different types. In other words, it's a tree of objects. Most often, you'll deal with trees of a more specific type, such as trees of integers. In the figure, you can see that a tree is a recursive structure. Each branch leads to a new tree (sometimes called a *subtree*). You can also see that some branches lead to a single element. This isn't a problem, because a single element is in fact a tree with empty branches. Also note the T element: it has a left branch, but no right one.

From this, you can infer the definition of a binary tree. A tree is one of the following:

- A single element
- An element with one branch (right or left)
- An element with two branches (right and left)

Each branch holds a (sub)tree. A tree in which all elements have either two branches or zero branches is called a *full* tree. The tree in figure 10.1 isn't full, but the left subtree is.

10.1.1 *Balanced and unbalanced trees*

Binary trees may be more or less balanced. A perfectly balanced tree is a tree in which the two branches of all subtrees contain the same number of elements. Figure 10.2 shows three examples of trees with the same elements. The first tree is perfectly balanced and the last tree is totally unbalanced. Perfectly balanced binary trees are sometimes called *perfect* trees.

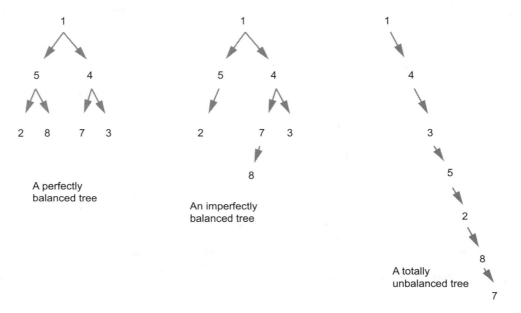

Figure 10.2   Trees can be more or less balanced.

In figure 10.2, the tree on the right is in fact a singly linked list. A singly linked list can be seen as a special case of a totally unbalanced tree.

10.1.2 *Size, height, and depth*

A tree can be characterized by the number of elements it contains and the number of levels on which these elements are located. The number of elements is called the *size*, and the number of levels, not counting the root, is called the *height*. In figure 10.2, all three trees have a size of 7. The first (perfectly balanced) tree has a height of 2, the second a height of 3, and the third a height of 6.

The word *height* is also used to characterize individual elements, and it refers to the length of the longest path from an element to a leaf. The height of the root is the height of the tree, and the height of an element is the height of the subtree having this element as its root.

The *depth* of an element is the length of the path from the root to the element. The first element, also called the *root*, has a depth of 0. In the perfectly balanced tree in figure 10.2, 5 and 4 have a depth of 1; and 2, 8, 7, and 3 have a depth of 2.

By convention, the height and depth of an empty tree are equal to -1. You'll see that this is necessary for some operations, such as balancing.

10.1.3 *Leafy trees*

Binary trees are sometimes represented in a different way, as shown in figure 10.3. In this representation, a tree is represented by branches that don't hold values. Only the terminal nodes hold values. Terminal nodes are called *leaves*; hence, the name *leafy trees*.

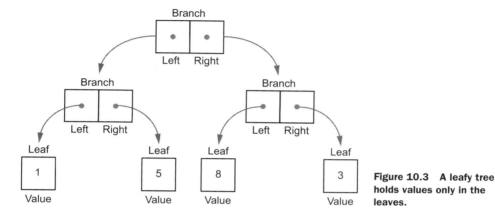

Figure 10.3   A leafy tree holds values only in the leaves.

The leafy tree representation is sometimes preferred because it makes implementing some functions easier. In this book, we'll consider only "classic" trees and not leafy trees.

10.1.4 *Ordered binary trees or binary search trees (BST)*

An ordered binary tree, also called a *binary search tree* (BST), is a tree containing elements that can be ordered, and where all elements in one branch have a lower value than the root element, while all elements in the other branch have a higher value than the root. The same condition holds for all subtrees. By convention, elements with lower values than the root are on the left branch, and elements with higher values are on the right branch. Figure 10.4 shows an example of an ordered tree.

One very important consequence of the definition of ordered binary trees is that they can never contain duplicates.

Ordered trees are particularly interesting because they allow fast retrieval of elements. To find out whether an element is contained in the tree, you follow these steps:

1 Compare the searched-for element with the root. If they are equal, you're done.

2 If the searched-for element is lower than the root, proceed recursively with the left branch.

3 If the searched-for element is higher than the root, proceed recursively with the right branch.

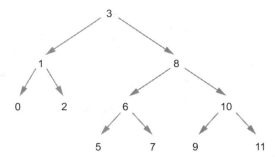

Figure 10.4   An example of an ordered tree, or binary search tree (BST)

Compared to a search in a singly linked list, you can see that searching a perfectly balanced ordered binary tree will take an amount of time proportional to the height of the tree, which means that it will take a time proportional to $\log2(n)$, with n being the size (number of elements) of the tree. By contrast, the search time in a singly linked list is proportional to the number of elements.

A direct consequence of this is that a recursive search in a perfectly balanced binary tree will never overflow the stack. As you saw in chapter 4, the standard stack size allows for 1,000 to 3,000 recursive steps. Because a perfectly balanced binary tree of height 1,000 contains $2^{1,000}$ elements, you'll never have enough main memory for such a tree.

This is good news. But the bad news is that not all binary trees are perfectly balanced. Because the totally unbalanced binary tree is in fact a singly linked list, it will have the same performance and the same problem for recursion as the list. This means that to get the most from trees, you'll have to find a way to balance them.

10.1.5   *Insertion order*

The structure of a tree (meaning how well balanced it is) depends on the insertion order of its elements. Insertion is done in the same way as searching:

1   Compare the element to be inserted with the root. If they're equal, you're done. There's nothing to insert because you can only insert an element lower or higher than the root. Note, however, that the reality will sometimes be different. If the objects inserted into the tree may be equal from the tree-ordering point of view but different based on other criteria, you'll probably want to replace the root with the element you're inserting. This will be the most frequent case, as you'll see.

2   If the element to be inserted is lower than the root, insert it recursively into the left branch.

3   If the element to be inserted is higher than the root, insert it recursively into the right branch.

This process leads to a very interesting observation: the balance of the tree depends on the order in which elements are inserted. It's obvious that inserting ordered elements will produce a totally unbalanced tree. On the other hand, many insertion orders will

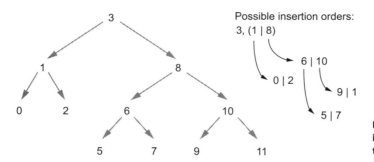

Figure 10.5 Many different insertion orders can produce the same tree.

produce identical trees. Figure 10.5 shows the possible insertion orders that will result in the same tree.

A set of 10 elements can be inserted into a tree in 3,628,800 distinct orders, but this will only produce 16,796 distinct trees. These trees will range from perfectly balanced to totally unbalanced. From a more pragmatic point of view, ordered trees are very efficient for storing and retrieving random data, but they're very bad for storing and retrieving preordered data. You'll soon learn how to solve this problem.

10.1.6 *Tree traversal order*

Given a specific tree as represented in figure 10.5, one common use case is to traverse it, visiting all elements one after the other. This is typically the case when mapping or folding trees, and to a lesser extent when searching a tree for a particular value. When we studied lists, you learned that there are two ways to traverse them: from left to right or from right to left. Trees offer many more approaches, and among them we'll make a distinction between recursive and nonrecursive ones.

RECURSIVE TRAVERSAL ORDERS

Consider the left branch of the tree in figure 10.5. This branch is itself a tree composed of the root 1, the left branch 0, and the right branch 2. You can traverse this tree in six orders:

- 1, 0, 2
- 1, 2, 0
- 0, 1, 2
- 2, 1, 0
- 0, 2, 1
- 2, 0, 1

You can see that three of these orders are symmetric with the other three. 1, 0, 2 and 1, 2, 0 are symmetric. You start from the root and then visit the two branches, from left to right or from right to left. The same holds for 0, 1, 2 and 2, 1, 0, which differ only by the order of the branches, and again for 0, 2, 1 and 2, 0, 1. You'll only consider the left to right direction (because the other direction is exactly the same, as if it were seen in a mirror), so you're left with three orders, which are named after the position of the root:

- Pre order (1 0 2 or 1 2 0)
- In order (0 1 2 or 2 1 0)
- Post order (0 2 1 or 2 0 1)

These terms are coined after the operator position in an operation. To better see the analogy, imagine the root (1) replaced with a plus (+) sign, producing this:

- Prefix (+ 0 2 or + 2 0)
- Infix (0 + 2 or 2 + 0)
- Postfix (0 2 + or 2 0 +)

Applied recursively to the whole tree, these orders result in traversing the tree while giving priority to height, leading to the traversal paths shown in figure 10.6. Note that this type of traversal is generally called *depth first* instead of the more logical *height first*. When talking about the whole tree, height and depth refer to the height of the root and depth of the deepest leaf. These two values are equal.

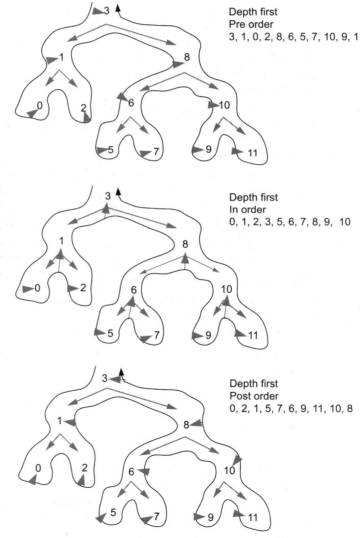

Depth first
Pre order
3, 1, 0, 2, 8, 6, 5, 7, 10, 9, 1

Depth first
In order
0, 1, 2, 3, 5, 6, 7, 8, 9, 10

Depth first
Post order
0, 2, 1, 5, 7, 6, 9, 11, 10, 8

Figure 10.6   Depth-first traversal consists in traversing the tree while giving priority to height. There are three main orders in which this may be applied.

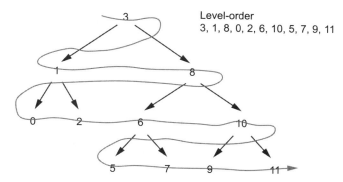

Level-order
3, 1, 8, 0, 2, 6, 10, 5, 7, 9, 11

Figure 10.7 Level-order traversal consists in visiting all the elements of a given level before going to the next level.

NONRECURSIVE TRAVERSAL ORDERS

Another way to traverse a tree is to first visit a complete level and then go to the next level. Again, this can be done from left to right or from right to left. This kind of traversal is called *level-order traversal*, or *breadth-first search*; one example is shown in figure 10.7.

10.2 *Implementing the binary search tree*

In this book, we'll consider traditional binary trees and not leafy trees. A binary tree is implemented the same way as a singly linked list, with a head (called `value`) and two tails (the branches, called `left` and `right`). You'll define an abstract `Tree` class with two subclasses named `T` and `Empty`. `T` represents a non-empty tree, whereas `Empty`, unsurprisingly, represents the empty tree. The following listing represents the minimal `Tree` implementation.

> **Listing 10.1 The `Tree` implementation**

The Tree class is parameterized, and the parameter type must extend Comparable.

The empty tree is represented by an unparameterized singleton.

The value method is public and returns the value of the tree root.

The left and right methods are package private. They'll only be used in the extending inner classes.

```java
public abstract class Tree<A extends Comparable<A>> {
    @SuppressWarnings("rawtypes")
    private static Tree EMPTY = new Empty();
    public abstract A value();
    abstract Tree<A> left();
    abstract Tree<A> right();

    private static class Empty<A extends Comparable<A>> extends Tree<A> {
        @Override
        public A value() {
            throw new IllegalStateException("value() called on empty");
        }
        @Override
```

The Empty subclass represents an empty tree.

```
    Tree<A> left() {
      throw new IllegalStateException("left() called on empty");
    }

    @Override
    Tree<A> right() {
      throw new IllegalStateException("right() called on empty");
    }

    @Override
    public String toString() {
      return "E";
    }
  }
```

The T subclass represents a non-empty tree.

```
  private static class T<A extends Comparable<A>> extends Tree<A> {
    private final Tree<A> left;
    private final Tree<A> right;
    private final A value;

    private T(Tree<A> left, A value, Tree<A> right) {
      this.left = left;
      this.right = right;
      this.value = value;
    }

    @Override
    public A value() {
      return value;
    }

    @Override
    Tree<A> left() {
      return left;
    }

    @Override
    Tree<A> right() {
      return right;
    }

    @Override
    public String toString() {
      return String.format("(T %s %s %s)", left, value, right);
    }
  }

  @SuppressWarnings("unchecked")
  public static <A extends Comparable<A>> Tree<A> empty() {
    return EMPTY;
  }
}
```

The empty method returns the EMPTY singleton and is defined to prevent compiler warnings about unchecked type assignments from leaking out of the Tree class.

This class is quite simple, but it's useless as long as you have no way to construct a real tree.

EXERCISE 10.1

Define an `insert` method to insert a value into a tree. The name of the method, `insert`, isn't very well chosen, because nothing should really be inserted. As usual, the `Tree` structure is immutable and persistent, so a new tree with the inserted value must be constructed, leaving the original tree untouched. But it's standard to call this method `insert` because it has the same function as insertion in traditional programming.

If the value is equal to the root, you must return a new tree with the inserted value as the root and the two original branches left unchanged. Otherwise, a value lower than the root is inserted in the left branch, and a value higher than the root is inserted in the right branch. Declare the method in the parent `Tree` class, and implement it in both subclasses. This is the method signature:

```
public abstract Tree<A> insert(A a);
```

SOLUTION 10.1

The `Empty` implementation constructs a new `T` with the inserted value as the root and two empty trees as the branches:

```
public Tree<A> insert(A insertedValue) {
  return new T<>(empty(), insertedValue, empty());
}
```

The `T` implementation is a bit more complex. First, it compares the inserted value with the root. If it's lower, it constructs a new `T` with the current root and the current right branch. The left branch is the result of recursively inserting the value into the original left branch.

If the value is higher than the root, it constructs a new `T` with the current root and the current left branch. The right branch is the result of recursively inserting the value into the original right branch.

Finally, if the value is equal to the root, you return a new tree composed of the inserted value as the root and the two original branches left untouched:

```
public Tree<A> insert(A insertedValue) {
  return insertedValue.compareTo(this.value) < 0
      ? new T<>(left.insert(insertedValue), this.value, right)
      : insertedValue.compareTo(this.value) > 0
          ? new T<>(left, this.value, right.insert(insertedValue))
          : new T<>(this.left, insertedValue, this.right);
}
```

Note that this is different from what happens in a Java `TreeSet`, which is unchanged if you try to insert an element that's equal to an element already in the set. Although this behavior might be acceptable for mutable elements, it's not acceptable when elements are immutable. You may think that it's a waste of time and memory space to construct a new instance of T with the same left branch, the same right branch, and a root equal to the current root, because you could simply return this. Returning this would be equivalent to returning

```
new T<>(this.left, this.value, this.right)
```

If this was what you intended, returning this would be a good optimization. This would work, but it would be tedious to obtain the same result as mutating a tree element. You'd have to remove the element before inserting an equal element with some changed properties. You'll encounter this use case when implementing a map in chapter 11.

You may be wondering whether you should implement stack-safe recursion, since the insert method is recursive. As I said previously, there's no need to do so with a balanced tree, because the height (which determines the maximum number of recursion steps), is generally much lower than the size. But you've seen that this isn't always the case, particularly if the elements to be inserted are ordered. This could eventually result in a tree with only one branch, which would have its height equal to its size (minus 1) and would overflow the stack.

For now, though, you won't bother with this problem. Rather than implementing stack-safe recursive operations, you'll find a way to automatically balance trees. The simple tree you're working on is only for learning. It will never be used in production. But balanced trees are more complex to implement, so you'll start with simple unbalanced trees.

EXERCISE 10.2

One operation often used on trees consists of checking whether a specific element is present in the tree. Implement a member method that performs this check. Here's its signature:

```
boolean member(A a)
```

HINT

Implement this as an abstract method in the Tree parent class with a specific implementation in each subclass.

SOLUTION 10.2

Let's start with the T subclass implementation. You have to compare the parameter with the tree value (which means the value at the root of the tree). If the parameter is lower, recursively apply the comparison to the left branch. If it's higher, recursively apply the comparison to the right branch. If the value and the parameter are equal, simply return true:

```
public boolean member(A value) {
  return value.compareTo(this.value) < 0
      ? left.member(value)
      : value.compareTo(this.value) > 0
          ? right.member(value)
          : true;
}
```

Note that this code can be simplified into the following:

```
public boolean member(A value) {
  return value.compareTo(this.value) < 0
      ? left.member(value)
      : value.compareTo(this.value) == 0 || right.member(value);
}
```

But you may find the first version clearer. Of course, the Empty implementation returns false.

EXERCISE 10.3

To simplify tree creation, write a static method that takes a vararg argument and inserts all elements into an empty tree. Here's its signature:

```
public static <A extends Comparable<A>> Tree<A> tree(A... as)
```

HINT

Start by implementing a method that takes a list as its argument. Then define the vararg method in terms of the list method.

SOLUTION 10.3

This is more an exercise about lists than about trees! Here's the solution:

```
public static <A extends Comparable<A>> Tree<A> tree(List<A> list) {
  return list.foldLeft(empty(), t -> t::insert);
}

@SafeVarargs
public static <A extends Comparable<A>> Tree<A> tree(A... as) {
  return tree(List.list(as));
}
```

EXERCISE 10.4

Write methods to compute the size and height of a tree. Here are their signatures in the Tree class:

```
public abstract int size();
public abstract int height();
```

SOLUTION 10.4

Of course, the Empty implementation of size returns 0. And as I said previously, the Empty implementation of the height method returns -1. The implementation of the size method in the T class returns 1 plus the size of each branch. The implementation of the height method returns 1 plus the maximum height of the two branches:

```
public int size() {
  return 1 + left.size() + right.size();
}

public int height() {
  return 1 + Math.max(left.height(), right.height());
}
```

Based on this, you can see why the height of an empty tree needs to be equal to -1. If it were 0, the height would be equal to the number of elements in the path, instead of the number of segments.

Note that these methods are just for illustration. In reality, you'd memoize the height and size as you did for `length` in `List`. Look at the code accompanying this book for a reminder of how this is done.

EXERCISE 10.5

Write `max` and `min` methods to compute the maximum and minimum values contained in a tree.

HINT

Think of what the methods should return in the `Empty` class.

SOLUTION 10.5

Of course, there are no minimum or maximum values in an empty tree. The solution is to return a `Result<A>`, and the `Empty` implementations will return `Result.empty()`. The implementation for the `T` class is a bit tricky. For the `max` method, the solution is to return the `max` of the right branch. If the right branch isn't empty, this will be a recursive call. If the right branch is empty, you'll get `Result.Empty`. You then know that the max value is the value of the current tree, so you can simply call the `orElse` method on the return value of the `right.max()` method:

```
public Result<A> max() {
   return right.max().orElse(() -> Result.success(value));
}
```

Recall that the `orElse` method evaluates its argument lazily, which means it takes a `Supplier<Result<A>>`. Of course, the `min` method is completely symmetrical:

```
public Result<A> min() {
   return left.min().orElse(() -> Result.success(value));
}
```

10.3   *Removing elements from trees*

Unlike singly linked lists, trees allow you to retrieve a specific element, as you saw when you developed the `member` method in exercise 10.2. This should also make it possible to remove a specific element from a tree.

EXERCISE 10.6

Write a `remove` method that removes an element from a tree. This method will take an element as its parameter. If this element is present in the tree, it will be removed, and the method will return a new tree without this element. Of course, this new tree will respect the requirements that all elements on a left branch will be lower than the root, and all elements on the right branch will be higher than the root. If the element isn't in the tree, the method will return the tree unchanged. The method signature will be

```
Tree<A> remove(A a)
```

HINT

You'll need to define a method to merge two trees with the particularity that all elements of one are either greater or smaller than all elements of the other. You'll also need an isEmpty method that returns true in the Empty class and false in the T class.

SOLUTION 10.6

Of course, the Empty implementation can't remove anything and will simply return this. For the T subclass implementation, here's the algorithm you'll need to implement:

- If a < this, remove from left.
- If a > this, remove from right.
- Else, the root is to be removed. Merge the left and right branches, discarding the root, and return the result.

The merge is a simplified merge because you know that all elements in the left branch are lower than all elements of the right branch.

First you must define the merge method. Define an abstract method in the Tree class:

```
protected abstract Tree<A> removeMerge(Tree<A> ta)
```

The implementation in the Empty class simply returns the parameter unchanged, because merging ta with an empty tree results in ta:

```
protected Tree<A> removeMerge(Tree<A> ta) {
  return ta;
}
```

The T implementation uses the following algorithm:

- If ta is empty, return this (this can't be empty).
- If ta < this, merge ta in the left branch.
- If ta > this, merge ta in the right branch.

Here's the implementation:

```
protected Tree<A> removeMerge(Tree<A> ta) {
  if (ta.isEmpty()) {
    return this;
  }
  if (ta.value().compareTo(value) < 0) {
    return new T<>(left.removeMerge(ta), value, right);
  } else if (ta.value().compareTo(value) > 0) {
    return new T<>(left, value, right.removeMerge(ta));
  }
  throw new IllegalStateException("We shouldn't be here");
}
```

Note that the method throws an exception if the roots of the two trees are equal, which should never happen because the two trees to be merged are supposed to be the left and right branches of the same original tree.

Now you can write the remove method:

```
public Tree<A> remove(A a) {
  if (a.compareTo(this.value) < 0) {
    return new T<>(left.remove(a), value, right);
  } else if (a.compareTo(this.value) > 0) {
    return new T<>(left, value, right.remove(a));
  } else {
    return left.removeMerge (right);
  }
}
```

10.4   *Merging arbitrary trees*

In the previous section, you used a restricted merging method that could only merge trees where all values in one tree were lower than all values of the other tree. Merging for trees is the equivalent of concatenation for lists. You need a more general method to handle merging for arbitrary trees.

EXERCISE 10.7 (HARD)

So far, you've only merged trees in which all elements in one tree were greater than all elements of the other. Write a merge method that merges arbitrary trees. Its signature will be

```
public abstract Tree<A> merge(Tree<A> a);
```

SOLUTION 10.7

The Empty implementation will simply return its parameter:

```
public Tree<A> merge(Tree<A> a) {
  return a;
}
```

The T subclass implementation will use the following algorithm, in which *this* means the tree in which the method is defined:

- If the parameter tree is empty, return this.
- If the root of the parameter is higher than this root, remove the left branch of the parameter tree and merge the result with this right branch. Then merge the result with the parameter's left branch.
- If the root of the parameter is lower than this root, remove the right branch of the parameter tree and merge the result with this left branch. Then merge the result with the parameter's right branch.
- If the root of the parameter is equal to this root, merge the left branch of the parameter with this left branch and merge the right branch of the parameter with this right branch.

Here's the implementation of this algorithm:

```
public Tree<A> merge(Tree<A> a) {
  if (a.isEmpty()) {
    return this;
  }
  if (a.value().compareTo(this.value) > 0) {
    return new T<>(left, value, right.merge(new T<>(empty(),
                            a.value(), a.right())))).merge(a.left());
  }
  if (a.value().compareTo(this.value) < 0) {
    return new T<>(left.merge(new T<>(a.left(), a.value(),
                         empty()))), value, right).merge(a.right());
  }
  return new T<>(left.merge(a.left()), value, right.merge(a.right()));
}
```

This algorithm is illustrated by figures 10.8 through 10.17.

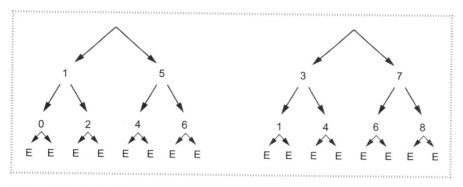

Figure 10.8 The two trees to be merged. On the left is `this` tree, and on the right is the parameter tree.

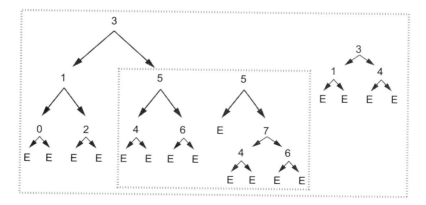

Figure 10.9 The root of the parameter tree is higher than the root of `this` tree. Merge the right branch of `this` tree with the parameter tree with its left branch removed. (The merging operation is represented by the dotted box.)

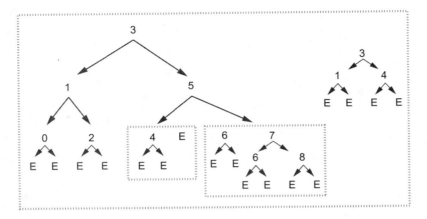

Figure 10.10   The roots of each tree to be merged being equal, you use `this` value for the result of the merge. The left branch will be the result of merging the two left branches, and the right branch will be the result of merging the two right branches.

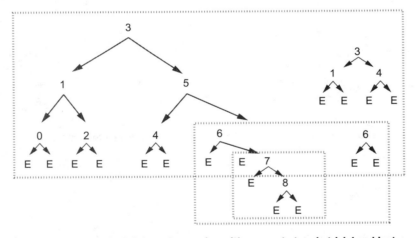

Figure 10.11   For the left branch, merging with an empty tree is trivial and just returns the original tree (root 4 and two empty branches). For the right branch, the first tree has empty branches and 6 as its root, and the second tree has 7 as its root, so you remove the left branch of the 7 rooted tree and use the result to merge with the empty right branch of the 6 rooted tree. The removed left branch will be merged with the result of the previous merge. Note that the 6 rooted tree on the right comes from the 7 rooted tree, where it has been replaced by an empty tree.

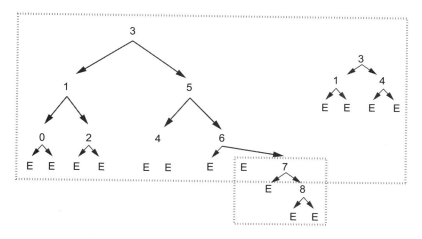

Figure 10.12 The two trees to be merged have equal roots (6) so you merge the branches (left with left and right with right). Because the tree to be merged has both branches empty, there is in fact nothing to do.

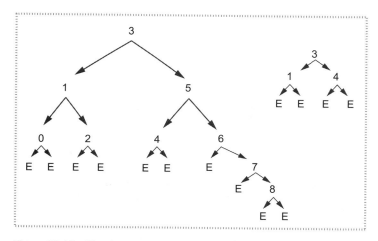

Figure 10.13 Merging an empty tree simply results in the tree to be merged. You're left with two trees with the same root to merge.

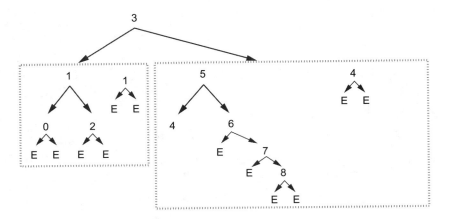

Figure 10.14   Merging two trees with the same root is simple: just merge right with right and left with left, and use the results as the new branches.

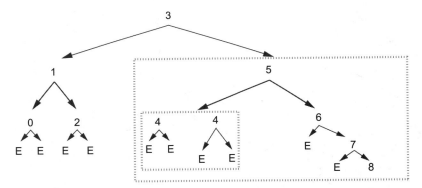

Figure 10.15   The left merge is trivial because the roots are equal and both branches of the tree to be merged are empty. On the right side, the tree to be merged has a lower root (4), so you remove the right branch (E) and merge what remains with the left branch of the original tree.

You can see in these figures that merging two trees gives a tree with a size (number of elements) that can be smaller than the sum of the sizes of the original trees, because duplicate elements are automatically removed.

On the other hand, the height of the result is higher than you might expect. Merging two trees of height 3 can lead to a resulting tree of height 5. It's easy to see that the optimal height shouldn't be higher than log2(size). In other words, the optimal height is the smallest power of 2 higher than the resulting size. In this example, the sizes of the two original trees were 7 and their heights were 3. The size of the merged tree is 9, and the optimal height would be 4 instead of 5. In such a small example, this

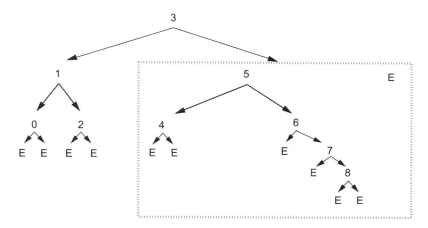

Figure 10.16   Merging two identical trees doesn't need any explanation.

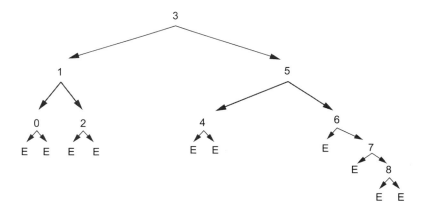

Figure 10.17   The final result after merging the last empty tree

might not be a problem. But when you're merging big trees, you could end up with badly balanced trees, resulting in suboptimal performance, and even possibly a stack overflow when using recursive methods.

10.5   *Folding trees*

No, this isn't a section about origami. Folding a tree is similar to folding a list; it consists of transforming a tree into a single value. For example, in a tree of numerical values, computing the sum of all elements can be represented through a fold. But folding a tree is more complicated than folding a list.

Computing the sum of the elements in a tree of integers is trivial because the addition is associative in both directions and commutative. In other words, the following expressions have the same values:

```
*  (((1 + 3) + 2) + ((5 + 7) + 6)) + 4
*  4 + ((2 + (1 + 3)) + (6 + (5 + 7)))
*  (((7 + 5) + 6) + ((3 + 1) + 2)) + 4
*  4 + ((6 + (7 + 5)) + (2 + (3 + 1)))
*  (1 +(2 + 3)) + (4 + (5 + (6 + (7))))
*  (7 + (6 + 5)) + (4 + (3 + (2 + 1)))
```

Examining these expressions, you can see that they represent some possible results of folding the following tree using addition:

Considering only the order in which the elements are processed, you can recognize the following orders:

- Post order left
- Pre order left
- Post order right
- Pre order right
- In order left
- In order right

Note that *left* and *right* mean *starting from the left* and *starting from the right.* You can verify this by computing the result for each expression. For example, the first expression can be reduced as follows:

```
(((1 + 3) + 2) + ((5 + 7) + 6 )) + 4
((   4    + 2) + ((5 + 7) + 6)) + 4 used: 1, 3
(        6    + ((5 + 7) + 6)) + 4 used: 1, 3, 2
(        6    + (   12   + 6)) + 4 used: 1, 3, 2, 5, 7
(        6    +        18  ) + 4 used: 1, 3, 2, 5, 7, 6
              24              + 4 used: 1, 3, 2, 5, 7, 6
                            28 used: 1, 3, 2, 5, 7, 6, 4
```

There are other possibilities, but these six are the most interesting. Although they're equivalent for addition, they may not be for other operations, such as adding characters to strings or adding elements to lists.

10.5.1 *Folding with two functions*

The problem when folding a tree is that the recursive approach will in fact be bi-recursive. You can fold each branch with the given operation, but you need a way to combine the two results into one. Does this remind you of list-folding parallelization?

Yes, you need an additional operation. If the operation needed to fold Tree<A> is a function from B to A to B, you need an additional function from B to B to B to merge the left and right results.

EXERCISE 10.8

Write a `foldLeft` method that folds a tree, given the two functions just described. Its signature in the `Tree` class will be as follows:

```
public abstract <B> B foldLeft(B identity,
                               Function<B, Function<A, B>> f,
                               Function<B, Function<B, B>> g)
```

SOLUTION 10.8

The implementation in the `Empty` subclass is straightforward and will simply return the identity element. The `T` subclass implementation is a bit more difficult. What you need to do is recursively compute the fold for each branch, and then combine the results with the root. The problem is that each branch fold returns a B, but the root is an A, and you have no function from A to B at your disposal. The solution might be as follows:

1 Recursively fold the left branch and the right branch, giving two B values.
2 Combine these two B values with the g function, and then combine the result with the root and return the result.

This could be one solution:

```
public <B> B foldLeft(B identity,
                      Function<B, Function<A, B>> f,
                      Function<B, Function<B, B>> g) {
  return g.apply(right.foldLeft(identity, f, g))
      .apply(f.apply(left.foldLeft(identity, f, g)).apply(this.value));
}
```

Simple? Not so. The problem is that the g function is a function from B to B to B, so you could easily swap the arguments:

```
public <B> B foldLeft(B identity,
                      Function<B, Function<A, B>> f,
                      Function<B, Function<B, B>> g) {
  return g.apply(*left*.foldLeft(identity, f, g))
      .apply(f.apply(*right*.foldLeft(identity, f, g)).apply(this.value));
}
```

Is this a problem? Yes, it is. If you fold a list with an operation that's commutative, like addition, the result won't change. But if you use an operation that isn't commutative, you're in trouble. The end result is that the two solutions will give you different results. For example, the following function,

```
Tree.tree(4, 2, 6, 1, 3, 5, 7)
          .foldLeft(List.list(), list -> a -> list.cons(a),
                                 x -> y -> y.concat(x)).toString();
```

will produce the following result with the first solution,

```
[4, 2, 1, 3, 6, 5, 7, NIL]
```

and the following result with the second solution:

```
[4, 6, 7, 5, 2, 3, 1, NIL]
```

Which is the right result? You can find the original result by switching the arguments of the second function:

```
Tree.tree(4, 2, 6, 1, 3, 5, 7)
           .foldLeft(List.list(), list -> a -> list.cons(a),
                                   x -> y -> x.concat(y)).toString();
```

In fact, both lists, although in different orders, represent the same tree. Figure 10.18 represents the two cases.

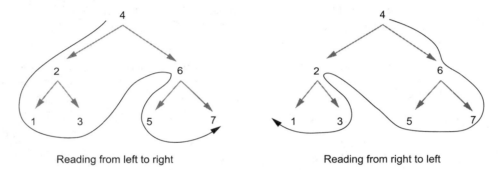

Reading from left to right   Reading from right to left

Figure 10.18 Reading the tree from left to right and from right to left

In the code accompanying this book, you'll find these two examples. Be aware that this isn't a comparable difference as foldLeft and foldRight for the List class. Folding from right to left is in fact a left fold of the reversed list. A right fold would look like this:

```
@Override
public <B> B foldRight(B identity,
                       Function<A, Function<B, B>> f,
                       Function<B, Function<B, B>> g) {
  return g.apply(f.apply(this.value).apply(left.foldRight(identity, f, g)))
      .apply(right.foldRight(identity, f, g));
}
```

Because there are many traversal orders, there are many possible implementations that will give different results with noncommutative operations. You'll find examples in the comments in the code accompanying this book.

10.5.2 *Folding with a single function*

It's also possible to fold with a single function taking an additional parameter, which means, for example, a function from B to A to B to B. Once again, there will be many possible implementations, depending upon the traversal order.

EXERCISE 10.9

Write three methods to fold a tree: `foldInOrder`, `foldPreOrder`, and `foldPostOrder`. Applied to the tree in figure 10.18, the elements should be processed as follows:

- In order: 1 2 3 4 5 6 7
- Pre order: 4 2 1 3 6 5 7
- Post order: 1 3 2 5 7 6 4

Here are the method signatures:

```
<B> B foldInOrder(B identity, Function<B, Function<A, Function<B, B>>> f);
<B> B foldPreOrder(B identity, Function<A, Function<B, Function<B, B>>> f);
<B> B foldPostOrder(B identity, Function<B, Function<B, Function<A, B>>> f);
```

SOLUTION 10.9

Here are the solutions. The `Empty` implementations all return `identity`. The implementations in the `T` class are as follows:

```
public <B> B foldInOrder(B identity,
                      Function<B, Function<A, Function<B, B>>> f) {
  return f.apply(left.foldInOrder(identity, f))
          .apply(value).apply(right.foldInOrder(identity, f));
}

public <B> B foldPreOrder(B identity,
                      Function<A, Function<B, Function<B, B>>> f) {
  return f.apply(value).apply(left.foldPreOrder(identity, f))
                      .apply(right.foldPreOrder(identity, f));
}

public <B> B foldPostOrder(B identity,
                      Function<B, Function<B, Function<A, B>>> f) {
  return f.apply(left.foldPostOrder(identity, f))
          .apply(right.foldPostOrder(identity, f)).apply(value);
}
```

10.5.3 *Which fold implementation to choose*

You've now written five different fold methods. Which one should you choose? To answer this question, let's consider what properties a fold method should have.

There's a relationship between the way a data structure is folded and the way it's constructed. You can construct a data structure by starting with an empty element and adding elements one by one. This is the reverse of folding. Ideally, you should be able to fold a structure using specific parameters that allow you to turn the fold into an identity function. For a list, this would be as follows:

```
list.foldRight(List.list(), i -> l -> l.cons(i));
```

You could also use `foldLeft`, but the function would be slightly more complex:

```
list1.foldLeft(List.list(), l -> i -> l.reverse().cons(i).reverse());
```

(This isn't surprising; if you look at the `foldRight` implementation, you'll see that it internally uses `foldLeft` and `reverse`.)

Can you do the same with tree folding? To achieve this, you'll need a new way to build trees by assembling a left tree, a root, and a right tree. That way, you'll be able to use any of the three fold methods taking only one function parameter.

EXERCISE 10.10 (HARD)

Create a method that combines two trees and a root to create a new tree. Its signature will be

```
Tree<A> tree(Tree<A> left, A a, Tree<A> right)
```

This method should allow you to reconstruct a tree identical to the original tree using any of these three folding methods: `foldPreOrder`, `foldInOrder`, and `foldPostOrder`.

HINT

You'll have to handle the two cases differently. If the trees to be merged are ordered, which means that the maximum value of the first one is lower than the root, and the minimum value of the second one is higher than the root, you can simply assemble the three using the `T` constructor. Otherwise, you should fall back to another way of constructing the result.

SOLUTION 10.10

There are several ways to implement this method. One is to first define a method that tests the two trees to check whether they're ordered. For this, you can first define methods to return the result of the value comparison:

```
public static <A extends Comparable<A>> boolean lt(A first, A second) {
  return first.compareTo(second) < 0;
}

public static <A extends Comparable<A>> boolean lt(A first, A second,
                                                    A third) {
  return lt(first, second) && lt(second, third);
}
```

Then you can define the ordered method that implements the tree comparison:

```
public static <A extends Comparable<A>> boolean ordered(Tree<A> left,
                                                 A a, Tree<A> right) {
  return left.max().flatMap(lMax -> right.min().map(rMin ->
        lt(lMax, a, rMin))).getOrElse(left.isEmpty() && right.isEmpty())
    || left.min().mapEmpty().flatMap(ignore -> right.min().map(rMin ->
        lt(a, rMin))).getOrElse(false)
    || right.min().mapEmpty().flatMap(ignore -> left.max().map(lMax ->
        lt(lMax, a))).getOrElse(false);
}
```

The first test (before the first || operator) returns `true` if both trees are not empty and the left `max`, a, and the right `min` are ordered. The second and third tests handle the cases where the left or the right tree is empty (but not both). Note that the `Result.mapEmpty` method returns `Success<Nothing>` if the `Result` is `Empty`, and a failure otherwise.

Using this method, writing the `tree` method is very simple:

```
public static <A extends Comparable<A>> Tree<A> tree(Tree<A> t1,
                                             A a, Tree<A> t2) {

   return ordered(t1, a, t2)
       ? new T<>(t1, a, t2)
       : ordered(t2, a, t1)
           ? new T<>(t2, a, t1)
           : Tree.<A>empty().insert(a).merge(t1).merge(t2);
}
```

Note that if the trees aren't ordered, you test the inverse order before falling back to the normal insert/merge algorithm.

Now you can fold a tree and obtain the same tree as the original one (provided you use the correct function). You'll find the following examples in the test code accompanying this book:

```
tree.foldInOrder(Tree.<Integer>empty(),
                       t1 -> i -> t2 -> Tree.tree(t1, i, t2));
tree.foldPostOrder(Tree.<Integer>empty(),
                       t1 -> t2 -> i -> Tree.tree(t1, i, t2));
tree.foldPreOrder(Tree.<Integer>empty(),
                       i -> t1 -> t2 -> Tree.tree(t1, i, t2));
```

You could also define a fold method that takes only one function with two parameters, as you did for `List`. The trick is to first transform the tree into a list, as shown in this example of `foldLeft`:

```
public <B> B foldLeft(B identity, Function<B, Function<A, B>> f) {
   return toListPreOrderLeft().foldLeft(identity, f);
}

protected List<A> toListPreOrderLeft() {
   return left().toListPreOrderLeft()
                   .concat(right().toListPreOrderLeft()).cons(value);
}
```

This might not be the fastest implementation, but it might still be useful.

10.6 *Mapping trees*

Like lists, trees can be mapped, but mapping trees is a bit more complicated. Applying a function to each element of a tree may seem trivial, but it's not. The problem is that not all functions will preserve ordering. Adding a given value to all elements of a tree of integers will be fine, but using the function f(x) = x * x will be much more complicated if the tree might contain negative values, because simply applying the function "in place" will not result in a binary search tree.

EXERCISE 10.11

Define a map method for trees. Try to preserve the tree structure if possible. For example, mapping a tree of integers by squaring values might produce a tree with a different structure, but mapping by adding a constant should not.

SOLUTION 10.11

Using one of the fold methods makes it very straightforward. There are several possible implementations using the various fold methods. Here's an example:

```
public <B extends Comparable<B>> Tree<B> map(Function<A, B> f) {
  return foldInOrder(Tree.<B>empty(),
                     t1 -> i -> t2 -> Tree.tree(t1, f.apply(i), t2));
}
```

Of course, the `Empty` implementation returns `empty()` (not `this`, because the type would be invalid).

10.7 Balancing trees

As I said earlier, trees will work well if they're balanced, which means that all paths from the root to a leaf element have nearly the same length. In a perfectly balanced tree, the difference in lengths will not exceed 1, which happens if the deeper level isn't full. (Only perfectly balanced trees of size $2n + 1$ have all paths from the root to a leaf element of the same length.)

Using unbalanced trees may lead to bad performance, because operations could need an amount of time proportional to the size of the tree instead of to log2(size). More dramatically, unbalanced trees can cause a stack overflow when using recursive operations. There are two ways to avoid this problem:

- Balance the unbalanced trees.
- Use self-balancing trees.

Once you have a way to balance trees, it's easy to make trees self-balancing by automatically launching the balancing process after each operation that could potentially change the tree structure.

10.7.1 Rotating trees

Before you can balance trees, you need to know how to incrementally change the structure of a tree. The technique used is called *rotating* the tree, and it's illustrated in figures 10.19 and 10.20.

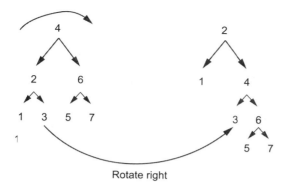

Figure 10.19   Rotating a tree to the right. During the rotation, the line between 2 and 3 is replaced with a line between 2 and 4, so element 3 is moved to become the left element of 4.

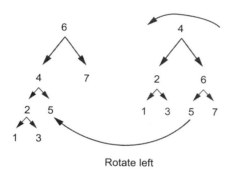

Rotate left

Figure 10.20   Rotating a tree to the left. The left element of 6 becomes 4 (formerly the parent of 6) so the 5 is moved to become the right element of 4.

EXERCISE 10.12

Write `rotateRight` and `rotateLeft` methods to rotate a tree in both directions. Be careful to preserve the branch order. Left elements must always be lower than the root, and right elements must always be higher than the root. Declare abstract methods in the parent class. Make them protected, because they'll only be used from inside the Tree class. Here are the signatures in the parent class:

```
protected abstract Tree<A> rotateLeft();
protected abstract Tree<A> rotateRight();
```

SOLUTION 10.12

The `Empty` implementations simply return `this`. In the `T` class, these are the steps for the right rotation:

1 Test the left branch for emptiness.
2 If the left branch is empty, just return `this`, because rotating right consists of promoting the left element to root. (You can't promote an empty tree.)

3   If the left element isn't empty, it becomes the root, so a new `T` is created with `left.value` as the root. The left branch of the left element becomes the left branch of the new tree. For the right branch, you construct a new tree with the original root as the root, the right branch of the original left as the left branch, and the original right as the right branch.

The left rotation is symmetrical:

```
protected Tree<A> rotateLeft() {
  return right.isEmpty()
      ? this
      : new T<>(new T<>(left, value, right.left()),
                                    right.value(), right.right());
}

protected Tree<A> rotateRight() {
  return left.isEmpty()
      ? this
      : new T<>(left.left(), left.value(),
                            new T<>(left.right(), value, right));
}
```

The explanation seems complex, but it's really very simple. Just compare the code with the figures to see what's happening.

    If you try to rotate a tree several times, you'll arrive at a point where one branch is empty, and the tree can't be rotated any longer in the same direction.

EXERCISE 10.13

To balance the tree, you'll also need methods to transform a tree into an ordered list. Write a method to change a tree into an in-order list from right to left (which means in descending order). If you want to try more exercises, don't hesitate to define a method for in-order left to right, as well as methods for pre order and post order.

    Here's the signature for the `toListInOrderRight` method:

```
public List<A> toListInOrderRight()
```

SOLUTION 10.13

This is very simple and is more related to lists than to trees. `Empty` implementations simply return an empty list. You might think of the following implementation:

```
public List<A> toListInOrderRight() {
  return right.toListInOrderRight().concat(List.list(value))
                              .concat((left.toListInOrderRight()));
}
```

Unfortunately, this method will overflow the stack if the tree is very badly balanced. You need this method to balance a tree, so it would be sad if it couldn't work with an unbalanced tree!

Here's a stack-safe recursive version:

```
public List<A> toListInOrderRight() {
  return unBalanceRight(List.list(), this).eval();
}

private TailCall<List<A>> unBalanceRight(List<A> acc, Tree<A> tree) {
  return tree.isEmpty()
      ? TailCall.ret(acc)
      : tree.left().isEmpty()
         ? TailCall.sus(() ->
                 unBalanceRight(acc.cons(tree.value()), tree.right()))
         : TailCall.sus(() -
    > unBalanceRight(acc, tree.rotateRight()));
}
```

❶ Adds the tree to the accumulator list

❷ Rotates the tree until the left branch is empty

The `unBalanceRight` method simply rotates the tree to the right until the left branch is empty ❷. Then it calls itself recursively to do the same thing to all the right sub-trees, after having added the tree value to the accumulator list ❶. Eventually the tree parameter is found empty and the method returns the list accumulator.

10.7.2 Balancing trees using the Day-Stout-Warren algorithm

The Day-Stout-Warren algorithm is simple. First, transform the tree into a totally unbalanced tree. Then apply rotations until the tree is fully balanced. Transforming the tree into a totally unbalanced one is a simple matter of making an in-order list and creating a new tree from it. Because you want to create the tree in ascending order, you'll have to create a list in descending order and then start to rotate the result left. Of course, you can choose the symmetric case.

Here's the algorithm for obtaining a fully balanced tree:

1 Rotate the tree left until the result has branches as equal as possible. This means that the branch sizes will be equal if the total size is odd, and will differ by 1 if the total size is even. The result will be a tree with two totally unbalanced branches of near to equal size.

2 Apply the same process recursively to the right branch. Apply the symmetric process (rotating right) to the left branch.

3 Stop when the height of the result is equal to log2(size). For this you'll need the following helper method:

```
public static int log2nlz(int n) {
  return n == 0
      ? 0
      : 31 - Integer.numberOfLeadingZeros(n);
}
```

EXERCISE 10.14

Implement the `balance` method to fully balance any tree. This will be a static method taking the tree to be balanced as its parameter.

HINT

This implementation will be based on several helper methods: A front method will create the totally unbalanced tree by calling the `toListInOrderRight` method. The resulting list will be folded left into a (totally unbalanced) tree, which will then be easier to balance.

You'll also need a method to test whether a tree is fully balanced or not, and one to recursively rotate a tree. Here's the method for rotating a tree:

```
public static <A> A unfold(A a, Function<A, Result<A>> f) {
  Result<A> ra = Result.success(a);
  return unfold(new Tuple<>(ra, ra), f).eval()._2.getOrElse(a);
}

private static <A> TailCall<Tuple<Result<A>, Result<A>>> unfold(Tuple<Result<A>,
                                            Result<A>> a, Function<A, Result<A>> f) {
  Result<A> x = a._2.flatMap(f::apply);
  return x.isSuccess()
      ? TailCall.sus(() -> unfold(new Tuple<>(a._2, x), f))
      : TailCall.ret(a);
}
```

This method is called `unfold` by analogy to `List.unfold` or `Stream.unfold`. It does the same job (except that the result type of the function is the same as its input type), but it forgets the results, keeping only the two last ones, so it's faster and uses less memory.

SOLUTION 10.14

First, you define the utility method that tests whether a tree is unbalanced. For it to be balanced, the difference between the heights of both branches must be 0 if the total size of branches is even, and 1 if the size is odd:

```
static <A extends Comparable<A>> boolean isUnBalanced(Tree<A> tree) {
  return Math.abs(tree.left().height() - tree.right().height())
                                      > (tree.size() - 1) % 2;
}
```

Then you can write the main balancing methods:

```
public static <A extends Comparable<A>> Tree<A> balance(Tree<A> tree) {
  return balance_(tree.toListInOrderRight().foldLeft(Tree.<A>empty(),
                              t -> a -> new T<>(empty(), a, t)));
}

public static <A extends Comparable<A>> Tree<A> balance_(Tree<A> tree) {
  return !tree.isEmpty() && tree.height() > log2nlz(tree.size())
      ? Math.abs(tree.left().height() - tree.right().height()) > 1
          ? balance_(balanceFirstLevel(tree))
```

```
            : new T<>(balance_(tree.left()), tree.value(),
                                        balance_(tree.right()))
        : tree;
}

private static <A extends Comparable<A>> Tree<A>
                                balanceFirstLevel(Tree<A> tree) {
    return unfold(tree, t -> isUnBalanced(t)
        ? tree.right().height() > tree.left().height()
            ? Result.success(t.rotateLeft())
            : Result.success(t.rotateRight())
        : Result.empty());
}
```

10.7.3 *Automatically balancing trees*

Although the `balance` method is designed to avoid stack overflow when handling big, unbalanced trees, you can't use it on such trees because it would itself overflow the stack during the balancing process. This can be seen in the tests. Testing the `balance` method with a fully unbalanced tree of more than 15,000 elements is impossible.

The solution is to use `balance` only on small fully unbalanced trees and on partially balanced trees of any size. This means that you must balance a tree before it becomes too big. The question is whether you can make the balancing automatic after each modification.

EXERCISE 10.15

Transform the tree you've developed to make it auto-balancing on insertions, merges, and removals.

SOLUTION 10.15

The obvious solution is to call `balance` after each operation that modifies the tree, as in the following code:

```
@Override
public Tree<A> insert(A a) {
    return balance(ins(a));
}

protected Tree<A> ins(A a) {
    return a.compareTo(this.value) < 0
        ? new T<>(left.ins(a), this.value, right)
        : a.compareTo(this.value) > 0
            ? new T<>(left, this.value, right.ins(a))
            : new T<>(this.left, value, this.right);
}
```

This will work for small trees (that, in fact, don't need to be balanced), but it won't work for large ones because it would be much too slow. One solution is to only partially balance trees. For example, you could run the balancing method only when the height is 20 times the ideal height of a fully balanced tree:

```
public Tree<A> insert(A a) {
  Tree<A> t = ins(a);
  return t.height() > log2nlz(t.size()) * 20 ? balance(t) : t;
}
```

10.7.4 Solving the right problem

The performance of the balancing solution may seem far from optimal, but it's a compromise. Creating a tree from an ordered list of 100,000 elements would take 7.5 seconds and produce a tree of height 59, compared with the ideal height of 16. Replacing the value 20 with 10 in the `insert` method will double the time with no benefit, because the resulting tree will have a height of 159. Note that the resulting height isn't proportional to the value you use. It's much better if the tree is balanced close to the last insertion, so it's better to use a high value, just to avoid stack overflow, and to explicitly balance the tree before using it.

But the real question is, what problem are you trying to solve? In fact, there are at least two very different requirements:

- You must be able to create a tree from a huge quantity of elements in any order without the risk of overflowing the stack.
- You must make the tree as well balanced as possible, because this minimizes the height, and the time needed for a search is proportional to the height.

For the first requirement, you don't need to make the tree perfectly balanced. A height of 2,000 is acceptable because this will not overflow the stack. You could simply balance the tree each time 2,000 elements have been inserted. You would then balance the tree again when the construction is finished.

The second requirement is a different story, and the use cases may vary. Some trees are almost never updated, whereas others change continuously. In the first case, it may be OK to balance the tree after each change. In the second, it's probably better to update only after a certain number of changes. Either way, an optimization would be to batch the tree modifications and balance only after each batch. You'll learn more about this in chapter 11.

10.8   Summary

- Trees are recursive data structures in which one element is linked to one or several subtrees.
- Binary search trees allow much faster retrieval of comparable elements.
- Trees may be more or less balanced. Fully balanced trees provide the best performance, whereas totally unbalanced trees have the same performance as lists.
- The size of a tree is the number of elements it contains; its height is the longest path in the tree.

- The tree structure depends on the order of insertion of the tree elements.
- Trees can be traversed in many different orders (pre order, in order, or post order), and in both directions (left to right, or right to left).
- Trees can be easily merged without traversing them.
- Trees can be mapped or rotated as well as folded in many ways.
- Trees can be balanced for better performance and to avoid stack overflows in recursive operations.

Solving real problems with advanced trees

This chapter covers

- Avoiding stack overflow with self-balancing trees
- Implementing the red-black tree
- Creating functional maps
- Designing a functional priority queue

In the previous chapter, you learned about the binary tree structure and basic tree operations. But you saw that to fully benefit from trees, you must either have very specific use cases, such as handling randomly ordered data, or a limited data set, in order to avoid any risk of stack overflows. Making trees stack-safe is much more difficult than it is for lists, because each computing step involves two recursive calls, which makes it impossible to create tail-recursive versions.

In this chapter, we'll study two specific trees:

- The red-black tree is a self-balancing, general-purpose tree with high performance. It's suitable for general use and data sets of any size.
- The leftist heap is a very specific tree suitable for implementing priority queues.

11.1 Better performance and stack safety with self-balancing trees

The Day-Stout-Warren balancing algorithm that you used in the previous chapter isn't well suited for balancing functional trees because it was designed for in-place modifications. In functional programming, in-place modifications are generally avoided, and instead, a new structure is created for each change. A much better solution is to define a balancing process that doesn't involve transforming the tree into a list before reconstructing a totally unbalanced tree and then finally balancing it. There are two ways to optimize this process:

- Directly rotate the original tree (eliminating the list/unbalanced tree process).
- Accept a certain amount of imbalance.

You could try to invent such a solution, but others have long since done that. One of the most efficient self-balancing tree designs is the red-black tree. This structure was invented in 1978 by Guibas and Sedgewick.[1] In 1999, Chris Okasaki published a functional version of the red-black tree algorithm in his book *Purely Functional Data Structures* (Cambridge University Press, 1999). The description was illustrated by an implementation in Standard ML, and a Haskell implementation was added later. It's this algorithm that you'll implement in Java.

If you're interested in functional data structures, I strongly encourage you to buy and read Okasaki's book. You can also read his 1996 thesis with the same title. It's much less complete than his book, but it's available as a free download (www.cs.cmu.edu/~rwh/theses/okasaki.pdf).

11.1.1 The basic tree structure

The red-black tree is a binary search tree (BST) with some additions to its structure and a modified insertion algorithm, which also balances the result. Unfortunately, Okasaki didn't describe removal, which happens to be a far more complex process. But Kimball Germane and Matthew Might described this "missing method" in 2014.[2]

In a red-black tree, each tree (including subtrees) has an additional property representing its color. Besides this, the structure is exactly the same as the BST structure, as shown in the following listing.

> **Listing 11.1 The red-black tree base structure**

```
public abstract class Tree<A extends Comparable<A>> {

    private static Tree E = new E();
    private static Color R = new Red();          Colors are used through
                                                 static singletons.
```

---

[1] Leo J. Guibas and Robert Sedgewick, "A dichromatic framework for balanced trees," *Foundations of Computer Science* (1978), http://mng.bz/Ly5Jl.

[2] Kimball Germane and Matthew Might, "Functional Pearl, Deletion: The curse of the red-black tree," *JFP 24*, 4 (2014): 423–433; http://matt.might.net/papers/germane2014deletion.pdf.

```
private static Color B = new Black();
protected abstract boolean isE();
protected abstract boolean isT();
protected abstract boolean isB();
protected abstract boolean isR();
protected abstract boolean isTB();
protected abstract boolean isTR();
public abstract boolean isEmpty();
protected abstract Tree<A> right();
protected abstract Tree<A> left();
protected abstract A value();
public abstract int size();
public abstract int height();

private static class E<A extends Comparable<A>> extends Tree<A> {

  @Override
  protected boolean isE() {
    return true;
  }

  @Override
  public int size() {
    return 0;
  }

  @Override
  public int height() {
    return -1;
  }

  @Override
  public Tree<A> right() {
    return E;
  }

  @Override
  public Tree<A> left() {
    return E;
  }

  @Override
  protected A value() {
    throw new IllegalStateException("value called on Empty");
  }

  @Override
  protected boolean isR() {
    return false;
  }

  @Override
  protected boolean isT() {
    return false;
  }

  @Override
  protected boolean isB() {
    return true;
  }
```

The isE method is (for now) just a shortcut for isEmpty.

Methods are defined to test each characteristic of a tree (emptiness, color, and some combinations of them).

The empty class is named E. This is just a convenience.

An empty tree is always black.

```
    @Override
    protected boolean isTB() {
      return false;
    }

    @Override
    protected boolean isTR() {
      return false;
    }

    @Override
    public boolean isEmpty() {
      return true;
    }

    @Override
    public String toString() {
      return "E";
    }
  }

  private static class T<A extends Comparable<A>> extends Tree<A> {
    private final Tree<A> left;
    private final Tree<A> right;
    private final A value;
    private final Color color;
    private final int length;
    private final int height;

    private T(Color color, Tree<A> left, A value, Tree<A> right) {
      this.color = color;
      this.left = left;
      this.right = right;
      this.value = value;
      this.length = left.size() + 1 + right.size();
      this.height = Math.max(left.height(), right.height()) + 1;
    }

    public boolean isR() {
      return this.color.isR();
    }

    public boolean isB() {
      return this.color.isB();
    }

    @Override
    protected boolean isTB() {
      return this.color.isB();
    }

    @Override
    protected boolean isTR() {
      return this.color.isR();
    }

    @Override
    protected boolean isE() {
```

The non-empty tree is constructed with a color.

```
      return false;
    }

    @Override
    protected boolean isT() {
      return true;
    }

    @Override
    public int size() {
      return length;
    }

    @Override
    public int height() {
      return height;
    }

    @Override
    public boolean isEmpty() {
      return false;
    }

    @Override
    protected Tree<A> right() {
      return right;
    }

    @Override
    protected Tree<A> left() {
      return left;
    }

    @Override
    protected A value() {
      return value;
    }

    @Override
    public String toString() {
      return String.format("(T %s %s %s %s)", color, left, value, right);
    }
  }

  private static abstract class Color {
    abstract boolean isR();
    abstract boolean isB();
  }

  private static class Red extends Color {

    @Override
    boolean isR() {
      return true;
    }

    @Override
    boolean isB() {
      return false;
    }
```

The color classes Red and Black extend the Color abstract class.

```
    @Override
    public String toString() {
      return "R";
    }
  }

  private static class Black extends Color {

    @Override
    boolean isR() {
      return false;
    }

    @Override
    boolean isB() {
      return true;
    }

    @Override
    public String toString() {
      return "B";
    }
  }

  public static <A extends Comparable<A>> Tree<A> empty() {
    return E;
  }
}
```

The `member` method hasn't been represented, nor the other methods such as `fold`, `map`, and so on, because they aren't different from the standard tree versions. As you'll see, only the `insert` and `remove` methods are different.

11.1.2 *Inserting an element into the red-black tree*

The main characteristic of a red-black tree is invariants that must always be verified. While modifying the tree, it will be tested to check whether these invariants are being broken and to restore them through rotations and color changes if necessary. These invariants are as follows:

- An empty tree is black. (This can't change, so there's no need to verify it.)
- The left and right subtrees of a red tree are black. In other words, it's not possible to find two successive reds while descending the tree.
- Every path from the root to an empty subtree has the same number of blacks.

Inserting an element in a red-black tree is then a somewhat complex process that includes checking the invariants after insertion (and rebalancing, if necessary). Here's the corresponding algorithm:

- An empty tree is always black.
- Insertion proper is done exactly as in an ordinary tree, but is followed by balancing.
- Inserting an element into an empty tree produces a red tree.
- After balancing, the root is blackened.

Figures 11.1 through 11.7 illustrate insertion of integers 1 through 7 into an initially empty tree. Figure 11.1 shows the insertion of element 1 into the empty tree. Because you're inserting into an empty tree, the initial color is red. Once the element is inserted, the root is blackened.

Start with an empty tree

Insert 1
Red, because it's inserted into an empty tree

Blacken the root

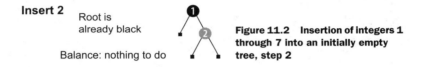

Figure 11.1   Insertion of integers 1 through 7 into an initially empty tree, step 1

Figure 11.2 shows the insertion of element 2. The inserted element is red, the root is already black, and there's still no need for balancing.

Insert 2
Root is already black

Balance: nothing to do

Figure 11.2   Insertion of integers 1 through 7 into an initially empty tree, step 2

Figure 11.3 illustrates insertion of element 3. The inserted element is red, and the tree is being balanced because it has two successive red elements. Because the red element now has two children, they are made black. (Children of a red element must always be black.) Eventually, the root is blackened.

Insert 3

Red, because it's inserted into an empty tree

Balance

Blacken the root

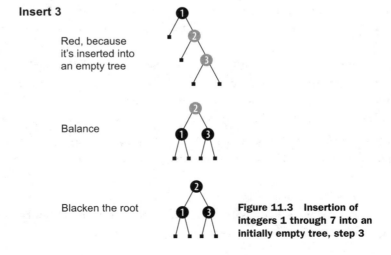

Figure 11.3   Insertion of integers 1 through 7 into an initially empty tree, step 3

Figure 11.4 shows the insertion of element 4. No further manipulation is needed.

Insert 4

Balance and blacken
the root: nothing to
change

**Figure 11.4   Insertion of
integers 1 through 7 into an
initially empty tree, step 4**

Figure 11.5 illustrates the insertion of element 5. You now have two successive red elements, so the tree must be balanced by making 3 the left child of 4. 4 becomes the right child of 2.

Insert 5

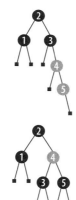

Balance

**Figure 11.5   Insertion of integers 1 through
7 into an initially empty tree, step 5**

Figure 11.6 shows the insertion of element 6. No further manipulation is needed.

Insert 6

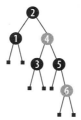

Balance: nothing to do

**Figure 11.6   Insertion of
integers 1 through 7 into an
initially empty tree, step 6**

In figure 11.7, element 7 is added to the tree. Because elements 6 and 7 are two successive red elements, the tree must be balanced. The first step is to make 5 the left child of 6, and 6 the right child of 4, which leaves again two successive red elements: 4 and 6. The tree is then balanced again, making 4 the root, 2 the left child of 4, and 3 the right child of 2. The last operation consists of blackening the root.

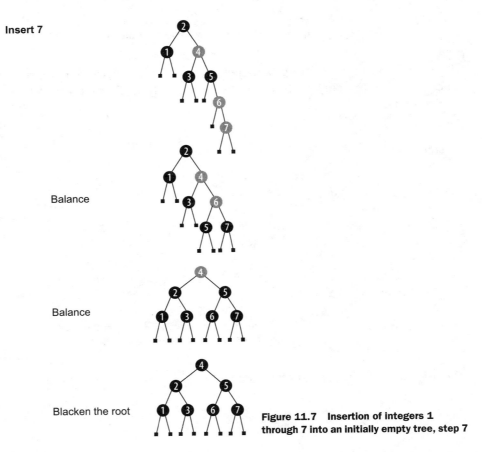

Figure 11.7   Insertion of integers 1 through 7 into an initially empty tree, step 7

The balance method takes the same arguments as the tree constructor: color, left, value, and right. These four parameters are tested for various patterns, and the result is constructed accordingly. In other words, the balance method replaces the tree constructor. Any process using the constructor should be modified to use this method instead.

The following list shows how each pattern of arguments is transformed by this method:

- (T B (T R (T R a x b) y c) z d) → (T R (T B a x b) y (T B c z d))
- (T B (T R a x (T R b y c)) z d) → (T R (T B a x b) y (T B c z d))
- (T B a x (T R (T R b y c) z d)) → (T R (T B a x b) y (T B c z d))

- $(T\ B\ a\ x\ (T\ R\ b\ y\ (T\ R\ c\ z\ d))) \rightarrow (T\ R\ (T\ B\ a\ x\ b)\ y\ (T\ B\ c\ z\ d))$
- $(T\ color\ a\ x\ b) \rightarrow (T\ color\ a\ x\ b)$

Each pair in parentheses corresponds to a tree. The letter T indicates a non-empty tree. B and R indicate the colors. Lowercase letters are placeholders for any value that could be valid at the corresponding place. Each left pattern (those to the left of the arrow, $\rightarrow$) is applied in descending order, which means that if a match is found, the corresponding right pattern is applied as the resulting tree. This way of presenting things is very similar to the `switch ... case` instruction, with the last line being the default case.

EXERCISE 11.1

Write the `insert`, `balance`, and `blacken` methods for implementing insertion into the red-black tree. Unfortunately, Java doesn't implement pattern matching, so you'll have to use conditional instructions instead.

HINT

Write an `ins` method that will perform a regular insertion, and then replace constructor calls with calls to the `balance` method. Next, write the `blacken` method, and finally write the `insert` method in the parent class, calling `blacken` on the result of `ins`. All these methods should be protected, except for the `insert` method, which will be public.

SOLUTION 11.1

For once, I don't recommended using the conditional operator. It's much easier to represent the patterns with a succession of `if` sections, each containing a `return`. Here's the `balance` method:

```
Tree<A> balance(Color color, Tree<A> left, A value, Tree<A> right) {
  if (color.isB() && left.isTR() && left.left().isTR()) {
    return new T<>(R, new T<>(B, left.left().left(), left.left().value(),
      left.left().right()), left.value(), new T<>(B, left.right(), value,
      right));
  }
  if (color.isB() && left.isTR() && left.right().isTR()) {
    return new T<>(R, new T<>(B, left.left(), left.value(),
        left.right().left()), left.right().value(), new T<>(B,
        left.right().right(), value, right));
  }
  if (color.isB() && right.isTR() && right.left().isTR()) {
    return new T<>(R, new T<>(B, left, value, right.left().left()),
        right.left().value(), new T<>(B, right.left().right(),
        right.value(), right.right()));
  }
  if (color.isB() && right.isTR() && right.right().isTR()) {
    return new T<>(R, new T<>(B, left, value, right.left()), right.value(),
        new T<>(B, right.right().left(), right.right().value(),
        right.right().right()));
  }
  return new T<>(color, left, value, right);
}
```

Each if section implements one of the patterns listed before this exercise. If you want to compare them, it's probably much easier to do so in a text editor than on a printed page.

The ins method is very similar to what you did in the standard BST, with the exception that the balance method replaces the T constructor (plus there's the additional color parameter). Here's the implementation in the T class:

```
protected Tree<A> ins(A value) {
  return value.compareTo(this.value) < 0
      ? balance(this.color, this.left.ins(value), this.value, this.right)
      : value.compareTo(this.value) > 0
          ? balance(this.color, this.left, this.value,
                                          this.right.ins(value))
          : this;
}
```

And here's the implementation in the E class:

```
protected Tree<A> ins(A value) {
  return new T<>(R, empty(), value, empty());
}
```

The blacken method is implemented in the Tree class:

```
protected static <A extends Comparable<A>> Tree<A> blacken(Tree<A> t) {
    return t.isEmpty()
        ? empty()
        : new T<>(B, t.left(), t.value(), t.right());
}
```

Finally, the insert method is defined in the Tree class and returns the blackened result of ins:

```
public Tree<A> insert(A value) {
  return blacken(ins(value));
}
```

REMOVING ELEMENTS FROM A RED-BLACK TREE   Removing an element from a red-black tree is discussed by Kimball Germane and Matthew Might in an article titled "The missing method: Deleting from Okasaki's red-black trees" (http://matt.might.net/articles/red-black-delete/). The implementation in Java is too long to include in this book, but it's included in the accompanying code (http://github.com/fpinjava/fpinjava). It will be used in the next exercise.

11.2   *A use case for the red-black tree: maps*

Trees of integers are not often useful (although sometimes they are). One very important use of binary search trees is *maps*, also called *dictionaries* or *associative arrays*. Maps are collections of key/value pairs that allow insertion, removal, and fast retrieval of each pair. Maps are familiar to Java programmers, and Java offers several implementations, among which the most common are the `HashMap` and the `TreeMap`. However, these maps can't be used in a multithreaded environment without using some protection mechanisms that are difficult to design correctly and to use (although concurrent versions are available for this kind of use).

11.2.1 Implementing Map

Functional trees, like the red-black tree you've developed, have the advantage of immutability, which allows you to use them in multithreaded environments without bothering about locks and synchronization. The next listing shows the interface of a `Map` that can be implemented using the red-black tree.

Listing 11.2   A functional map

```java
public class Map<K extends Comparable<K>, V> {

  public Map<K, V> add(K key, V value) {
    . . .
  }

  public boolean contains(K key) {
    . . .
  }

  public Map<K, V> remove(K key) {
    . . .
  }

  public Result<MapEntry<K, V>> get(K key) {
    . . .
  }

  public boolean isEmpty() {
    . . .
  }

  public static <K extends Comparable<K>, V> Map<K, V> empty() {
    return new Map<>();
  }
}
```

EXERCISE 11.2

Complete the `Map` class by implementing all methods.

HINT

You should use a delegate. From this delegate, all methods can be implemented in one line of code. The only (very easy) problem is choosing how you'll store data in the map.

SOLUTION 11.2

The solution is to create a component to represent the key/value pair, and to store instances of this component in a tree. This component is very similar to a `Tuple`, with an important difference: it must be comparable, and the comparison must be based on the key. The equals and hashCode methods will also be based on key equality and hash codes. Here's a possible implementation:

```
public class MapEntry<K extends Comparable<K>, V>
                                implements Comparable<MapEntry<K, V>> {
  public final K key;
  public final Result<V> value;

  private MapEntry(K key, Result<V> value) {
    this.key = key;
    this.value = value;
  }

  @Override
  public String toString() {
    return String.format("MapEntry(%s, %s)", key, value);
  }

  @Override
  public int compareTo(MapEntry<K, V> me) {
    return this.key.compareTo(me.key);
  }

  @Override
  public boolean equals(Object o) {
    return o instanceof MapEntry && this.key.equals(((MapEntry) o).key);
  }

  @Override
  public int hashCode() {
    return key.hashCode();
  }

  public static <K extends Comparable<K>, V> MapEntry<K, V>
                                      mapEntry(K key, V value) {
    return new MapEntry<>(key, Result.success(value));
  }

  public static <K extends Comparable<K>, V> MapEntry<K, V>
                                                  mapEntry(K key) {
    return new MapEntry<>(key, Result.empty());
  }
}
```

Implementing the Map component is now just a matter of delegating all operations to a Tree<MapEntry<Key, Value>>. Here's a possible implementation:

```
import static com.fpinjava.advancedtrees.exercise11_02.MapEntry.*;

public class Map<K extends Comparable<K>, V> {

  protected final Tree<MapEntry<K, V>> delegate;

  private Map() {
    this.delegate = Tree.empty();
  }
```

```
private Map(Tree<MapEntry<K, V>> delegate) {
  this.delegate = delegate;
}

public Map<K, V> add(K key, V value) {
  return new Map<>(delegate.insert(mapEntry(key, value)));
}

public boolean contains(K key) {
  return delegate.member(mapEntry(key));
}

public Map<K, V> remove(K key) {
  return new Map<>(delegate.delete(mapEntry(key)));
}

public MapEntry<K, V> max() {
  return delegate.max();
}

public MapEntry<K, V> min() {
  return delegate.min();
}

public Result<MapEntry<K, V>> get(K key) {
  return delegate.get(mapEntry(key));
}

public boolean isEmpty() {
  return delegate.isEmpty();
}

public static <K extends Comparable<K>, V> Map<K, V> empty() {
  return new Map<>();
}
}
```

11.2.2 *Extending maps*

Not all tree operations have been delegated because some operations don't make much sense in the current conditions. But you may need additional operations in some special use cases. Implementing these operations is easy: extend the Map class and add delegating methods. For example, you might need to find the object with the maximal or minimal key. Another possible need is to fold the map, perhaps to get a list of the contained values. Here's an example of delegating the foldLeft method:

```
public <B> B foldLeft(B identity, Function<B,
        Function<MapEntry<K, V>, B>> f, Function<B, Function<B, B>> g) {
  return delegate.foldLeft(identity, b -> me -> f.apply(b).apply(me), g);
}
```

Generally, folding maps occur in very specific use cases that deserve to be abstracted inside the Map class.

EXERCISE 11.3

Write a values method in the Map class that returns a list of the values contained in the map in ascending key order.

HINT

You might have to create a new folding method in the `Tree` class and delegate to it from the `Map` class.

SOLUTION 11.3

There are several possible implementations of the `values` method. It would be possible to delegate to the `foldInOrder` method, but this method iterates over the tree values in ascending order. Using this method to construct a list would result in a list in descending order. You could reverse the result, but this wouldn't be very efficient.

A much better solution is to add a `foldInReverseOrder` method into the `Tree` class. Recall the `foldInOrder` method:

```
public <B> B foldInOrder(B identity,
                         Function<B, Function<A, Function<B, B>>> f) {
  return f.apply(left.foldInOrder(identity, f))
        .apply(value)
        .apply(right.foldInOrder(identity, f));
}
```

All you have to do is reverse the order:

```
public <B> B foldInReverseOrder(B identity,
                                Function<B, Function<A, Function<B, B>>> f) {
  return f.apply(right.foldInReverseOrder(identity, f))
        .apply(value).apply(left
        .foldInReverseOrder(identity, f));
}
```

As usual, the `Empty` implementation returns `identity`. Now you can delegate to this method from inside the `Map` class:

```
public List<V> values() {
  return List.sequence(delegate.foldInReverseOrder(List.<Result<V>>list(),
    lst1 -> me -> lst2 -> List.concat(lst2,
                          lst1.cons(me.value)))).getOrElse(List.list());
}
```

If you have a problem with the types, you can write the function with explicit types:

```
Function<List<Result<V>>, Function<MapEntry<K, V>,
            Function<List<Result<V>>, List<Result<V>>>>> f =
        lst1 -> me -> lst2 -> List.concat(lst2, lst1.cons(me.value));
```

11.2.3 Using Map with noncomparable keys

The `Map` class is useful and relatively efficient, but it has a big disadvantage compared to the maps you may be used to: the keys must be comparable. The types used for keys are usually comparable, such as integers or strings, but what if you need to use a noncomparable type for the keys?

EXERCISE 11.4

Implement a version of Map that works with noncomparable keys.

HINT

There are two things to modify. First, the MapEntry class should be made comparable, although the key is not. Second, non-equal values might happen to be held in equal map entries, so collisions should be resolved by keeping both colliding entries.

SOLUTION 11.4

The first thing to do is to modify the MapEntry class by removing the need for the key to be comparable:

```
public class MapEntry<K, V> implements Comparable<MapEntry<K, V>> {
```

Note that the MapEntry class is still comparable, although the K type is not.

Second, you must use a different implementation for the compareTo method. One possibility is to compare the map entries based on key hash code comparison:

```
public int compareTo(MapEntry<K, V> that) {

  int thisHashCode = this.hashCode();
  int thatHashCode = that.hashCode();

  return thisHashCode < thatHashCode
      ? -1
      : thisHashCode > thatHashCode
          ? 1
          : 0;
}
```

Then you must handle collisions that happen when two map entries have different keys with the same hash code. In such cases, you should keep both of them. The simplest solution is to store the map entries in a list, and to do this, you must modify the Map class.

First, the tree delegate will have a modified type:

```
protected final Tree<MapEntry<Integer, List<Tuple<K, V>>>> delegate;
```

Then, you must change the constructor that takes the delegate as a parameter:

```
public Map(Tree<MapEntry<Integer, List<Tuple<K, V>>>> delegate) {
  this.delegate = delegate;
}
```

Next, you'll need a method to retrieve the list of key/value tuples corresponding to the same key hash code:

```
private Result<List<Tuple<K, V>>> getAll(K key) {
  return delegate.get(mapEntry(key.hashCode()))
                     .flatMap(x -> x.value.map(lt -> lt.map(t -> t)));
}
```

You can next define the add, contains, remove, and get methods in terms of the getAll method. Here's the add method:

```
public Map<K, V> add(K key, V value) {
  Tuple<K, V> tuple = new Tuple<>(key, value);
  List<Tuple<K, V>> ltkv = getAll(key).map(lt ->
              lt.foldLeft(List.list(tuple), l -> t -> t._1.equals(key)
                  ? l
                  : l.cons(t))).getOrElse(() -> List.list(tuple));
  return new Map<>(delegate.insert(mapEntry(key.hashCode(), ltkv)));
}
```

Here's the contains method:

```
public boolean contains(K key) {
  return getAll(key).map(lt -> lt.exists(t ->
                          t._1.equals(key))).getOrElse(false);
}
```

And here's the remove method:

```
public Map<K, V> remove(K key) {
  List<Tuple<K, V>> ltkv = getAll(key).map(lt ->
      lt.foldLeft(List.<Tuple<K, V>>list(), l -> t -> t._1.equals(key)
          ? l
          : l.cons(t))).getOrElse(List::list);
  return ltkv.isEmpty()
        ? new Map<>(delegate.delete(MapEntry.mapEntry(key.hashCode())))
        : new Map<>(delegate.insert(mapEntry(key.hashCode(), ltkv)));
}
public Result<Tuple<K, V>> get(K key) {
  return getAll(key).flatMap(lt -> lt.first(t -> t._1.equals(key)));
}
```

Finally, the min and max methods need to be removed.

With these modifications, the Map class can be used with noncomparable keys. Using a list for storing the key/value tuples may not be the most efficient implementation, because searching in a list takes an amount of time proportional to the number of elements. But in most cases the list will contain only one element, so the search will return in no time.

One thing to note about this implementation is that the remove method tests whether the resulting list of tuples is empty. If it is, it calls the remove method on the delegate. Otherwise, it calls the insert method to re-insert the new list from which the corresponding entry has been deleted. Recall exercise 10.1 from chapter 10. This is possible only because you decided to implement insert in such a way that an element found equal to an element present in the map would be inserted in place of the original one. If you hadn't done this, you'd have had to first remove the element and then insert the new one with the modified list.

11.3 *Implementing a functional priority queue*

As you know, a queue is a kind of list with a specific access protocol. Queues can be single-ended, like the singly linked list you've used so often in previous chapters. In that case, the access protocol is last in, first out (LIFO). A queue can also be double-ended, allowing the first in, first out (FIFO) access protocol. But there are also data structures with more-specialized protocols. Among them is the *priority queue*.

11.3.1 *The priority queue access protocol*

Values can be inserted in a priority queue in any order, but they can only be retrieved in a very specific order. All values have a priority level, and only the element with the highest priority is available. Priority is represented by an ordering of the elements, which implies that the elements must be comparable in some way.

The priority corresponds to the position of the elements in a theoretical waiting queue. The highest priority belongs to the element with the lowest position (the first element). So, by convention, the highest priority is represented by the lowest value.

Because a priority queue will contain comparable elements, this makes it a good fit for a tree-like structure. But from the user's perspective, the priority queue is seen as a list, with a head (the element with the highest priority, meaning the lowest value) and a tail (the rest of the queue).

11.3.2 *Priority queue use cases*

The priority queue has many different use cases. One that comes to mind quickly is sorting. You could insert elements into a priority queue in random order and retrieve them sorted. This isn't the main use case for this structure, but it may be useful for sorting small data sets.

Another very common use case is reordering elements after asynchronous parallel processing. Let's say you have a number of pages of data to process. To speed processing, you can distribute the data to several threads that will work in parallel. But there's no guarantee that the threads will give back their work in the same order that they received it. To resynchronize the pages, you can put them in a priority queue. The process that is supposed to consume the pages will then poll the queue to check if the available element (the head of the queue) is the expected one. For example, if pages 1, 2, 3, 4, 5, 6, 7, and 8 are given to eight threads to be processed in parallel, the consumer will poll the queue to see if page 1 is available. If it is, it will consume it. If not, it will just wait.

In such a scenario, the queue acts both as a buffer and as a way to reorder the elements. This will generally imply limited variation in size, because elements will be removed from the queue more or less at the same speed they're inserted. Of course, this is true if the consumer consumes elements at approximately the same pace as they're produced by the eight threads. If it isn't the case, it may be possible to use several consumers.

As I said earlier, choosing an implementation is generally a matter of trading space against time or time against time. Here, the choice you have to make is between insertion and retrieval times. In the general use case, retrieval time must be optimized over insertion time because the ratio between the numbers of insertion and retrieval operations will generally be largely in favor of retrieval. (Often the head will be read but not removed.)

11.3.3 *Implementation requirements*

You could implement a priority queue based on the red-black tree, because finding the minimum value is fast. But retrieval doesn't mean removal. If you search for the minimum value and find that it's not the one you want, you'll have to come back later and search again. One solution to this problem could be to memoize the lowest value on insertion. The other change you may want to make is in regard to removal. Removing an element is relatively fast, but because you'll always be removing the lowest element, you might be able to optimize the data structure for this operation.

Another important problem would be in regard to duplicates. Although the red-black tree doesn't allow duplicates, the priority queue must, because it's perfectly possible to have several elements with the same priority. The solution can be the same as for maps—storing lists of elements (instead of single elements) with the same priority—but this will probably not be optimal for performance.

11.3.4 *The leftist heap data structure*

To meet your requirements for the priority queue, you'll use the "leftist heap" described by Okasaki in his book, *Purely Functional Data Structures*.[3] This data structure meets the requirements for the priority queue. Okasaki defines the leftist heap as a "heap-ordered tree with an additional leftist property":

- A heap-ordered tree is a tree in which each branch of an element is greater than or equal to the element itself. This guarantees that the lowest element in the tree is always the root element, making access to the lowest value instantaneous.
- The "leftist" property means that, for each element, the left branch *rank* is greater than or equal to the right branch rank.
- The *rank* of an element is the length of the right path (also called the right *spine*) to an empty element. The leftist property guarantees that the shortest path from any element to an empty element is the right path. A consequence of this is that elements are always found in ascending order along any descending path.

Figure 11.8 shows an example of a leftist tree.

As you can see, retrieving the highest priority element is possible in constant time because it will always be the root of the tree. This element will be called the "head" of the structure. Removing an element, by analogy with a list, will consist of returning the

---

[3] Leftist heaps were first described by Clark Allan Crane in "Linear lists and priority queues as balanced binary trees," (1972), but Okasaki was one of the first to publish a purely functional implementation.

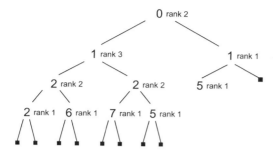

Figure 11.8   A heap-ordered leftist tree, showing that each branch of an element is higher than or equal to the element itself, and each left branch rank is greater than or equal to the corresponding right branch rank

rest of the tree once the root has been removed. This returned value will be called the "tail" of the structure.

11.3.5 *Implementing the leftist heap*

The leftist heap main class will be called `Heap` and will be a tree implementation. The basic structure is shown in listing 11.3. The main difference from the trees you've been developing up to now is that methods such as `right`, `left`, and `head` (equivalent to what you called `value` in previous examples) will return a `Result` instead of raw values. Note also that the number of elements is called `length` (by analogy with a queue) and that the memoized `length` and `rank` will be computed by the callers of the constructor instead of by the constructor itself. This is an unmotivated design choice, just to show another way of doing things. The constructors are private, so the difference won't leak outside the `Heap` class.

Listing 11.3   The leftist heap structures

```
public abstract class Heap<A extends Comparable<A>> {

  @SuppressWarnings("rawtypes")
  protected static final Heap EMPTY = new Empty();
  protected abstract Result<Heap<A>> left();
  protected abstract Result<Heap<A>> right();
  protected abstract int rank();
  public abstract Result<A> head();
  public abstract int length();
  public abstract boolean isEmpty();

  public static class Empty<A extends Comparable<A>> extends Heap<A> {

    private Empty() {}

    @Override
    protected int rank() {
      return 0;
    }

    @Override
    public Result<A> head() {
      return Result.failure(new NoSuchElementException(
                            "head() called on empty heap"));
    }
```

Methods left, right, and head all return a Result.

The length of the tree is simply the number of elements it contains.

```
    @Override
    public int length() {
      return 0;
    }

    @Override
    protected Result<Heap<A>> left() {
      return Result.success(empty());
    }

    @Override
    protected Result<Heap<A>> right() {
      return Result.success(empty());
    }

    @Override
    public boolean isEmpty() {
      return true;
    }
  }

  public static class H<A extends Comparable<A>> extends Heap<A> {

    private final int length;
    private final int rank;
    private final A head;
    private final Heap<A> left;
    private final Heap<A> right;

    private H(int length, int rank, Heap<A> left, A head, Heap<A> right) {
      this.length = length;
      this.rank = rank;                         The rank and length
      this.head = head;                         properties are computed
      this.left = left;                         outside of the H subclass.
      this.right = right;
    }

    @Override
    protected int rank() {
      return this.rank;
    }

    @Override
    public Result<A> head() {
      return Result.success(this.head);
    }

    @Override
    public int length() {
      return this.length;
    }

    @Override
    protected Result<Heap<A>> left() {
      return Result.success(this.left);
    }

    @Override
    protected Result<Heap<A>> right() {
      return Result.success(this.right);
    }
```

```
    @Override
    public boolean isEmpty() {
      return false;
    }
  }

  @SuppressWarnings("unchecked")
  public static <A extends Comparable<A>> Heap<A> empty() {
    return EMPTY;
  }
}
```

EXERCISE 11.5

The first functionality you'll want to add to your Heap implementation is the ability to add an element. Define an add method for this. Make it an instance method in the Heap class with the following signature:

```
public Heap<T> add(T element)
```

The requirement is that if the value is smaller than any element in the heap, it should become the root of the new heap. Otherwise, the root of the heap shouldn't change. Also, the other requirements about rank and length of the right path should be respected.

HINT

Define a static method to create a Heap from an element, and another to create a heap by merging two heaps, with the following signatures:

```
public static <A extends Comparable<A>> Heap<A> heap(A element)
public static <A extends Comparable<A>> Heap<A> merge(Heap<A> first,
                                                      Heap<A> second)
```

Then define the add method in terms of those two.

SOLUTION 11.5

The method for creating a heap from a single element is simple. Just create a new tree with length 1, rank 1; the parameter element as the head; and two empty heaps as the left and right branches:

```
public static <A extends Comparable<A>> Heap<A> heap(A element) {
  return new H<>(1, 1, empty(), element, empty());
}
```

Creating a heap by merging two heaps is a bit more complicated. For this, you'll need an additional helper method that creates a heap from one element and two heaps:

```
protected static <A extends Comparable<A>> Heap<A> heap(A head,
                                          Heap<A> first, Heap<A> second) {
  return first.rank() >= second.rank()
      ? new H<>(first.length() + second.length() + 1,
                              second.rank() + 1, first, head, second)
```

```
    : new H<>(first.length() + second.length() + 1,
                        first.rank() + 1, second, head, first);
}
```

This code first checks whether the first heap's rank is greater than or equal to the second one. If the first heap's rank is greater than or equal, the new rank is set to the rank of the second heap + 1, and the two heaps are used in first, second order. Otherwise, the new rank is set to the rank of the first heap + 1, and the two heaps are used in reverse order (second, first).

Now the method to merge two heaps can be written as follows:

```
public static <A extends Comparable<A>> Heap<A> merge(Heap<A> first,
                                                     Heap<A> second) {
  return first.head().flatMap(
    fh -> second.head().flatMap(
      sh -> fh.compareTo(sh) <= 0
      ? first.left().flatMap(
          fl -> first.right().map(
            fr -> heap(fh, fl, merge(fr, second)))))
      : second.left().flatMap(
          sl -> second.right().map(
            sr -> heap(sh, sl, merge(first, sr))))))
                  .getOrElse(first.isEmpty() ? second : first);
}
```

Of course, if one of the heaps to be merged is empty, you return the other one. Otherwise, you compute the result of the merge.

If you find this code difficult to understand (and by now I hope you don't), it's simply the fully functional equivalent of the following less-functional implementations:

```
public static <A extends Comparable<A>> Heap<A> merge(Heap<A> first, Heap<A>
      second) {
  return first.isEmpty()
      ? second
      : second.isEmpty()
        ? first
        : first.head().successValue()
                    .compareTo(second.head().successValue()) <= 0
            ? heap(first.head().successValue(), first.left()
                .successValue(), merge(first.right()
                                    .successValue(), second))
            : heap(second.head().successValue(), second.left()
                .successValue(), merge(second.right()
                                    .successValue(), first));
}

public static <A extends Comparable<A>> Heap<A> merge(Heap<A> first,
                                                     Heap<A> second) {
  try {
    return first.head().successValue()
                .compareTo(second.head().successValue()) <= 0
      ? heap(first.head().successValue(), first.left().successValue(),
                        merge(first.right().successValue(), second))
```

```
                   : heap(second.head().successValue(), second.left().successValue(),
                              merge(second.right().successValue(), first));
        } catch(IllegalStateException e) {
         return first.isEmpty() ? second : first;
        }
    }
}
```

As a general rule, you should always remember that calling `successValue`, like `getOrThrow`, could throw an exception if the `Result` is `Empty`. You could either test for emptiness first (as in the first example above), or include the code in a try ... catch block (as in the second example), but none of these solutions is really functional.

By the way, you should try to avoid calling `successValue` and `getOrThrow`. The `successValue` method should only be used inside the `Result` class. The best solution for enforcing this would be to make it protected, but it's useful to use it while learning, to see what's happening.

With these methods defined, it's easy to create the add method:

```
public Heap<A> add(A element) {
  return merge(this, heap(element));
}
```

11.3.6 *Implementing the queue-like interface*

Although it's implemented as a tree, the heap, from the user's perspective, is like a priority queue, which means a kind of linked list where the head is always the smallest element. By analogy, the root element of the tree is called the head, and what remains after having "removed" the head is called the tail.

EXERCISE 11.6

Define a `tail` method that returns what's left after removing the head. This method, like the head method, returns a `Result` in order to make it safe when it's called on an empty queue. Here's its signature in the Heap parent class:

```
Result<Heap<A>> tail()
```

SOLUTION 11.6

The `Empty` implementation is obvious and returns a `Failure`:

```
public Result<Heap<A>> tail() {
  return Result.failure(new NoSuchElementException("tail() called
                                            on empty heap"));
}
```

The H implementation is no more complex, given the methods you defined in the previous exercise. It simply returns the result of merging the left and right branches:

```
public Result<Heap<A>> tail() {
  return Result.success(Heap.merge(left, right));
}
```

EXERCISE 11.7

Implement a get method that takes an int parameter and returns the nth element by priority order. This method will return a Result to handle the case where no element is found. Here's its signature in the Heap parent class:

```
public abstract Result<A> get(int index)
```

SOLUTION 11.7

The Empty implementation is obvious and will return a failure:

```
public Result<A> get(int index) {
  return Result.failure(new NoSuchElementException("Index out of range"));
}
```

The H implementation is equally simple. It starts by testing the index. If it's 0, it returns a Success of the head value. Otherwise, it recursively searches for the element of index $n - 1$ in the tail. Because the tail doesn't really exist, but is only the value returned by the getTail method (which is a Result), this result is flat-mapped with a recursive call to get:

```
public Result<A> get(int index) {
  return index == 0
      ? head()
      : tail().flatMap(x -> x.get(index - 1));
}
```

11.4 *A priority queue for noncomparable elements*

To insert elements into a priority queue, you must be able to compare their priorities. But priority isn't always a property of elements; not all elements implement the Comparable interface. Elements that don't implement this interface can still be compared using a Comparator, so can you do this for your priority queue?

EXERCISE 11.8

Modify the Heap class so that it can be used either with Comparable elements or with a separate Comparator.

SOLUTION 11.8

First, you can add a method to the Heap class that will return the Comparator. Because the comparator is optional, this method will return a Result<Comparator> that will potentially be empty.

```
protected abstract Result<Comparator<A>> comparator();
```

You can then implement it in both subclasses. The Empty implementation will return the value of an added property that will be initialized in a constructor:

```
private final Result<Comparator<A>> comparator;

private Empty(Result<Comparator<A>> comparator) {
  this.comparator = comparator;
}
```

```
protected Result<Comparator<A>> comparator() {
  return this.comparator;
}
```

You will, of course, do the same in the H class, with the difference that you'll modify the existing constructor rather than create a new one:

```
private final Result<Comparator<A>> comparator;

private H(int length, int rank, Heap<A> left, A head, Heap<A> right,
                                    Result<Comparator<A>> comparator) {
  this.length = length;
  this.rank = rank;
  this.head = head;
  this.left = left;
  this.right = right;
  this.comparator = comparator;
}

protected Result<Comparator<A>> comparator() {
  return this.comparator;
}
```

You'll then have to update the factory methods. But before you do that, you must change the type parameter for the classes, replacing this

```
public abstract class Heap<A extends Comparable<A>>
```

with this:

```
public abstract class Heap<A>>
```

The same modification should be applied to the subclass constructors.

The static factory method for creating an empty Heap will take an additional Result<Comparator> argument, and you'll need to add a new method using a default Result.Empty:

```
public static <A> Heap<A> empty(Comparator<A> comparator) {
  return empty(Result.success(comparator));
}

public static <A> Heap<A> empty(Result<Comparator<A>> comparator) {
  return new Empty<>(comparator);
}
```

Note that I have also added a method taking a Comparator<A> instead of a Result<Comparable> in order to make using the Heap class easier. This method will be used mainly from outside of the Heap class.

You will, however, keep an empty method taking no parameter. This method will still need to be parameterized with a Comparable type. Otherwise, you'd risk getting a ClassCastException later.

```
public static <A extends Comparable<A>> Heap<A> empty() {
  return empty(Result.empty());
}
```

By using a Comparable type, you can be sure you get a compiler error instead of a run-time exception.

You can now do the same for the methods that create a Heap from a single element:

```java
public static <A extends Comparable<A>> Heap<A> heap(A element) {
  return heap(element, Result.empty());
}

public static <A> Heap<A> heap(A element, Result<Comparator<A>> comparator) {
  Heap<A> empty = empty(comparator);
  return new H<>(1, 1, empty, element, empty, comparator);
}

public static <A> Heap<A> heap(A element, Comparator<A> comparator) {
  Heap<A> empty = empty(comparator);
  return new H<>(1, 1, empty, element, empty, Result.success(comparator));
}
```

The method taking an element and two heaps needs to be modified accordingly, but this time, you'll extract the comparator from the heap arguments:

```java
protected static <A> Heap<A> heap(A head, Heap<A> first, Heap<A> second) {
  Result<Comparator<A>> comparator = first.comparator()
                                   .orElse(second::comparator);
  return first.rank() >= second.rank()
      ? new H<>(first.length() + second.length() + 1,
                  second.rank() + 1, first, head, second, comparator)
      : new H<>(first.length() + second.length() + 1,
                  first.rank() + 1, second, head, first, comparator);
}
```

For the merge method, you can use the Comparator from either of the two trees to be merged. If none have a Comparator, you can use a Result.Empty. In order to not extract the comparator from the arguments on each recursive call, you can split the method in two:

```java
public static <A> Heap<A> merge(Heap<A> first, Heap<A> second) {
    Result<Comparator<A>> comparator =
                    first.comparator().orElse(second::comparator);
    return merge(first, second, comparator);
}

  public static <A> Heap<A> merge(Heap<A> first, Heap<A> second,
                                    Result<Comparator<A>> comparator) {
    return first.head().flatMap(fh -> second.head()
                        .flatMap(sh -> compare(fh, sh, comparator) <= 0
        ? first.left().flatMap(fl -> first.right().map(fr ->
                        heap(fh, fl, merge(fr, second, comparator))))
        : second.left().flatMap(sl -> second.right().map(sr ->
                        heap(sh, sl, merge(first, sr, comparator))))))
                    .getOrElse(first.isEmpty()
                        ? second
                        : first);
}
```

The second method uses a helper method called compare:

```
@SuppressWarnings("unchecked")
public static <A> int compare(A first, A second,
                              Result<Comparator<A>> comparator) {
  return comparator.map(comp -> comp.compare(first, second))
         .getOrElse(() -> ((Comparable<A>) first).compareTo(second));
}
```

This method performs a cast of one of its arguments, but you know you aren't risking a ClassCastException being thrown because you ensured that no heap could be created without a comparator if the type parameter didn't extend Comparable.

Now the static final EMPTY singleton can be removed. The add method must also be modified as follows:

```
public Heap<A> add(A element) {
  return merge(this, heap(element, this.comparator()));
}
```

Finally, the left and right methods in the Empty class must be changed as follows:

```
public Result<Heap<A>> left() {
  return Result.success(empty(this.comparator));
}

protected Result<Heap<A>> right() {
  return Result.success(empty(this.comparator));
}
```

EXERCISE 11.9

So far, the only way you had to add an element to a Heap is through the merge method. Implement an insert method that adds an element without resorting to merge. Define an abstract method in the Heap parent class with the following signature:

```
public abstract Heap<A> insert(A a)
```

HINT

You should reuse the compare method from the previous exercise.

SOLUTION 11.9

The Empty implementation just calls the heap factory method, passing it the value to be inserted and two references to this:

```
public Heap<A> insert(A a) {
  return heap(a, this, this);
}
```

In the H class, the algorithm you need to implement is simple. Let's call a the element to be inserted. You must build a new H with a head, a left, and a right:

- If this head is lower than a, keep it as the current head. Else use a.
- Keep the left branch as is.

- If the head is higher than a, recursively insert the head into the right branch.
- Else, recursively insert a into the right branch.

Here's the code:

```
public Heap<A> insert(A a) {
  return heap(compare(head, a, comparator) < 0
      ? head
      : a, left, right.insert(compare(head, a, comparator) > 0
          ? head
          : a));
}
```

This code isn't optimized because you call compare twice with the same argument. You could call it once and cache the result, which also makes the code easier to read:

```
public Heap<A> insert(A a) {
  int comp = compare(head, a, comparator);
  return heap(comp < 0
              ? head
              : a, left, right.insert(comp > 0 ? head : a));
}
```

Looks nice? Not so.

EXERCISE 11.10
Running the solution to exercise 11.9 on a Heap<Integer> will work, but it has a bug. Find it and fix it. Of course, if you did exercise 11.9 and directly found the correct solution, you may take a break.

HINT
Think about what happens if the value inserted has the same priority as the head.

SOLUTION 11.10
If the priority of the head is equal to the priority of the inserted element a, a is used for the new head and is then inserted into the new right branch. This isn't a big deal with a heap of integers, but it will probably be a big bug with most other types. Consider the following type:

```
class Point implements Comparable<Point> {

  public final int x;
  public final int y;

  private Point(int x, int y) {
    this.x = x;
    this.y = y;
  }

  public String toString() {
    return "(" + x + "," + y + ")";
  }

  @Override
  public int compareTo(Point that) {
```

```
        return this.x < that.x ? -1 : this.x > that.x ? 1 : 0;
    }
}
```

This type represents points that can be compared using only their x coordinate. Now, consider this program simulating insertions of points into a heap:

```
List<Tuple<Integer, Integer>> points =
                List.list(1, 2, 2, 2, 6, 7, 5, 0, 5, 1).zipWithPosition();
Heap<Point> heap = points.foldLeft(Heap.empty(), h -> t ->
                                        h.insert(new Point(t._1, t._2)));
List<Point> lp = List.unfold(heap, hp -> hp.head()
                    .flatMap(h -> hp.tail().map(t -> new Tuple<>(h, t))));
System.out.println(points);
System.out.println(lp);
```

After the points are inserted, they're extracted again by priority order into a list. Here's the result (with the first line showing the original points):

```
[(1,0), (2,1), (2,2), (2,3), (6,4), (7,5), (5,6), (0,7), (5,8), (1,9), NIL]
[(0,7), (1,9), (1,9), (2,3), (2,1), (2,3), (5,8), (5,6), (6,4), (7,5), NIL]
```

In the second line, you can see that you get two points with x = 1, but instead of (1,0) and (1,9), you get (1,9) twice. You have the same problem with points where x = 2. This problem wouldn't be apparent if you were only inserting integers into the heap.

Here's the correct implementation:

```
public Heap<A> insert(A a) {
    int comp = compare(head, a, comparator);
    return heap(comp < 0
                ? head
                : a, left, right.insert(comp >= 0
                                        ? head
                                        : a));
}
```

With this tiny modification, the result is much more correct.

Now you'll get the following (correct) result:

```
[(1,0), (2,1), (2,2), (2,3), (6,4), (7,5), (5,6), (0,7), (5,8), (1,9), NIL]
[(0,7), (1,9), (1,0), (2,3), (2,1), (2,2), (5,8), (5,6), (6,4), (7,5), NIL]
```

11.5 *Summary*

- Trees can be balanced for better performance and to avoid stack overflows in recursive operations.
- The red-black tree is a self-balancing tree structure that frees you from caring about tree balancing.
- Maps can be implemented by delegating to a tree that stores key/value tuples.
- Maps with noncomparable keys must handle collisions in order to store elements with the same key representation.

- Priority queues are structures that allow elements to be retrieved by priority order.
- Priority queues can be implemented using a leftist heap, which is a heap-ordered binary tree.
- Priority queues of noncomparable elements can be constructed using an additional comparator.

Handling state mutation in a functional way

In this chapter, you'll learn how to handle state in a purely functional way. In the previous chapters, state mutation was avoided as much as possible, and you might have come to believe that state mutation is incompatible with functional programming. This isn't true. In functional programming, it's perfectly possible to handle state mutation. The only difference from what you may be used to is that you have to handle state mutation functionally, which means without resorting to side effects.

For a programmer, there are many reasons for handling state mutations. One of the simplest examples is the random number generator. A random number generator is a component with a method that returns a random number. If the random

321

number generator had no state (which means, in reality, no changing state), it would always return the same number. This is not what you expect.

On the other hand, because I've said many times in the previous chapters that a function, given the same argument, should return the same value, it might be difficult to imagine how such a generator would work.

12.1   *A functional random number generator*

There are many uses for a random number generator, but they can be grouped into two main categories:

- Generating numbers that are evenly distributed over a given range
- Generating truly "random" numbers, which means numbers that you can't predict

In the first case, you don't need the numbers to be really random. What you need is that they be randomly distributed. So randomness, in this case, doesn't apply to a single number, but to a series. Moreover, you want to be able to reproduce the series if needed. This will allow you to test your programs. If the generated numbers were really random (in the sense of being unpredictable), you wouldn't be able to test the generator or the programs using it, because you wouldn't know which values to expect.

In the second case, you really want the numbers to be unpredictable. For example, if you wanted to generate random test data to test other programs, it would be useless to generate the same data each time the tests were run.

Java has a random number generator. You can use it by calling the `nextInt` method (among others):

```
Random rng = new Random();
System.out.println(rng.nextInt());
System.out.println(rng.nextInt());
System.out.println(rng.nextInt());
```

This program prints ... well, you don't know. On each run, it will print a different result, like this:

```
773282358
-496891854
-47242220
```

Although this is sometimes what you want, this isn't functional. The `nextInt` method of the random number generator isn't a function because it doesn't always return the same value when called with the same argument.

> **FUNCTIONS WITHOUT ARGUMENTS**   The fact that `nextInt` doesn't take an argument is irrelevant. To be a function, it must simply always return the same value. Not taking an argument means, in fact, that it could take any argument, and this argument would have no influence on the returned value. This doesn't contradict the definition of a function. This kind of function is simply a constant.

Let's think about what's happening. If the method takes no argument and returns a value, this value must come from somewhere. Of course, you'd guess that this somewhere is inside the random number generator. The fact that the value changes on each call means that the generator changes between each call; it has a mutable state. So the question is whether the value returned by the `nextInt` method depends only on the state of the generator, or whether it depends on something else.

If the returned value were to depend only on the state of the generator, it would be easy to make it functional. You'd just have to pass the state of the generator as an argument to the method. Of course, since the state will change as the method returns a result (in order for the generator to not always return the same value), the method would have to return the state of the generator together with the generated value. You know how to do this by simply returning a tuple, so the `nextInt` method signature would change as follows:

```
public Tuple<Integer, Random> nextInt(Random)
```

The problem here is that the Java `Random` generator doesn't work this way. The `next-Int` method returns a value that's not only dependent on the state of the generator, but also on the system clock: the system clock is used to initialize the generator. In fact, the Java `Random` generator takes a `long` value to initialize itself. From this point, the series of generated numbers won't vary, but this `long` value, called the *seed*, is by default based on the number of nanoseconds returned by the system clock. (Look at the `Random.java` source code for more details.) What's important is that the approach taken by Java is to return unpredictable numbers unless a specific seed is provided to initialize the generator. So you can still use it for generating random numbers in a functional way.

12.1.1 *The random number generator interface*

You'll now implement a functional random number generator. This won't be the best example of a number generator, but because you're just learning how to handle state mutation in a functional way, it will serve as an example of functional state handling.

First, you need to define the interface of the generator. Generating random numbers can be done in many different ways, so you could use different implementations. The quality of a generator, from the business point of view, is based on the impossibility of predicting the next number just by looking at the previous ones. So you might define a simple generator that produces somewhat predictable data at a low cost, or you might define a complex implementation for use cases where unpredictability is a matter of security.

Here's the interface of your generator:

```
import com.fpinjava.common.Tuple;

public interface RNG {
  Tuple<Integer, RNG> nextInt();
}
```

12.1.2　*Implementing the random number generator*

In this section, you'll implement the random number generator as simply as possible by using the Java Random class. You must initialize it with a seed in order for the random number series to be reproducible. Here's a possible implementation:

```java
import com.fpinjava.common.Tuple;
import java.util.Random;

public class JavaRNG implements RNG {

  private final Random random;

  private JavaRNG(long seed) {
    this.random = new Random(seed);
  }

  @Override
  public Tuple<Integer, RNG> nextInt() {
    return new Tuple<>(random.nextInt(), this);
  }

  public static RNG rng(long seed) {
    return new JavaRNG(seed);
  }
}
```

All that's left to do is to create a front-end component to make the random number generator more functional:

```java
import com.fpinjava.common.Tuple;

public class Generator {
  public static Tuple<Integer, RNG> integer(RNG rng) {
    return rng.nextInt();
  }
}
```

To see how this class can be used, let's look at a unit test:

```java
public void testInteger() throws Exception {
  RNG rng = JavaRNG.rng(0);
  Tuple<Integer, RNG> t1 = Generator.integer(rng);
  assertEquals(Integer.valueOf(-1155484576), t1._1);
  Tuple<Integer, RNG> t2 = Generator.integer(t1._2);
  assertEquals(Integer.valueOf(-723955400), t2._1);
  Tuple<Integer, RNG> t3 = Generator.integer(t2._2);
  assertEquals(Integer.valueOf(1033096058), t3._1);
}
```

As you can see, the integer method of the Generator class is functional. You can run this test as many times as you want; it will always produce the same values. So although the value returned by the generator depends on the generator's mutable state, the method is still referentially transparent.

If you need to produce really unpredictable numbers, you can call the `JavaRNG.rng` method with a "random" long value; for example, the value returned by `System.nanoTime()`. Be aware, however, that the value returned doesn't have the resolution of 1 nanosecond, so several successive invocations might return the same value. This can be avoided by caching the value returned by `nanoTime` and calling it again if the value hasn't changed, until a different value is obtained. The `Random` class offers this service, so the simplest solution would be to create a second method initializing the random field with an unparameterized `Random()`. But once again, this chapter isn't about generators, but about functionally handling state.

EXERCISE 12.1

Write a method in the `Generator` class that returns a random positive integer lower than a value passed as a parameter, but greater than or equal to 0. Here's the signature:

```
public static Tuple<Integer, RNG> integer(RNG rng, int limit)
```

SOLUTION 12.1

Simply get the next random value from the generator. For the first tuple member, create a new tuple using the absolute value of the rest of the division by the parameter. Leave the second member unchanged.

```
public static Tuple<Integer, RNG> integer(RNG rng, int limit) {
  Tuple<Integer, RNG> random = rng.nextInt();
  return new Tuple<>(Math.abs(random._1 % limit), random._2);
}
```

EXERCISE 12.2

Write a method returning a list of *n* random integers. It will also have to return the current state, which translates to the last RNG, so it can generate the next integer. Here's the signature:

```
Tuple<List<Integer>, RNG> integers(RNG rng, int length)
```

HINT

Try not to use explicit recursion. Use methods from the `List` class, starting by creating a list of the requested size and folding it. Note that if you generate a list of random numbers, you might as well return it in reverse order (if that's simpler). But you must ensure that the returned generator is up to date, which means it must be the last one returned by the `nextInt` method.

SOLUTION 12.2

The idea is to create a list of the intended length, and then to fold it with the right function. You'll do this with a list of integers:

```
List.range(0, length).foldLeft(identity, f);
```

This is a common pattern for replacing the indexed loops of imperative programming. Here, the `f` function ignores the integers in the list. This function adds the value produced by the generator to a list, starting with an empty list. So it seems it should be a function of the following type:

```
Function<List<Tuple<Integer, RNG>>, Function<Integer,
                                        List<Tuple<Integer, RNG>>
```

But if you do this, you'll have a problem. You might easily transform the resulting `List<Tuple<Integer, RNG>>` into a `List<Integer>`, but to reconstruct a `Tuple<List<Integer>, RNG>`, you'll have to get the last RNG in the list. That's because folding a list into another list reverses the order of the elements. The fact that the random values are in reverse order is irrelevant, but you need access to the last returned RNG, which, due to the fold, will be in last position. To access it, you'd have to reverse the list, which is neither efficient nor smart.

A better solution is to carry the current RNG while folding the list of integers. The result will be a `Tuple<List<Tuple<Integer, RNG>>, RNG>`, and the function used to fold will be the following:

```
Function<Tuple<List<Tuple<Integer, RNG>>, RNG>, Function<Integer,
            Tuple<List<Tuple<Integer, RNG>>, RNG>>> f = tuple -> i -> {
  Tuple<Integer, RNG> t = integer(tuple._2);
  return new Tuple<>(tuple._1.cons(t), t._2);
};
```

The type may look intimidating, but despite that, you shouldn't make it explicit. The compiler will be able to infer this type, so you don't have to write it. Here's the complete fold:

```
Tuple<List<Tuple<Integer, RNG>>, RNG> result = List.range(0, length)
                .foldLeft(new Tuple<>(List.list(), rng), tuple -> i -> {
  Tuple<Integer, RNG> t = integer(tuple._2);
  return new Tuple<>(tuple._1.cons(t), t._2);
});
```

Now that you get a `Tuple<List<Tuple<Integer, RNG>>, RNG>`, it's easy to construct the expected result:

```
public static Tuple<List<Integer>, RNG> integers(RNG rng, int length) {
  Tuple<List<Tuple<Integer, RNG>>, RNG> result = List.range(0, length)
                .foldLeft(new Tuple<>(List.list(), rng), tuple -> i -> {
    Tuple<Integer, RNG> t = integer(tuple._2);
    return new Tuple<>(tuple._1.cons(t), t._2);
  });
  List<Integer> list = result._1.map(x -> x._1);
  return new Tuple<>(list, result._2);
}
```

As you can see, the resulting list of random numbers is still in reverse order because of the way the singly linked list is constructed, but you don't need to reverse the list. You don't care about the first-generated number coming last. The only important thing is that the returned RNG will produce the correct number.

If you prefer, you could implement the method this way:

```
public static Tuple<List<Integer>, RNG> integers2(RNG rng, int length) {
  List<Tuple<Integer, RNG>> result = List.range(0, length).
                  foldLeft(List.list(), lst -> i -> lst.cons(integer(rng)));
  List<Integer> list = result.map(x -> x._1);
  Result<Tuple<List<Integer>, RNG>> result2 =
                  result.headOption().map(tr -> new Tuple<>(list, tr._2));
  return result2.getOrElse(new Tuple<>(List.list(), rng));
}
```

In the normal case (length > 0), tr._2 is the RNG you return.

Here, you return rng with an empty list as the default value, corresponding to the case where length == 0.

Alternatively, you can use explicit recursion:

```
public static Tuple<List<Integer>, RNG> integers3(RNG rng, int length) {
  return integers3_(rng, length, List.list()).eval();
}

private static TailCall<Tuple<List<Integer>, RNG>> integers3_(RNG rng,
                                        int length, List<Integer> xs) {
  if (length <= 0)
    return TailCall.ret(new Tuple<>(xs, rng));
  else {
    Tuple<Integer, RNG> t1 = rng.nextInt();
    return TailCall.sus(() ->
                  integers3_(t1._2, length - 1, xs.cons(t1._1)));
  }
}
```

Be aware, however, that functional programmers generally consider using explicit recursion a bad practice. They instead favor abstracting recursion by using folds.

12.2 A generic API for handling state

As I said, the way you implemented RNG isn't the best way to implement generators. This was just an example to show you how state can be handled in a functional way. What you can learn from that example is that your RNG represents the current state of the generator.

But if you want to generate integers, you probably aren't really interested in RNG. You'd probably prefer to make it transparent. In other words, what you've used so far is a function taking an RNG and returning the generated value, be it an Integer, a List, or whatever, as well as the new RNG:

```
Function<RNG, Tuple<A, RNG>>
```

Wouldn't it be better if you could get rid of the RNG? Is it possible to abstract the RNG handling in such a way that you don't have to worry about it anymore?

To abstract the RNG handling, you need to create a new type encapsulating the RNG parameter:

```
public interface Random<A> extends Function<RNG, Tuple<A, RNG>>
```

You can now redefine the generating operations in terms of this new type. For example, you can replace the following method

```
public static Tuple<Integer, RNG> integer(RNG rng) {
  return rng.nextInt();
}
```

with a function:

```
public static Random<Integer> integer = RNG::nextInt;
```

12.2.1 *Working with state operations*

Having abstracted the RNG, you're left with something that looks very similar to the parameterized types you've studied in previous chapters. What you get here is a computational context for some simple types. Remember List and Result? Those types were acting like computational contexts for other types.

A List of integers is a computational context for the Integer type. For example, it allows you to apply, to a list of integers, a function from Integer to another type, without caring about the number of elements in the list.

Result is no different. It creates a computational context for a value, allowing you to apply a function to that value without caring whether a value is really present. In the same manner, Random allows you to apply computations to a value without having to handle the fact that the value is random.

Can you define for Random the same abstractions you defined for List and Result? Let's try.

To start with, you need a way to create a Random from a single value. Although this might seem mostly useless in real life, it's needed to create the other abstractions. You'll call this method unit:

```
public static <A> Random<A> unit(A a) {
  return rng -> new Tuple<>(a, rng);
}
```

The name unit is used by convention. You could have also used this name for Result, Stream, List, Heap, and so on, but you chose more business-related names instead, such as list and success. It's the same concept applied to different types.

Let's try going further. Can you use a function from A to B to transform a Random<A> into a Random<B>? Sure you can. For other types, this was called map. Let's define a map method for Random:

```
static <A, B> Random<B> map(Random<A> s, Function<A, B> f) {
  return rng -> {
    Tuple<A, RNG> t = s.apply(rng);
    return new Tuple<>(f.apply(t._1), t._2);
  };
}
```

This method can be defined anywhere, such as in the Random interface.

EXERCISE 12.3

Use the map method to generate a random Boolean. Do this by creating a function in the Random interface.

HINT

Use the following function, which you just created:

```
Random<Integer> intRnd = RNG::nextInt;
```

SOLUTION 12.3

The solution consists of mapping the result returned by the intRnd function with a function that converts an int into a boolean. Of course, if you want the result to have a 50% probability of being true, you must choose the function accordingly. The commonly used algorithm for this is to test whether the remainder of the division by 2 is 0:

```
Random<Boolean> booleanRnd = Random.map(intRnd, x -> x % 2 == 0);
```

EXERCISE 12.4

Implement a function that returns a randomly generated Double.

SOLUTION 12.4

This works exactly like the booleanRnd function. The only difference is the function to map:

```
Random<Double> doubleRnd =
            map(intRnd, x -> x / (((double) Integer.MAX_VALUE) + 1.0));
```

12.2.2 Composing state operations

In the previous section, you composed state operations with ordinary functions. What if you need to compose two or more state operations? This is what you did in exercise 12.2 to produce a List of randomly generated integers. Can you abstract this in the Random type? As a starting point, you might need a method to combine two Random instances, such as to generate a pair of random numbers.

EXERCISE 12.5

Implement a function that takes an RNG and returns a pair of integers.

HINT

First define a map2 method in the Random interface that composes two calls to the random generator to produce a pair of values of generic types A and B, and then use them as parameters for a function that returns a third type C. Here's its signature:

```
static <A, B, C> Random<C> map2(Random<A> ra, Random<B> rb,
                          Function<A, Function<B, C>> f) {
```

SOLUTION 12.5

This isn't any more difficult than implementing map. You first have to pass the rng parameter to the first function. Then, extract the returned RNG from the result, and pass it to the second function. Finally, use the two values as input to the f function, and return the result together with the resulting RNG:

```
static <A, B, C> Random<C> map2(Random<A> ra, Random<B> rb,
                                Function<A, Function<B, C>> f) {
  return rng -> {
    Tuple<A, RNG> t1 = ra.apply(rng);
    Tuple<B, RNG> t2 = rb.apply(t1._2);
    return new Tuple<>(f.apply(t1._1).apply(t2._1), t2._2);
  };
}
```

Using this method, you can define a function that returns a pair of random integers, as in the following example:

```
Random<Tuple<Integer, Integer>> intPairRnd =
              map2(intRnd, intRnd, x -> y -> new Tuple<>(x, y));
```

Don't use the same RNG for both values. Doing so would produce a pair of two identical integers!

EXERCISE 12.6

Implement a function that takes an RNG and returns a list of randomly generated integers.

HINT

The overall process is quite simple to describe. First, you have to generate a List <Random<Integers>>. Then, you must transform this into a Random<List<Integer>>. Does this remind you of something? It's the same abstraction you implemented for Result, changing a List<Result> into a Result<List>, which you called sequence.

You can start by implementing a sequence method in the Random class. Here's its signature:

```
static <A> Random<List<A>> sequence(List<Random<A>> rs)
```

To generate the list, you can use the List.fill() method that's defined in the List class with the following signature:

```
public static <A> List<A> fill(int n, Supplier<A> s)
```

SOLUTION 12.6

You can guess that you'll have to iterate over the list. You don't need to use explicit recursion for this, and you shouldn't! You should instead use a fold. The starting value will be a Random constructed with an empty list. This is where the unit method starts to be a useful tool. Use a foldLeft or foldRight with a function that applies map2 to the current accumulator value and the element of the list to process.

This is much more difficult to describe than to code. Here's an example using foldLeft:

```
static <A> Random<List<A>> sequence(List<Random<A>> rs) {
  return rs.foldLeft(unit(List.list()), acc -> r ->
                         map2(r, acc, x -> y -> y.cons(x)));
}
```

Then define the function returning a list of random integers. This time, the type is no longer Random<Integer>, because you have to deal with the additional int parameter representing the desired length of the list:

```
Function<Integer, Random<List<Integer>>> integersRnd =
                length -> sequence(List.fill(length, () -> intRnd));
```

It's interesting to compare this implementation with the solution of exercise 12.2:

```
public static Tuple<List<Integer>, RNG> integers(RNG rng, int length) {
  Tuple<List<Tuple<Integer, RNG>>, RNG> result = List.range(0, length)
                .foldLeft(new Tuple<>(List.list(), rng), tuple -> i -> {
    Tuple<Integer, RNG> t = integer(tuple._2);
    return new Tuple<>(tuple._1.cons(t), t._2);
  });
  List<Integer> list = result._1.map(x -> x._1);
  return new Tuple<>(list, result._2);
}
```

You can see that the fold has been abstracted into the sequence method, and the intermediary result handling has been abstracted into the map2 method. The resulting code is very clean and easy to understand (provided you understood the two abstractions). In the integersRnd function, you don't have to manipulate the RNG generator. The same is true for the sequence and map2 methods. As you can see, you're very close to implementing a generic state–handling tool.

12.2.3 *Recursive state operations*

So far, you've seen how to call the generator several times to return several values. But you might have to handle a different use case. Imagine that you want to generate integers that shouldn't be multiples of 5.

If you were writing an imperative program, you could simply generate a number and test it. If it wasn't a multiple of 5, you'd return it. Otherwise, you'd generate the next number. In this implementation, you'd have to generate a second number in an average of one case out of five. You might think about something like this:

```
Random<Integer> notMultipleOfFiveRnd = Random.map(intRnd, x -> {
  return x % 5 != 0
      ? x
      : Random.notMultipleOfFiveRnd.apply(???);
});
```

But how can you access the RNG that must be passed to the recursive call to the notMultipleOfFiveRnd function? This is the RNG resulting from the first call to the function.

You *could* solve this problem by explicitly handling the result of the first function call:

```
Random<Integer> notMultipleOfFiveRnd = rng -> {
    Tuple<Integer, RNG> t = intRnd.apply(rng);
```

```
   return t._1 % 5 != 0
       ? t
       : Random.notMultipleOfFiveRnd.apply(t._2);
};
```

But it seems you're returning to where you started from. What you really need here is a flatMap method.

EXERCISE 12.7

Write a flatMap method and use it to implement the notMultipleOfFiveRnd function. Here's the flatMap method signature:

```
static <A, B> Random<B> flatMap(Random<A> s, Function<A, Random<B>> f)
```

SOLUTION 12.7

The flatMap method is very similar to the map method:

```
static <A, B> Random<B> flatMap(Random<A> s, Function<A, Random<B>> f) {
  return rng -> {
    Tuple<A, RNG> t = s.apply(rng);
    return f.apply(t._1).apply(t._2);
  };
}
```

The difference is that instead of constructing a tuple and returning it, you simply pass the generated value to the f function, which gives you a Random<B>. Remember that this is, in reality, a Function<RNG, Tuple<A, RNG>>, so you pass the RNG resulting from the application of s to that function, which gives you a Tuple<A, RNG> that you can return.

Now you can implement the notMultipleOfFiveRnd function in terms of flatMap:

```
Random<Integer> notMultipleOfFiveRnd = Random.flatMap(intRnd, x -> {
    int mod = x % 5;
    return mod != 0
        ? unit(x)
        : Random.notMultipleOfFiveRnd;
});
```

EXERCISE 12.8

Implement map and map2 in terms of flatMap.

HINT

There's a relationship between map, flatMap, and unit: flatMap is a combination of map and unit.

SOLUTION 12.8

Here are the two new implementations:

```
static <A, B> Random<B> map(Random<A> s, Function<A, B> f) {
  return flatMap(s, a -> unit(f.apply(a)));
}
```

```
static <A, B, C> Random<C> map2(Random<A> ra, Random<B> rb,
                                Function<A, Function<B, C>> f) {
  return flatMap(ra, a -> map(rb, b -> f.apply(a).apply(b)));
}
```

As you can see, `flatMap` gives you an additional level of abstraction, which allows you to write much clearer method implementations.

12.3 *Generic state handling*

So far, all the methods and functions you've developed in this chapter have been used to generate random numbers. But you started with code that was specific to generating random numbers, and you ended with tools that are absolutely unrelated to random number generation. The methods of the `Random` interface are connected to random number generation only by the fact that this interface extends `Function` `<RNG, Tuple<A, RNG>>`. You could, in fact, redefine this interface to handle any kind of state:

```
interface State<S, A> extends Function<S, Tuple<A, S>> {}
```

You're certainly aware that composition is better than inheritance, so you might prefer to define the `State` class using a delegate:

```
public class State<S, A> {

  public final Function<S, Tuple<A, S>> run;

  public State(Function<S, Tuple<A, S>> run) {
    super();
    this.run = run;
  }
}
```

Now you can redefine `Random` as a specific case of `State`:

```
public class Random<A> extends State<RNG, A> {

  public Random(Function<RNG, Tuple<A, RNG>> run) {
    super(run);
  }
}
```

EXERCISE 12.9

Complete the `State` class by re-implementing the methods of the `Random` interface in a generic way.

HINT

Define the methods as instance methods, except, of course, for the `unit` method, which needs to be static. Each method will have to create a new `State`.

SOLUTION 12.9

Here are your new methods:

```
public static <S, A> State<S, A> unit(A a) {
  return new State<>(state -> new Tuple<>(a, state));
}

public <B> State<S, B> map(Function<A, B> f) {
  return flatMap(a -> State.unit(f.apply(a)));
}

public <B, C> State<S, C> map2(State<S, B> sb, Function<A,
                                         Function<B, C>> f) {
  return flatMap(a -> sb.map(b -> f.apply(a).apply(b)));
}

public <B> State<S, B> flatMap(Function<A, State<S, B>> f) {
  return new State<>(s -> {
    Tuple<A, S> temp = run.apply(s);
    return f.apply(temp._1).run.apply(temp._2);
  });
}

public static <S, A> State<S, List<A>> sequence(List<State<S, A>> fs) {
  return fs.foldRight(State.unit(List.<A>list()),
                    f -> acc -> f.map2(acc, a -> b -> b.cons(a)));
}
```

You can now replace your Random interface with an alias for State<RNG, A>:

```
public class Random<A> extends State<RNG, A> {
  public Random(Function<RNG, Tuple<A, RNG>> run) {
    super(run);
  }
  public static State<RNG, Integer> intRnd = new Random<>(RNG::nextInt);
}
```

12.3.1 State patterns

Imagine you need to generate three random integers to initialize a three-dimensional (3D) point:

```
public class Point {
  public final int x;
  public final int y;
  public final int z;
  public Point(int x, int y, int z) {
    this.x = x;
    this.y = y;
    this.z = z;
  }

  @Override
  public String toString() {
    return String.format("Point(%s, %s, %s)", x, y, z);
  }
}
```

You can create a random `Point` as follows:

```
State<RNG, Point> ns =
    intRnd.flatMap(x ->
        intRnd.flatMap(y ->
            intRnd.map(z -> new Point(x, y, z))));
```

This code simply modifies a state. But this modification could be simplified if you had a get method for reading the state and a set method for writing it. Then you could combine them to modify the state using a function f as follows:

```
public static <S> State<S, Nothing> modify(Function<S, S> f) {
    return State.<S>get().flatMap(s -> set(f.apply(s)));
}
```

This method returns a `State<S, Nothing>` because it doesn't return a value. You're only interested in the modified state. `Nothing` is a type you have to define as follows:

```
public final class Nothing {

    private Nothing() {}

    public static final Nothing instance = new Nothing();
}
```

Instead of using the `Nothing` type, you could have returned `Void`, but instantiating `Void` is a bit tricky, using a dirty hack, so a cleaner solution is preferable.

The get method creates a function that simply returns the argument's state both as the state and the value:

```
public static <S> State<S, S> get() {
    return new State<>(s -> new Tuple<>(s, s));
}
```

The set method creates a function that returns the parameter's state as the new state and the `Nothing` singleton as the value:

```
public static <S> State<S, Nothing> set(S s) {
    return new State<>(x -> new Tuple<>(Nothing.instance, s));
}
```

12.3.2 *Building a state machine*

One of the most common tools for composing state mutations is the state machine. A state machine is a piece of code that processes inputs by conditionally switching from one state to another. Many business problems can be represented by such conditional state mutations.

By creating a parameterized state machine, you can abstract all the details about state handling. That way, you'll be able to handle any such problem by simply listing the condition/transition pairs, and then feeding in the list of inputs to get the resulting state. The machine will handle the composition of the various transitions transparently.

First, you'll define two interfaces to represent the conditions and the corresponding transitions. These interfaces aren't absolutely necessary, because they're simple functions, but they'll simplify coding:

```
interface Condition<I, S> extends Function<StateTuple<I, S>, Boolean> {}

interface Transition<A, S> extends Function<StateTuple<A, S>, S> {}
```

The `StateTuple` class is also a helper class to simplify coding. It's simply a tuple in which the two fields are called `value` and `state`. This is easier to read than `_1` and `_2` or `left` and `right`, because it's easy to forget which of those is which.

```
public class StateTuple<A, S> {

  public final A value;
  public final S state;

  public StateTuple(A a, S s) {
    value = a;
    state = s;
  }
}
```

The `StateMachine` class simply holds a function of type `Function<A, State<S, Nothing>>`. Returning the final value as part of the state is a matter of choice. Here, the final value is included in the state, so you don't need to carry the value separately.

The state machine is constructed from a list of `<Tuple<Condition<A, S>, Transition<A, S>>`. In the constructor, the function is built as follows:

```
public class StateMachine<A, S> {

  Function<A, State<S, Nothing>> function;

  public StateMachine(List<Tuple<Condition<A, S>,
                            Transition<A, S>>> transitions) {
    function = a -> State.sequence(m ->
      Result.success(new StateTuple<>(a, m)).flatMap((StateTuple<A, S> t) ->
        transitions.filter((Tuple<Condition<A, S>, Transition<A, S>> x) ->
          x._1.apply(t)).headOption().map((Tuple<Condition<A, S>,
            Transition<A, S>> y) -> y._2.apply(t))).getOrElse(m));
  }
}
```

The `State.sequence` method is defined like this:

```
public static <S> State<S, Nothing> sequence(Function<S, S> f) {
  return new State<>(s -> new StateTuple<>(Nothing.instance, f.apply(s)));
}
```

This code may seem complex, but it simply builds a function that will compose all the conditional transitions received as the constructor's parameter.

The StateMachine class also defines a process method that receives a list of inputs to produce the resulting state:

```
public State<S, S> process(List<A> inputs) {
    List<State<S, Nothing>> a = inputs.map(function);
    State<S, List<Nothing>> b = State.compose(a);
    return b.flatMap(x -> State.get());
  }
}
```

The State.compose() method is defined as follows:

```
public static <S, A> State<S, List<A>> compose(List<State<S, A>> fs) {
  return fs.foldRight(State.unit(List.<A>list()),
                      f -> acc -> f.map2(acc, a -> b -> b.cons(a)));
}
```

EXERCISE 12.10

Write an Atm class that simulates an automated teller machine. The inputs will be represented by the following interface:

```
public interface Input {

  Type type();

  boolean isDeposit();

  boolean isWithdraw();

  int getAmount();

  enum Type {DEPOSIT,WITHDRAW}
}
```

The Input interface will have two implementations, Deposit and Withdraw:

```
public class Deposit implements Input {

  private final int amount;

  public Deposit(int amount) {
    super();
    this.amount = amount;
  }

  @Override
  public Type type() {
    return Type.DEPOSIT;
  }

  @Override
  public boolean isDeposit() {
    return true;
  }

  @Override
  public boolean isWithdraw() {
    return false;
  }
```

```
    @Override
  public int getAmount() {
    return this.amount;
  }
}

public class Withdraw implements Input {

  private final int amount;

  public Withdraw(int amount) {
    super();
    this.amount = amount;
  }

  @Override
  public Type type() {
    return Type.WITHDRAW;
  }

  @Override
  public boolean isDeposit() {
    return false;
  }

  @Override
  public boolean isWithdraw() {
    return true;
  }

  @Override
  public int getAmount() {
    return this.amount;
  }
}
```

To simplify the code, use an additional Outcome class representing the result tuple:

```
public class Outcome {
  public final Integer account;
  public final List<Integer> operations;

  public Outcome(Integer account, List<Integer> operations) {
    super();
    this.account = account;
    this.operations = operations;
  }
  public String toString() {
    return "(" + account.toString() + "," + operations.toString() + ")";
  }
}
```

As you can see in this class, Atm produces an integer value representing the resulting balance of the account, and a list of integers representing the amounts of the operations (positive for a deposit, negative for a withdrawal).

The exercise is to implement the Atm class, which basically contains a method that constructs a StateMachine:

```
public class Atm {
  public static StateMachine<Input, Outcome> createMachine() {
    ...
  }
}
```

HINT

The createMachine implementation must first construct a list of tuples of conditions and corresponding transitions. These tuples will have to be ordered, with the more specific coming first. The last tuple will need a catch-all condition. This is like the default case in a switch structure (and also like the default case in exercise 3.2). This catch-all condition isn't always needed, but it's safer to always have one. The list of tuples will be used as the argument to the StateMachine constructor.

You'll have to run the resulting state machine to get an observable result. This can be done by applying the run function to a starting state, which will produce a resulting state, from which you can extract the value:

```
Outcome out = Atm.createMachine().process(inputs)
                  .run.apply(new Outcome(0, List.list())).value;
```

The running part of this code (the second line) can be abstracted into the State class by adding the following method:

```
public A eval(S s) {
  return run.apply(s).value;
}
```

With this added method, running the state machine is much neater:

```
Outcome out = Atm.createMachine().process(inputs)
                        .eval(new Outcome(0, List.list()));
```

SOLUTION 12.10

The solution is like a program in an imperative language. It can be described in pseudo code like this:

```
process operation
  if the operation is a deposit
    add the amount to the account and add the operation
                                            to the operation list
    process next operation
  if the operation is a withdraw and the amount is less
                                            than the account balance
    remove the amount from the account and add the operation
                                            to the operation list
    process next operation
  else
    do not change account nor operation list
```

Implementing this is easy:

```
public static StateMachine<Input, Outcome> createMachine() {

    Condition<Input, Outcome> predicate1 = t -> t.value.isDeposit();
    Transition<Input, Outcome> transition1 =
            t -> new Outcome(t.state.account + t.value.getAmount(),
                             t.state.operations.cons(t.value.getAmount())));

    Condition<Input, Outcome> predicate2 = t -> t.value.isWithdraw()
                             && t.state.account >= t.value.getAmount();
    Transition<Input, Outcome> transition2 =
        t -> new Outcome(t.state.account - t.value.getAmount(),
                         t.state.operations.cons(- t.value.getAmount())));

    Condition<Input, Outcome> predicate3 = t -> true;
    Transition<Input, Outcome> transition3 = t -> t.state;

    List<Tuple<Condition<Input, Outcome>,
               Transition<Input, Outcome>>> transitions = List.list(
        new Tuple<>(predicate1, transition1),
        new Tuple<>(predicate2, transition2),
        new Tuple<>(predicate3, transition3));

    return new StateMachine<>(transitions);
}
```

If you want to see the machine in action, just run the unit test that comes with the code accompanying this book.

This code works exactly like an imperative program, which, by the way, it is. It is imperative programming done functionally. Of course, using this kind of code to deal with such a simple problem would be overkill. The main drawback of this approach isn't the complexity of the code (this code is very simple), but its verbosity. On the other hand, the benefit is that it can be extended at near to zero cost. All you have to do is insert the right condition/transition in the right place.

EXERCISE 12.11
Modify the previous program so that errors such as trying to withdraw more than the account balance are reported.

SOLUTION 12.11
I have no written solution for this exercise, but I've provided one possible solution, along with the corresponding JUnit test, in the code accompanying this book.

12.3.3 *When to use state and the state machine*

It might seem that handling state functionally is an overly complex version of imperative programming. This is true for the very simple and small examples that can be described in a book. But if you think about complex programs that have a huge number of rules, the high level of abstraction of functional state handling is clearly beneficial. But this isn't the only advantage—the main advantage is scalability. You can evolve an application simply by changing the rules or adding more of them without ever risking messing with the implementation.

You can make this even simpler. Describing the rules (the condition/transition) in Java is very verbose, but it's possible to write them in a more concise form. You'd then just have to read them and translate them into Java.

This could evolve into creating a domain-specific language (DSL). Of course you'd need a parser to process the programs written using this DSL, but such a parser could easily be created using the functional state machine. (A state machine is not the best solution for parsing all types of grammar, but that's another story.)

12.4 Summary

- Generating random numbers involves managing the state of a generator.
- You can manage state in a functional way by using a representation for state operations.
- You can compose state operations with the help of methods like `map` and `flat-Map`.
- You can compose state operations recursively.
- The `State` type is a generic representation for state operations, which can be used as the basis for implementing a state machine.

Functional input/output

13

This chapter covers

- Applying effects safely from inside contexts
- Adding effect application to `Result` and `List`
- Combining effects for successes and failures
- Reading data safely from the console, from file, or from memory, with the `Reader` abstraction
- Handling input/output with the `IO` type

So far, you've learned how to write functional programs that haven't really produced any usable results. You learned how to compose true functions to build more-powerful functions. More interestingly, you learned how to use nonfunctional operations in a safe, functional way. Nonfunctional operations are operations producing side effects, like throwing exceptions, changing the outside world, or simply depending on the outside world to produce a result. For example, you learned how to take an integer division, which is a potentially unsafe operation, and turn it into a safe one by using it inside a computational context.

You've already encountered several such computational contexts:

- The `Result` type you developed in chapter 7 is such a computational context, allowing you to use a function that could produce an error in a safe, error-free way.

- The `Option` type from chapter 6 is also a computational context used to safely apply functions that could sometimes (for some arguments) produce no data.
- The `List` class you studied in chapters 5 and 8 is a computational context, but rather than dealing with errors, it allows the use of functions that work on single elements in the context of a collection of elements. It also deals with the absence of data represented by an empty list.

While studying these types, as well as others like `Stream`, `Map`, `Heap`, and `State`, you didn't care about producing a useful result. In this chapter, however, you'll learn several techniques for producing useful results from your functional programs. This includes displaying a result for a human user or passing a result to another program.

13.1 Applying effects in context

Recall what you did to apply a function to the result of an integer operation. Let's say you want to write an `inverse` function that computes the inverse of an integer value:

```
Function<Integer, Result<Double>> inverse = x -> x != 0
    ? Result.success((double) 1 / x)
    : Result.failure("Division by 0");
```

This function can be applied to an integer value, but when composed with other functions, the value will be the output of another function, so it will usually already be in context, and often the same type of context. Here's an example:

```
Result<Integer> ri = ...
Result<Double> rd = ri.flatMap(inverse);
```

It's important to note that you don't take the value in `ri` out of its context to apply the function. It works the other way around: you pass the function to the context (the `Result` type) so that it can be applied inside it, producing a new context, possibly wrapping the resulting value. Here, you pass the function to the `ri` context, producing the new `rd` result.

This is very neat and safe. No bad things can happen; no exceptions can be thrown. This is the beauty of functional programming: you have a program that will always work, whatever data you use as input. But the question is, how can you use this result? Suppose you want to display the result on the console—how can you do this?

13.1.1 What are effects?

I defined pure functions as functions without any observable side effects. An effect is anything that can be observed from outside the program. The role of a function is to return a value, and a side effect is anything, besides the returned value, that's observable from the outside of the function. It's called a *side effect* because it comes in addition to the value that's returned. An *effect* (without "side") is like a side effect, but it's the main (and generally unique) role of a program. Functional programming is about writing programs with pure functions (with no side effects) and pure effects in a functional way.

The question is, what does it mean to handle effects in a functional way? The closest definition I can give at this stage is "handling effects in a way that doesn't interfere with the principles of functional programming, the most important principle being referential transparency." There are several ways to approach or reach this goal, and reaching this goal fully can be complex. Often, approaching it is sufficient. It's up to you to decide which technique you want to use. Applying effects to contexts is the simplest (although not fully functional) way to make otherwise functional programs produce observable effects.

13.1.2 *Implementing effects*

As I just said, an effect is anything that's observable from outside the program. Of course, to be valuable, this effect must generally reflect the result of the program, so you'll generally need to take the result of the program and do something observable with it. Note that "observable" doesn't always mean observable by a human operator. Often the result is observable by another program, which might then translate this effect into something observable by a human operator, either in synchronous or asynchronous form. Printing to the computer screen can be seen by the operator. Writing to a database, on the other hand, might not always be directly visible to a human user. Sometimes the result will be looked up by a human, but usually it will be read later by another program. In chapter 14, you'll learn how such effects can be used by programs to communicate with other programs.

Because an effect is generally applied to a value, a pure effect can be modeled as a special kind of function, returning no value. I represent this in the book by the following interface:

```
public interface Effect<T> {
  void apply(T t);
}
```

Note that this is equivalent to Java's `Consumer` interface. Only the name of the class and the name of the method are different. In fact, as I mentioned several times in the beginning of this book, names are irrelevant, but meaningful names are better.

The `Effect` interface is what Java calls a functional interface, which roughly means an interface with a single abstract method (SAM). To define an effect consisting of printing a `Double` value to the screen, you can write this:

```
Effect<Double> print = x -> System.out.println(x);
```

Or better, you can use a method reference:

```
Effect<Double> print = System.out::println;
```

Note that this creates an object of type `Effect<Double>`, so it's generally not the most efficient way to handle effects. Naming effects is similar to naming functions: anonymous lambdas (not to be confused with anonymous classes) generally compile to a few additional instructions added to the underlying code, whereas named lambdas compile to objects. So it's generally better to use effects as anonymous lambdas or anonymous method references. Moreover, using anonymous lambdas relieves us of the need to declare the type explicitly.

What you need is something like this, where rd is the Result from the example in section 13.1:

```
rd.map(x -> System.out.println(x));
```

Unfortunately, this doesn't compile because the expression System.out.println(x) returns void, and it would have to return a value to make the code compile.

You could use a function that returns a value and prints as a side effect. You'd just have to ignore the returned value. But you can do better, as you saw in chapter 7. In that chapter, you wrote a forEach method in the Result class that takes an effect and applies it to the underlying value. This method was implemented in the Empty class as follows:

```
public void forEach(Effect<T> ef) {
  // Do nothing
}
```

In the Success class, it was implemented like this:

```
public void forEach(Effect<T> ef) {
  ef.apply(value);
}
```

Of course, you can't write unit tests for this method. To verify that it works, you can run the program shown in the following listing and look at the result on the screen.

Listing 13.1 Outputting data

```
public class ResultTest {

  public static void main(String... args) {

    Result<Integer> ra = Result.success(4);      Simulates data returned by
    Result<Integer> rb = Result.success(0);      functions that could fail

    Function<Integer, Result<Double>> inverse = x -> x != 0
        ? Result.success((double) 1 / x)
        : Result.failure("Division by 0");

    Effect<Double> print = System.out::println;

    Result<Double> rt1 = ra.flatMap(inverse);
    Result<Double> rt2 = rb.flatMap(inverse);

    System.out.print("Inverse of 4: ");          Outputs the
    rt1.forEach(print);                          resulting value

    System.out.print("Inverse of 0: ");          Doesn't produce any output,
    rt2.forEach(print);                          because there's no value
  }
}
```

This program produces the following result:

```
Inverse of 4: 0.25
Inverse of 0:
```

EXERCISE 13.1

Write a `forEach` method in the `List` class that takes an effect and applies it to all the elements of the list.

SOLUTION 13.1

The implementation for the `Nil` class is the same as for `Result.Empty`:

```
public void forEach(Effect<A> ef) {
  // Do nothing
}
```

The simplest recursive implementation for the `Cons` class would be as follows:

```
public void forEach(Effect<A> ef) {
  ef.apply(head);
  tail.forEach(ef);
}
```

Unfortunately, this implementation will blow the stack if you have more than a few thousand elements.

There are many different solutions to this problem. You can't use the `TailCall` class directly to make recursion stack-safe, but you can use a helper function with a side effect and ignore the result:

```
public void forEach(Effect<A> ef) {
  forEach(this, ef).eval();
}

private static <A> TailCall<List<A>> forEach(List<A> list, Effect<A> ef) {
  return list.isEmpty()
      ? TailCall.ret(list)
      : TailCall.sus(() -> {
        ef.apply(list.head());
        return forEach(list.tail(), ef);
      });
}
```

This implementation uses a side effect of the `forEach` helper function, but because you're implementing the application of an effect, it doesn't really matter much. Another (more efficient) solution is simply to use a `while` loop. Choosing the implementation is up to you.

13.1.3 *More-powerful effects for failures*

Although it makes sense to do nothing when a list is empty (and the same is true for `Option.None` and `Result.Empty`), it's certainly not enough for processing results that might be errors. In that case you might need to apply an effect to the errors.

Your `Result` class will contain an `Exception` in case of error. You might think of two different effects for this case. The first effect is to throw the exception, and the second is to handle the exception in some other way, avoiding throwing.

In chapter 7, you wrote the `forEachOrThrow` method in the `Result` class, which took an `Effect` as its argument and applied it to the underlying value if it was present, or threw an exception if it was a `Failure`.

The `Empty` implementation of `forEachOrThrow` does nothing and is similar to the `forEach` implementation. The `Failure` implementation simply throws the contained exception:

```
public void forEachOrThrow(Effect<T> c) {
  throw this.exception;
}
```

The `Success` implementation is again similar to `forEach` and will apply the effect to the contained value:

```
public void forEachOrThrow(Effect<T> e) {
  e.apply(this.value);
}
```

Throwing an exception in the case of a failure isn't what you generally want to do, at least in the `Result` class. Generally it's up to the client to decide what to do, and you might want to do something less radical than throwing an exception. For example, you might want to log the exception before continuing.

Logging isn't very functional, because logging is generally a side effect. No programs are written with logging as their main goal. Applying an effect with a method like `forEach` is breaking the functional contract. This isn't a problem in itself, but when you log, you're suddenly ceasing to be functional—this is in some respects the end of a functional program. After the effect is applied, you're ready to start another new functional program.

The frontier between imperative and functional programming won't be very clear if your application logs in every method. But because logging is generally a requirement, at least in the Java world, you may want a clean way to do it. You have no simple way to log an exception in case of a failure. What you need is to transform a failure into a success of its exception. For this, you need direct access to the exception, which can't be done from outside the `Result` context.

Why logging is dangerous

In functional programming, you won't see much logging. This is because functional programming makes logging mostly useless. Functional programs are built by composing pure functions, meaning functions that always return the same value given the same argument, so there can't be any surprises. On the other hand, logging is ubiquitous in imperative programming because in imperative programs you can't predict

> *(continued)*
>
> the output for a given input. Logging is like saying "I don't know what the program might produce at this point, so I'll write it to a log file. If everything goes well, I won't need this log file, but if something goes wrong, I'll be able to look at the logs to see what the program's state was at this point." This is nonsense.
>
> In functional programming, there's no need for such logs. If all functions are correct, which can generally be proved, you don't need to know the intermediate states. Furthermore, logging in imperative programs is often made conditional, which means that some logging code will only be executed in very rare and unknown states. This code is often untested. If you've ever seen an imperative Java program that worked well in INFO mode suddenly break when run in TRACE mode, you know what I mean.

EXERCISE 13.2

In chapter 7, you wrote a forEachOrException method in the Result type that worked like forEach in Empty and Success, with the addition that it would return a Result.Empty, and that returned a Result.Success<Exception> in the Failure class.

Write a forEachOrFail method that will return a Result<String> with the exception message, instead of the exception itself.

Note that these two methods aren't functional. Although they return a value, they might have a side effect.

SOLUTION 13.2

The implementation in Empty does nothing and returns Empty:

```
public Result<String> forEachOrFail(Effect<T> c) {
  return empty();
}
```

The implementations in Success applies the effect and returns Empty:

```
public Result<String> forEachOrFail(Effect<T> e) {
  e.apply(this.value);
  return empty();
}
```

The Failure implementations just return a Success of the contained exception or of its message:

```
public Result<String> forEachOrFail(Effect<T> c) {
  return success(exception.getMessage());
}

public Result<RuntimeException> forEachOrException(Effect<T> c) {
  return success(exception);
}
```

These methods, although not functional, greatly simplify the use of `Result` values:

```
public class ResultTest {

  public static void main(String... args) {

    Result<Integer> ra = Result.success(4);
    Result<Integer> rb = Result.success(0);

    Function<Integer, Result<Double>> inverse = x -> x != 0
        ? Result.success((double) 1 / x)
        : Result.failure("Division by 0");

    Result<Double> rt1 = ra.flatMap(inverse);
    Result<Double> rt2 = rb.flatMap(inverse);

    System.out.print("Inverse of 4: ");
    rt1.forEachOrFail(System.out::println).forEach(ResultTest::log);

    System.out.print("Inverse of 0: ");
    rt2.forEachOrFail(System.out::println).forEach(ResultTest::log);
  }

  private static void log(String s) {
    System.out.println(s);
  }
}
```

This program will print the following:

```
Inverse of 4: 0.25
Inverse of 0: Division by 0
```

13.2 Reading data

So far, you've only dealt with output. As you saw, outputting data occurs at the end of the program, once the result is computed. This allows most of the program to be written functionally, with all the benefits of that paradigm. Only the output part isn't functional. I also said that output could be done by sending data to other programs, but you haven't looked at how to input data into your programs. Let's do that now.

Later we'll look at a functional way to input data. But first, as we did for output, we'll discuss how to input data in a clean (although nonfunctional and imperative) way that fits nicely with the functional parts.

13.2.1 Reading data from the console

As an example, you'll read data from the console in a way that, although imperative, allows testing by making your programs deterministic. The approach you'll use is similar to what you did with the random generator in chapter 12.

You'll first develop an example that reads integers and strings. The following listing shows the interface you need to implement.

Listing 13.2   An interface for inputting data

```
public interface Input {

  Result<Tuple<String, Input>> readString();

  Result<Tuple<Integer, Input>> readInt();

  default Result<Tuple<String, Input>> readString(String message) {
    return readString();
  }

  default Result<Tuple<Integer, Input>> readInt(String message) {
    return readInt();
  }
}
```

Methods readInt and readString will input an integer and a string, respectively.

These methods allow you to pass a message as a parameter, which can be useful for prompting the user, but the provided default implementations ignore the message.

You could write a concrete implementation for this interface, but first you'll write an abstract one (because you might want to read data from some other source, such as a file). You'll put the common code in an abstract class and extend it for each type of input. The following listing shows this implementation.

Listing 13.3   The `AbstractReader` implementation

```
import com.fpinjava.common.Result;
import com.fpinjava.common.Tuple;
import java.io.BufferedReader;

public class AbstractReader implements Input {

  protected final BufferedReader reader;

  protected AbstractReader(BufferedReader reader) {
    this.reader = reader;
  }

  @Override
  public Result<Tuple<String, Input>> readString() {
    try {
      String s = reader.readLine();
      return s.length() == 0
          ? Result.empty()
          : Result.success(new Tuple<>(s, this));
    } catch (Exception e) {
      return Result.failure(e);
    }
  }

  @Override
  public Result<Tuple<Integer, Input>> readInt() {
    try {
      String s = reader.readLine();
      return s.length() == 0
          ? Result.empty()
          : Result.success(new Tuple<>(Integer.parseInt(s), this));
```

The class will be built with a reader, allowing for different sources of input.

The readString method will read a line from the reader and return a Result.Empty if the line was empty, a Result.Success if some data was obtained, or a Result.Failure if something went wrong.

```
      } catch (Exception e) {
        return Result.failure(e);
      }
    }
  }
}
```

Now you just have to implement the concrete class in order to read from the console. This class will be responsible for providing the `reader`. Additionally, you'll re-implement the two default methods from the interface to display a prompt to the user.

Listing 13.4 The `ConsoleReader` implementation

```
import com.fpinjava.common.Result;
import com.fpinjava.common.Tuple;
import java.io.BufferedReader;
import java.io.InputStreamReader;

public class ConsoleReader extends AbstractReader {

  protected ConsoleReader(BufferedReader reader) {
    super(reader);
  }

  @Override
  public Result<Tuple<String, Input>> readString(String message) {
    System.out.print(message + " ");
    return readString();
  }

  @Override
  public Result<Tuple<Integer, Input>> readInt(String message) {
    System.out.print(message + " ");
    return readInt();
  }

  public static ConsoleReader consoleReader() {
    return new ConsoleReader(new BufferedReader(
                             new InputStreamReader(System.in)));
  }
}
```

> **The two default methods are re-implemented to display the user prompt.**

> **The static factory method provides a reader to the underlying abstract class.**

Now you can use your `ConsoleReader` class with what you've learned to write a complete program, from input to output.

Listing 13.5 A complete program, from input to output

```
public class TestReader {

  public static void main(String... args) {

    Input input = ConsoleReader.consoleReader();

    Result<String> rString =
            input.readString("Enter your name: ").map(t -> t._1);

    Result<String> result =
            rString.map(s -> String.format("Hello, %s!", s));
```

> **The reader is created.**

> **The readString method is called (with a user prompt) and returns a Result<Tuple<String, Input>>, which is mapped to produce a Result<String>.**

```
result.forEachOrFail(System.out::println)
        .forEach(System.out::println);
    }
}
```

This line represents the business part of the program. It may be functionally pure.

The pattern from the previous section is applied to output either the result or an error message.

This isn't very impressive. It's the equivalent of the ubiquitous "hello" program that's usually the second example (just after "hello world") in most programming courses! Of course, this is only an example. What's interesting is how easy it is to evolve it into something more useful.

EXERCISE 13.3

Write a program that repeatedly asks the user to input an integer ID, a first name, and a last name, and that later displays the list of people on the console. Data input stops as soon as the user enters a blank ID, and the list of entered data is then displayed.

HINT

You'll need a class to hold each line of data. Use the Person class shown in the following listing.

Listing 13.6 The Person class

```
public class Person {

  private static final String FORMAT =
                  "ID: %s, First name: %s, Last name: %s";
  public final int id;
  public final String firstName;
  public final String lastName;

  private Person(int id, String firstName, String lastName) {
    this.id = id;
    this.firstName = firstName;
    this.lastName = lastName;
  }

  public static Person apply(int id, String firstName, String lastName) {
    return new Person(id, firstName, lastName);
  }

  @Override
  public String toString() {
    return String.format(FORMAT, id, firstName, lastName);
  }
}
```

Implement the solution in the main method of a ReadConsole class. Use the Stream.unfold method to produce a stream of persons. You might find it easier to create a separate method for inputting the data corresponding to a single person, and use a method reference as the argument of unfold. This method could have the following signature:

```
public static Result<Tuple<Person, Input>> person(Input input)
```

SOLUTION 13.3

The solution is very simple. Considering that you have a method for inputting the data for a single person, you can create a stream of persons and print the result as follows (ignoring any error in this case):

```
Input input = ConsoleReader.consoleReader();
Stream<Person> stream = Stream.unfold(input, ReadConsole::person);
stream.toList().forEach(System.out::println);
```

All you need now is the person method. This method will simply ask for the ID, the first name, and the last name, producing three Result instances that can be combined using the comprehension pattern you learned in previous chapters:

```
public static Result<Tuple<Person, Input>> person(Input input) {
  return input.readInt("Enter ID:")
     .flatMap(id -> id._2.readString("Enter first name:")
        .flatMap(firstName -> firstName._2.readString("Enter last name:")
           .map(lastName -> new Tuple<>(Person.apply(id._1, firstName._1,
                                   lastName._1), lastName._2))));
}
```

Note that the comprehension pattern is probably one of the most important patterns in functional programming, so you really want to master it. Other languages such as Scala or Haskell have syntactic sugar for it, but Java doesn't. This corresponds, in pseudo code, to something like this:

```
for {
  id in input.readInt("Enter ID:")
  firstName in id._2.readString("Enter first name:")
  lastName in firstName._2.readString("Enter last name:")
} return new Tuple<>(Person.apply(id._1, firstName._1,
                                lastName._1), lastName._2))
```

But you don't really need the syntactic sugar. The flatMap idiom is perhaps more difficult to master at first, but it really shows what's happening.

By the way, many programmers know this pattern as the following:

```
a.flatMap(b -> flatMap(c -> map(d -> getSomething(a, b, c, d))))
```

They often think it's always a series of flatMaps ending with a map. This is absolutely not the case. Whether it ends with map or flatMap depends solely on the return type. It often happens that the last method (here, getSomething) returns a bare value, which is why the pattern ends with a map. But if getSomething were to return a context (such as a Result), the pattern would be as follows:

```
a.flatMap(b -> flatMap(c -> flatMap(d -> getSomething(a, b, c, d))))
```

13.2.2 *Reading from a file*

The way you've designed the program makes it very simple to adapt it to reading files. The `FileReader` class is very similar to the `ConsoleReader`. The only difference is that the static factory method must handle an `IOException` so it returns a `Result<Input>` instead of a bare value.

> **Listing 13.7   The `FileReader` implementation**

```
import com.fpinjava.common.Result;
import java.io.*;

public class FileReader extends AbstractReader {

  private FileReader(BufferedReader reader) {
    super(reader);
  }

  public static Result<Input> fileReader(String path) {
    try {
      return Result.success(new FileReader(new BufferedReader(
        new InputStreamReader(new FileInputStream(new File(path))))));
    } catch (Exception e) {
      return Result.failure(e);
    }
  }
}
```

EXERCISE 13.4

Write a `ReadFile` program, similar to `ReadConsole`, but that reads from a file containing the entries, each one on a separate line. An example file is provided with the code accompanying this book (http://github.com/fpinjava/fpinjava).

HINT

Although it's similar to the `ReadConsole` program, you'll have to deal with the fact that the factory method returns a `Result`. Try to reuse the same `person` method.

SOLUTION 13.4

The solution is given in listing 13.8. Note how the `Result` returned by the factory method is handled before calling the `person` method, allowing you to use the same method as for the `ConsoleReader`. (You could also use the `read` methods that don't take any parameters.)

> **Listing 13.8   The `ReadFile` implementation**

Change the path to the file location on your system.

```
public class ReadFile {

  private static String path = "path to data file";

  public static void main(String... args) {
    Result<Input> rInput = FileReader.fileReader(path);
    Result<Stream<Person>> rStream =
        rInput.map(input -> Stream.unfold(input, ReadFile::person));
    rStream.forEachOrFail(stream -> stream.toList()
```

The Result<Input> is handled here.

```
                    .forEach(System.out::println)).forEach(System.out::println);
    }
    public static Result<Tuple<Person, Input>> person(Input input) {
      return input.readInt("Enter ID:")
        .flatMap(id -> id._2.readString("Enter first name:")
          .flatMap(firstName -> firstName._2.readString("Enter last name:")
            .map(lastName -> new Tuple<>(Person.apply(id._1,
                          firstName._1, lastName._1), lastName._2))));
    }
  }
```

13.2.3 *Testing with input*

One of the benefits of the approach you took in the preceding solution is that the program is easily testable. Of course, it would be possible to test your programs by providing files instead of user input at the console, but it's just as easy to interface your program with another program that produces a script of the input commands. The following listing shows an example ScriptReader that could be used for testing.

Listing 13.9   A `ScriptReader` that allows you to use a list of input commands

```
public class ScriptReader implements Input {

  private final List<String> commands;

  public ScriptReader(List<String> commands) {
    super();
    this.commands = commands;
  }

  public ScriptReader(String... commands) {
    super();
    this.commands = List.list(commands);
  }

  public Result<Tuple<String, Input>> readString() {
    return commands.isEmpty()
      ? Result.failure("Not enough entries in script")
      : Result.success(new Tuple<>(commands.headOption().getOrElse(""),
                              new ScriptReader(commands.drop(1))));
  }

  @Override
  public Result<Tuple<Integer, Input>> readInt() {
    try {
      return commands.isEmpty()
        ? Result.failure("Not enough entries in script")
        : Integer.parseInt(commands.headOption().getOrElse("")) >= 0
          ? Result.success(new Tuple<>(Integer.parseInt(
                            commands.headOption().getOrElse("")),
                              new ScriptReader(commands.drop(1))))
          : Result.empty();
    } catch(Exception e) {
      return Result.failure(e);
    }
  }
}
```

The next listing shows an example of using the `ScriptReader` class. In the code accompanying this book, you'll find examples of unit testing.

Listing 13.10   **Using the `ScriptReader` to enter data**

```
public class ReadScriptReader {

  public static void main(String... args) {
    Input input = new ScriptReader(
        "0", "Mickey", "Mouse",
        "1", "Minnie", "Mouse",
        "2", "Donald", "Duck",
        "3", "Homer", "Simpson"
    );

    Stream<Person> stream =
                Stream.unfold(input, ReadScriptReader::person);
    stream.toList().forEach(System.out::println);
  }

  public static Result<Tuple<Person, Input>> person(Input input) {
    return input.readInt("Enter ID:")
      .flatMap(id -> id._2.readString("Enter first name:")
        .flatMap(firstName -> firstName._2.readString("Enter last name:")
          .map(lastName -> new Tuple<>(Person.apply(id._1, firstName._1,
                                      lastName._1), lastName._2))));
  }
}
```

13.3   *Really functional input/output*

What you've learned so far is sufficient for most Java programmers. Separating the functional part of the program from the nonfunctional parts is essential, and also sufficient. But it's interesting to see how Java programs can be made even more functional.

Whether you use the following techniques in Java programs in production is up to you. It might not be worth the additional complexity. It is, however, useful and interesting to learn these techniques so you can make an educated choice.

13.3.1   *How can input/output be made fully functional?*

There are several answers to this question. The shortest answer is this: it can't. According to our definition of a functional program, which is "a program that has no other observable effect than returning a value," there's no way to do any input or output.

But many programs don't need to do any input or output. For example, many libraries fall into that category. Libraries are programs that are designed to be used by other programs. They receive argument values, and they return values resulting from computations based on their arguments. What you did in the first two sections of this chapter was separate your programs into three parts: one doing the input, one doing the output, and a third part acting as a library and being fully functional.

Another way to handle the problem is to write this library part, and produce, as the final return value, another (nonfunctional) program that handles all the input and output. This is very similar in concept to laziness. You can handle input and output as something that will happen later, in a separate program that will be the returned value of your pure functional program.

13.3.2 *Implementing purely functional input/output*

In this section, you'll see how to implement purely functional input/output. Let's start with output. Imagine that you simply want to display a welcome message to the console. For now, you'll assume you already know the name to use for the message. Instead of writing this

```
static void sayHello(String name) {
    System.out.println("Hello, " + name + "!");
}
```

we could make the `sayHello` method return a program that, once run, will have the same effect. To do so, you might use a lambda and the `Runnable` interface, like this:

```
static Runnable sayHello(String name) {
    return () -> System.out.println("Hello, " + name + "!");
}
```

You can use this method as follows:

```
public static void main(String... args) {
  Runnable program = sayHello("Georges");
}
```

This code is purely functional. You could argue that it doesn't do anything visible, and this is true. It produces a program that can be run to produce the desired effect. This program can be run by calling the `run` method on the `Runnable` it produces. The returned program isn't functional, but you don't care. Your program is functional.

Is this cheating? No. Think of a program written in any "functional" language. In the end, it's compiled into an executable program that's absolutely not functional and that can be run on your computer. You're doing exactly the same thing, except that the program you're producing might seem to be written in Java. In fact, it's not. It's written in some kind of DSL (domain-specific language) that your program is constructing.

To execute this program, you can simply write

```
program.run();
```

Be aware that most code-checker programs won't like the fact that `run` is called on a `Runnable`. This is why, in previous chapters, you created the `Executable` interface to do the same thing.

Here, you need something much more powerful, so you'll create a new interface named `IO`. You'll start with a single `run` method. At this stage, it's no different from `Runnable`:

```
public interface IO {
  void run();
}
```

Suppose you have the three following methods:

```
static IO println(String message) {
  return () -> System.out.print(message);
}

static <A> String toString(Result<A> rd) {
  return rd.map(Object::toString).getOrElse(rd::toString);
}

static Result<Double> inverse(int i) {
  return i == 0
      ? Result.failure("Div by 0")
      : Result.success(1.0 / i);
}
```

You might write the following purely functional program:

```
IO computation = println(toString(inverse(3)));
```

This program produces another program that can later be executed:

```
computation.run();
```

13.3.3 *Combining IO*

With your IO interface, you can potentially build any program, but as a single unit. It would be interesting to be able to combine such programs. The simplest combination you could use consists of grouping two programs into one. This is what you'll do in the following exercise.

EXERCISE 13.5
Create a method in the IO interface allowing you to group two IO instances into one. This method will be called add, and it will have a default implementation. Here's the signature:

```
default IO add(IO io)
```

SOLUTION 13.5
The solution is simply to return a new IO with a run implementation that will first execute the current IO, and then the argument IO:

```
default IO add(IO io) {
  return () -> {
    IO.this.run();
    io.run();
  };
}
```

You'll later need a "do nothing" IO to serve as a neutral element for some IO combinations. This can easily be created in the IO interface as follows:

```
IO<Nothing> empty = () -> Nothing.instance;
```

Using these new methods, you can create more-sophisticated programs by combining IO instances:

```
String name = getName();

IO instruction1 = println("Hello, ");
IO instruction2 = println(name);
IO instruction3 = println("!\n");

IO script = instruction1.add(instruction2).add(instruction3);
script.run();
```

> These three lines don't print anything. They're like instructions in the DSL.

> **Execute it.**

> **Combine the three instructions to create a program.**

Of course, you can simplify the process:

```
println("Hello, ").add(println(name)).add(println("!\n")).run();
```

You can also create a program from a list of instructions:

```
List<IO> instructions = List.list(
    println("Hello, "),
    println(name),
    println("!\n")
);
```

Does this look like an imperative program? In fact, it is. To "compile it," you might use a right fold:

```
IO program = instructions.foldRight(IO.empty(), io -> io::add);
```

Or a left fold:

```
IO program = instructions.foldLeft(IO.empty(), acc -> acc::add);
```

You can see why you needed a "do nothing" implementation. Finally, you can run the program as usual:

```
program.run();
```

13.3.4 Handling input with IO

At this point, your IO type can only handle output. To make it handle input, one necessary change is to parameterize it with the type of the input value, so that it can be used to handle this value. Here's the new parameterized IO type:

```
public interface IO<A> {

  A run();

  IO<Nothing> empty = () -> Nothing.instance;

  static <A> IO<A> unit(A a) {
    return () -> a;
  }
}
```

> **The IO interface is type-annotated.**

> **The empty instance has no type parameter, so you make it return the Nothing singleton.**

> **The unit method takes a bare value and returns it in the IO context.**

As you can see, the IO interface creates a context for computations in the same way Option, Result, List, Stream, State, and the like did. It similarly has a method returning an empty instance, as well as a method that puts a bare value in context.

In order to perform computations on IO values, you now need methods like map and flatMap to bind functions to the IO context.

EXERCISE 13.6

Define a map method in IO<A> that takes as its argument a function from A to B and returns an IO<B>. Make this a default implementation in the IO interface.

SOLUTION 13.6

Here's the implementation, which applies the function to the value of this, and returns the result in a new IO context:

```
default <B> IO<B> map(Function<A, B> f) {
  return () -> f.apply(this.run());
}
```

EXERCISE 13.7

Write a flatMap method that takes a function from A to IO<B> as its argument and returns an IO<B>.

HINT

Don't worry about a potential stack problem. You'll deal with this later.

SOLUTION 13.7

Applying the function to the value obtained by running thisIO would give an IO<IO<B>>. You need to flatten this result, which can be done very simply by running it, as follows:

```
default <B> IO<B> flatMap(Function<A, IO<B>> f) {
  return () -> f.apply(this.run()).run();
}
```

As you can see, this is kind of recursive. It won't be a problem at first, because there's only one recursion step, but it could become a problem if you were to chain a huge number of flatMap calls.

To see your new methods in action, use the following Console class.

Listing 13.11   The Console class

```
import com.fpinjava.common.Nothing;
import java.io.BufferedReader;
import java.io.IOException;
import java.io.InputStreamReader;

public class Console {

  private static BufferedReader br =
                 new BufferedReader(new InputStreamReader(System.in));

  public static IO<String> readLine(Nothing nothing) {
```

The readLine method takes a Nothing as its parameter and returns an IO<String>.

```
    return () -> {
      try {
        return br.readLine();
      } catch (IOException e) {
        throw new IllegalStateException((e));
      }
    };
  }

  public static IO<Nothing> printLine(Object o) {
    return () -> {
      System.out.println(o.toString());
      return Nothing.instance;
    };
  }
}
```

> You rethrow any exception wrapped in a runtime exception. Keep in mind that this isn't the readLine method throwing.

> The printLine method takes an Object as its argument and returns a Nothing.

> The string representation of the object parameter is printed to the screen. Keep in mind that the printLine method isn't doing the printing. It returns a lambda that will do the actual printing when executed.

It's important to note that these two methods are purely functional. They don't throw any exceptions, nor do they read from or print to the console. They only return programs that do those things.

To see this at work, you can run the following example program.

Listing 13.12 Reading from and printing to the console in a purely functional way

```
public class Main {

  public static void main(String... args) {
    IO<Nothing> script = sayHello();
    script.run();
  }

  private static IO<Nothing> sayHello() {
    return Console.printLine("Enter your name: ")
        .flatMap(Console::readLine)
        .map(Main::buildMessage)
        .flatMap(Console::printLine);
  }

  private static String buildMessage(String name) {
    return String.format("Hello, %s!", name);
  }
}
```

> The sayHello method returns a program.

> This program can be executed by calling run on it.

> These lines are the instructions from which you build a program.

13.3.5 *Extending the IO type*

By using the IO type, you can create impure programs (programs with effects) in a purely functional way. But at this stage, these programs only allow us to read from and print to an element such as your Console class. You can extend your DSL by adding instructions to create control structures, such as loops and conditionals.

First, you'll implement a loop similar to the for indexed loop. This will take the form of a repeat method that takes the number of iterations and the IO to repeat as its parameters.

EXERCISE 13.8

Implement repeat as a static method in the IO interface with the following signature:

```
static <A> IO<List<A>> repeat(int n, IO<A> io)
```

HINT

You should create a collection of IO instances representing each iteration, and then fold this collection by combining the IO instances. To do this, you'll need something more powerful than the add method. Start by implementing a map2 method with the following signature:

```
static <A, B, C> IO<C> map2(IO<A> ioa, IO<B> iob,
                               Function<A, Function<B, C>> f)
```

SOLUTION 13.8

The map2 method can be implemented as follows:

```
static <A, B, C> IO<C> map2(IO<A> ioa, IO<B> iob,
                               Function<A, Function<B, C>> f) {
  return ioa.flatMap(a -> iob.map(b -> f.apply(a).apply(b)));
}
```

This is a simple application of the ubiquitous comprehension pattern. With this method at hand, you can easily implement repeat as follows:

```
static <A> IO<List<A>> repeat(int n, IO<A> io) {
  return Stream.fill(n, () -> io)
    .foldRight(() -> unit(List.list()), ioa -> sioLa -> map2(ioa,
                        sioLa.get(), a -> la -> List.cons(a, la)));
}
```

Note that you create a stream using the Stream.fill() method, which has the following signature:

```
public static <T> Stream<T> fill(int n, Supplier<T> elem)
```

It returns a Stream of *n* (lazily evaluated) instances of T.

This may look a bit complex, but that's partly because of the line being wrapped for printing, and partly because it's written as a one-liner for optimization. It's equivalent to this:

```
static <A> IO<List<A>> repeat(int n, IO<A> io) {
  Stream<IO<A>> stream = Stream.fill(n, () -> io);
  Function<A, Function<List<A>, List<A>>> f = a -> la -> List.cons(a, la);
  Function<IO<A>, Function<Supplier<IO<List<A>>>, IO<List<A>>>> g =
                        ioa -> sioLa -> map2(ioa, sioLa.get(), f);
  Supplier<IO<List<A>>> z = () -> unit(List.list());
  return stream.foldRight(z, g);
}
```

If you're using an IDE, it's relatively easy to find the types. For example, in IntelliJ, you just have to put the mouse pointer on a reference while holding down the Ctrl key to display the type.

With these methods you can now write the following:

```
IO program = IO.repeat(3, sayHello());
```

This will give you a program corresponding to calling the following method as say-Hello(3):

```
private static void sayHello(int n) throws IOException {
  BufferedReader br = new BufferedReader(new InputStreamReader(System.in));

  for (int i = 0; i < n; i++) {
    System.out.println("Enter your name: ");
    String name = br.readLine();
    System.out.println(buildMessage(name));
  }
}
```

The very important difference, however, is that calling sayHello(3) will execute the effect three times eagerly, whereas IO.repeat(3, sayHello()) will simply return a (non-evaluated) program that will do the same only when its run method is called.

It's possible to define many other control structures. You'll find examples in the accompanying code that can be downloaded from http://github.com/fpinjava/fpinjava. The following listing shows an example of using when and doWhile methods that do exactly the same thing as if and while in imperative Java.

Listing 13.13   Using IO to wrap imperative programming

```
public class Main {

  public static void main(String... args) throws IOException {
    IO program = program(buildMessage,
                    "Enter the names of the persons to welcome:");
    program.run();
  }

  public static IO<Nothing> program(Function<String, IO<Boolean>> f,
                                              String title) {
    return IO.sequence(
        Console.printLine(title),
        IO.doWhile(Console.readLine(), f),
        Console.printLine("bye!")
    );
  }

  private static Function<String, IO<Boolean>> buildMessage =
          name -> IO.when(name.length() != 0,
              () -> IO.unit(String.format("Hello, %s!", name))
    .flatMap(Console::printLine));
}
```

This example isn't meant to suggest that you should program like this. It's certainly better to use the IO type only for input and output, doing all the computations in functional programming. After all, if you choose to learn functional programming, it's probably not to implement an imperative language in functional code. But it's interesting to do it as an exercise, to understand how it works.

13.3.6 *Making the IO type stack-safe*

In the previous exercises, you might not have noticed that some of the IO methods used the stack in the same way recursive methods do. The repeat method, for example, will overflow the stack if the number of repetitions is too high. How much "too high" is depends on the stack size and how full it is when the program returned by the method is run. (By now, I expect you understand that calling the repeat method won't blow the stack. Only running the program it returns might do so.)

EXERCISE 13.9

In order to experiment with blowing the stack, create a forever method that takes an IO as its argument and returns a new IO executing the argument in an endless loop. Here's the corresponding signature:

```
static <A, B> IO<B> forever(IO<A> ioa)
```

SOLUTION 13.9

This is as simple to implement as it is useless! All you have to do is make the constructed program infinitely recursive. Be aware that the forever method itself should not be recursive. Only the returned program should be. The solution is to use a Supplier, and to flatMap the IO argument with an IO executing get on this Supplier:

```
static <A, B> IO<B> forever(IO<A> ioa) {
  Supplier<IO<B>> t = () -> forever(ioa);
  return ioa.flatMap(x -> t.get());
}
```

This method can be used as follows:

```
public static void main(String... args) {
  IO program = IO.forever(IO.unit("Hi again!")
                         .flatMap(Console::printLine));
  program.run();
}
```

It will blow the stack after a few thousand iterations. Note that this is equivalent to the following:

```
IO.forever(Console.printLine("Hi again!")).run();
```

If you don't see why it blows the stack, consider the following pseudo code (which won't compile!) where the t variable is replaced by the corresponding expression:

```
static <A, B> IO<B> forever(IO<A> ioa) {
```

```
    return ioa.flatMap(x -> (() -> forever(ioa)).get());
}
```

Now let's replace the recursive call with the corresponding code:

```
static <A, B> IO<B> forever(IO<A> ioa) {
  return ioa.flatMap(x -> (() -> ioa.flatMap(x -> (() -
    > forever(ioa)).get())).get());
}
```

You could continue forever recursively. (Remember, you shouldn't try to compile this code!) What you may notice is that the calls to `flatMap` would be nested, resulting in the current state being pushed onto the stack with each call, which would indeed blow the stack after a few thousand steps. Unlike in imperative code, where you'd execute one instruction after the other, you call the `flatMap` method recursively.

To make `IO` stack-safe, you can use the same technique you used in chapter 4 to create stack-safe recursive methods and functions. First, you'll need to represent three states of your program:

- `Return` will represent a computation that's finished, meaning that you just have to return the result.
- `Suspend` will represent a suspended computation, when some effect has to be applied before resuming the current computation.
- `Continue` will represent a state where the program has to first apply a subcomputation before continuing with the next one.

These states will be represented by the three classes shown in listing 13.14.

> **NOTE** Listings 13.14 through 13.16 are parts of a whole. They aren't supposed to be used with the code constructed so far, but together.

Listing 13.14   The three classes needed to make `IO` stack-safe

```
final static class Return<T> implements IO<T> {

  public final T value;                          ┐ This value will be returned
                                                 ┘ by the computation.
  protected Return(T value) {
    this.value = value;
  }

  @Override
  public boolean isReturn() {          ◄─┐
    return true;                          │  Helper methods are used to
  }                                       │  determinate the nature of an IO. The
                                          │  corresponding abstract methods are
  @Override                               │  declared in the IO interface.
  public boolean isSuspend()    ◄────────┘
    return false;
  }
}

final static class Suspend<T> implements IO<T> {
```

```
  public final Supplier<T> resume;

  protected Suspend(Supplier<T> resume) {
    this.resume = resume;
  }

  @Override
  public boolean isReturn() {
    return false;
  }

  @Override
  public boolean isSuspend() {
    return true;
  }
}

final static class Continue<T, U> implements IO<T> {

  public final IO<T> sub;
  public final Function<T, IO<U>> f;

  protected Continue(IO<T> sub, Function<T, IO<U>> f) {
    this.sub = sub;
    this.f = f;
  }

  @Override
  public boolean isReturn() {
    return false;
  }

  @Override
  public boolean isSuspend() {
    return false;
  }
}
```

This Supplier acts as a function taking no argument, applying a (side) effect and returning a value.

Helper methods are used to determinate the nature of an IO. The corresponding abstract methods are declared in the IO interface.

This IO is executed first, producing a value.

The computation continues by applying this function to the returned value.

Helper methods are used to determinate the nature of an IO. The corresponding abstract methods are declared in the IO interface.

Some modifications must be made to the enclosing IO interface, as shown in listings 13.15 and 13.16.

Listing 13.15   Changes in the stack-safe version of IO

```
import com.fpinjava.common.*;
import static com.fpinjava.common.TailCall.ret;
import static com.fpinjava.common.TailCall.sus;

public abstract class IO<A> {

  protected abstract boolean isReturn();
  protected abstract boolean isSuspend();

  private static IO<Nothing> EMPTY =
                 new IO.Suspend<>(() -> Nothing.instance);

  public static IO<Nothing> empty() {
    return EMPTY;
  }
}
```

The IO type is now an abstract class.

The empty IO is now a Suspend. It's made private, and a corresponding public accessor is added.

```java
public A run() {
    return run(this);
}
```

The run method now simply calls the helper method run(this).

```java
public A run(IO<A> io) {
    return run_(io).eval();
}
```

The run(this) method, in turn, calls the run_ helper method that will return a TailCall.

```java
private TailCall<A> run_(IO<A> io) {
    ... // see listing 13.16
}
```

The run_ helper method is shown in listing 3.16.

```java
public <B> IO<B> map(Function<A, B> f) {
    return flatMap(f.andThen(Return::new));
}
```

The map method is now defined in terms of applying flatMap to the composition of f and the Return constructor.

```java
@SuppressWarnings("unchecked")
public <B> IO<B> flatMap(Function<A, IO<B>> f) {
    return (IO<B>) new Continue<>(this, f);
}
```

The flatMap method returns a Continue that's cast into an IO<A>.

```java
static <A> IO<A> unit(A a) {
    return new IO.Suspend<>(() -> a);
}
```

The unit method returns a Suspend.

Listing 13.16 The stack-safe `run` method

The method returns a TailCall that will be evaluated by the caller method.

```java
private TailCall<A> run_(IO<A> io) {
    if (io.isReturn()) {
        return ret(((Return<A>) io).value);
    } else if(io.isSuspend()) {
        return ret(((Suspend<A>) io).resume.get());
    } else {
        Continue<A, A> ct = (Continue<A, A>) io;
        IO<A> sub = ct.sub;
        Function<A, IO<A>> f = ct.f;
        if (sub.isReturn()) {
            return sus(() -> run_(f.apply(((Return<A>) sub).value)));
        } else if (sub.isSuspend()) {
            return sus(() -> run_(f.apply(((Suspend<A>) sub).resume.get())));
        } else {
            Continue<A, A> ct2 = (Continue<A, A>) sub;
            IO<A> sub2 = ct2.sub;
            Function<A, IO<A>> f2 = ct2.f;
            return sus(() -> run_(sub2.flatMap(x ->
                                        f2.apply(x).flatMap(f))));
        }
    }
}
```

If the received IO is a Return, the computation is over.

If the received IO is a Suspend, the contained effect is executed before returning the resume value.

If the received IO is a Continue, the contained sub IO is read.

If sub is a continue, the IO it contains is extracted (sub2), and it's flatMapped with sub, thus creating the chaining.

If sub is a Return, the method is called recursively, with the result of applying the enclosed function to it.

If sub is a Suspend, the enclosed function is applied to it, possibly producing the function's effect, if there is one.

The new stack-safe version can be used as follows.

Listing 13.17   The new `Console` class using the stack-safe version

```
public class Console {

  private static BufferedReader br = new BufferedReader(new InputStreamReader(System.in));

  public static IO<String> readLine(Nothing nothing) {
    return new IO.Suspend<>(() -> {
      try {
        return br.readLine();
      } catch (IOException e) {
        throw new IllegalStateException((e));
      }
    });
  }

  /**
   * A possible implementation of readLine as a function
   */
  public static Function<Nothing, IO<String>> readLine_ = x -> new IO.Suspend<>(() -> {
    try {
      return br.readLine();
    } catch (IOException e) {
      throw new IllegalStateException((e));
    }
  });

  /**
   * A simpler implementation of readLine as a function using a method reference
   */
  public static Function<Nothing, IO<String>> readLine = Console::readLine;

  /**
   * A convenience helper method allowing calling the readLine method without
   * providing a Nothing.
   */
  public static IO<String> readLine() {
    return readLine(Nothing.instance);
  }

  public static IO<Nothing> printLine(Object s) {
    return new IO.Suspend<>(() -> println(s));
  }

  private static Nothing println(Object s) {
    System.out.println(s);
    return Nothing.instance;
  }

  public static IO<Nothing> printLine_(Object s) {
    return new IO.Suspend<>(() -> {
      System.out.println(s);
      return Nothing.instance;
    });
  }
```

```
public static Function<String, IO<Nothing>> printLine_ =
        s -> new IO.Suspend<>(() -> {
            System.out.println(s);
            return Nothing.instance;
        });

public static Function<String, IO<Nothing>> printLine = Console::printLine;
}
```

Now you can use `forever` or `doWhile` without the risk of overflowing the stack. You can also rewrite `repeat` to make it stack-safe. I won't show the new implementation here, but you'll find it in the accompanying code (http://github.com/fpinjava/fpinjava).

Keep in mind that this is not the recommended way to write functional programs. Take it as an example of what can ultimately be done, rather than as good practice. Also note that "ultimately," here, applies to Java programming. With a more functional-friendly language, you can craft much more powerful programs.

13.4 *Summary*

- Effects can be passed into `List`, `Result`, and other contexts to be safely applied to values, rather than extracting values from these contexts and applying the effects outside, which might produce errors if there are no values.
- Handling two different effects for success and failure can be abstracted inside the `Result` type.
- Reading data can be done in the same way as random numbers were generated in chapter 12.
- Reading from files is done in exactly the same way as reading from the console or from memory through the `Reader` abstraction.
- More-functional input/output can be obtained through the `IO` type.
- The `IO` type can be extended to a more generic type that makes it possible to perform any imperative task in a functional way by building a program that will be executed later.
- The `IO` type can be made stack-safe by using the same techniques we used for stack-safe recursive methods.

14

Sharing mutable state with actors

This chapter covers

- Understanding the actor model
- Using asynchronous messaging
- Building an actor framework
- Putting actors to work
- Optimizing actor performance

In working through this book, you first learned that functional programming often deals with immutable data, which results in programs that are safer, more reliable, and easier to design and scale. Then you learned how mutable state can be handled in a functional way by passing the state along as an argument to functions. You saw several examples of this technique:

- Passing the generator while generating random numbers allowed for increased testability.
- Passing the console as a parameter allowed you to send functional output to the screen and receive input from the keyboard.

This technique can be widely applied to many domains. In imperative programming, parsing a file is generally handled by continuously mutating the state of a component that represents the result of the parsing. To make this process compatible with functional programming, you just have to pass the state as an additional argument to all parsing functions. Logging can be done the same way, as well as monitoring performance: instead of writing to a log file in each function, you can make the function receive the log file as an argument, and return the augmented file as part of the result.

The benefit of this approach is that it relieves you from caring about synchronization and locking when accessing resources. But this security is obtained by preventing data sharing. This is good because it forces you to find other, safer ways of doing things. Using immutable lists doesn't automatically add safety to operations involving sharing those lists. It just prevents you from sharing mutable state. It allows you to fake a list mutation in a way that more or less corresponds to making defensive copies, but without the performance penalty. This is useful, but sometimes it's not what you need.

Imagine you want to count how many times a function is called. In a single-threaded application, you might do this by adding the counter to the function arguments and returning the incremented counter as part of the result. But most imperative programmers would rather increment the counter as a side effect. This would work seamlessly, because there's only a single thread, so no locking is necessary to prevent potential concurrent access. This is the same as living on a desert island. If you're the only inhabitant, there's really no need for locks on your doors.

But in a multithreaded program, how can you increment the counter in a safe way, avoiding concurrent access? The answer is generally to use locks or to make operations atomic, or both.

In functional programming, sharing resources has to be done as an effect, which means, more or less, that each time you access a shared resource, you have to leave the functional safety and treat this access as you did for input/output in chapter 13. Does this mean that you must then manage locks and synchronization? Not at all. As you learned in the previous chapters, functional programming is also about pushing abstraction to the limit. Sharing mutable state can be abstracted in such a way that you can use it without bothering about the gory details. One way to achieve this is to use an actor framework.

Unlike in previous chapters, here you're not going to develop a real, complete actor framework. Creating a complete actor framework is such a tremendous job that you should probably use an existing one. Here, you'll develop a minimal actor framework that will give you the feeling of what an actor framework brings to functional programming.

14.1 The actor model

In the actor model, a multithreaded application is divided into basically single-threaded components called *actors*. If each actor is single threaded, it doesn't need to share data using locks or synchronization. Actors communicate with other actors by way of effects, as if such communication were input/output. This means that actors rely on a mechanism for serializing the messages they receive. (Here, *serialization* means handling one message after the other. This isn't to be confused with Java serialization.) Due to this mechanism, they can process messages one at a time without having to bother about concurrent access to their resources. As a result, an actor system can be seen as a series of functional programs communicating with each other through effects. Each actor can be single threaded, so there's no concurrent access to resources inside. Concurrency is abstracted inside the framework.

14.1.1   Asynchronous messaging

As part of message processing, actors can send messages to other actors. Messages are sent asynchronously, which means there's no answer to wait for. As soon as a message is sent, the sender can continue its job, which mostly consists of processing, one at a time, a queue of messages it receives. Of course, handling the message queue means that there are some concurrent accesses to the queue to manage. But this management is abstracted in the actor framework, so you, the programmer, don't need to worry about this.

Of course, answers to messages might be needed. Suppose an actor is responsible for a long computation. The client can take advantage of asynchronicity by continuing its own job while the computation is handled for it. But once the computation is done, there must be a way for the client to receive the result. This is simply done by having the actor responsible for the computation call back its client and send it the result, once again in an asynchronous way. Note that the client may be the original sender, though that need not always be the case.

14.1.2   Handling parallelization

The actor model allows tasks to be parallelized by using a manager actor that's responsible for breaking the task into subtasks and distributing them to a number of worker actors. Each time a worker actor returns a result to the manager, it's given a new subtask. This model offers an advantage over other parallelization models in that no worker actor will ever be idle until the list of subtasks is empty. The downside is that the manager actor won't participate in the computation. But in a real application, this generally makes no noticeable difference.

For some tasks, the results of the subtasks may need to be reordered when they're received. In such a case, the manager actor will probably send the results to a specific actor responsible for this job. You'll see an example of this in section 14.2.3. In small programs, the manager itself can handle this task. In figure 14.1, this actor is called `Receiver`.

14.1.3   Handling actor state mutation

Actors can be stateless (immutable) or stateful, meaning they're supposed to change their state according to the messages they receive. For example, a synchronizer actor may receive the results of computations that have to be reordered before being used.

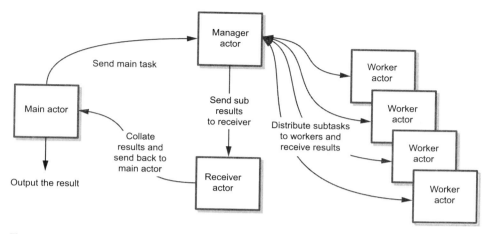

Figure 14.1 The `Main` actor produces the main task and sends it to the `Manager` actor, which splits it into subtasks that are processed in parallel by several `Worker` actors. Sub results are sent back to the `Manager`, which passes them to the `Receiver`. After collating the sub results, the `Receiver` sends the final result to the `Main` actor.

Imagine, for example, that you have a list of data that must go through heavy computation in order to provide a list of results. In short, this is a mapping. It could be parallelized by breaking the list into several sublists and giving these sublists to worker actors for processing. But there's no guarantee that the worker actors will finish their jobs in the same order that those jobs were given to them. One solution for resynchronizing the results is to number the tasks. When a worker sends back a result, it adds the corresponding task number, so that the receiver can put the results in a priority queue. Not only does this allow automatic sorting, but it also makes it possible to process the results as an asynchronous stream. Each time the receiver receives a result, it compares the task number to the expected number. If there's a match, it passes the result to the client and then looks into the priority queue to see if the first available result corresponds to the new expected task number. If there's a match again, the dequeuing process continues until there's no longer a match. If the received result doesn't match the expected result number, it's simply added to the priority queue.

In such a design, the receiving actor has to handle two mutable pieces of data: the priority queue and the expected result number. Does this mean the actor has to use mutable properties? This wouldn't be a big deal, but because actors are single threaded, it's not even necessary. As you'll see, the handling of property mutations can be included and abstracted into a general state-mutation process, allowing the programmer to use only immutable data.

14.2 Building the actor framework

In this section, you'll learn how to build a minimal but fully functional actor framework. While building this framework, you'll learn how an actor framework allows for safe sharing of mutable state, easy and secure parallelization and reserialization, and modular architecture of applications. At the end of this chapter, you'll see some general things you can do with actor frameworks.

Your actor framework will be made of four components:

- The `Actor` interface will determine the behavior of an actor.
- The `AbstractActor` class will contain all the stuff that's common to all actors. This class will have to be extended by business actors.
- The `ActorContext` will act as a way to access actors. In your implementation, this component will be very minimalist, and will be used primarily to access actor behavior. This component isn't really necessary in such a small implementation, but most serious implementations will use such a component. This context allows, for example, searching for available actors.
- The `MessageProcessor` interface will be the interface you'll implement for any component that has to handle a received message.

14.2.1 Limitations of this actor framework

As I said, the implementation you'll create here is minimalist; consider it a way to understand and practice using the actor model. You'll be missing many (most?) of the functions of a real actor system, particularly those related to the actor context. One other simplification is that each actor will be mapped to a single thread. In a real actor system, actors are mapped to pools of threads, allowing thousands or even millions of actors to run on a few dozen threads.

Another limitation of your implementation is that most actor frameworks allow distributed actors to be handled in a transparent way, meaning that you can use actors that are running on different machines without having to care about communication. This, of course, makes actor frameworks an ideal way to build scalable applications. We won't deal with this aspect.

14.2.2 Designing the actor framework interfaces

First, you need to define the interfaces that will constitute your actor framework. The most important is, of course, the `Actor` interface that will define several methods. The main method of this interface is

```
void tell(T message, Result<Actor<T>> sender)
```

This method is used to send a message to this actor (meaning the actor holding the method). Of course, this means that to send a message to an actor, you must have a reference to it. (This is different from real actor frameworks, in which messages aren't sent to actors but to actor references, proxies, or some other substitute. Without this enhancement, it wouldn't be possible to send messages to remote actors.) This method takes a `Result<Actor>` as the second parameter. It's supposed to represent the sender, but it's sometimes set to nobody (the empty result) or to a different actor.

Other methods are used to manage the actor lifecycle to ease the use of actors, as shown in listing 14.1. Note that this code isn't intended to use the results of the exercises from previous chapters, but the `fpinjava-common` module that's available in the code accompanying this book (https://github.com/fpinjava/fpinjava). This is mostly the same code as the solutions to the exercises, but with some additional methods.

Listing 14.1 The `Actor` interface

```
public interface Actor<T> {

  static <T> Result<Actor<T>> noSender() {
    return Result.empty();
  }

  Result<Actor<T>> self();

  ActorContext<T> getContext();

  default void tell(T message) {
    tell(message, self());
  }

  void tell(T message, Result<Actor<T>> sender);

  void shutdown();

  default void tell(T message, Actor<T> sender) {
    tell(message, Result.of(sender));
  }

  enum Type {SERIAL, PARALLEL}
}
```

The noSender method is a helper method to provide a Result.Empty with the Result<Actor> type.

The self method returns a reference to this actor.

The getContext method allows you to access the actor context.

This is a convenience method to simplify sending messages without having to indicate the sender.

This is another convenience method allowing you to send a message with an actor reference instead of a Result<Actor>.

In some specific cases, Actors can be configured to be multithreaded.

The shutdown method allows you to tell the actor that it should terminate itself. In your minimal framework, it will allow you to terminate the actor thread.

The following listing shows the two other necessary interfaces: `ActorContext` and `MessageProcessor`.

Listing 14.2 The `ActorContext` and `MessageProcessor` interfaces

```
public interface ActorContext<T> {

  void become(MessageProcessor<T> behavior);

  MessageProcessor<T> getBehavior();
}
public interface MessageProcessor<T> {

  void process(T t, Result<Actor<T>> sender);
}
```

The become method allows an actor to change its behavior by registering a new MessageProcessor.

This method allows access to the actor's behavior.

The MessageProcessor interface has only one method, which represents the processing of one message.

The most important element here is the `ActorContext` interface. The become method allows an actor to change its behavior, meaning the way it processes messages. As you can see, the behavior of an actor looks like an effect, taking as its argument a pair composed of the message to process and the sender.

During the life of the application, the behavior of each actor will be allowed to change. Generally, this change of behavior will be caused by a modification to the state of the actor, replacing the original behavior with a new one. This will be clearer once you see the implementation.

14.2.3 The AbstractActor implementation

The `AbstractActor` implementation represents the part of an actor implementation that's common to all actors. All the message management operations are common and are provided by the actor framework, so that you'll only have to implement the business part. The `AbstractActor` implementation is shown in the following listing.

Listing 14.3 The `AbstractActor` implementation

```
import com.fpinjava.common.Result;
import java.util.concurrent.ExecutorService;
import java.util.concurrent.Executors;
import java.util.concurrent.RejectedExecutionException;

public abstract class AbstractActor<T> implements Actor<T> {

  private final ActorContext<T> context;
  protected final String id;
  private final ExecutorService executor;

  public AbstractActor(String id, Actor.Type type) {
    super();
    this.id = id;
    this.executor = type == Type.SERIAL
      ? Executors.newSingleThreadExecutor(new DaemonThreadFactory())
      : Executors.newCachedThreadPool(new DaemonThreadFactory());

    this.context = new ActorContext<T>() {
      private MessageProcessor<T> behavior =
                              AbstractActor.this::onReceive;
      @Override
      public synchronized void become(MessageProcessor<T> behavior) {
        this.behavior = behavior;
      }

      @Override
      public MessageProcessor<T> getBehavior() {
        return behavior;
      }
    };
  }

  public abstract void onReceive(T message, Result<Actor<T>> sender);

  public Result<Actor<T>> self() {
    return Result.success(this);
  }
```

The context property is initialized to a new ActorContext.

The underlying ExecutorService is initialized.

The default behavior is delegated to the onReceive method.

To change its behavior, the ActorContext simply registers the new behavior. This is where the mutation occurs, but it's hidden by the framework.

The onReceive method will hold the business processing and will be implemented by the user of the API.

```
public ActorContext<T> getContext() {
  return this.context;
}

@Override
public void shutdown() {
  this.executor.shutdown();
}

public synchronized void tell(final T message, Result<Actor<T>> sender) {
  executor.execute(() -> {
    try {
      context.getBehavior().process(message, sender);
    } catch (RejectedExecutionException e) {
      /*
       * This is probably normal and means all pending tasks
       * were canceled because the actor was stopped.
       */
    } catch (Exception e) {
      throw new RuntimeException(e);
    }
  });
}
}
```

The tell method is how an actor receives a message. It's synchronized to ensure that messages are processed one at a time.

When a message is received, it's processed by the current behavior returned by the actor context.

Note that the Executor is initialized with a single-thread executor if the actor is to be single threaded, which is the most general case, or a cached thread pool if it's to be multithreaded. Thread pools are created with a daemon thread factory to allow automatic shutdown when the main thread terminates.

Your actor framework is now complete, though as I mentioned before, this is not production code. This is a minimal example to show you how an actor framework might work.

14.3 Putting actors to work

Now that you have an actor framework at your disposal, it's time to apply it to some concrete problems. Actors are useful when multiple threads are supposed to share some mutable state, as when a thread produces the result of a computation and this result must be passed to another thread for further processing. Usually, such mutable state sharing is done by storing values in shared mutable properties, which implies locking and synchronization. We'll first look at a minimal actor example, which can be considered as the "Hello, World!" of actors. We'll then study a more complete application where an actor is used to distribute tasks to other actors working in parallel.

The first example is a minimal, traditional example that's used to test actors. It consists of two ping-pong players and a referee. The game starts when the ball, represented by an integer, is given to one player. Each player then sends the ball to the other until this has happened ten times, at which point the ball is given back to the referee.

14.3.1 *Implementing the ping-pong example*

First, you'll implement the referee. All you have to do is create an actor, implementing its onReceive method. In this method, you'll display a message:

```
Actor<Integer> referee =
        new AbstractActor<Integer>("Referee", Actor.Type.SERIAL) {
    @Override
    public void onReceive(Integer message, Result<Actor<Integer>> sender) {
        System.out.println("Game ended after " + message + " shots");
    }
};
```

Next, you have to create the two players. Because there are two instances, you won't create them as an anonymous class. You'll create a Player class.

Listing 14.4   The Player actor

The sound String is a message that will be displayed by the players when they receive the ball (either "Ping" or "Pong").

Each player is created with a reference to the referee so that a player can give the ball back to the referee when the game is over.

```
static class Player extends AbstractActor<Integer> {
    private final String sound;
    private final Actor<Integer> referee;

    public Player(String id, String sound, Actor<Integer> referee) {
        super(id, Actor.Type.SERIAL);
        this.referee = referee;
        this.sound = sound;
    }

    @Override
    public void onReceive(Integer message, Result<Actor<Integer>> sender) {
        System.out.println(sound + " - " + message);
        if (message >= 10) {
            referee.tell(message, sender);
        } else {
            sender.forEachOrFail(actor -> actor.tell(message + 1, self()))
                    .forEach(ignore -> referee.tell(message, sender));
        }
    }
}
```

This is the "business" part of the actor.

Otherwise, send back the ball to the other player, if it's present. If the other player isn't present, register an issue with the referee.

If the game is over, give the ball back to the referee.

With the Player class created, you can finalize your program. But you need a way to keep the application running until the game is over. Without this, the main application thread will terminate as soon as the game is started, and the players won't be given the opportunity to play their game. This can be achieved through the use of a semaphore, as shown next.

Listing 14.5　The ping-pong example

```
private static final Semaphore semaphore = new Semaphore(1);          A semaphore
                                                                      is created
public static void main(String... args) throws InterruptedException {  with 1 permit.
  Actor<Integer> referee =
                new AbstractActor<Integer>("Referee", Actor.Type.SERIAL) {

    @Override
    public void onReceive(Integer message, Result<Actor<Integer>> sender) {
      System.out.println("Game ended after " + message + " shots");
      semaphore.release();
    }
  };

  Actor<Integer> player1 = new Player("Player1", "Ping", referee);
  Actor<Integer> player2 = new Player("Player2", "Pong", referee);

  semaphore.acquire();
  player1.tell(1, Result.success(player2));
  semaphore.acquire();

}
```

When the game is over, the
semaphore is released, making one
new permit available, thus allowing
the main thread to resume.

The single available
permit is acquired
by the current
thread, and the
game is started.

The main thread tries to acquire a new
permit. Because none are available, it
blocks until the semaphore is released.

When resuming, the main thread
terminates. All actor threads are daemons,
so they also stop automatically.

The program displays the following output:

```
Ping - 1
Pong - 2
Ping - 3
Pong - 4
Ping - 5
Pong - 6
Ping - 7
Pong - 8
Ping - 9
Pong - 10
Game ended after 10 shots
```

14.3.2　A more serious example: running a computation in parallel

It's now time to look at a more serious example of the actor framework in action: running a computation in parallel. To simulate a long-running computation, you'll
choose a list of random numbers between 0 and 30, and compute the corresponding
Fibonacci value using a slow algorithm. The application will be composed of three

kinds of actors: a Manager, in charge of creating a given number of worker actors and distributing the tasks to them; several instances of workers; and a client, which will be implemented in the main program class as an anonymous actor. The following listing shows the simplest of these classes, the Worker actor.

> **Listing 14.6   The Worker actor, in charge of running parts of the computation**

```
import com.fpinjava.actors.AbstractActor;
import com.fpinjava.actors.Actor;
import com.fpinjava.common.Result;
import com.fpinjava.common.TailCall;

public class Worker extends AbstractActor<Integer> {

  public Worker(String id, Type type) {
    super(id, type);
  }

  @Override

  public void onReceive(Integer message, Result<Actor<Integer>> sender) {
    sender.forEach(a -> a.tell(fibo(message), self()));
  }

  private static int fibo(int number) {
    return fibo_(0, 1, number).eval();
  }

  private static TailCall<Integer> fibo_(int acc1, int acc2, int x) {
    if (x == 0) {
      return TailCall.ret(1);
    } else if (x == 1) {
      return TailCall.ret(acc1 + acc2);
    } else {
      return TailCall.sus(() -> fibo_(acc2, acc1 + acc2, x - 1));
    }
  }
}
```

When the Worker receives a number, it reacts by computing the corresponding Fibonacci value and sending it back to the caller.

The fibo method uses a tail-recursive helper method.

You use a very inefficient algorithm on purpose to create long-lasting tasks.

As you can see, this actor is stateless. It computes the result and sends it back to the sender for which it has received a reference. Note that this might be a different actor than the caller. Because the numbers are chosen randomly between 0 and 30, the time needed to compute the result will be highly variable. This simulates tasks that take variable amounts of time to execute. Unlike the example of automatic parallelization in chapter 8, all threads/actors will be kept busy until the whole computation is finished, except when there are no more tasks to start.

The Manager class is a bit more complicated. The following listing shows the constructor of the class and the properties that are initialized.

Listing 14.7 The constructor and properties of the `Manager` class

The initial list will be a list of tuples of integers,
holding both the number to process (._l) and
the position in the list (._2).

The workList is the list of tasks remaining
to be executed once all worker actors
have been given their first task.

The Manager stores the references to
its client, to which it will send the
result of the computation.

```java
import com.fpinjava.actors.AbstractActor;
import com.fpinjava.actors.Actor;
import com.fpinjava.actors.MessageProcessor;
import com.fpinjava.common.*;

public class Manager extends AbstractActor<Integer> {

    private final Actor<Result<List<Integer>>> client;
    private final int workers;
    private final List<Tuple<Integer, Integer>> initial;
    private final List<Integer> workList;
    private final List<Integer> resultList;
    private final Function<Manager, Function<Behavior,
                                    Effect<Integer>>> managerFunction;

    public Manager(String id, List<Integer> list,
                       Actor<Result<List<Integer>>> client, int workers) {
        super(id, Type.SERIAL);
        this.client = client;
        this.workers = workers;
        Tuple<List<Integer>, List<Integer>> splitLists =
                                        #list.splitAt(this.workers);
```

The number of
workers to use
is stored.

The managerFunction is the heart of the
Manager, determining what it will be able to do.
This function will be applied each time the
manager receives a result from a worker.

The list of values to be processed is
split at the number of workers in
order to obtain a list of initial tasks
and a list of remaining tasks.

The resultList will hold the
results of the computations.

(Listing continued on next page)

The resultList is initialized to an empty list.

The manager function, representing the work of the manager, is a curried function of the manager itself, its behavior, and the received message (i), which will be the result of a subtask.

The list of initial tasks (numbers for which the Fibonacci value will be computed) is zipped with the position of its elements. The position (numbers from 0 to n) will only be used to name the worker actors from 0 to n.

The workList is set to the remaining tasks.

```
this.initial = splitLists._1.zipWithPosition();
this.workList = splitLists._2;
this.resultList = List.list();

managerFunction = manager -> behavior -> i -> {
  List<Integer> result = behavior.resultList.cons(i);
  if (result.length() == list.length()) {
    this.client.tell(Result.success(result.reverse()));
  } else {
    manager.getContext()
        .become(new Behavior(behavior.workList
                                .tailOption()
                                .getOrElse(List.list()), result));
  }
};
}
```

Otherwise, the become method of the context is called to change the behavior of the Manager. Here, this change of behavior is in fact a change of state. The new behavior is created with the tail of the workList and the current list of results (to which the received value has been added).

If the resultList length is equal to the input list length, the computation is finished, so the result is reversed and sent to the client.

When a result is received, it's added to the list of results, which is fetched from the manager behavior.

As you can see, if the computation is finished, the result is added to the result list and sent to the client. Otherwise, the result is added to the current result list. In traditional programs, this would be done by mutating the list of results that would be held by the Manager. This is exactly what happens here, except for two differences:

- The list of results is stored in the behavior.
- Neither the behavior nor the list is mutated. Instead, a new behavior is created, and the context is mutated to hold this new behavior as a replacement for the old one. However, you don't have to deal with this mutation. As far as you're concerned, everything is immutable because the mutation is abstracted by the actor framework.

The following listing shows the Behavior class, implemented as an inner class.

```
class Behavior implements MessageProcessor<Integer> {

  private final List<Integer> workList;
  private final List<Integer> resultList;

  private Behavior(List<Integer> workList, List<Integer> resultList) {
    this.workList = workList;
    this.resultList = resultList;
  }

  @Override
  public void process(Integer i, Result<Actor<Integer>> sender) {
    managerFunction.apply(Manager.this).apply(Behavior.this).apply(i);
    sender.forEach(a -> workList.headOption().forEachOrFail(x ->
                        a.tell(x, self())).forEach(x -> a.shutdown())));
  }
}
```

The Behavior is constructed with the workList (from which the head has been removed prior to calling the constructor) and the resultList (to which a result has been added).

The process method, which will be called upon reception of a message, first applies the managerFunction to the received message. Then it sends the next task (the head of the workList) to the sender (a Worker actor that will process it) or, if the workList is empty, it simply instructs the worker actor to shut down.

That covers the main parts of the `Manager`. The rest is composed of utility methods that are mainly used for starting the work.

```
public class Manager extends AbstractActor<Integer> {

  . . .

  public void start() {
    onReceive(0, self());
    initial.sequence(this::initWorker)
           .forEachOrFail(this::initWorkers)
           .forEach(this::tellClientEmptyResult);
  }

  private Result<Executable> initWorker(Tuple<Integer, Integer> t) {
    return Result.success(() ->
          new Worker("Worker " + t._2, Type.SERIAL).tell(t._1, self()));
  }

  private void initWorkers(List<Executable> lst) {
    lst.forEach(Executable::exec);
  }
```

In order to start, the Manager sends a message to itself. What the message is makes no difference, because the behavior has yet to be initialized.

The workers are then created and initialized.

This method creates an Executable that creates a worker actor.

This method performs the actor creation.

```
    private void tellClientEmptyResult(String string) {
        client.tell(Result.failure(string + " caused by empty input list."));
    }

    @Override
    public void onReceive(Integer message, Result<Actor<Integer>> sender) {
        getContext().become(new Behavior(workList, resultList));
    }
}
```

This is the initial behavior of the Manager. As part of its initialization, it switches behavior, starting with the workList containing the remaining tasks and the empty resultList.

If there was an error, the client is informed.

It's important to understand that the onReceive method represents what the actor will do when it receives its first message. This method won't be called when the workers send their results to the manager.

The last part of the program is shown in listing 14.10. The WorkersExample class represents the client code for the application. But unlike the Manager and the Worker, it's not an actor. Instead, it *has* an actor. This is an implementation choice. There's no specific reason for choosing one solution or the other. But a client actor is necessary in order to receive the result.

Listing 14.10 The client application

The number of tasks is initialized.

The list of tasks is created by randomly generating numbers between 0 and 30.

A semaphore is created to allow the main thread to wait for the actors to complete their work.

The number of worker actors is set here.

```
public class WorkersExample {

    private static final Semaphore semaphore = new Semaphore(1);
    private static int listLength = 200_000;
    private static int workers = 8;
    private static final List<Integer> testList =
            SimpleRNG.doubles(listLength, new SimpleRNG.Simple(3))
                     ._1.map(x -> (int) (x * 30)).reverse();

    public static void main(String... args) throws InterruptedException {
        semaphore.acquire();
        final AbstractActor<Result<List<Integer>>> client =
        new AbstractActor<Result<List<Integer>>>("Client", Actor.Type.SERIAL) {
            @Override
            public void onReceive(Result<List<Integer>> message,
                                  Result<Actor<Result<List<Integer>>>> sender) {
                message.forEachOrFail(WorkersExample::processSuccess)
                       .forEach(WorkersExample::processFailure);
                semaphore.release();
            }
        };
```

The semaphore is acquired when the program starts.

A client actor is created as an anonymous class.

The client releases the semaphore when it receives the result.

The only responsibility of the client is to process the result or any occurring error.

```
  final Manager manager =
                new Manager("Manager", testList, client, workers);
  manager.start();
  semaphore.acquire();
}
```

The semaphore is acquired again to wait for the job to finish.

The manager is instantiated and started.

```
private static void processFailure(String s) {
  System.out.println(s);
}


public static void processSuccess(List<Integer> lst) {
  System.out.println("Result: " + lst.takeAtMost(40));
}
}
```

You can run this program with various lengths for the list of tasks, and various numbers of worker actors. On my eight-core Linux box, running with a task length of 200,000 gives the following results:

- One worker actor: 3.5 sec
- Two worker actors: 1.5 sec
- Three worker actors: 1.1 sec
- Four worker actors: 0.8 sec
- Six worker actors: 0.8 sec
- Eight worker actors: 0.8 sec
- Sixteen worker actors: 0.8 sec

These figures are, of course, not very precise, but they show that using a number of threads corresponding to the number of available cores is useless. The result displayed by the program is as follows (only the first 40 results are displayed):

```
Input: [0, 11, 28, 13, 20, 5, 15, 8, 24, 19, 12, 7, 11, 4, 18, 20, 26,
    21, 15, 21, 29, 16, 15, 8, 22, 11, 26, 1, 22, 13, 25, 3, 13, 24, 29,
    10, 7, 26, 24, 1, NIL]
Time: 797
Result: [1, 8, 28657, 34, 196418, 34, 987, 987, 1597, 832040, 28657,
    17711, 987, 377, 1, 17711, 196418, 377, 10946, 4181, 5, 6765, 144,
    21, 75025, 233, 832040, 89, 144, 75025, 514229, 21, 377, 1, 10946,
    3, 17711, 196418, 144, 1597, NIL]
```

As you can see, we have a problem!

14.3.3 *Reordering the results*

As you may have noticed, the result isn't correct. This is obvious when looking at the third and fifth random values (28 and 29) and at the corresponding results (28,657 and 196,418). You can also compare values and results for 4 and 6. The results are both 34 when the argument values are 13 and 5. Note that if you run the program on your computer, you'll obtain different results.

What's happening here is that not all tasks take the same amount of time to execute. I chose the computation to perform this way, so that some tasks (computations for low argument values) return quickly, while others (computations for higher values) take much longer. As a result, the returned values aren't in the correct order.

To fix this problem, you need to sort the results in the same order as their corresponding arguments. One solution is to use the `Heap` data type you developed in chapter 11. You could number each task and use this number as the priority in a priority queue.

The first thing you have to change is the type of the worker actors. Instead of working on integers, they'll have to work on tuples of integers: one integer representing the argument or the computation, and one representing the number of the task. The following listing shows the corresponding changes in the `Worker` class.

Listing 14.11 The `Worker` actor keeping track of the task number

```
public class Worker extends AbstractActor<Tuple<Integer, Integer>> {      ◁──┐

  public Worker(String id, Type type) {
    super(id, type);                          The type parameter is changed from
  }                                           Integer to Tuple<Integer, Integer>.

  @Override
  public void onReceive(Tuple<Integer, Integer> message,                 ◁──┐
                        Result<Actor<Tuple<Integer, Integer>>> sender) {
    sender.forEach(a -> a.tell(new Tuple<>(fibo(message._1),
                                           message._2), self())));
  }
  ...
}
```

The return message is changed to include the task number. (annotation pointing to `sender.forEach` line)

The signature of the onReceive method is changed to reflect the new actor type.

Note that the task number is the second element of the tuple. This isn't easy to read and remember, given that the task number and the argument of the computation are of the same type (`Integer`). In real life, this shouldn't happen, because you should be using a specific type for the task. But if you prefer, you can also use a specific type instead of `Tuple` to wrap both the task and the task number, such as a `Task` type with a number property.

Changes in the `Manager` class are more numerous. First, you have to change the type of the class and the types of the `workList` and result properties:

```
public class Manager extends AbstractActor<Tuple<Integer, Integer>> {

  ...

  private final List<Tuple<Integer, Integer>> workList;
  private final Heap<Tuple<Integer, Integer>> resultHeap;
```

These properties are initialized in the constructor as follows:

```
Tuple<List<Tuple<Integer, Integer>>, List<Tuple<Integer, Integer>>>
        splitLists = list.zipWithPosition().splitAt(this.workers);
```

```
this.initial = splitLists._1;
this.workList = splitLists._2;
this.resultHeap = Heap.empty((t1, t2) -> t1._2.compareTo(t2._2));
```

The workList now contains tuples (as was the case for the initial list in the former example), and the result is a priority queue (Heap) of tuples. Note that this Heap is initialized with a Comparator based on the comparison of the second element of the tuples. Using a Task type that wraps both the task and the task number would have allowed you to make this type Comparable, so that a Comparator would have been useless. (I leave this optimization as an exercise for you.)

Of course, the managerFunction is different too:

```
private final Function<Manager, Function<Behavior, Effect<Tuple<Integer,
                                               Integer>>>> managerFunction;
```

It's initialized in the constructor like this:

```
managerFunction = manager -> behavior -> i -> {
  Heap<Tuple<Integer, Integer>> result = behavior.resultHeap.insert(i);    <--- The received result is now inserted into the Heap.
  if (result.length() == list.length()) {
    this.client.tell(Result.success(result.toList()
                           .map(x -> x._1).reverse()));    <---
  } else {
    ...
  }
};
```

> The received result is now inserted into the Heap.

> Once the computation is complete, the Heap is converted into a list before being returned to the client.

The Behavior inner class must be changed to reflect the actor type change:

> The type of the result is now Heap<Tuple<Integer, Integer>>.

> The type parameter of the Behavior class is now Tuple<Integer, Integer>.

> The type of the workList is now List<Tuple<Integer, Integer>>.

```
class Behavior implements MessageProcessor<Tuple<Integer, Integer>> {

  private final List<Tuple<Integer, Integer>> workList;
  private final Heap<Tuple<Integer, Integer>> resultHeap;

  private Behavior(List<Tuple<Integer, Integer>> workList,
                   Heap<Tuple<Integer, Integer>> resultHeap) {    <---
    this.workList = workList;
    this.resultHeap = resultHeap;
  }
```

> The constructor signature is changed accordingly.

```
  @Override
  public void process(Tuple<Integer, Integer> i,
                  Result<Actor<Tuple<Integer, Integer>>> sender) {    <---
    managerFunction.apply(Manager.this).apply(Behavior.this).apply(i);
    ...
  }
}
```

> The signature of the process method is modified to reflect the change of parameter type.

There are still some minor changes to apply in the rest of the Manager class. The start method must be modified:

```
public void start() {
  onReceive(new Tuple<>(0, 0), self());
  initial.sequence(this::initWorker)
        .forEachOrFail(this::initWorkers)
        .forEach(this::tellClientEmptyResult);
}
```

> The type of the start message must match the type parameter of the Manager actor.

The Worker initialization process is slightly different too:

```
private Result<Executable> initWorker(Tuple<Integer, Integer> t) {
  return Result.success(() -> new Worker("Worker " + t._2,
              Type.SERIAL).tell(new Tuple<>(t._1, t._2), self()));
}
```

Last, the onReceive method is modified:

```
@Override
public void onReceive(Tuple<Integer, Integer> message,
                      Result<Actor<Tuple<Integer, Integer>>> sender) {
  getContext().become(new Behavior(workList, resultHeap));
}
```

Now the results are displayed in the correct order. But you have a new problem: the time needed for the computation is now 15 sec with one worker actor, and 13 sec with four worker actors. What's happening?

The answer is simple: the bottleneck is the Heap. The Heap data structure isn't meant for sorting. It has good performance as long as the number of elements is kept low, but here you're inserting all 200,000 results into the heap, sorting the full data set on each insertion. This isn't efficient.

14.3.4 *Fixing the performance problem*

Obviously, this inefficiency isn't an implementation problem, but a problem about using the right tool for the job. You'd get much better performance by storing all results and sorting them once when the computation is over, though you'd need to use the right tool for sorting.

Another option is to fix your implementation. One of the problems you're having with the current design is that not only does insertion into the Heap take a long time, but it's done by the Manager thread, so that instead of distributing tasks to the worker actors as soon as they've finished a computation, the Manager makes them wait until it has finished the insertion into the heap. One possible solution would be to use a separate actor for inserting into the Heap.

But sometimes a better way to go is to use the right job for the tool. The fact that you consume the result synchronously might not be a requirement. If it isn't, you're just adding an implicit requirement that makes the problem harder to solve. One possibility would be to pass the results individually to the client. This way, the Heap would be used only when the results are out of order, preventing it from becoming too big.

This kind of use is, in fact, how a priority queue is intended to be used. To take this into account, you can add a `Receiver` actor to your program.

Listing 14.12 The `Receiver` actor, in charge of receiving the results asynchronously

The Receiver class is an actor parameterized by the type of data it's meant to receive: Integer.

The Receiver client is an actor parameterized by the type List<Integer>.

```java
public class Receiver extends AbstractActor<Integer> {

    private final Actor<List<Integer>> client;
    private final Function<Receiver, Function<Behavior,
                                Effect<Integer>>> receiverFunction;

    public Receiver(String id, Type type, Actor<List<Integer>> client) {
        super(id, type);
        this.client = client;
        receiverFunction = receiver -> behavior -> i -> {
            if (i == -1) {
                this.client.tell(behavior.resultList.reverse());
                shutdown();
            } else {
                receiver.getContext()
                        .become(new Behavior(behavior.resultList.cons(i)));
            }
        };
    }

    @Override
    public void onReceive(Integer i, Result<Actor<Integer>> sender) {
        getContext().become(new Behavior(List.list(i)));
    }

    class Behavior implements MessageProcessor<Integer> {

        private final List<Integer> resultList;

        private Behavior(List<Integer> resultList) {
            this.resultList = resultList;
        }

        @Override
        public void process(Integer i, Result<Actor<Integer>> sender) {
            receiverFunction.apply(Receiver.this).apply(Behavior.this).apply(i);
        }
    }
}
```

The Receiver function receives an Integer. If it's -1, meaning the computation is complete, it sends the result to its client and shuts itself down.

Otherwise, it changes its behavior by adding the result to the result list.

The initial onReceive implementation consists of replacing the actor behavior with one that uses a new list containing the first result.

The behavior holds the current list of results.

The main class (`WorkersExample`) isn't much different from the previous example. The only difference is the addition of the `Receiver`:

```java
public static void main(String... args) throws InterruptedException {
    semaphore.acquire();
    final AbstractActor<List<Integer>> client =
                new AbstractActor<List<Integer>>("Client", Actor.Type.SERIAL) {
```

```
    @Override
    public void onReceive(List message, Result<Actor<List<Integer>>> sender) {
      System.out.println("Result: " + message.takeAtMost(40));
      semaphore.release();
    }
  };

  final Receiver receiver = new Receiver("Receiver", Actor.Type.SERIAL, client);
  final Manager manager = new Manager("Manager", testList, receiver, workers);
  manager.start();
  semaphore.acquire();
}
```

The Worker actor is exactly the same as in the previous example. This leaves you with the Manager class holding the most important changes. The first change is that the Manager will have a client of type Actor<Integer> and will keep track of the length of the list of tasks:

```
private final Actor<Integer> client;
...
private final int limit;
...
public Manager(String id, List<Integer> list, Actor<Integer> client,
                                                  int workers) {
  super(id, Type.SERIAL);
  this.client = client;
  this.workers = workers;
  this.limit = list.length() - 1;
```

Also note that the client is now the Receiver, so it's of type Actor<Integer>, receiving results asynchronously, one by one.

The managerFunction, of course, is different:

This function now calls the streamResult method, returning a Tuple3. The first element is the Heap of results, to which the received result has been added. The second element is the next expected result number, and the third element is a List of results that are in expected order.

```
managerFunction = manager -> behavior -> t -> {
  Tuple3<Heap<Tuple<Integer, Integer>>, Integer, List<Integer>> result =
           streamResult(behavior.resultHeap.insert(t),
                       behavior.expected, List.list());
  result._3.reverse().forEach(this.client::tell);
  if (result._2 > limit) {
    this.client.tell(-1);
  } else {
    manager.getContext()
          .become(new Behavior(behavior.workList.tailOption()
                  .getOrElse(List.list()), result._1, result._2));
  }
};
```

If all the tasks have been executed, the client is sent a special termination code.

As you can see, most of the work is done in the `streamResult` method:

```
private Tuple3<Heap<Tuple<Integer, Integer>>, Integer,
  List<Integer>> streamResult(Heap<Tuple<Integer, Integer>> result,
                            int expected, List<Integer> list) {
  Tuple3<Heap<Tuple<Integer, Integer>>, Integer, List<Integer>> tuple3 =
                            new Tuple3<>(result, expected, list);
  Result<Tuple3<Heap<Tuple<Integer, Integer>>, Integer,
        List<Integer>>> temp = result.head().flatMap(head ->
                result.tail().map(tail -> head._2 == expected
                ? streamResult(tail, expected + 1, list.cons(head._1))
                : tuple3));
  return temp.getOrElse(tuple3);
}
```

This method may seem difficult to decipher, but that's only because the type notation in Java is so verbose. The `streamResult` method takes as its argument the `Heap` of results, the next expected task number, and a list of integers that's initially empty:

- If the head of the result heap is different from the expected task result number, nothing needs to be done, and the three parameters are returned as a `Tuple3`.
- If the head of the result heap matches the expected task result number, it's removed from the heap and added to the list. Then the method is called recursively until the head no longer matches, thus constructing a list of the results in expected order, leaving the others in the heap.

By processing this way, the heap is always kept small. For example, when computing 200,000 tasks, the maximal size of the heap was found to be 121. It was over 100 on 12 occasions, and more than 95% of the time it was less than 2.

Figure 14.2 shows the overall process of receiving the results from the `Manager` point of view.

The `tellClientEmptyResult` method is modified according to the client type:

```
private void tellClientEmptyResult(String ignore) {
  client.tell(-1);
}
```

The `onReceive` method is different because, on starting, you expect result number 0:

```
getContext().become(new Behavior(workList, resultHeap, 0));
```

The last change is to the `Behavior` class, which now holds the expected task number:

```
class Behavior implements MessageProcessor<Tuple<Integer, Integer>> {

  private final List<Tuple<Integer, Integer>> workList;
  private final Heap<Tuple<Integer, Integer>> resultHeap;
  private final int expected; // Change

  private Behavior(List<Tuple<Integer, Integer>> workList,
          Heap<Tuple<Integer, Integer>> resultHeap, int expected) {
    this.workList = workList;
    this.resultHeap = resultHeap;
    this.expected = expected;
  }

  ...
```

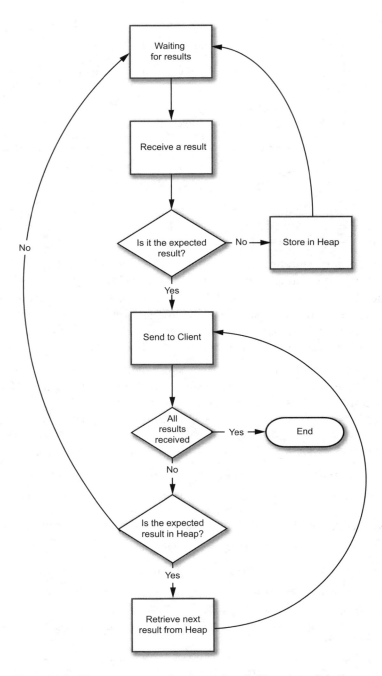

Figure 14.2   The Manager receives a result and either stores it in the Heap (if it doesn't correspond to the expected number) or sends it to the client. In the latter case, it then looks at the Heap to see if the next expected result has already been received.

With these modifications, the application is much faster. For example, under the same conditions as in the previous example, the time needed to process 200,000 numbers with one worker actor was 7.5 seconds, whereas it dropped to 5.3 seconds with four worker actors.

This process is obviously not as fast as storing all the values unsorted and sorting them afterwards, which brought the time down to 3.5 seconds with one actor and 1.19 seconds with four. But there's still plenty of room for optimization. For example, instead of putting each result into the Heap, you could pass it to the streamResult method, where it would be put directly into the result list if it matches the expected task number.

Anyway, this was just an example to show how actors can be used. Solving this kind of problem is much better handled by other means, such as automatic parallelization of lists (as shown in chapter 8), or even a simple map. The main use of actors is not for parallelization, but for the abstraction of sharing mutable state. In these examples, you used lists that were shared between tasks. Without actors, you'd have had to synchronize access to the workList and resultHeap to handle concurrency. Actors allow you to abstract synchronization and mutation in the framework. If you look at the business code you wrote (apart from the actor framework itself), you'll find no mutable data, and thus no need to care about synchronization and no risks of thread starvation or deadlocks. Although they're not functional, actors provide a good way to make functional parts of your code work together, sharing mutable state in an abstracted manner.

Your actor framework is really minimal and isn't intended to be used in any serious code. For such uses, you can use one of the available actor frameworks for Java, particularly Akka. Although Akka is written in Scala, a more functional-friendly language than Java, it can be used in Java programs as well. When using Akka, you'll never see a line of Scala code unless you want to. To learn more about actors, and Akka in particular, refer to Raymond Roestenburg, Rob Bakker, and Rob Williams's *Akka in Action* (Manning, 2016).

14.4 Summary

- Actors are components that receive messages in an asynchronous way and process them one after the other.
- Sharing mutable state can be abstracted into actors.
- Abstracting mutable state sharing relieves you of synchronization and concurrency problems.
- The actor model is based on asynchronous messaging and is a nice complement to functional programming.
- The actor model offers easy and safe parallelization.
- Actor mutations are abstracted from the programmer by the framework.
- Several actor frameworks are available to Java programmers.
- Akka is one of the most-used actor frameworks for Java programming.

Solving common problems functionally

This chapter covers

- Using assertions
- Reading property files
- Adapting imperative libraries

You now have at your disposal many functional tools that can make your life as a programmer easier. But knowing the tools isn't enough. To become efficient in functional programming, you must make it second nature. You need to think functionally. Initially you'll keep your imperative reflexes, and you'll probably have to think about how you might translate an imperative solution into functional coding. You'll have become a proficient functional programmer when your first approach to a programming problem is to think about a functional solution first (and perhaps have some difficulties translating it into imperative!).

To reach this stage, there's no other way than practicing. And because, at least in the Java world, a huge majority of the known solutions to common problems are imperative, it can be a good exercise to look at some common problems and see how they can be solved in a functional way.

Lots of examples are available on the internet about solving mathematical problems in a functional way. These examples are very interesting, but they're sometimes counterproductive in the sense that they make programmers believe that functional programming is only good for solving mathematical problems. Worse yet, it leads some into thinking that mathematical skills are necessary for practicing functional programming. This isn't the case. Mathematical skills are necessary for solving mathematical problems, but most programming problems you need to solve aren't related to mathematics. And they're often simpler to solve in a functional way.

In this chapter, we'll look at some common problems programmers have to solve in everyday professional life and see how they can be approached differently using the functional paradigm.

15.1 Using assertions to validate data

Java has had assertions since version 1.4. Assertions are used to check invariants such as preconditions, post-conditions, control-flow conditions, and class conditions. In functional programming, there's generally no control flow, and classes are usually immutable, so the only conditions to check are pre- and post-conditions, which, for the same reasons (immutability and absence of control flow), consist in testing the arguments received by methods and functions, and testing their results before returning them.

Testing the argument value is necessary in partial functions such as this:

```
double inverse(int x) {
  return 1.0 / x;
}
```

This method returns a usable value for any input, except for 0, for which it returns "infinity." Because you probably can't do anything with this value, you might prefer to handle it in a specific way. In imperative programming, you could write this:

```
double inverse(int x) {
  assert x == 0;
  return 1.0 / x;
}
```

But in Java you can disable assertions at runtime, so the common trick is to prevent the program from running with assertions disabled by using a static initializer:

```
static {
  boolean assertsEnabled = false;
  assert assertsEnabled = true;
  if (!assertsEnabled) {
    throw new RuntimeException("Asserts must be enabled!!!");
  }
}
```

This is what Oracle suggests. Of course, it's simpler to write this:

```
double inverse(int x) {
   if (x != 0) throw new IllegalArgumentException("div. By 0");
   return 1.0 / x;
}
```

In functional programming, the function should be transformed into a total function, as follows:

```
Result<Double> inverse(int x) {
   return x == 0
       ? Result.failure("div. By 0")
       : Result.success(1.0 / x);
}
```

There's then no need to check the argument, because this test is part of the function implementation. And, of course, there's no need to check the returned value.

One condition that must often be checked is that arguments aren't null. Java has `Objects.requireNonNull` for this. There are variants of this method taking an additional error message, or a `Supplier` of an error message. These methods can sometimes be useful:

```
public static <T, U> Tuple<T, U> t(T t, U u) {
   return new Tuple<>(Objects.requireNonNull(t), Objects.requireNonNull(u));
}
```

But in a functional program, the most generic form of assertion consists of testing an argument against a specific condition, returning a `Result.Failure` if the condition isn't matched, and a `Result.Success` otherwise. Take the example of a factory method for a `Person` type:

```
public static Person apply(int id, String firstName, String lastName) {
   return new Person(id, firstName, lastName);
}
```

This method might be used with data extracted from a database:

```
Person person = Person.apply(rs.getInt("personId"),
               rs.getString("firstName"), rs.getString("lastName"));
```

In such a case, you might want to validate the data before calling the `apply` method. For example, you might want to check that the ID is positive, and that the first and last names aren't `null` or empty and that they start with an uppercase letter. In imperative Java, this could be done through the use of assertion methods:

```
Person person = Person.apply(
    assertPositive(rs.getInt("personId"), "Negative id"),
    assertValidName(rs.getString("firstName"), "Invalid first name:"),
    assertValidName(rs.getString("lastName"), "Invalid last name:"));
```

```
private static int assertPositive(int i, String message) {
  if (i < 0) {
    throw new IllegalStateException(message);
  } else {
    return i;
  }
}

private static String assertValidName(String name, String message) {
  if (name == null || name.length() == 0
         || name.charAt(0) < 65 || name.charAt(0) > 91) {
    throw new IllegalStateException(message);
  }
  return name;
}
```

In functional programming, you don't throw exceptions; you use special contexts such as `Result` for error handling. This kind of validation is abstracted into the `Result` type. All you have to do is write the validating functions, which means you just have to write methods and use method references. Generic validation function can be grouped into a special class:

```
public class Assertion {
  public static boolean isPositive(int i) {
    return i >= 0;
  }

  public static boolean isValidName(String name) {
    return name != null && name.length() != 0
                 && name.charAt(0) >= 65 && name.charAt(0) <= 91;
  }
}
```

You can then validate the data:

```
Result<Person> person =
   Result.of(Assertion::isPositive, getInt("personId"), "Negative id")
      .flatMap(id -> Result.of(Assertion::isValidName,
                     getString("firstName"), "Invalid first name")
         .flatMap(firstName -> Result.of(Assertion::isValidName,
                     getString("lastName"), "Invalid last name")
            .map(lastName -> Person.apply(id, firstName, lastName))));
```

But you can also simplify things by abstracting more of the process in the `Assertion` class:

```
public static Result<Integer> assertPositive(int i, String message) {
  return Result.of(Assertion::isPositive, i, message);
}

public static Result<String> assertValidName(String name, String message) {
  return Result.of(Assertion::isValidName, name, message);
}
```

And you can create a `Person` as follows:

```
Result<Integer> rId = Assertion.assertPositive(getInt("personId"), "Negative id");
Result<String> rFirstName =
        Assertion.assertValidName(getString("firstName"), "Invalid first name");
Result<String> rLastName =
        Assertion.assertValidName(getString("lastName"), "Invalid first name");
Result<Person> person =
    rId.flatMap(id -> rFirstName
         .flatMap(firstName -> rLastName
             .map(lastName -> Person.apply(id, firstName, lastName))));
```

The following listing shows the `Assertion` class with some example methods.

Listing 15.1   Examples of functional assertions

```
public final class Assertion {

  private Assertion() {
  }

  public static <T> Result<T> assertCondition(T value,
                                      Function<T, Boolean> f) {
    return assertCondition(value, f,
          "Assertion error: condition should evaluate to true");
  }

  public static <T> Result<T> assertCondition(T value,
                      Function<T, Boolean> f, String message) {
    return f.apply(value)
        ? Result.success(value)
        : Result.failure(message, new IllegalStateException(message));
  }

  public static Result<Boolean> assertTrue(boolean condition) {
    return assertTrue(condition,
                  "Assertion error: condition should be true");
  }

  public static Result<Boolean> assertTrue(boolean condition,
                                      String message) {
    return assertCondition(condition, x -> x, message);
  }

  public static Result<Boolean> assertFalse(boolean condition) {
    return assertFalse(condition,
                  "Assertion error: condition should be false");
  }

  public static Result<Boolean> assertFalse(boolean condition,
                                      String message) {
    return assertCondition(condition, x -> !x, message);
  }

  public static <T> Result<T> assertNotNull(T t) {
    return assertNotNull(t, "Assertion error: object should not be null");
  }
```

```java
  public static <T> Result<T> assertNotNull(T t, String message) {
    return assertCondition(t, x -> x != null, message);
  }

  public static Result<Integer> assertPositive(int value) {
    return assertPositive(value,
        String.format("Assertion error: value %s must be positive", value));
  }
  public static Result<Integer> assertPositive(int value, String message) {
    return assertCondition(value, x -> x > 0, message);
  }

  public static Result<Integer> assertInRange(int value, int min,
                                                         int max) {
    return assertCondition(value, x -> x >= min && x < max,
         String.format("Assertion error: value %s should be between %s and
                        %s (exclusive)", value, min, max));
  }

  public static Result<Integer> assertPositiveOrZero(int value) {
    return assertPositiveOrZero(value,
      String.format("Assertion error: value %s must not be negative", 0));
  }

  public static Result<Integer> assertPositiveOrZero(int value,
                                                   String message) {
    return assertCondition(value, x -> x >= 0, message);
  }

  public static <A> void assertType(A element, Class<?> clazz) {
    assertType(element, clazz,
        String.format("Wrong type: %s, expected: %s",
                element.getClass().getName(), clazz.getName()));
  }

  public static <A> Result<A> assertType(A element, Class<?> clazz,
                                                   String message) {
    return assertCondition(element, e -> e.getClass().equals(clazz)
                                                   ,message);
  }
}
```

15.2   Reading properties from file

Most software applications are configured using property files that are read at startup. Properties are key/value pairs, and both keys and values are written as strings. Whatever the chosen property format (key=value, XML, JSON, YAML, and so on), the programmer always has to read strings and transform them into Java objects or primitives. This process is tedious and error prone. You can use a specialized library for this, but if something goes wrong, you'll find yourself throwing exceptions. To get more functional behavior, you'll have to write your own library.

15.2.1 Loading the property file

Whatever format you use, the process is exactly the same: reading the file and handling any IOException that could arise in that process. In the following example, you'll read a Java property file.

The first thing to do is to read the file and return a Result<Properties>.

Listing 15.2 Reading a Java property file

```java
import com.fpinjava.common.Result;
import java.io.InputStream;
import java.util.Properties;

public class PropertyReader {

  private final Result<Properties> properties;

  public PropertyReader(String configFileName) {
    this.properties = readProperties(configFileName);
  }

  private Result<Properties> readProperties(String configFileName) {
    try (InputStream inputStream = getClass().getClassLoader()
                        .getResourceAsStream(configFileName)) {
      Properties properties = new Properties();
      properties.load(inputStream);
      return Result.of(properties);
    } catch (Exception e) {
      return Result.failure(e);
    }
  }
}
```

A Result<Properties> is stored in the PropertyReader class.

The PropertyReader class is created with a string referencing a property file.

The file is loaded from the classpath.

You catch Exception and not IOException to handle the case of a null InputStream ❶.

In the case of an exception, you return a Result.Failure containing the exception.

❶ The property file is loaded, possibly causing an IOException. Be aware that if the file isn't found, this won't produce an IOException but a null inputStream, causing a NullPointerException.

In this example, you load the property file from the classpath. It could, of course, be loaded from anywhere on disk, or read from a remote URL, or any other source.

15.2.2 Reading properties as strings

The simple use case consists in reading the properties as strings. This is very straightforward. You just have to add a readProperty method to the PropertyReader class, taking the property name as its argument and returning a Result<String>. But be aware that the following won't work:

```java
public Result<String> getProperty(String name) {
  return properties.map(props -> props.getProperty(name));
}
```

If the property doesn't exist, the getProperty method returns null. (In Java 8, it should return an Optional, but it doesn't.) Note that the Properties class can be constructed with a default property list, and that the getProperty method can itself be called with a default value. But not all properties have default values.

To handle this problem, you can create a helper method:

```
public Result<String> getProperty(String name) {
  return properties.flatMap(props ->getProperty(props, name));
}

private Result<String> getProperty(Properties properties, String name) {
  return Result.of(properties.getProperty(name));
}
```

Now, let's say you have a property file in the classpath, containing the following properties:

```
host=acme.org
port=6666
name=
temp=71.3
price=$45
list=34,56,67,89
person=3,Jeanne,Doe
```

You can access properties in a safe way:

```
PropertyReader propertyReader = new PropertyReader("com/fpinjava/properties/c
    onfig.properties");

propertyReader.getProperty("host")
              .forEachOrFail(System.out::println)
              .forEach(System.out::println);

propertyReader.getProperty("name")
              .forEachOrFail(System.out::println)
              .forEach(System.out::println);

propertyReader.getProperty("year")
              .forEachOrFail(System.out::println)
              .forEach(System.out::println);
```

Given your property file, you'll get the following result:

```
acme.org

Null value
```

The first line corresponds to the host property, which is correct. The second line corresponds to the name property, and it's an empty string, which might or might not be correct; you don't know. It depends on whether the name is optional from the business point of view. The third line corresponds to the missing year property, but the "Null value" message isn't very informative. Of course, it's contained in a Result

`<String>` that could be assigned to a year variable, so you could know which property is missing. But it would be better to have the name of the property as part of the message. Furthermore, if the file isn't found, you get a very uninformative error message:

```
java.lang.NullPointerException
```

15.2.3 *Producing better error messages*

The problem you're facing here is a very good example of what should never happen. Using the Java standard library, you're confident that things will go as expected. In particular, you expect that if a file isn't found, or if it can't be read, you'll get an `IOException`. You would even hope to be told the full path of the file, because a "missing" file is often just a file that's not in the right place (or is a file that Java isn't looking for in the right place). A good error message in such a case would be "I am looking for file 'abc' in location 'xyz' but can't find it."

Now, look at the code for the `ClassLoader.getResourceAsStream` method:

```java
public InputStream getResourceAsStream(String name) {
  URL url = getResource(name);
  try {
    return url != null ? url.openStream() : null;
  } catch (IOException e) {
    return null;
  }
}
```

No, you're not dreaming. This is how Java 8 is written. The conclusion is that you, as a programmer, should never use a method from the Java standard library without looking at the corresponding code.

Note that the Javadoc says that the method returns "An input stream for reading the resource, or `null` if the resource could not be found." This means that many things can go wrong. An `IOException` might occur if the file isn't found, or if there's a problem while reading it. Or the filename could be `null`. Or the `getResource` method could throw an exception or return `null`. (Look at the code for this method to see what I mean.)

The minimum that you should do is provide a different message for each case. And despite the fact that an `IOException` is very unlikely to be thrown, you must still handle this case, as well as the general case of an unexpected exception:

```java
private Result<Properties> readProperties(String configFileName) {
  try (InputStream inputStream =
      getClass().getClassLoader().getResourceAsStream(configFileName)) {
    Properties properties = new Properties();
    properties.load(inputStream);
    return Result.of(properties);
  } catch (NullPointerException e) {
    return Result.failure(String.format("File %s not found in classpath",
                                        configFileName));
  } catch (IOException e) {
```

```
      return Result.failure(String.format("IOException reading classpath
                                  resource %s", configFileName));
  } catch (Exception e) {
      return Result.failure(String.format("Exception reading classpath
                                  resource %s", configFileName), e);
  }
}
```

Now, if the file isn't found, the message is

```
File com/fpinjava/properties/config.properties not found in classpath
```

You also have to deal with property-related error messages. When using code like this

```
Result<String> year = propertyReader.getProperty("year");
```

it's clear that if you get the `Null` value error message, it means the `year` property wasn't found. But in the following example, the `Null` value message gives no information about which property was missing:

```
PropertyReader propertyReader =
            new PropertyReader("com/fpinjava/properties/config.properties");
Result<Person> person =
  propertyReader.getProperty("id").map(Integer::parseInt)
    .flatMap(id -> propertyReader.getProperty("firstName")
      .flatMap(firstName -> propertyReader.getProperty("lastName")
        .map(lastName -> Person.apply(id, firstName, lastName))));
person.forEachOrFail(System.out::println).forEach(System.out::println);
```

To solve this problem, you have several options at your disposal. The simplest is to map the failure in the `getProperty` helper method of the `PropertyReader` class:

```
private Result<String> getProperty(Properties properties, String name) {
  return Result.of(properties.getProperty(name))
        .mapFailure(String.format("Property \"%s\" no found", name));
}
```

The preceding example produces the following error message, indicating clearly that the `id` property wasn't present in the property file:

```
Property "id" not found
```

Another potential source of failure is a parsing error while converting the string `id` property into an integer. For example, if the property was

```
id=three
```

the error message will be

```
For input string: "three"
```

This doesn't give you meaningful information, and that's because it's the standard Java 8 error message for a parsing error. Most standard Java error messages are like this. It's like a `NullPointerException`. It says that a reference was found `null`, but it doesn't say which one. Here, it doesn't even say which error was encountered. The nature of the error was carried by the exception. Printing the stack trace would have given you this:

```
Exception in thread "main" java.lang.NumberFormatException: For input string:
    "three"
at java.lang.NumberFormatException.forInputString(NumberFormatException.java:
    48) ...
```

What you really need is the name of the property that caused the exception. Something like this:

```
propertyReader.getProperty("id")
    .map(Integer::parseInt)
        .mapFailure(String.format("Invalid format for property \"id\": ", ???))
```

But you have to write the name of the property twice, and you'd like to replace "???" with the value found (this isn't possible because the value is already lost). Because you'll have to parse property values for all non-string properties, you should abstract this inside the `PropertyReader` class.

To do so, you'll first rename the `getProperty` method:

```
public Result<String> getAsString(String name) {
  return properties.flatMap(props -> getProperty(props, name));
}
```

Then, you'll add a `getAsInteger` method:

```
public Result<Integer> getAsInteger(String name) {
  Result<String> rString =
      properties.flatMap(props ->getProperty(props, name));
  return rString.flatMap(x -> {
    try {
      return Result.success(Integer.parseInt(x));
    } catch (NumberFormatException e) {
      return Result.failure(String.format("Invalid value while parsing
                                          property %s: %s", name, x));
    }
  });
}
```

Now, you don't need to worry about errors while converting to integers:

```
Result<Person> person =
  propertyReader.getAsInteger("id")
    .flatMap(id -> propertyReader.getAsString("firstName")
      .flatMap(firstName -> propertyReader.getAsString("lastName")
        .map(lastName -> Person.apply(id, firstName, lastName))));
person.forEachOrFail(System.out::println).forEach(System.out::println);
```

15.2.4 *Reading properties as lists*

You could do the same thing you've done for integers for other numeric types, such as `long` or `double`. But you can do much more than this. You can read properties as lists:

```
list=34,56,67,89
```

You just have to add a specialized method to handle this case. You can use the following method to get a property as a list of integers:

```
public Result<List<Integer>> getAsIntegerList(String name) {
  Result<String> rString =
          properties.flatMap(props ->getProperty(props, name));
  return rString.flatMap(s -> {
    try {
      return Result.success(List.fromSeparatedString(s,',')
                                      .map(Integer::parseInt));
    } catch (NumberFormatException e) {
      return Result.failure(String.format("Invalid value while parsing
                                    property %s: %s", name, s));
    }
  });
}
```

Of course, you'll need to add the `fromSeparatedString` method to the `List` class. As I said in the previous chapter, this code isn't intended to use the result of the exercises of previous chapters but the `fpinjava-common` module that's available in the code accompanying this book (https://github.com/fpinjava/fpinjava). This is mostly the same code as in the solutions to the exercises, but with some additional methods, such as `List.fromCollection(...)` in the following example:

```
public static List<String> fromSeparatedString(String string,
                                                char separator) {
  return List.fromCollection(Arrays.asList(string.split("\\s*"
                                    + separator + "\\s*")));
}
```

But you can do much more. You can read a property as a list of any numerical values by providing the conversion function:

```
public <T> Result<List<T>> getAsList(String name, Function<String, T> f) {
  Result<String> rString
              = properties.flatMap(props ->getProperty(props, name));
  return rString.flatMap(s -> {
    try {
      return Result.success(List.fromSeparatedString(s, ',').map(f));
    } catch (NumberFormatException e) {
      return Result.failure(String.format("Invalid value while parsing
                                    property %s: %s", name, s));
    }
  });
}
```

And now you can define functions for all sorts of number formats in terms of getAsList:

```
public Result<List<Integer>> getAsIntegerList(String name) {
  return getAsList(name, Integer::parseInt);
}

public Result<List<Double>> getAsDoubleList(String name) {
  return getAsList(name, Double::parseDouble);
}

public Result<List<Boolean>> getAsBooleanList(String name) {
  return getAsList(name, Boolean::parseBoolean);
}
```

15.2.5 *Reading enum values*

One frequent use case is reading a property as an enum value, which is a particular case of reading a property as any type. You can first create a method to convert a property to any type T, taking a function from String to a Result<T>:

```
public <T> Result<T> getAsType(final Function<String, Result<T>> function,
                                                     final String name) {
  Result<String> rString =
              properties.flatMap(props -> getProperty(props, name));
  return rString.flatMap(s -> {
    try {
      return function.apply(s);
    } catch (Exception e) {
      return Result.failure(String.format("Invalid value while parsing
                                    property %s: %s", name, s));
    }
  });
}
```

You can now create a getAsEnum method in terms of getAsType:

```
public <T extends Enum<?>> Result<T> getAsEnum(final String parameterName,
                                                  final Class<T> enumClass) {
  Function<String, Result<T>> f = t -> {
    try {
      T constant = enumClass.getEnumConstants()[0];    ⟵ This is a trick...
      @SuppressWarnings("unchecked")
      T value = (T) Enum.valueOf(constant.getClass(), t);  ⟵┐ ...to allow the use of
      return Result.success(value);                         │  the class of T here.
    } catch (Exception e) {
      return Result.failure(String.format("Error parsing property %s: value
        %s can't be parsed to %s.", t, parameterName, enumClass.getName()));
    }
  };
  return getAsType(f, parameterName);
}
```

Given the following property

```
type=SERIAL
```

and the following enum,

```
public enum Type {
  SERIAL,
  PARALLEL
}
```

you can now read the property using the following code:

```
Result<Type> type = propertyReader.getAsEnum("type", Type.class);
```

15.2.6 *Reading properties of arbitrary types*

So far, you've been reading properties as strings, primitives (int, double, boolean, and so on), or enums. It may also be interesting to read properties as arbitrary objects. For this, you'll have to write the object properties in a kind of serialized form in the property file, and then load these properties and deserialize them.

You can use the getAsType method to read a property as any type. For example, you could read the following property to get a Person:

```
person=id:3,firstName:Jane,lastName:Doe
```

All you have to do is provide a function from String to Result<Person>. This function should be able to create a Person from the string id:3,firstName:Jane,last-Name:Doe.

To simplify its use, you could create a getAsPerson method. But because it's type-specific, you shouldn't put it inside the PropertyReader. A static factory method taking a PropertyReader and the property name as its arguments can be added to the Person class.

There are several ways to implement it. One way is to get the property as a list and then split each element, putting the key/value pairs in a map. It would then be easy to create a Person from this map. Another way to go would be to create a second PropertyReader that reads from the string after having replaced the commas with newline characters. The following listing shows the Person class with two specific methods for constructing instances from a property string.

Listing 15.3 Methods that allow you to read properties as objects or lists of objects

```
public class Person {
  ...
  public static Result<Person> getAsPerson(String propertyName,
                              PropertyReader propertyReader) {
    Result<String> rString =
              propertyReader.getAsPropertyString(propertyName);
    Result<PropertyReader> rPropReader =
              rString.map(PropertyReader::stringPropertyReader);
    return rPropReader.flatMap(Person::readPerson);
  }

  public static Result<List<Person>> getAsPersonList(String propertyName,
                              PropertyReader propertyReader) {
```

```
        Result<List<String>> rList =
                            propertyReader.getAsStringList(propertyName);
        return rList.flatMap(list -> List.sequence(list.map(s ->
            readPerson(PropertyReader.stringPropertyReader(PropertyReader
                                        .toPropertyString(s))))));
    }

    private static Result<Person> readPerson(PropertyReader propReader) {
        return propReader.getAsInteger("id")
            .flatMap(id -> propReader.getAsString("firstName")
                .flatMap(firstName -> propReader.getAsString("lastName")
                    .map(lastName -> Person.apply(id, firstName, lastName))));
    }
}
```

The getAsPersonList method allows you to read vector properties written as follows:

```
employees:\
  id:3;firstName:Jane;lastName:Doe,\
  id:5;firstName:Paul;lastName:Smith,\
  id:8;firstName:Mary;lastName:Winston
```

These methods necessitate some changes in the PropertyReader class.

Listing 15.4   Static factory methods added to the PropertyReader class

The PropertyReader is now constructed
with a Result<Properties>.

The source is registered in order
to be used in error messages.

```
public class PropertyReader {

    private final Result<Properties> properties;
    private final String source;

    private PropertyReader(Result<Properties> properties, String source) {
        this.properties = properties;
        this.source = source;
    }

    ...

    public static String toPropertyString(String s) {
        return s.replace(";", "\n");
    }

    public Result<String> getAsPropertyString(String propertyName) {
        return getAsString(propertyName).map(PropertyReader::toPropertyString);
    }

    private static Result<Properties> readPropertiesFromFile(String
                                            configFileName) {
        try (InputStream inputStream = PropertyReader.class.getClassLoader()
                                .getResourceAsStream(configFileName)) {
            Properties properties = new Properties();
            properties.load(inputStream);
            return Result.of(properties);
        } catch (NullPointerException e) {
```

This method converts a
single property value into
a property string that can
be used as input for a
nested PropertyReader.

This is the
original
method for
reading a
property file.

This method reads a property and
converts the value into a property string.

```
        return Result.failure(String.format("File %s not found in classpath",
                                                    configFileName));
    } catch (IOException e) {
        return Result.failure(String.format("IOException reading classpath
                                    resource %s", configFileName));
    } catch (Exception e) {
        return Result.failure(String.format("Exception reading classpath
                                    resource %s", configFileName), e);
    }
}

private static Result<Properties> readPropertiesFromString(String
                                            propString) {
    try (Reader reader = new StringReader(propString)) {
        Properties properties = new Properties();
        properties.load(reader);
        return Result.of(properties);
    } catch (Exception e) {
        return Result.failure(String.format("Exception reading property
                                    string %s", propString), e);
    }
}

public static PropertyReader filePropertyReader(String fileName) {
    return new PropertyReader(readPropertiesFromFile(fileName),
                            String.format("File: %s", fileName));
}

public static PropertyReader stringPropertyReader(String propString) {
    return new PropertyReader(readPropertiesFromString(propString),
                            String.format("String: %s", propString));
}
}
```

This is a new method to read properties from a property string.

This static factory method creates a PropertyReader from a filename.

This static property method creates a PropertyReader from a property string.

Of course, the same thing can be done for XML property files (which are handled by Java out of the box) or for other formats, such as JSON or YAML.

15.3 *Converting an imperative program: the XML reader*

Writing new functional programs for any task you have to accomplish is exciting, but you generally don't have time for this. Often, you'll want to use existing imperative programs in your own code. This is the case each time you want to use a Java library. Of course, you may find it more interesting to start from scratch and build a completely new, 100% functional solution. But you have to be realistic. You generally don't have the time or budget to do this, and you'll have to use existing nonfunctional libraries.

As you'll soon discover, once you're comfortable with functional techniques, it's really a pain to go back to the old imperative coding style. The solution is generally to build a thin functional wrapper around these imperative libraries. As an example, we'll examine a very common library for reading XML files, JDOM 2.0.6. This is the most commonly used Java library for this task.

You'll start with the example program in listing 15.5. This program comes from one of the numerous sites proposing tutorials about how to use JDOM (http://mng.bz/4p3x). I've chosen this example because it's minimal and fits easily in the book.

Listing 15.5   Reading XML data with JDOM: imperative version

```java
import org.jdom2.Document;
import org.jdom2.Element;
import org.jdom2.JDOMException;
import org.jdom2.input.SAXBuilder;
import java.io.File;
import java.io.IOException;
import java.util.List;

public class ReadXmlFile {

  public static void main(String[] args) {
    SAXBuilder builder = new SAXBuilder();
    File xmlFile = new File("path_to_file");
    try {
      Document document = (Document) builder.build(xmlFile);
      Element rootNode = document.getRootElement();
      List list = rootNode.getChildren("staff");
      for (int i = 0; i < list.size(); i++) {
        Element node = (Element) list.get(i);
        System.out.println("First Name : " +
                                  node.getChildText("firstname"));
        System.out.println("\tLast Name : " +
                                  node.getChildText("lastname"));
        System.out.println("\tNick Name : " +
                                  node.getChildText("email"));
        System.out.println("\tSalary : " + node.getChildText("salary"));
      }
    } catch (IOException io) {
      System.out.println(io.getMessage());
    } catch (JDOMException jdomex) {
      System.out.println(jdomex.getMessage());
    }
  }
}
```

The data file used with this example is shown in the following listing.

Listing 15.6   The XML file to read

```xml
<?xml version="1.0"?>
<company>
  <staff>
    <firstname>Paul</firstname>
    <lastname>Smith</lastname>
    <email>paul.smith@acme.com</email>
    <salary>100000</salary>
  </staff>
```

```
<staff>
  <firstname>Mary</firstname>
  <lastname>Colson</lastname>
  <email>mary.colson@acme.com</email>
  <salary>200000</salary>
</staff>
</company>
```

First, you'll look at the benefits you can get from rewriting this example in a functional way. The first problem you might have is that no part of the program can be reused. Of course, it's only an example, but even as an example, it should be written in a reusable way, at least so it's testable. Here, the only way to test the program is to look at the console, which will display either the expected result or an error message. As you'll see, it might even display an erroneous result.

15.3.1 *Listing the necessary functions*

To make this program more functional, you should start by listing the fundamental functions you need, write them as autonomous, reusable, and testable units, and then code the example by composing these functions. Here are the main functions of the program:

1 Read a file and return the content as an XML string.
2 Convert the XML string into a list of elements.
3 Convert a list of elements into a list of string representations of these elements.

You'll also need an effect for displaying the list of strings to the computer screen.

> **NOTE** The description of the main functions of this program is only suitable for a small file that can be loaded entirely in memory.

The first function you need can be implemented as the following method:

```
public static Result<String> readFile2String(String path)
```

This method won't throw any exceptions, but returns a `Result<String>`.

The second method converts an XML string into a list of elements, so it needs to know the name of the root XML element. It will have the following signature:

```
private static Result<List<Element>> readDocument(String rootElementName,
                                                   String stringDoc)
```

The third function you need will receive a list of elements as its argument and return a list of string representations of those elements. This will be implemented by a method with the following signature:

```
private static List<String> toStringList(List<Element> list, String format)
```

Eventually, you'll need to apply an effect to the data, so you'll have to define it as a method with the following signature:

```
private static <T> void processList(List<T> list)
```

This decomposition in functions doesn't look much different from what you could do in imperative programming. After all, it's also good practice to decompose imperative programs into methods with a single responsibility each. It is, however, more different than it might look. Note that the readDocument method takes as its first parameter a string that's returned by a method that could (in the imperative world) throw an exception. Thus, you'd have to deal with the additional method:

```
private static Result<String> getRootElementName()
```

In the same way, the file path could be returned by the same kind of method:

```
private static Result<String> getXmlFilePath()
```

The important thing to note is that the argument types and return types of these functions don't match! This is the explicit translation of the fact that the imperative versions of these functions would be partial, which means they'd possibly throw exceptions. Methods throwing exceptions don't compose well. In contrast, your functions compose perfectly.

15.3.2   Composing the functions and applying an effect

Although the argument and return types don't match, your functions can be composed easily, using the comprehension pattern:

```
final static String format = "First Name : %s\n" +
      "\tLast Name : %s\n" +
      "\tEmail : %s\n" +
      "\tSalary : %s";
...
final Result<String> path = getXmlFilePath();
final Result<String> rDoc = path.flatMap(ReadXmlFile::readFile2String);
final Result<String> rRoot = getRootElementName();
final Result<List<String>> result = rDoc.flatMap(doc -> rRoot
    .flatMap(rootElementName -> readDocument(rootElementName, doc))
    .map(list -> toStringList(list, format)));
```

To display the result, you simply apply the corresponding effect:

```
result.forEachOrException(ReadXmlFile::processList)
      .forEach(Throwable::printStackTrace);
```

Your functional version of the program is much cleaner, and it's fully testable—or it will be when you've implemented all the necessary functions.

15.3.3   Implementing the functions

Your program is relatively elegant, but you still have to implement the functions and effects you're using in order to make it work. The good news is that each function is very simple and can be easily tested.

First, you'll implement the getXmlFilePath and getRootElementName functions. In our example, these are constants that would be replaced in a real application:

```
private static Result<String> getXmlFilePath() {
  return Result.of("<path_to_file>");
}

private static Result<String> getRootElementName() {
  return Result.of("staff");
}
```

Then you have to implement the readFile2String method. Here's one of the many possible implementations:

```
public static Result<String> readFile2String(String path) {
  try {
    return Result.success(new String(Files.readAllBytes(Paths.get(path))));
  } catch (IOException e) {
    return Result.failure(String.format("IO error while reading file %s",
                                                              path), e);
  } catch (Exception e) {
    return Result.failure(String.format("Unexpected error while reading
                                          file %s", path), e);
  }
}
```

Note that you catch IOException and Exception separately. This isn't mandatory, but it allows you to provide better error messages. In any case, you must always catch Exception. (You could get a SecurityException here, for example.)

Next, you need to implement the readDocument method. This method takes as its parameters an XML string containing the XML data and the name of the root element:

```
private static Result<List<Element>> readDocument(String rootElementName,
                                                    String stringDoc) {
  final SAXBuilder builder = new SAXBuilder();
  try {
    final Document document =
            builder.build(new StringReader(stringDoc));
    final Element rootElement = document.getRootElement();
    return Result.success(List.fromCollection(
                      rootElement.getChildren(rootElementName)));
  } catch (IOException | JDOMException io) {
    return Result.failure(String.format("Invalid root element name '%s'
                      or XML data %s", rootElementName, stringDoc), io);
  } catch (Exception e) {
    return Result.failure(String.format("Unexpected error while reading XML
          data %s with root element %s", stringDoc, rootElementName), e);
  }
}
```

This line might throw a NullPointerException.

This line might throw an IllegalStateException.

You first catch IOException (which is very unlikely to be thrown, because you're reading from a string) and JDOMException, both of which are checked exceptions and return a failure with the corresponding error message. But by looking at the JDOM code (no one should call a library method without first looking at how it is implemented), you see that the code might throw an IllegalStateException or a NullPointerException. Once again, you have to catch Exception.

The toStringList method simply maps the list to a function responsible for the conversion:

```
private static List<String> toStringList(List<Element> list,
                                          String format) {
  return list.map(e -> processElement(e, format));
}
private static String processElement(Element element, String format) {
  return String.format(format, element.getChildText("firstname"),
      element.getChildText("lastname"),
      element.getChildText("email"),
      element.getChildText("salary"));
}
```

Finally, you need to implement the effect that will be applied to the result:

```
private static <T> void processList(List<T> list) {
  list.forEach(System.out::println);
}
```

15.3.4 *Making the program even more functional*

Your program is now much more modular and testable, and its parts are reusable. But you can still do better. You're still using four nonfunctional elements: the file path, the name of the root element, the format used to convert the elements to string, and the effect that's applied to the result. To make your program fully functional, you should make these elements parameters of your program.

The processElement method also used specific data in the form of the element names, which correspond to the parameters of the format string used to display them. You can replace the format parameter with a Tuple of the format string and a list of parameters. This way, the processElement method will become the following:

```
private static List<String> toStringList(List<Element> list,
                                 Tuple<String, List<String>> format) {
  return list.map(e -> processElement(e, format));
}

private static String processElement(Element element, Tuple<String,
                                          List<String>> format) {
  String formatString = format._1;
  List<String> parameters = format._2.map(element::getChildText);
  return String.format(formatString, parameters.toJavaList().toArray());
}
```

Now your program can be a pure function, taking four arguments and returning a new (nonfunctional) executable program as its result. This version of the program is represented in the following listing.

Listing 15.7 The fully functional XML reader program

The path and root element name are now received as Supplier instances. The format includes the parameter names, and the method takes an executable as an additional parameter.

The method returns an executable applying the effect received as a parameter to the result. Note that this method throws exceptions. There's nothing better to do, because it's an effect and thus can't return a value.

```
import com.fpinjava.common.*;
import org.jdom2.Document;
import org.jdom2.Element;
import org.jdom2.JDOMException;
import org.jdom2.input.SAXBuilder;
import java.io.IOException;
import java.io.StringReader;
import java.nio.file.Files;
import java.nio.file.Paths;

public class ReadXmlFile {

    public static Executable readXmlFile(Supplier<Result<String>> sPath,
                                         Supplier<Result<String>> sRootName,
                                         Tuple<String, List<String>> format,
                                         Effect<List<String>> e) {
        final Result<String> path = sPath.get();
        final Result<String> rDoc = path.flatMap(ReadXmlFile::readFile2String);
        final Result<String> rRoot =sRootName.get();
        final Result<List<String>> result = rDoc.flatMap(doc -> rRoot
            .flatMap(rootElementName -> readDocument(rootElementName, doc))
            .map(list -> toStringList(list, format)));
        return () -> result.forEachOrThrow(e);
    }

    public static Result<String> readFile2String(String path) {
     try {
      return Result.success(new String(Files.readAllBytes(Paths.get(path))));
      } catch (IOException e) {
        return Result.failure(String.format("IO error while reading file %s",
                                                              path), e);
      } catch (Exception e) {
        return Result.failure(String.format("Unexpected error while reading
                                                      file %s", path), e);
      }
    }

    private static Result<List<Element>> readDocument(String rootElementName,
                                                      String stringDoc) {
       final SAXBuilder builder = new SAXBuilder();
       try {
         final Document document = builder.build(new StringReader(stringDoc));
         final Element rootElement = document.getRootElement();
         return Result.success(List.fromCollection(
```

Suppliers are evaluated to get the actual parameters.

```
                                 rootElement.getChildren(rootElementName)));
        } catch (IOException | JDOMException io) {
          return Result.failure(String.format("Invalid root element name '%s'
                          or XML data %s", rootElementName, stringDoc), io);
        } catch (Exception e) {
          return Result.failure(String.format("Unexpected error while reading
                                  XML data %s", stringDoc), e);
        }
      }

      private static List<String> toStringList(List<Element> list,
                               Tuple<String, List<String>> format) {
        return list.map(e -> processElement(e, format));
      }

      private static String processElement(Element element,       <──────────┐
                               Tuple<String, List<String>> format) {         │
        String formatString = format._1;                                     │
        List<String> parameters = format._2.map(element::getChildText);      │
        return String.format(formatString, parameters.toJavaList().toArray());│
      }                                                                      │
    }                                                                        │
```

**The processElement method
is no longer specific.**

At this point, this program can be tested with the client code shown in the following listing.

Listing 15.8 The client program to test the XML reader

```
public class Test {

  private final static Tuple<String, List<String>> format =
      new Tuple<>("First Name : %s\n" +
          "\tLast Name : %s\n" +
          "\tEmail : %s\n" +
          "\tSalary : %s", List.list("firstname", "lastname", "email", "salary"));

  public static void main(String... args) {
    Executable program = ReadXmlFile.readXmlFile(Test::getXmlFilePath,
                          Test::getRootElementName, format, Test::processList);
    program.exec();
  }

  private static Result<String> getXmlFilePath() {
    return Result.of("file.xml"); // <- adjust path
  }

  private static Result<String> getRootElementName() {
    return Result.of("staff");
  }

  private static <T> void processList(List<T> list) {
    list.forEach(System.out::println);
  }
}
```

This program isn't ideal because you haven't handled the potential error that could arise from invalid element names. For example, if you use a wrong element name, you might get the following result:

```
First Name : null
  Last Name : Smith
  email : paul.smith@acme.com
  Salary : 100000
First Name : null
  Last Name : Colson
  email : mary.colson@acme.com
  Salary : 200000
```

You can guess what the error is by seeing that all the first names are null, but it would be better to replace the word "null" with an explicit message containing the erroneous element name. A more important problem is that if you forget one of the element names in the list, you'll get an exception from the String.format method because of the following code:

```
List<String> parameters = format._2.map(element::getChildText);
return String.format(formatString, parameters.toJavaList().toArray());
```

In this code, the array of parameters will have only three elements instead of the expected four. But it will be difficult to locate the source of the error from the exception trace.

   In fact, the real cause of the problem is that you've taken all the specific data out of the ReadXmlFile class, such as the root element name, the file path, and the effect to apply, but the processElement method is still specific to the client business use case. The ReadXmlFile class only allows you to read all elements that are direct children of the root element, gathering some of their direct child elements' values (those whose names are passed along with the format).

   A third problem is that the readXmlFile method takes two arguments of the same type. This is a source of error if arguments are swapped, which won't be detected by the compiler.

15.3.5 *Fixing the argument type problem*

The third problem is very easy to fix by using the value types technique described in chapter 3. Instead of using Result<String> arguments, you can use Result<File-Path> and Result<ElementName>. FilePath and ElementName are just value classes for string values:

```
public class FilePath {

  public final Result<String> value;

  private FilePath(Result<String> value) {
    this.value = value;
  }
```

```
    public static FilePath apply(String value) {
      return new FilePath(Result.of(FilePath::isValidPath, value,
                                   "Invalid file path: " + value));
    }

    private static boolean isValidPath(String path) {
      // Replace with validation code
      return true;
    }
}
```

The ElementName class is similar. Of course, you have to add the validation code if you want some validation to happen. The simplest way is to check the value against a regular expression. To use these new classes, the readXmlFile method can be modified as follows:

```
public static Executable readXmlFile(Supplier<FilePath> sPath,
                                     Supplier<ElementName> sRootName,
                                     Tuple<String, List<String>> format,
                                     Effect<List<String>> e) {
  final Result<String> path = sPath.get().value;
  final Result<String> rDoc = path.flatMap(ReadXmlFile::readFile2String);
  final Result<String> rRoot =sRootName.get().value;
```

As you see, the changes are minimal. Note that you can use getters instead of public properties in the value type classes if you think having public properties is inappropriate.

The client class must also be modified:

```
private static FilePath getXmlFilePath() {
  return FilePath.apply("<path_to_file>");
}

private static ElementName getRootElementName() {
  return ElementName.apply("staff");
}
```

With these changes, it's now impossible to switch the order of the arguments without being warned by the compiler.

15.3.6 *Making the element-processing function a parameter*

The two remaining problems can be solved with a single change: passing the element-processing function as a parameter to the readXmlFile method. This way, this method will have a single task: read the list of first-level elements in the file, apply them to a configurable function, and return the result. The main difference is that the method will no longer produce a list of strings and apply a string effect.

You'll need to make the method generic. This means only the following changes:

The method is made generic.

The Tuple<String, List<String>> format argument has disappeared, and a new function argument replaces it. This is the function that will be applied to convert the list of elements to a list of T.

```
public static <T> Executable readXmlFile(Supplier<FilePath> sPath,
                                         Supplier<ElementName> sRootName,
                                         Function<Element, T> f,
                                         Effect<List<T>> e) {
    final Result<String> path = sPath.get().value;
    final Result<String> rDoc = path.flatMap(ReadXmlFile::readFile2String);
    final Result<String> rRoot =sRootName.get().value;
    final Result<List<T>> result = rDoc.flatMap(doc -> rRoot
        .flatMap(rootElementName -> readDocument(rootElementName, doc))
        .map(list -> list.map(f)));
    return () -> result.forEachOrThrow(e);
}
```

The effect to be applied is now parameterized by List<T>.

The toStringList and processElement methods have been removed. They're replaced with an application of the received function.

The client program can now be modified accordingly. This relieves you of using the Tuple trick to pass both the format string and the list of parameter names:

```
private final static String format = "First Name : %s\n" +
    "\tLast Name : %s\n" +
    "\tEmail : %s\n" +
    "\tSalary : %s";
```

The format is now again set as a simple string.

```
    private final static List<String> elementNames =
            List.list("firstname", "lastname", "email", "salary");
    public static void main(String... args) {
      Executable program =
        ReadXmlFile.readXmlFile(Test::getXmlFilePath,
                                Test::getRootElementName,
                                Test::processElement,
                                Test::processList);
      program.exec();
    }
```

The list of element names is also set separately.

The processElement function is passed as an argument.

```
    private static String processElement(Element element) {
      return String.format(format, elementNames.map(element::getChildText)
                                               .toJavaList()
                                               .toArray());
    }
    ...
```

The processElement method is now implemented by the client.

Note that the processList effect has not changed. Now it's up to the client to provide a function to convert one element, and an effect to apply to this element.

15.3.7 *Handling errors on element names*

Now you're left with the problem of errors happening while you read the elements. The function that you pass to the readXmlFile method returns a raw type, meaning that it should be a total function, but it's not. It was in our initial example, because an error produced the "null" string. Now that you're using a function from Element to T, you could use Result<String> as the realization of T, but this wouldn't be very practical because you'd end up with a List<Result<T>>, and you'd have to transform it to a Result<List<T>>. Not a big deal, but this should definitely be abstracted.

The solution is to use a function from Element to Result<T>, and use the List.sequence method to transform the result into a Result<List<T>>. Here's the new method:

```
public static <T> Executable readXmlFile(Supplier<FilePath> sPath,
                                         Supplier<ElementName> sRootName,
                            ▷            Function<Element, Result<T>> f,
                                         Effect<List<T>> e) {
    final Result<String> path = sPath.get().value;
    final Result<String> rDoc = path.flatMap(ReadXmlFile::readFile2String);
    final Result<String> rRoot =sRootName.get().value;
    final Result<List<T>> result = rDoc.flatMap(doc -> rRoot
        .flatMap(rootElementName -> readDocument(rootElementName, doc))
        .flatMap(list -> List.sequence(list.map(f))));    ◁
    ...
```

The function received as an argument is now a function from Element to Result<T>.

The result is "sequenced," producing a Result<List<T>>. Of course, you had to change the map method for flatMap.

The only additional change to be made is to handle the error that might occur in the process element method. The best approach is to examine the code of the getChild-Text method from JDOM. This method is implemented as follows:

```
/**
 * Returns the textual content of the named child element, or null if
 * there's no such child. This method is a convenience because calling
 * <code>getChild().getText()</code> can throw a NullPointerException.
 *
 * @param cname the name of the child
 * @return text   content for the named child, or null if no such child
 */
public String getChildText(final String cname) {
    final Element child = getChild(cname);
    if (child == null) {
        return null;
    }
    return child.getText();
}
```

As you can see (as you continue examining the code for the getChild method), this method won't throw any exceptions, but it will return null if the element doesn't exist. So you can modify your processElement method:

**You now use a custom method
for returning the element text.**

```
private static Result<String> processElement(Element element) {
  try {
    return Result.of(String.format(format, elementNames.map(name ->
            getChildText(element, name)).toJavaList().toArray()));  ⟵
  } catch (Exception e) {
    return Result.failure("Exception while formatting element. " +   ⟵
        "Probable cause is a missing element name in element list " +
            elementNames);
  }
}
```

**You catch the exception that might occur
while formatting the result in order to
provide an explicit error message.**

```
private static String getChildText(Element element, String name) {
  String string = element.getChildText(name);
  return string != null                        ⟵  If the returned value
      ? string                                     is null, you replace it
      : "Element " + name + " not found";          with an explicit error
}
```

Now, most potential errors are handled in a functional way. Note, however, that not all errors can be handled functionally. As I said earlier, exceptions that are thrown by the effect passed to the readXmlFile method can't be handled this way. These are exceptions thrown by the program that's returned by the method. When the method returns the program, it hasn't yet been executed. These exceptions must be caught while executing the resulting program:

```
public static void main(String... args) {
  Executable program = ReadXmlFile.readXmlFile(Test::getXmlFilePath,
                                               Test::getRootElementName,
                                               Test::processElement,
                                               Test::processList);

  try {
    program.exec();
  } catch (Exception e) {
    System.out.println(e.getMessage());
  }
}
```

You'll find the complete example in the code accompanying this book (http://github .com/fpinjava/fpinjava).

15.4 *Summary*

- Putting values in the Result context is the functional equivalent of assertions.
- Property files can be read in a safe manner using the Result context.
- Functional property reading relieves you of handling conversion errors.
- Properties can be read as any type, enum, or collection in an abstracted way.
- Functional wrappers can be built around legacy imperative libraries.

appendix A
Using Java 8
functional features

When Java 8 was released, it was presented by Oracle as a step towards more-functional programming. Among the functional-friendly features listed in Oracle's "What's New in JDK 8" note were the following:

- "Lambda Expressions, a new language feature, has been introduced in this release. They enable you to treat functionality as a method argument, or code as data. Lambda expressions let you express instances of single-method interfaces (referred to as functional interfaces) more compactly." This is a very important aspect of the functional paradigm.
- "Method references provide easy-to-read lambda expressions for methods that already have a name." The latter part of that sentence probably refers to "existing methods," because methods that don't already have a name don't exist.
- "Type Annotations provide the ability to apply an annotation anywhere a type is used, not just on a declaration."
- "Improved type inference."
- "Classes in the new `java.util.stream` package provide a Stream API to support functional-style operations on streams of elements. The Stream API is integrated into the Collections API, which enables such as sequential or parallel map-reduce transformations."

You can read these statements (along with many others not related to functional programming) in Oracle's original "What's new in JDK 8" document (http://mng .bz/27na).

In this presentation, Oracle didn't list several elements and omitted one important fact:

- The `Function` package
- The `Optional` class
- The `CompletableFuture` class
- The fact that most collections were modified by adding the `stream()` method, making it possible to transform them into `Stream` instances.

All this, including the fact that `Optional`, `Stream`, and `CompletableFuture` are monadic structures (see appendix B for what this means) makes it very clear that Oracle's intention was to make it easier to use Java for functional programming.

In this book, I made heavy use of some of these functional-friendly features, such as lambdas and functional interfaces, and I indirectly benefited from better type inference and extended type annotations. However, I didn't use the other functional elements like `Optional` or `Stream`. In this appendix, I'll explain why.

A.1   *The Optional class*

The `Optional` class is similar to the `Option` class you developed in chapter 6. It's supposed to solve the problem of the `null` reference, but it's not a great help for functional programming. Obviously, something has been done wrong. The `Optional` class has a `get` method that will return the "enclosed" value if there is one, and `null` otherwise. Of course, calling this method defeats the original goal.

If you want to use the `Optional` class, you should remember to *never* call `get`. You might object that the `Option` class has the `getOrThrow` method which, although never returning `null`, will throw an exception if no data is available. But this method is protected, and the class can't be extended from outside. This makes a huge difference. This method is equivalent to the `head` or `tail` methods in `List`: they should *never* be called from outside.

Besides this, the `Optional` class suffers from the same limitations as `Option`: `Optional` can be used for truly optional data, but generally the absence of data is due to an error. `Optional`, like `Option`, doesn't allow you to carry the error cause, so it's only useful for truly optional data, which means when the cause for the absence of data is obvious, such as returning a value from a map, or the position of a character in a string. If the `get(key)` method of a map returns no value, whether it means `null` or an empty `Optional`, it should be obvious that the key wasn't found. And if the `indexOf(char)` method returns no value or an empty `Optional`, it should mean that the character isn't present in the string.

But even this isn't true. The `get(key)` method of a map could return `null` because the `null` value was stored under that key. Or it could return no value because the key was `null` (provided `null` isn't a valid key). The `indexOf(char)` method could also return no value for many reasons, such as a negative argument. Returning `Optional` in these cases wouldn't indicate the nature of the error. Furthermore, this `Optional` would be difficult to compose with values returned by other methods that could produce errors.

For all these reasons, `Optional`, like our version of `Option`, is useless. That's why we developed the `Return` type, which you can use to represent the absence of optional data as well as errors.

A.2   Streams

Streams are another new element of Java 8 that mixes three different concepts:

- Lazy collections
- Monadic collections
- Automatic parallelization

These three concepts are independent, and there's no obvious reason why they were mixed. Unfortunately, as with many other tools that are supposed to do several different things, they are less than optimal at each of them.

Monadic data structures are essential to functional programming, and Java collections aren't monadic. You could create such structures by simply calling the newly added `stream()` method on such collections. That could be an acceptable solution if streams had all the necessary methods for functional processing. But streams were designed to make it possible to automatically switch from serial to parallel processing. Such a process is quite complex, and it's probably the reason why some important methods weren't implemented in streams. For example, Java 8 streams have no `takeWhile` or `dropWhile` methods.

This might be an acceptable price to pay for access to automatic parallelization, but even this feature isn't really usable. (This issue is addressed in Java 9.) All parallel streams use a single fork/join pool containing as many threads as there are physical threads available on the computer, minus one (the main thread). Tasks are distributed to waiting queues for each worker thread in the pool. Once a thread has exhausted its task queue, it "steals" work from other threads. The main thread itself participates by stealing work from worker threads.

The overall result isn't optimal because, of course, the computer may have lots of other tasks to do at the same time. Think about a Java EE application receiving requests from clients. These requests are already processed in parallel, so there's very little to gain from further parallelizing each request. Usually, in such a context, there will be no benefit at all.

Worse yet, because all parallel streams share the same fork/join pool, if one stream blocks, it might block all other streams! It's possible to use a specific pool for each stream, but this is a bit complex, and it should be done only if you're using pools of smaller sizes, meaning with fewer threads. If you're interested in such techniques, take a look at the following articles I've posted on DZone:

- "What's Wrong in Java 8, Part III: Streams and Parallel Streams" (https://dzone.com/articles/whats-wrong-java-8-part-iii)
- "What's Wrong in Java 8, Part VII: Streams Again" (https://dzone.com/articles/whats-wrong-java-8-part-vii)

Probably the worst thing about Java 8 streams is that they're usable only once. As soon as a terminal method has been called on them, they can no longer be used. Any further access will produce an exception. This has two consequences.

The first is that memoization isn't possible. Instead of accessing a stream a second time, you can only create a new one. The result is that if the values were lazily evaluated, they'll have to be evaluated again.

The second consequence is even worse: Java 8 streams can't be used in the comprehension pattern. Imagine you want to write a function to verify the Pythagorean relation $a^2 + b^2 = c^2$ using a `Triple` class implementation such as this:

```
public class Triple {
  public final int a;
  public final int b;
  public final int c;
  Triple(int a, int b, int c) {
    this.a = a;
    this.b = b;
    this.c = c;
  }

  @Override
  public String toString() {
    return String.format("(%s,%s,%s)", a, b, c);
  }
}
```

In imperative Java, the `pyths` method could be implemented as follows:

```
static List<Triple> pyths(int n) {
  List<Triple> result = new ArrayList<>();
  for (int a = 1; a <= n; a++) {
    for (int b = 1; b <= n; b++) {
      for (int c = 1; c <= n; c++) {
        if (a * a + b * b == c * c) {
          result.add(new Triple (a, b, c));
        }
      }
    }
  }
  return result;
}
```

The "functional" version, using streams, should look like this:

```
static Stream<Triple> pyths(int n) {
  Stream<Integer> stream = IntStream.rangeClosed(1, n).boxed();
  return stream.flatMap(a -> stream
      .flatMap(b -> stream
          .flatMap(c -> a * a + b * b == c * c
              ? Stream.of(new Triple (a, b, c))
              : Stream.empty())));
}
```

Unfortunately, in Java 8, this will produce the following exception:

```
java.lang.IllegalStateException: stream has already been operated upon or closed
```

By contrast, you can write this example using the List class you developed in chapter 5.

Another limitation of Java 8 streams is that folding is a terminal operation, meaning that a fold (called `reduce` in Java 8 streams) will cause the evaluation of all stream elements. To understand the difference, recall the `Stream.foldRight` method you developed in chapter 9. With this method, you could write an implementation of the `identity` function as follows:

```
public Stream<A> identity() {
  return foldRight(Stream::empty, a -> b -> cons(() -> a, b));
}
```

This method was totally lazy, which allowed you to use it to implement methods such as map, flatMap, and many others. This is completely impossible with Java 8 streams.

Does this mean that you should never use Java 8 streams? Absolutely not. Java 8 streams are a good choice to complement imperative programs when performance is the most important criterion, especially when you need to deal with primitives. Parallel streams, however, should generally be avoided in production contexts. And for most functional uses, truly functional streams are a better choice.

If you want (or need) to use Java 8 Stream in a functional context, be aware that although the Stream type has a reduce method (in fact, three versions of this method) that is supposed to be used for folding, it's not the best way to fold a stream. Folding should be done with a Collector implementation. Collector is an interface that defines five methods:

```
@Override
public Supplier<A> supplier();

@Override
public BiConsumer<A, T> accumulator();

@Override
public BinaryOperator<A> combiner();

@Override
public Function<List<List<T>>, List<List<T>>> finisher();

@Override
public Set<Characteristics> characteristics();
```

The supplier method returns a Supplier<A> for the identity element. The accumulator method returns a BiConsumer<A, T>, which is the nonfunctional replacement for the folding function. The corresponding folding function would be BiFunction <A, T, A>, which combines an element with the current result. Instead of returning the result, the consumer is supposed to store it somewhere (in the Collector). In other words, it's a state-mutation-based version of a fold. The finisher is an optional function that will be applied to the final result. Finally, characteristics returns a set of characteristics of the Collector used to optimize its work. There are three possible characteristics—CONCURRENT, IDENTITY_FINISH, and UNORDERED:

- CONCURRENT means that the accumulator function supports concurrency and may be used by several threads.
- IDENTITY_FINISH means that the finisher function is the identity and can thus be ignored.
- UNORDERED means that the stream is unordered, which allows more freedom for parallelization.

Here's an example of a Collector for folding a Stream<String> into a List<List<String>>, simulating the grouping of words on lines of a given maximum length. First, you define a generic GroupingCollector:

```java
import java.util.ArrayList;
import java.util.List;
import java.util.function.*;
import java.util.stream.Collector;

import static java.util.stream.Collector.Characteristics.IDENTITY_FINISH;

public class GroupingCollector<T> {

  private final BiPredicate<List<T>, T> p;

  public GroupingCollector(BiPredicate<List<T>, T> p) {
    this.p = p;
  }

  public void accumulator(List<List<T>> llt, T t) {
    if (! llt.isEmpty()) {
      List<T> last = llt.get(llt.size() - 1);
      if (p.test(last, t)) {
        llt.get(llt.size() - 1).add(t);
      } else {
        addNewList(llt, t);
      }
    } else {
      addNewList(llt, t);
    }
  }

  public List<List<T>> combiner(List<List<T>> list1, List<List<T>> list2) {
    List<List<T>> result = new ArrayList<>();
    result.addAll(list1);
    result.addAll(list2);
    return result;
  }

  public static <T> void addNewList(List<List<T>> llt, T t) {
    List<T> list = new ArrayList<>();
    list.add(t);
    llt.add(list);
  }

  public Collector<T, List<List<T>>, List<List<T>>> collector() {
```

```
    return Collector.of(ArrayList::new, this::accumulator, this::combiner, ID
    ENTITY_FINISH);
  }
}
```

Then, you create a specific grouping collector for strings:

```
import java.util.List;
import java.util.function.BiPredicate;
import java.util.stream.Collector;

public class StringGrouperCollector {

  private StringGrouperCollector() {
  }

  public static Collector<String, List<List<String>>, List<List<String>>> get
      Instance(int length) {
    BiPredicate<List<String>, String> p = (ls, s) -
    > length(ls) + s.length() <= length;
    return new GroupingCollector<>(p).collector();
  }

  public static int length(List<String> list) {
    int length = 0;
    for (String s : list) {
      length += s.length();
    }
    return length;
  }
}
```

Finally, you can create the client code for testing the collector:

```
public class Client {

  public static void main(String...args) {

    List<String> words2 = Arrays.asList("Once", "upon", "a", "time", "there",
      "was", "a", "prince",
        "who", "lived", "in", "a", "magnificent", "castle");
      words2.stream().collect(StringGrouperCollector.getInstance(20))
        .forEach(System.out::println);
  }
}
```

This program prints the following:

```
[Once, upon, a, time, there]
[was, a, prince, who, lived, in]
[a, magnificent, castle]
```

The principle is exactly the same as for a fold, abstracting the iteration over the stream elements.

appendix B
Monads

After reading this book, you might be surprised (and possibly frustrated) by the fact that I didn't talk about monads. Monads are a hot topic, and you can find many so-called "Monad tutorials" on the web. The topic of monads seems to be very intimidating, and many programmers read these tutorials one after the other in the hope that they'll eventually understand what monads are. Of course, many other programmers do understand monads, but very few are able to explain monads in simple terms.

The reason why there are so many monad tutorials is probably because there's no definitive tutorial, so people keep trying to roll their own. This appendix is not another monad tutorial. I wouldn't want to write one for two reasons:

- If you have read this book, you don't need a monad tutorial. Although I never used the term *monad*, you already know what a monad is. You know the concept and have made heavy use of it throughout this book. You just have to name it.
- There's an old saying about monads having a kind of magic: as soon as you understand them, you lose the ability to explain them to others.

But let's see what others say about monads. Searching on the internet, you can find many definitions:

- "A monad is just a monoid in the category of endofunctors."
- "A monad is a computational context for some value."
- "A monad is a class with a `unit` method and a `flatmap` method."

You may also find some more exotic definitions:

- "Monads are burritos."
- "Monads are elephants."

In the first list, the definitions are valid… in some contexts. The first one is probably the most rigorous definition in the context of category theory, a branch of mathematics about which most programmers don't care. (They should, but that's another story.)

The third definition is probably the most easily understood by Java programmers. The names of the methods are unimportant. What matters are the rules these methods must respect.

The second definition is probably the most useful for understanding monads. Monads are computational contexts, and functional programming is programming with functions. Safe functional programming is programming with total functions. Functions that aren't total are said to be partial, which means that they don't always have a value (see chapter 2). And when they have no value, they aren't happy and start doing awful things. And they stop being pure.

Consider the following function:

```
f(x, y) = x + y
```

Is this a pure function? No one can say. It depends on the programming language used. In some languages, it could throw an arithmetic overflow exception, so it wouldn't be a total function because it wouldn't be defined for all pairs (x, y). It wouldn't be a pure function because throwing an exception is a side effect.

In Java, using integers, however, this function is pure. This means that whatever pair of integers you give to the function, it will always return a value, and always the same value for the same pair. So you can trust the function. This doesn't mean the result will always be correct. In the case of overflow, the result might not be what you intended, but that's another problem. There will always be a result (meaning that the program won't hang in the wild) and this result will always be the same.

What about this function?

```
g(x, y) = x / y
```

In the context of Java and integers, which means a function taking a pair of integers as its argument and returning an integer, this isn't a total function. It might have no result for some pairs of integers. If the second argument is 0, there's no result and the function throws an exception. This is because g isn't a total function if considered as a function from (integer, integer) to integer.

There are two ways to make g a total function: change the domain, making it a function of (integer, non-null integer), or change the codomain, making it a function of (integer, integer) to (integer | exception).

To implement the first option, you'd have to create a new type: `NonNullInteger`. This is perfectly possible.

To implement the second option, you'd again have to create a new type: `IntegerOrException`.

Functional programmers prefer the second approach.

But if you change function g to return `IntegerOrException`, you can no longer compose it with f. More precisely, f . g (x), or f(g(x)) if you prefer this notation, will no longer compile because the types no longer match.

The solution is to create a computational context in which the functions can be safely executed. If you like metaphors, you can think about the context as a safe box.

So, what you need is

- A safe box
- A way to put the parameter value inside the box
- A way to put the modified function inside the box so that it can be applied to the parameter value

And that's it. The result will be a box containing the result of the function.

To take a simple example in Java, you'll have to slightly modify the requirements, because Java doesn't offer such a safe box. It offers three types of safe boxes, but not one suitable for this use case, so you have to modify the requirement by saying that in case of error, the result won't throw an exception but will simply return nothing. (Note that Java has a type for this: `Void`. But instantiating this type is a bit tricky.)

The type of safe box you can use for returning a result or nothing is the `Option` you developed in chapter 6, or (better) the `Result` type from chapter 7. In standard Java 8, it could be the `Optional` type.

In functional languages, the method that will put a value into the box is generally named `unit` or `return`, but you named it `of` for `Option` and `Result`, as Java 8 designers did for `Optional`. That doesn't change anything.

The method that allows you to apply the modified function to the value inside the box is called `flatMap`. Let's take the example of a simpler function taking a `String` and returning the first character. A "normal" method could look like this:

```
public static char firstChar(String a) {
  if (a == null || a.length() == 0) {
    throw new IllegalArgumentException();
  } else {
    return a.charAt(0);
  }
}
```

To make this function return either the first character or nothing, you must change it into this:

```
public static Optional<Character> firstChar(String a) {
  return a == null || a.length() == 0
      ? Optional.empty()
      : Optional.of(a.charAt(0));
}
```

To use these tools, you need to put a `String` in context:

```
Optional<String> data = Optional.of("Hello!");
```

```
Optional<Character> character = data.flatMap(ThisClass::firstChar);
```

The unit (of) and flatMap methods are all that's needed to make Optional a monad.

There are, however, other use cases that are frequent enough to have been added in most monad implementations. For example, you might have to use a function returning a raw value, like this:

```
public static int toUpper(char c) {
  return c >= 'a' && c <= 'z'
      ? c - 32
      : c;
}
```

You could do it with

```
Optional<Integer> upperChar = character.flatMap(x -> Optional.of(toUpper(x)));
```

But this isn't very efficient, because the function will wrap the result in an Optional, just for the flatMap method to unwrap it. So there's a map method for this use case:

```
Optional<Integer> upperChar = character.map(ThisClass::toUpper);
```

Note that if you were to use map with a function returning an Optional, such as the following, you'd obtain an Optional<Optional<Character>>:

```
Optional<String> data = Optional.of("Hello!");
Optional<???> character = data.map(ThisClass::firstChar);
```

This can be changed into an Optional<Character> using a method called flatten (or join), but this method is missing in Optional. As you can see, there's a strong relation between unit (of), flatMap, map, and flatten. The flatten method can be implemented as follows:

```
public static <T> Optional<T> flatten(Optional<Optional<T>> oot) {
  return oot.flatMap(Function.identity());
}
```

Lots of other use cases can be abstracted inside monads, but they're not necessary to make a type a monad. One of the most often used is fold. This method is generally seen as specific to vector types, such as List or Stream, but it's not. For Option, for example, fold can be implemented in None<T> as

```
public <U> U fold(U z, Function<U, Function<T, U>> f) {
  return z;
}
```

and in Some<T> as

```
public <U> U fold(U z, Function<U, Function<T, U>> f) {
  return f.apply(z).apply(value);
}
```

(Technically, this is a left fold, but the difference is irrelevant for this example.)

You can't add this method to the Java 8 class `Optional`, which is `final`. But you can write an external implementation:

```
public static <T, U> U fold(U z, Function<U, Function<T, U>> f, Optional<T> ot) {
  return ot.isPresent() ? f.apply(z).apply(ot.get()) : z;
}
```

Here, you use `Optional.get()`, which is awfully bad. (It's forbidden to access the value from outside of the context, which means this method shouldn't be public.) There's no smart solution to this problem. You know that the `get` method will never be called if the value isn't present, so you could write this:

```
public static <T, U> U fold(U z, Function<U, Function<T, U>> f, Optional<T> ot) {
  return ot.isPresent() ? f.apply(z).apply(ot.orElse(null)) : z;
}
```

But this is ugly. The less ugly implementation would probably look like this:

```
public static <T, U> U fold(U z, Function<U, Function<T, U>> f, Optional<T> ot) {
  return ot.isPresent()
    ? f.apply(z).apply(ot.orElseThrow(() ->
        new IllegalStateException("This exception is (never) thrown by dead code!")))
    : z;
}
```

Anyway, folding an `Optional` is useless, except to understand that the `orElse` method is in fact a `fold` and could be defined as follows:

```
public static <T> T orElse(Optional<T> ot, T defaultValue) {
  return fold(defaultValue, ignore -> t -> t, ot);
}
```

Yes, again this is totally useless, but it's helpful to understand it when studying other monads such as `Stream` or `List` (but not the `java.util.List`, of course).

Lots of other methods could have been added to `Optional` and are missing, and you can't add them because `Optional` is final. This is a good reason to develop a totally new `Option` monad. But at the same time, `Optional` is almost useless because it can't carry the reason for the absence of data. This is why another monad is needed. In this book, we called it `Result`, and it roughly corresponds to the Scala `Try` class.

appendix C
Where to go from here

You've now had some experience writing functional programs in Java. The extent to which you apply what you've learned to everyday Java programming is up to you. Aiming to be 100% functional is probably too much for many Java programmers. Using fully functional I/O, for example, is probably not something that every reader will want to do in their production code. But if you want to adopt the functional programming paradigm for professional projects, you have choices to make.

C.1 Choosing a new language

The first choice is the language you'll use. Often, choosing a different (more functional-friendly) language isn't an option. But sometimes it is. We've only scratched the surface of the subject, and with the right tools you can go much further. Choosing a functional language may seem complex, but it's not. Switching to a different language will only be interesting if you choose a much more powerful language in the domain. If you've read this book and want to go further, you won't be interested in a weakly typed language. So you have three possible choices: Haskell, Scala, and Kotlin (or possibly a fourth, Frege).

C.1.1 Haskell

Haskell is the de facto standard language for functional programming. Haskell is a strongly typed, lazy functional language, with nearly all the features an aspiring functional programmer might dream of, and many more-sophisticated features that you'll have trouble understanding at first. Most of the modern articles and books about functional programming use Haskell for their examples. Moreover, they use a specific version of Haskell: the Glasgow Haskell Compiler (GHC).

Whether or not you get to pick the language of your choice, which is unlikely if you work in a team or if you have to use legacy code, learning Haskell will be profitable. When you use Java to write functional programs, you often have to fight against the language. Using Haskell, you'll have to fight against it to write imperative programs. Learning Haskell will train your mind into functional thinking like no other language can do. Even if you continue using Java, prototyping functions with Haskell is really rewarding.

The main problem with Haskell (for a Java programmer) is that everything is new. You won't be able to use any of your regular Java tools (besides your code editor) or any of the numerous libraries you've been used to. Of course, there are lots of Haskell libraries, but you'll have to learn everything anew, including how to find, download, and manage them, how to build your programs, how to handle documentation, and everything else.

C.1.2 Scala

Another solution is to switch to Scala. Scala is not a strictly functional language. With Scala, you can write programs in both imperative and functional styles. Switching to Scala is easy because you can write Scala programs with a Java-like design, much as it was possible, when Java first appeared, to write Java programs exactly as C programs were written. Of course, this isn't the best way to go, and many of the problems we have in Java are due to this C heritage. And as more and more Java programmers switch to Scala, we'll see more and more imperative programs written in this language.

As a result, writing functional programs in Scala is a discipline, but nearly nothing is missing (if you use some advanced functional libraries). And the great advantage is that you'll be able to reuse most of what you know. You can write Scala programs in Eclipse, NetBeans, or IntelliJ. Although Scala has its own build tool (sbt), you can build Scala programs with Gradle, or even with Maven or Ant (although who would ever want to do this?). Moreover, you can use all the existing Java libraries from a Scala program. (And, of course, Scala libraries can be used from Java.) These features make Scala a good first choice if you need to deal with legacy Java code and tools.

C.1.3 Kotlin

Kotlin is a new language designed by JetBrains, the publisher of the IntelliJ IDE, which is the best IDE for Java as well as many other languages. Kotlin is what Java should have become. It has many functional-friendly features such as function types (allowing you to write (A) -> (B) -> C instead of Function<A, Function<B, C>>), data classes (automatically generating constructors, accessors, and equals and hashCode methods), and implicit method calls (allowing you to call a function as f(x) instead of the more verbose Java syntax f.apply(x)). Moreover, Kotlin is fully compatible with Java, and it's possible to mix Java and Kotlin in the same project. Since nothing is perfect (yet!), Kotlin has no functional collections (meaning immutable, persistent, and data-sharing), but uses the Java standard collections with a special mechanism—*extension functions*—that allows you to "add" methods to existing classes. (In fact, it allows calling static methods as if they were instance methods and using the this reference to refer to the "extended" instance.) Kotlin is so well integrated with Java that it's possible to start by adding a Kotlin class to a Java project. All you have to do is modify your build system to add Kotlin compilation. And for development, even that isn't necessary because IntelliJ allows compiling and running mixed Java/Kotlin projects transparently. As of this writing,

Kotlin is in version 1.0.5, so many things will change in the near future. Version 1.1 is in beta and should be available by the time you read this. This is really something you should look at if you're interested in functional programming in the Java ecosystem.

C.1.4   Frege

Another promising solution is the Frege language (named after the German mathematician and philosopher Gottlob Frege, and pronounced somewhat like "frey-guh"). Frege is a very young language and might not be mature enough for production code, but it's evolving rapidly and could become the language of choice for pure functional programming on the JVM. Frege is in fact "Haskell on the JVM." It's as close to Haskell as it can be, while retaining the possibility of using all existing Java libraries. Because it can mix with Java (like Scala can), it's a very good choice for a smooth transition. And if you decide to learn Haskell or Kotlin as a prototyping language, why not also use Frege? You can find more information about Frege at https://github.com/Frege/frege and http://fregepl.blogspot.fr/.

C.1.5   What about dynamically typed functional languages?

Dynamically typed functional languages are different from the previous ones because, instead of relying on the type system to help the programmer write correct programs, they free the programmer from the tyranny of types, allowing them to write ill-typed programs that compile.

To make this sound like a benefit, such languages are often called "Dynamically typed languages." Everyone knows that being dynamic is better than being static, so it should be a quality feature. Unfortunately, these languages would be better called "weakly typed" in contrast with "strongly typed" languages such as Java, Haskell, or Scala. This isn't to say that weakly typed languages are bad. They just have a very important difference: if you mess with the types, you won't generally be warned by the compiler. The program will only crash at runtime. This is a choice. See for yourself.

C.2   Staying with Java

You could stick to Java. To make the transition from learning the functional paradigm to applying it in Java production code, you'll need a Java functional library. You can use the one you developed while reading this book, but you need to be aware that maintaining a library is a huge task. If you're the only user, this is probably the best choice, because you'll be able to tailor the library to your own needs. Every time you discover a new function that could be abstracted into the library, you'll be free to do it. But if you're working in a team, it's another story. You'll have to take care of everyone's needs, be careful you don't break anything, and be backward compatible at all times. This is a really heavy job.

The alternative is to use one of the existing open source libraries developed and tested by many people. You won't have the same freedom to add new features you might need, but you'll be productive in no time. And if you really want a new feature, you can add it yourself and propose it to the community.

C.2.1 Functional Java

Functional Java was one of the earliest open source Java functional libraries that's still in use. It predates Java 8 and was first written using anonymous classes to represent functions. It's probably the functional library with the most fundamentalist approach. This is a good thing if you aim to become a fundamentalist functional programmer yourself. And even if you don't, using it and looking at how it's coded is a very rewarding experience. Note, however, that the documentation is scarce. You'll have to figure out by yourself how to use it, although what you've learned in this book will help you greatly.

Also note that this library has been developed by many great functional programmers, some of whom have now turned their interest toward more functional-friendly languages. You can find more information on this site: http://www.functionaljava .org/.

C.2.2 Javaslang

Javaslang is a more recent, less extreme functional library for Java. It has much better documentation, including basic examples, although the documentation is only a single (big) page. Here again, what you've learned in this book will be a great help when using Javaslang. As I said, Javaslang's approach is less fundamentalist, which probably makes it an easier transition, particularly for teams with various level of interest in the functional paradigm. One little glitch is that, although it has streams, those streams suffer one of the same problems of Java 8 streams: they don't have lazy folds. However, the issues state that there are plans to implement them. On the other hand, it offers a usable pattern-matching mechanism. You can find information about this library at http://javaslang.io/.

C.2.3 Cyclops

Cyclops is presented as "powerful, lightweight & modular extensions for JDK 8," but it's more than this. It is, in fact, full, functional libraries for Java with additional support for leveraging the standard Java data types to make them really usable. For example, it adds functional methods to standard Java collections, and it also provides immutable persistent collections like those you developed in this book. Cyclops also offers the missing methods for the Java 8 `Stream` interface, such as `takeWhile` and `dropWhile`. Cyclops is really full of interesting stuff, such as replayable streams, memoization, trampolining, pattern matching, tuples, and more. And it has probably the best documentation of all the available Java functional libraries. Finally, it's designed to work hand in hand with other libraries like Functional Java or Javaslang (or even Guava). Cyclops can be found at https://github.com/aol/cyclops.

C.2.4   *Other functional libraries*

There were once other Java functional libraries, such as Fun4j, LambdaJ, op4j, and Apache Commons Functor. All these libraries appeared before Java 8, and none have evolved since the release of Java 8, which mostly made them obsolete.

Guava has continued to evolve because it's not a functional library but a library that, among other things, contained functions. But the functional features of Guava haven't evolved much and are now obsolete.

C.3   *Further reading*

If you want to learn more about functional programming, you'll find lots of resources on the internet. Many articles and books have been written about functional programming, but not so many about functional programming in Java. You might, however, find some useful articles written about general functional programming with examples in "functional languages," because many concepts are applicable to Java.

Here's a non-exhaustive list of articles that you might find interesting:

John Hughes, "Why Functional Programming matters," from "Research Topics in Functional Programming," ed. D. Turner (Addison-Wesley, 1990), http://mng .bz/qp3B.

This very interesting article is mainly about higher-order functions and laziness and explains why these features are so important if you want to write better and safer programs.

Philip Walder,"Theorems for free!" (University of Glasgow, 1989), http://mng.bz/ my25.

This article is more difficult to read, but worth the effort if you want to determine what a strong type system can offer you as a programmer.

Chris Okasaki, "Purely Functional Data Structures" (thesis, School of Computer Science, Carnegie Mellon University, 1996), http://mng.bz/8Gz4.

This easier-to-read university thesis is about how to build purely functional data structures. Examples are written in Standard ML, a functional language. Okasaki has written a book based on this paper that is even easier to read and has examples in Haskell. If you're interested in functional (immutable and persistent) data structures, this is the book you must read.

Kimball Germane and Matthew Might, "Deletion: the curse of the red-black tree," *JFP* 24, 4 (2014): 423–433, http://mng.bz/yl57.

This paper complements Okasaki's presentation of the functional red-black tree. In his book, Okasaki doesn't give the implementation of element removal from this structure, and leaves it as an exercise for the reader. This article is about that implementation.

Graham Hutton, "A tutorial on the universality and expressiveness of fold," *J. Functional Programming* 9, 4 (1999): 355–372, http://mng.bz/me7Z.

> This is one of the most interesting articles about functional programming, and very easy to read. A must if you want to fully understand folds.

Ralf Hinze and Ross Patterson, "Finger trees: a simple general-purpose data structure," http://mng.bz/AYZS.

> An article about a very interesting functional data structure that allows all types of accesses and operations with good performance, although it's not as simple as the title says. Implementing it in Java is a rewarding challenge. (There are several known implementations.)

index